April 25, 1945

A BOOK OF OPERAS

THE MACMILLAN COMPANY
NEW YORK · BOSTON · CHICAGO · DALLAS
ATLANTA · SAN FRANCISCO

MACMILLAN AND CO., Limited
LONDON · BOMBAY · CALCUTTA · MADRAS
MELBOURNE

**THE MACMILLAN COMPANY
OF CANADA, Limited**
TORONTO

MOZART

(After a painting owned by the Author)

A BOOK OF OPERAS

THEIR HISTORIES, THEIR PLOTS, AND THEIR MUSIC

BY

HENRY EDWARD KREHBIEL

TWO VOLUMES IN ONE

Combining "A Book of Operas" and
"A Second Book of Operas"

ILLUSTRATED

New York

THE MACMILLAN COMPANY
1944

PRINTED IN THE UNITED STATES OF AMERICA
AMERICAN BOOK—STRATFORD PRESS, INC., NEW YORK

𝕿𝖔

LUCIEN WULSIN

AN OLD FRIEND

" Old friends are best." — SELDEN.

" I love everything that's old, — old friends, old times, old manners, old books, old wine." — GOLDSMITH.

" Old wood to burn ! Old wine to drink ! Old friends to trust ! Old authors to read ! " — MELCHIOR.

LIST OF ILLUSTRATIONS

A BOOK OF OPERAS

A SECOND BOOK OF OPERAS

A BOOK OF OPERAS

THE BOOK OF OPERAS

CONTENTS AND INDEX

CHAPTER I

"IL BARBIERE DI SIVIGLIA"

CHAPTER II

"LE NOZZE DI FIGARO"

xi

CHAPTER III

"DIE ZAUBERFLÖTE"

CHAPTER IV

"DON GIOVANNI"

CHAPTER V

"FIDELIO"

CHAPTER VI

" FAUST "

CHAPTER VII

" MEFISTOFELE "

CHAPTER VIII

"La Damnation de Faust"

CHAPTER IX

"La Traviata"

CHAPTER XIII

"Tristan und Isolde"

CHAPTER XIV

"Parsifal"

CHAPTER XV

"Die Meistersinger von Nürnberg"

CHAPTER XVI

"LOHENGRIN"

CHAPTER XVII

"HÄNSEL UND GRETEL"

A BOOK OF OPERAS

CHAPTER I

"IL BARBIERE DI SIVIGLIA"

THE history of what is popularly called Italian opera begins in the United States with a performance of Rossini's lyrical comedy "Il Barbiere di Siviglia"; it may, therefore, fittingly take the first place in these operatic studies. The place was the Park Theatre, in Park Row, opposite the present Post Office, and the date November 29, 1825. It was not the first performance of Italian opera music in America, however, nor yet of Rossini's merry work. In the early years of the nineteenth century New York was almost as fully abreast of the times in the matter of dramatic entertainments as London. New works produced in the English capital were heard in New York as soon as the ships of that day could bring over the books and the actors. Especially was this true of English ballad operas and English transcriptions, or adaptations, of French, German, and Italian operas. New York was five months ahead of Paris in making the acquaintance of the operatic version of Beaumarchais's "Barbier de Séville." The first performance of

Rossini's opera took place in Rome on February 5, 1816. London heard it in its original form at the King's Theatre on March 10, 1818, with Garcia, the first *Count Almaviva*, in that part. The opera "went off with unbounded applause," says Parke (an oboe player, who has left us two volumes of entertaining and instructive memoirs), but it did not win the degree of favor enjoyed by the other operas of Rossini then current on the English stage. It dropped out of the repertory of the King's Theatre and was not revived until 1822 — a year in which the popularity of Rossini in the British metropolis may be measured by the fact that all but four of the operas brought forward that year were composed by him. The first Parisian representation of the opera took place on October 26, 1819. Garcia was again in the cast. By that time, in all likelihood, all of musical New York that could muster up a pucker was already whistling "Largo al factotum" and the beginning of "Una voce poco fà," for, on May 17, 1819, Thomas Phillipps had brought an English "Barber of Seville" forward at a benefit performance for himself at the same Park Theatre at which more than six years later the Garcia company, the first Italian opera troupe to visit the New World, performed it in Italian on the date already mentioned. At Mr. Phillipps's performance the beneficiary sang the part of *Almaviva*, and Miss Leesugg, who afterward became the wife of the comedian Hackett, was the *Rosina*. On November 21, 1821, there was another performance for Mr.

Phillipps's benefit, and this time Mrs. Holman took the part of *Rosina*. Phillipps and Holman — brave names these in the dramatic annals of New York and London a little less than a century ago! When will European writers on music begin to realize that musical culture in America is not just now in its beginnings?

It was Manuel Garcia's troupe that first performed "Il Barbiere di Siviglia" in New York, and four of the parts in the opera were played by members of his family. Manuel, the father, was the *Count*, as he had been at the premières in Rome, London, and Paris; Manuel, son, was the *Figaro* (he lived to read about eighty-one years of operatic enterprise in New York, and died at the age of 101 years in London in 1906); Signora Garcia, *mère*, was the *Berta*, and *Rosina* was sung and played by that "cunning pattern of excellent nature," as a writer of the day called her, Signorina Garcia, afterward the famous Malibran. The other performers at this representation of the Italian "Barber" were Signor Rosich (*Dr. Bartolo*), Signor Angrisani (*Don Basilio*), and Signor Crivelli, the younger (*Fiorello*). The opera was given twenty-three times in a season of seventy-nine nights, and the receipts ranged from $1843 on the opening night and $1834 on the closing, down to $356 on the twenty-ninth night.

But neither Phillipps nor Garcia was the first to present an operatic version of Beaumarchais's comedy to the American people. French operas by

Rousseau, Monsigny, Dalayrac, and Grétry, which may be said to have composed the staple of the opera-houses of Europe in the last decades of the eighteenth century, were known also in the contemporaneous theatres of Charleston, Baltimore, Philadelphia, and New York. In 1794 the last three of these cities enjoyed "an opera in 3 acts," the text by Colman, entitled, "The Spanish Barber; or, The Futile Precaution." Nothing is said in the announcements of this opera touching the authorship of the music, but it seems to be an inevitable conclusion that it was Paisiello's, composed for St. Petersburg about 1780. There were German "Barbers" in existence at the time composed by Benda (Friedrich Ludwig), Elsperger, and Schulz, but they did not enjoy large popularity in their own country, and Isouard's "Barbier" was not yet written. Paisiello's opera, on the contrary, was extremely popular, throughout Europe. True, he called it "The Barber of Seville," not "The Spanish Barber," but Colman's subtitle, "The Futile Precaution," came from the original French title. Rossini also adopted it and purposely avoided the chief title set by Beaumarchais and used by Paisiello; but he was not long permitted to have his way. Thereby hangs a tale of the composition and first failure of his opera which I must now relate.

On December 26, 1815, the first day of the carnival season, Rossini produced his opera, "Torvaldo e Dorliska," at the Teatro Argentina, in Rome, and at the same time signed a contract with Ce-

sarini, the impresario of the theatre, to have the first
act of a second opera ready on the twentieth day
of the following January. For this opera Rossini
was to receive 400 Roman scudi (the equivalent of
about $400) after the first three performances,
which he was to conduct seated at the pianoforte
in the orchestra, as was then the custom. He
seems to have agreed to take any libretto submitted by the impresario and approved by the public censor; but there are indications that Sterbini,
who was to write the libretto, had already suggested a remodelling of Paisiello's "Barber." In
order to expedite the work of composition it was
provided in the contract that Rossini was to take
lodgings with a singer named Zamboni, to whom
the honor fell of being the original of the town
factotum in Rossini's opera. Some say that Rossini completed the score in thirteen days; some in
fifteen. Castil-Blaze says it was a month, but the
truth is that the work consumed less than half
that period. Donizetti, asked if he believed that
Rossini had really written the score in thirteen
days, is reported to have replied, no doubt with a
malicious twinkle in his eyes: "It is very possible;
he is so lazy." Paisiello was still alive, and so was
at least the memory of his opera, so Rossini, as a
precautionary measure, thought it wise to spike,
if possible, the guns of an apprehended opposition.
So he addressed a letter to the venerable composer,
asking leave to make use of the subject. He got
permission and then wrote a preface to his libretto

(or had Serbini write it for him), in which, while flattering his predecessor, he nevertheless contrived to indicate that he considered the opera of that venerable musician old-fashioned, undramatic, and outdated. "Beaumarchais's comedy, entitled 'The Barber of Seville, or the Useless Precaution,'" he wrote, "is presented at Rome in the form of a comic drama under the title of 'Almaviva, ossia l'inutile Precauzione,' in order that the public may be fully convinced of the sentiments of respect and veneration by which the author of the music of this drama is animated with regard to the celebrated Paisiello, who has already treated the subject under its primitive title. Himself invited to undertake this difficult task, the maestro Gioachino Rossini, in order to avoid the reproach of entering rashly into rivalry with the immortal author who preceded him, expressly required that 'The Barber of Seville' should be entirely versified anew, and also that new situations should be added for the musical pieces which, moreover, are required by the modern theatrical taste, entirely changed since the time when the renowned Paisiello wrote his work."

I have told the story of the fiasco made by Rossini's opera on its first production at the Argentine Theatre on February 5, 1816, in an extended preface to the vocal score of "Il Barbiere," published in 1900 by G. Schirmer, and a quotation from that preface will serve here quite as well as a paraphrase; so I quote (with an avowal of gratitude for the privilege to the publishers): —

Paisiello gave his consent to the use of the subject, believing that the opera of his young rival would assuredly fail. At the same time he wrote to a friend in Rome, asking him to do all in his power to compass a fiasco for the opera. The young composer's enemies were not sluggish. All the whistlers of Italy, says Castil-Blaze, seemed to have made a rendezvous at the Teatro Argentina on the night set down for the first production. Their malicious intentions were helped along by accidents at the outset of the performance. Details of the story have been preserved for us in an account written by Signora Giorgi-Righetti, who sang the part of *Rosina* on the memorable occasion. Garcia had persuaded Rossini to permit him to sing a Spanish song to his own accompaniment on a guitar under *Rosina's* balcony in the first act. It would provide the needed local color, he urged. When about to start his song, Garcia found that he had forgotten to tune his guitar. He began to set the pegs in the face of the waiting public. A string broke, and a new one was drawn up amid the titters of the spectators. The song did not please the auditors, who mocked at the singer by humming Spanish fiorituri after him. Boisterous laughter broke out when *Figaro* came on the stage also with a guitar, and "Largo al factotum" was lost in the din. Another howl of delighted derision went up when *Rosina's* voice was heard singing within: "Segui o caro, deh segui così" ("Continue, my dear, continue thus"). The audience continued "thus." The representative of *Rosina* was popular, but the fact that she was first heard in a trifling phrase instead of an aria caused disappointment. The duet, between *Almaviva* and *Figaro*, was sung amid hisses, shrieks, and shouts. The cavatina "Una voce poco fà" got a triple round of applause, however, and Rossini, interpreting the fact as a compliment to the personality of the singer rather than to the music, after bowing to the public, exclaimed: "Oh natura!"

"Thank her," retorted Giorgi-Righetti; "but for her you would not have had occasion to rise from your chair." The turmoil began again with the next duet, and the finale was mere dumb show. When the curtain fell, Rossini faced the mob, shrugged his shoulders, and clapped his hands to show his contempt. Only the musicians and singers heard the second act, the din being incessant from beginning to end. Rossini remained imperturbable, and when Giorgi-Rhigetti, Garcia, and Zamboni hastened to his lodgings to offer their condolences as soon as they could don street attire, they found him asleep. The next day he wrote the cavatina "Ecco ridente in cielo" to take the place of Garcia's unlucky Spanish song, borrowing the air from his own "Aureliano," composed two years before, into which it had been incorporated from "Ciro," a still earlier work. When night came, he feigned illness so as to escape the task of conducting. By that time his enemies had worn themselves out. The music was heard amid loud plaudits, and in a week the opera had scored a tremendous success.

And now for the dramatic and musical contents of "Il Barbiere." At the very outset Rossini opens the door for us to take a glimpse at the changes in musical manner which were wrought by time. He had faulted Paisiello's opera because in parts it had become antiquated, for which reason he had had new situations introduced to meet the "modern theatrical taste"; but he lived fifty years after "Il Barbiere" had conquered the world, and never took the trouble to write an overture for it, the one originally composed for the opera having been lost soon after the first production. The overture which leads us into the opera nowadays is all very well in its way and a striking example of how a

piece of music may benefit from fortuitous circumstances. Persons with fantastic imaginations have
rhapsodized on its appositeness, and professed to
hear in it the whispered plottings of the lovers and
the merry raillery of *Rosina*, contrasted with the
futile ragings of her grouty guardian; but when
Rossini composed this piece of music, its mission was
to introduce an adventure of the Emperor Aurelian
in Palmyra in the third century of the Christian
era. Having served that purpose, it became the
prelude to another opera which dealt with Queen
Elizabeth of England, a monarch who reigned
some twelve hundred years after Aurelian. Again,
before the melody now known as that of *Almaviva's* cavatina (which supplanted Garcia's unlucky
Spanish song) had burst into the efflorescence which
now distinguishes it, it came as a chorus from the
mouths of Cyrus and his Persians in ancient Babylon.
Truly, the verities of time and place sat lightly
on the Italian opera composers of a hundred years
ago. But the serenade which follows the rising
of the curtain preserves a custom more general
at the time of Beaumarchais than now, though
it is not yet obsolete. *Dr. Bartolo*, who is guardian
of the fascinating *Rosina*, is in love with her, or at
least wishes for reasons not entirely dissociated
from her money bags to make her his wife, and therefore keeps her most of the time behind bolts and
bars. The *Count Almaviva*, however, has seen her
on a visit from his estates to Seville, becomes enamoured of her, and she has felt her heart warmed

toward him, though she is ignorant of his rank and knows him only under the name of *Lindoro*. Hoping that it may bring him an opportunity for a glance, mayhap a word with his inamorata, *Almaviva* follows the advice given by *Sir Proteus* to *Thurio* in "The Two Gentlemen of Verona"; he visits his lady's chamber window, not at night, but at early dawn, with a "sweet concert," and to the instruments of *Fiorello's* musicians tunes "a deploring dump." It is the cavatina "Ecco ridente in cielo." The musicians, rewarded by *Almaviva* beyond expectations, are profuse and long-winded in their expression of gratitude, and are gotten rid of with difficulty. The *Count* has not yet had a glimpse of *Rosina*, who is in the habit of breathing the morning air from the balcony of her prison house, and is about to despair when *Figaro*, barber and Seville's factotum, appears trolling a song in which he recites his accomplishments, the universality of his employments, and the great demand for his services. ("Largo al factotum dello città.") The *Count* recognizes him, tells of his vain vigils in front of *Rosina's* balcony, and, so soon as he learns that *Figaro* is a sort of man of all work to *Bartolo*, employs him as his go-between. *Rosina* now appears on the balcony. *Almaviva* is about to engage her in conversation when *Bartolo* appears and discovers a billet-doux which *Rosina* had intended to drop into the hand of her *Lindoro*. He demands to see it, but she explains that it is but a copy of the words of an aria from an opera entitled "The

Futile Precaution," and drops it from the balcony, as if by accident. She sends *Bartolo* to recover it, but *Almaviva*, who had observed the device, secures it, and *Bartolo* is told by his crafty ward that the wind must have carried it away. Growing suspicious, he commands her into the house and goes 'way to hasten the preparations for his wedding, after giving orders that no one is to be admitted to the house save *Don Basilio*, *Rosina's* singing-master, and *Bartolo's* messenger and general mischief-maker.

The letter which *Rosina* had thus slyly conveyed to her unknown lover begged him to contrive means to let her know his name, condition, and intentions respecting herself. *Figaro*, taking the case in hand at once, suggests that *Almaviva* publish his answer in a ballad. This the *Count* does ("Se il mio nome saper"), protesting the honesty and ardor of his passion, but still concealing his name and station. He is delighted to hear his lady-love's voice bidding him to continue his song. (It is the phrase, "Segui, o caro, deh segui così," which sounded so monstrously diverting at the first representation of the opera in Rome.) After the second stanza *Rosina* essays a longer response, but is interrupted by some of the inmates of the house. *Figaro* now confides to the *Count* a scheme by which he is to meet his fair enslaver face to face: he is to assume the rôle of a drunken soldier who has been billeted upon *Dr. Bartolo*, a plan that is favored by the fact that a company of soldiers has come to Seville that very day which is under the command of the *Count's* cousin. The plan is promptly put into execution. Not long after, *Rosina* enters *Dr. Bartolo's* library singing the famous cavatina, "Una voce poco fà," in which she tells of her love for *Lindoro* and proclaims her determination to have her own way in the matter of her heart, in spite of all that her tyrannical guardian or anybody else can do. This cavatina has been the show piece of hundreds of singers ever since it was written. Signora Giorgi-Righetti, the first *Rosina*, was a contralto, and sang the music in the key of E, in which it was written. When it became one of Jenny Lind's display airs, it was transposed to F and tricked out with a great abundance of fiorituri. Adelina Patti in her youth used so to overburden its already florid measures with ornament that the story goes that once when she sang it for Rossini, the old master dryly remarked : "A very pretty air; who composed it?" *Figaro* enters at the conclusion of *Rosina's* song, and the two are about to exchange confidences when *Bartolo* enters with *Basilio*, who confides to the old doctor his suspicion that the unknown lover of *Rosina* is the *Count Almaviva*, and suggests that the latter's presence in Seville be made irksome by a few adroitly spread innuendoes against his character. How a calumny, ingeniously published, may grow from a whispered zephyr to a crashing, detonating tempest, *Basilio* describes in the buffo air "La calunnia" — a marvellous example of the device of crescendo which in this form is one of Rossini's

inventions. *Bartolo* prefers his own plan of com-
pelling his ward to marry him at once. He goes
with *Basilio* to draw up a marriage agreement,
and *Figaro,* who has overheard their talk, acquaints
Rosina with its purport. He also tells her that
she shall soon see her lover face to face if she will
but send him a line by his hands. Thus he secures
a letter from her, but learns that the artful minx
had written it before he entered. Her ink-stained
fingers, the disappearance of a sheet of paper from
his writing desk, and the condition of his quill pen
convince *Bartolo* on his return that he is being
deceived, and he resolves that henceforth his ward
shall be more closely confined than ever. And so
he informs her, while she mimics his angry gestures
behind his back. In another moment there is a
boisterous knocking and shouting at the door, and
in comes *Almaviva,* disguised as a cavalry soldier
most obviously in his cups. He manages to make
himself known to *Rosina,* and exchanges letters
with her under the very nose of her jailer, affects
a fury toward *Dr. Bartolo* when the latter claims
exemption from the billet, and escapes arrest only
by secretly making himself known to the officer
commanding the soldiers who had been drawn into
the house by the disturbance. The sudden and
inexplicable change of conduct on the part of the
soldiers petrifies *Bartolo;* he is literally "astonied,"
and *Figaro* makes him the victim of several laugh-
able pranks before he recovers his wits.

Dr. Bartolo's suspicions have been aroused about

the soldier, concerning whose identity he makes
vain inquiries, but he does not hesitate to admit
to his library a seeming music-master who announces
himself as *Don Alonzo*, come to act as substitute
for *Don Basilio*, who, he says, is ill. Of course it
is *Almaviva*. Soon the ill-natured guardian grows
impatient of his garrulity, and *Almaviva*, to allay
his suspicions and gain a sight of his inamorata,
gives him a letter written by *Rosina* to *Lindoro*,
which he says he had found in the *Count's* lodgings.
If he can but see the lady, he hopes by means of
the letter to convince her of *Lindoro's* faithlessness.
This device, though it disturbs its inventor, is successful, and *Bartolo* brings in his ward to receive
her music lesson. Here, according to tradition,
there stood in the original score a trio which was lost
with the overture. Very welcome has this loss appeared to the *Rosinas* of a later day, for it has enabled them to introduce into the "lesson scene"
music of their own choice, and, of course, such as
showed their voices and art to the best advantage.
Very amusing have been the anachronisms which
have resulted from these illustrations of artistic
vanity, and diverting are the glimpses which they
give of the tastes and sensibilities of great prime
donne. Grisi and Alboni, stimulated by the example of Catalani (though not in this opera), could
think of nothing nobler than to display their skill
by singing Rode's Air and Variations, a violin piece.
This grew hackneyed, but, nevertheless, survived
till a comparatively late day. Bosio, feeling that

variations were necessary, threw Rode's over in favor of those on "Gia della mente involarmi" — a polka tune from Alary's "A Tre Nozze." Then Mme. Gassier ushered in the day of the vocal waltz — Venzano's, of amiable memory. Her followers have not yet died out, though Patti substituted Arditi's "Il Bacio" for Venzano's; Mme. Sembrich, Strauss's "Voce di Primavera," and Mme. Melba, Arditi's "Se saran rose." Mme. Viardot, with a finer sense of the fitness of things, but either forgetful or not apprehensive of the fate which befell her father at the first performance of the opera in Rome, introduced a Spanish song. Mme. Patti always kept a ready repertory for the scene, with a song in the vernacular of the people for whom she was singing to bring the enthusiasm to a climax and a finish: "Home, Sweet Home" in New York and London, "Solovei" in St. Petersburg. Usually she began with the bolero from "Les Vêpres Siciliennes," or the shadow dance from "Dinorah." Mme. Sembrich, living in a period when the style of song of which she and Mme. Melba are still the brightest exemplars, is not as familiar as it used to be when they were children, also found it necessary to have an extended list of pieces ready at hand to satisfy the rapacious public. She was wont at first to sing Proch's Air and Variations, but that always led to a demand for more, and whether she supplemented it with "Ah! non giunge," from "La Sonnambula," the bolero from "The Sicilian Vespers," "O luce di quest anima," from "Linda," or the vocalized waltz by Strauss, the applause always was riotous, and so remained until she sat down to the pianoforte and sang Chopin's "Maiden's Wish," in Polish, to her own accompaniment. As for Mme. Melba, not to be set in the shade simply because Mme. Sembrich is almost as good a pianist as she is a singer, she supplements Arditi's waltz or Massenet's "Sevillana" with Tosti's "Mattinata," to which she also plays an exquisite accompaniment.

But this is a long digression; I must back to my intriguing lovers, who have made good use of the lesson scene to repeat their protestations of affection and lay plots for attaining their happiness. In this they are helped by *Figaro*, who comes to shave *Dr. Bartolo* in spite of his protests, and, contriving to get hold of the latter's keys, "conveys" the one which opens the balcony lock, and thus makes possible a plan for a midnight elopement. In the midst of the lesson the real *Basilio* comes to meet his appointment, and there is a moment of confusion for the plotters, out of which *Figaro* extricates them by persuading *Basilio* that he is sick of a raging fever, and must go instantly home, *Almaviva* adding a convincing argument in the shape of a generously lined purse. Nevertheless, *Basilio* afterwards betrays the *Count* to *Bartolo*, who commands him to bring a notary to the house that very night so that he may sign the marriage contract with *Rosina*. In the midst of a tempest *Figaro* and the *Count* let themselves into the house at midnight to carry off *Rosina*, but find her in a whimsy, her mind having been poisoned against her lover by *Bartolo* with the aid of the unfortunate letter. Out of this dilemma *Almaviva* extricates himself by confessing his identity, and the pair are about to steal away when the discovery is made that the ladder to the balcony has been carried away. As they are tiptoeing toward the window, the three sing a trio in which there is such obvious use of a melodic phrase which belongs to Haydn that every writer on "Il Barbiere" seems to have thought it his duty to point out an instance of "plagiarism" on the part of Rossini. It is a trifling matter. The trio begins thus:—

Zit - ti, zit - ti, pia - no pia - no, non fac-

cia - mo con - fu - sion - ne

which is a slightly varied form of four measures from *Simon's* song in the first part of "The Seasons":—

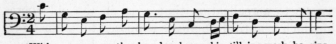

With ea-ger-ness the hus-band-man his till-ing work be-gins.

With these four measures the likeness begins and ends. A venial offence, if it be an offence at all. Composers were not held to so strict and scrupulous an accountability touching melodic *meum* and *tuum* a century ago as they are now; yet there

was then a thousand-fold more melodic inventiveness. Another case of "conveyance" by Rossini
has also been pointed out; the air of the duenna
in the third act beginning "Il vecchiotto cerca
moglie" is said to be that of a song which Rossini
heard a Russian lady sing in Rome. I have searched
much in Russian song literature and failed to find
the alleged original. To finish the story: the notary
summoned by *Bartolo* arrives on the scene, but is
persuaded by *Figaro* to draw up an attestation
of a marriage agreement between *Count Almaviva*
and *Rosina*, and *Bartolo*, finding at the last that
all his precautions have been in vain, comforted
not a little by the gift of his ward's dower, which
the *Count* relinquishes, gives his blessing to the
lovers.

I have told the story of "Il Barbiere di Siviglia"
as it appears in the book. It has grown to be the
custom to omit in performance several of the incidents which are essential to the development and
understanding of the plot. Some day — soon, it is
to be hoped — managers, singers, and public will
awake to a realization that, even in the old operas
in which beautiful singing is supposed to be the be-all
and end-all, the action ought to be kept coherent.
In that happy day Rossini's effervescent lyrical
arrangement of Beaumarchais's vivacious comedy
will be restored to its rights.

CHAPTER II

BEAUMARCHAIS wrote a trilogy of Figaro comedies, and if the tastes and methods of a century or so ago had been like those of the present, we might have had also a trilogy of Figaro operas — "Le Barbier de Seville," "Le Mariage de Figaro," and "La Mère coupable." As it is, we have operatic versions of the first two of the comedies, Mozart's "Nozze di Figaro" being a sequel to Rossini's "Il Barbiere," its action beginning at a period not long after the precautions of *Dr. Bartolo* had been rendered inutile by *Figaro's* cunning schemes and *Almaviva* had installed *Rosina* as his countess. "Le Nozze" was composed a whole generation before Rossini's opera. Mozart and his public could keep the sequence of incidents in view, however, from the fact that Paisiello had acquainted them with the beginning of the story. Paisiello's opera is dead, but Rossini's is very much alive, and it might prove interesting, some day, to have the two living operas brought together in performance in order to note the effect produced upon each other by comparison of their scores. One effect, I fancy,

19

would be to make the elder of the operas sound younger than its companion, because of the greater variety and freshness, as well as dramatic vigor, of its music. But though the names of many of the characters would be the same, we should scarcely recognize their musical physiognomies. We should find the sprightly *Rosina* of "Il Barbiere" changed into a mature lady with a countenance sicklied o'er with the pale cast of a gentle melancholy; the *Count's* tenor would, in the short interval, have changed into barytone; *Figaro's* barytone into a bass, while the buffo-bass of *Don Basilio* would have reversed the process with age and gone upward into the tenor region. We should meet with some new characters, of which two at least would supply the element of dramatic freshness and vivacity which we should miss from the company of the first opera — *Susanna* and *Cherubino*.

We should also, in all likelihood, be struck by the difference in the moral atmosphere of the two works. It took Beaumarchais three years to secure a public performance of his "Mariage de Figaro" because of the opposition of the French court, with Louis XVI at its head, to its too frank libertinism. This opposition spread also to other royal and imperial personages, who did not relish the manner in which the poet had castigated the nobility, exalted the intellectuality of menials, and satirized the social and political conditions which were generally prevalent a short time before the French Revolution. Neither of the operas, however, met the obstacles which blocked the progress of the comedies on which they are founded, because Da Ponte, who wrote the book for Mozart, and Sterbini, who was Rossini's librettist, judiciously and deftly elided the objectionable political element. "Le Nozze" is by far the more ingeniously constructed play of the two (though a trifle too involved for popular comprehension in the original language), but "Il Barbiere" has the advantage of freedom from the moral grossness which pollutes its companion. For the unspoiled taste of the better class of opera patrons, there is a livelier as well as a lovelier charm in the story of *Almaviva's* adventures while outwitting *Dr. Bartolo* and carrying off the winsome *Rosina* to be his countess than in the depiction of his amatory intrigues after marriage. In fact, there is something especially repellent in the *Count's* lustful pursuit of the bride of the man to whose intellectual resourcefulness he owed the successful outcome of his own wooing.

It is, indeed, a fortunate thing for Mozart's music that so few opera-goers understand Italian nowadays. The play is a moral blister, and the less intelligible it is made by excisions in its dialogue, the better, in one respect, for the virtuous sensibilities of its auditors. One point which can be sacrificed without detriment to the music and at only a trifling cost to the comedy (even when it is looked upon from the viewpoint which prevailed in Europe at the period of its creation) is that which Beaumarchais relied on chiefly to add piquancy to the

conduct of the *Count. Almaviva,* we are given to
understand, on his marriage with *Rosina* had voluntarily abandoned an ancient seignorial right,
described by *Susanna* as "certe mezz' ore che il
diritto feudale," but is desirous of reviving the
practice in the case of the *Countess's* bewitching
maid on the eve of her marriage to his valet. It is
this discovery which induces *Figaro* to invent his
scheme for expediting the wedding, and lends a
touch of humor to the scene in which *Figaro* asks
that he and his bride enjoy the first-fruits of the
reform while the villagers lustily hymn the merits
of their "virtuous" lord; but the too frank discussion of the subject with which the dialogue teems
might easily be avoided. The opera, like all the
old works of the lyrical stage, is in sad need of
intelligent revision and thorough study, so that its
dramatic as well as its musical beauties may be
preserved. There is no lovelier merit in Mozart's
music than the depth and tenderness with which
the honest love of *Susanna* for *Figaro* and the *Countess* for her lord are published; and it is no demerit
that the volatile passion of the adolescent *Cherubino*
and the frolicsome, scintillant, vivacious spirit of
the plotters are also given voice. Mozart's music
could not be all that it is if it did not enter fully
and unreservedly into the spirit of the comedy; it
is what it is because whenever the opportunity presented itself, he raised it into the realm of the ideal.
Yet Mozart was no Puritan. He swam along gayly
and contentedly on the careless current of life as

it was lived in Vienna and elsewhere in the closing decades of the eighteenth century, and was not averse, merely for the fun of the thing, to go even a step beyond his librettist when the chance offered. Here is an instance in point: The plotters have been working a little at cross-purposes, each seeking his own advantages, and their plans are about to be put to the test when *Figaro* temporarily loses confidence in the honesty of *Susanna*. With his trust in her falls to the ground his faith in all womankind. He rails against the whole sex in the air, beginning: "Aprite un po' quegl' occhi?" in the last act. Enumerating the moral blemishes of women, he at length seems to be fairly choked by his own spleen, and bursts out at the end with "Il resto nol dico, gia ognuno lo sa" ("The rest I'll not tell you — everybody knows it"). The orchestra stops, all but the horns, which with the phrase

Corni.

aided by a traditional gesture (the singer's forefingers pointing upward from his forehead), complete his meaning. It is a pity that the air is often omitted, for it is eloquent in the exposition of the spirit of the comedy.

The merriest of opera overtures introduces "Le

Nozze di Figaro," and puts the listener at once into
a frolicsome mood. It seems to be the most careless
of little pieces, drawing none of its material from
the music of the play, making light of some of the
formulas which demanded respect at the time (there
is no free fantasia), laughing and singing its innocent life out in less than five minutes as if it were
breathing an atmosphere of pure oxygen. It romps;
it does not reflect or feel. Motion is its business,
not emotion. It has no concern with the deep and
gentle feelings of the play, but only with its frolic.
The spirit of playful torment, the disposition of a
pretty tease, speaks out of its second subject:—

and one may, if one wishes, hear the voice of only
half-serious admonition in the phrase of the basses,
which the violins echo as if in mockery:—

Bassi Viola & Fag.

But, on the whole, the overture does not ask for
analysis or interpretation; it is satisfied to express
untrammelled joy in existence.

The curtain is withdrawn, and we discover the
lovers preparing for their wedding. *Figaro* is

taking the dimensions of a room, and the first motive of a duet illustrates his measured paces; *Susanna* is trimming a hat, and her happiness and her
complacent satisfaction with her handiwork are
published in the second motive, whose innocent
joy explodes in scintillant semi-quavers in the fiddles
at the third measure. His labors ended, *Figaro*
joins *Susanna* in her utterances of joy. But there
is a fly in the ointment. Why has *Figaro* been so
busily measuring the room? To test its fitness
as their chamber, for the *Count* has assigned it to
them, though it is one of the best rooms in the palace.
He points out its convenient location (duet: "Se
a caso madama"); so near the room of the *Countess*
that her maid can easily answer the "din din" of
her bell, and near enough to the room of the *Count*
that his "don don" would never sound in vain
should he wish to send his valet on an errand. Altogether too convenient, explains *Susanna;* some
fine day the *Count's* "don don" might mean a three-
mile journey for the valet, and then the devil would
fetch the dear *Count* to her side in three paces.
Has he not been making love violently to her for
a space, sending *Don Basilio* to give her singing
lessons and to urge her to accept his suit? Did
Figaro imagine it was because of his own pretty
face that the *Count* had promised her so handsome
a dowry? *Figaro* had pressed such a flattering
unction to his soul, but now recalls, with not a little
jealous perturbation, that the *Count* had planned
to take him with him to London, where he was to

go on a mission of state: "He as ambassador, *Figaro*
as a courier, and *Susanna* as ambassadress in secret.
Is that your game, my lord? Then I'll set the pace
for your dancing with my guitar" (Cavatina: "Se
vuol ballare").

Almaviva's obedient valet disappears, and presto!
in his place we see our old friend, the cunning, resourceful barber and town factotum of the earlier
days, who shall hatch out a plot to confound his
master and shield his love from persecution. First
of all he must hasten the wedding. He sets about
this at once, but all unconscious of the fact that
Dr. Bartolo has never forgiven nor forgotten the
part he played in robbing him of his ward *Rosina*.
He comes now to let us know that he is seeking revenge against *Figaro* and at the same time, as he
hopes, rid himself of his old housekeeper, *Marcellina,*
to whom he is bound by an obligation that is becoming irksome. The old duenna has been casting amatory glances in *Figaro's* direction, and has
a hold on him in the shape of a written obligation
to marry her in default of repayment of a sum of
money borrowed in a time of need. She enlists
Bartolo as adviser, and he agrees to lay the matter
before the *Count*. Somewhat early, but naturally
enough in the case of the conceited dotard, he gloats
over his vengeance, which seems as good as accomplished, and celebrates his triumph in an air ("La
vendetta!"). As she is about to leave the room,
Marcellina meets *Susanna*, and the two make a
forced effort to conceal their mutual hatred and

jealousy in an amusing duettino ("Via resti servita, madama brillante!"), full of satirical compliments and curtsies. *Marcellina* is bowed out of the room with extravagant politeness, and *Susanna* turns her attention to her mistress's wardrobe, only to be interrupted by the entrance of *Cherubino*, the *Count's* page. Though a mere stripling, *Cherubino* is already a budding voluptuary, animated with a wish, something like that of Byron's hero, that all womankind had but a single mouth and he the privilege of kissing it. He adores the *Countess;* but not her alone. *Susanna* has a ribbon in her hand with which, she tells him, she binds up her mistress's tresses at night. Happy *Susanna!* Happy ribbon! *Cherubino* seizes it, refuses to give it up, and offers in exchange his latest ballad. "What shall I do with the song?" asks *Susanna*. "Sing it to the *Countess!* Sing it yourself! Sing it to *Barbarina*, to *Marcellina*, to all the ladies in the palace!" He tells *Susanna* (Air: "Non so più cosa son") of the torments which he endures. The lad's mind is, indeed, in a parlous state; he feels his body alternately burning and freezing; the mere sight of a maiden sends the blood to his cheeks, and he needs must sigh whenever he hears her voice; sleeping and waking, by lakeside, in the shadow of the woods, on the mountain, by stream and fountain, his thoughts are only of love and its sweet pains. It is quite impossible to describe the eloquence with which Mozart's music expresses the feverish unrest, the turmoil, and the longing which fill the lad's

soul.   Otto Jahn has attempted it, and I shall quote
his effort: —

The vibration of sentiment, never amounting to actual
passion, the mingled anguish and delight of the longing
which can never be satisfied, are expressed with a power
of beauty raising them out of the domain of mere sensuality.
Very remarkable is the simplicity of the means by which
this extraordinary effect is attained.   A violin accompaniment passage, not unusual in itself, keeps up the
restless movement; the harmonies make no striking
progressions; strong emphasis and accents are sparingly
used, and yet the soft flow of the music is made suggestive
of the consuming glow of passion.   The instrumentation
is here of a very peculiar effect and quite a novel coloring;
the stringed instruments are muted, and clarinets occur
for the first time, and very prominently, both alone and
in combination with the horns and bassoons.

Cherubino's philandering with *Susanna* is interrupted by the *Count*, who comes with protestations
of love, which the page hears from a hiding-place
behind a large arm-chair, where *Susanna*, in her
embarrassment, had hastily concealed him on the
Count's entrance.   The *Count's* philandering, in turn,
is interrupted by *Basilio*, whose voice is heard long
enough before his entrance to permit the *Count*
also to seek a hiding-place.   He, too, gets behind
the chair, while *Cherubino*, screened by *Susanna's*
skirts, ensconces himself in the seat, and finds cover
under one of the *Countess's* gowns which *Susanna*
hurriedly throws over him.   *Don Basilio* comes
in search of the *Count*, but promptly begins his
pleas in behalf of his master.   Receiving nothing

but indignant rejoinders, he twits *Susanna* with loving the lad, and more than intimates that *Cherubino* is in love with the *Countess*. Why else does he devour her with his eyes when serving her at table? And had he not composed a canzonetta for her? Far be it from him, however, to add a word to what "everybody says." "Everybody says what?" demands the *Count*, discovering himself. A trio follows ("Cosa sento!"). The *Count*, though in a rage, preserves a dignified behavior and orders the instant dismissal of the page from the palace. *Susanna* is overwhelmed with confusion, and plainly betrays her agitation. She swoons, and her companions are about to place her in the arm-chair when she realizes a danger and recovers consciousness. *Don Basilio* cringes before the *Count*, but is maliciously delighted at the turn which affairs have taken.

The *Count* is stern. *Cherubino* had once before incurred his displeasure by poaching in his preserves. He had visited *Barbarina*, the pretty daughter of his gardener, and found the door bolted. The maid appeared confused, and he, seeking an explanation, drew the cover from the table and found the page hiding under. He illustrates his action by lifting the gown thrown over the chair, and there is the page again! This, then, is the reason of *Susanna's* seeming prudery—the page, her lover! He accuses *Susanna*, who asserts her innocence, and truthfully says that *Cherubino* had come to ask her to procure the *Countess's* intercession in his behalf, when his entrance had thrown them both into such confusion that *Cherubino* had concealed himself. Where? Behind the arm-chair. But the *Count* himself had hidden there. True, but a moment before the page had slipped around and into the chair. Then he had heard all that the *Count* had said to *Susanna*? *Cherubino* says he had tried his best not to overhear anything. *Figaro* is sent for and enters with the villagers, who hymn the virtues of their lord. To the *Count's* question as to the meaning of the demonstration, *Figaro* explains that it is an expression of their gratitude for the *Count's* surrender of seignorial rights, and that his subjects wish him to celebrate the occasion by bestowing the hand of *Susanna* on *Figaro* at once and himself placing the bridal veil upon her brow. The *Count* sees through *Figaro's* trick, but believing it will be frustrated by *Marcellina's* appeal, he promises to honor the bride, as requested, in due season. *Cherubino* has begged for the *Count's* forgiveness, and *Susanna* has urged his youth in extenuation of his fault. Reminded that the lad knows of his pursuit of *Susanna*, the *Count* modifies his sentence of dismissal from his service to banishment to Seville as an officer in his regiment. *Figaro* playfully inducts him into the new existence.

The air "Non più andrai," in which this is done, is in vigorous march rhythm. Benucci, the original *Figaro* in Vienna, had a superbly sonorous voice, and Michael Kelly, the English tenor (who sang the two rôles of *Don Basilio* and *Don Curzio*), tells us how thrillingly he sang the song at the first rehearsal with the full band. Mozart was on the stage in a crimson pelisse and cocked hat trimmed with gold lace, giving the time to the orchestra. *Figaro* gave the song with the greatest animation and power of voice. "I was standing close to Mozart," says Kelly, "who, *sotto voce*, was repeating: 'Bravo, bravo, Benucci!' and when Benucci came to the fine passage, 'Cherubino, alla vittoria, alla gloria militar,' which he gave out with stentorian lungs, the effect was electricity itself, for the whole of the performers on the stage, and those in the orchestra, as if actuated by one feeling of delight, vociferated: 'Bravo, bravo, maestro! Viva, viva, grande Mozart!' Those in the orchestra I thought would never have ceased applauding by beating the bows of their violins against the music desks. The little man acknowledged by repeated obeisances his thanks for the distinguished mark of enthusiastic applause bestowed upon him."

This ends the first act. At the opening of the second the *Countess* asks our sympathy because of the unhappiness caused by her errant husband. (Cavatina: "Porgi amor.") She prays the god of love to restore her to his affections. *Susanna* entering, the *Countess* asks her to continue her tale of the *Count's* pursuit of her. There is nothing to add, says the maid; the *Count* wooed as noblemen woo women of her class — with money. *Figaro* appears to tell that the *Count* is aiding *Marcellina*

in her scheme and of the trick which he has devised to circumvent him. He had sent *Basilio* to
his lordship with a letter warning him that the
Countess had made an appointment to meet a lover
at the ball to be given in the evening. This would
fan the fires of his jealousy and so enrage him that
he would forget his designs against *Susanna* until
she was safely married, when he would discover
that he had been outwitted. In the meantime,
while he is reflecting on the fact that two could play
at the game, *Susanna* is to apprise the *Count* that
she will meet him in the garden in the evening.
Cherubino, whose departure to Seville had been
delayed for the purpose, is to meet the *Count* disguised as *Susanna*, and the *Countess*, appearing on
the scene, is to unmask him. The *Count* is supposed
to have gone a-hunting, and the plotters have two
hours for preparation. *Figaro* leaves them to find
Cherubino, that he may be put into petticoats.
When the page comes, the *Countess* first insists on
hearing the song which he had given to *Susanna*,
and *Cherubino*, stammering and blushing at first,
sings it to *Susanna's* guitar. (Canzone: "Voi che
sapete.") Again I call upon Otto Jahn for a description of the music. "*Cherubino* is not here directly expressing his feelings; he is depicting them
in a romance, and he is in the presence of the *Countess*,
toward whom he glances with all the bashfulness
of boyish passion. The song is in ballad form, to
suit the situation, the voice executing the clear,
lovely melody, while the stringed instruments carry

on a simple accompaniment pizzicato, to imitate
the guitar: this delicate outline is, however, shaded
and animated in a wonderful degree by solo wind
instruments. Without being absolutely necessary
for the progress of the melodies and the complete-
ness of the harmonies, they supply the delicate
touches of detail, reading between the lines of the
romance, as it were, what is passing in the heart
of the singer. We know not whether to admire
most the gracefulness of the melodies, the delicacy
of the disposition of the parts, the charm of the tone
coloring, or the tenderness of the expression — the
whole is of entrancing beauty."

Susanna finds that she and *Cherubino* are of the
same height, and begins to array him in garments
belonging to her, first locking the door against possible intruders. The *Countess* views the adventure
with some misgivings at first, but, after all, *Cherubino* is a mere boy, and she rejoices him with approval of his songs, and smiles upon him till he is
deliriously happy. *Basilio* has given him his commission in the *Count's* regiment, and the *Countess*
discovers that it lacks a seal to secure which would
cause a longer and desired delay. While *Susanna*
is playing the rôle of dressing-maid to *Cherubino,*
and instructing him in a ladylike bearing, the *Count*
raps for admission to the room. *Figaro's* decoy
letter caused him uneasiness, and he had abandoned
the hunt. *Cherubino* hurries into the chamber, and
the *Countess* turns the key upon him before ad-
mitting his lordship, who enters in an ill-humor

which is soon turned into jealous rage. *Cherubino* has awkwardly overturned a chair in the chamber, and though the *Countess* explains that *Susanna* is within, she refuses to open the door, on the plea that her maid is making her toilet. The *Count* goes for tools to break open the door, taking the *Countess* with him. *Susanna*, who has heard all from an alcove, hastens to *Cherubino's* rescue, who escapes by leaping from the window of the *Countess's* apartment into the garden below. *Susanna* takes his place in the chamber. Then begins the most marvellously ingenious and beautiful finale in the whole literature of opera. Fast upon each other follow no fewer than eight independent pieces of music, each a perfect delineation of the quickly changing moods and situations of the comedy, yet each built up on the lines of musical symmetry, and developing a musical theme which, though it passes from mouth to mouth, appears each time to belong peculiarly to the person uttering it. The *Countess* throws herself upon the mercy of the *Count,* confesses that *Cherubino*, suspiciously garbed, is in the chamber, but pleads for his life and protests her innocence of wrong. She gives the key to her enraged husband, who draws his sword, unlocks the door, and commands the page to stand forth. *Susanna* confronts the pair with grave unconsciousness upon her features. The *Countess* is no less amazed than her lord.

The *Count* goes into the chamber to search for the page, giving *Susanna* a chance to explain, and the nimble-witted women are ready for him when

he comes back confused, confounded, and ready
to ask forgiveness of his wife, who becomes tearful
and accusing, telling him at length that the story
of the page's presence was all an invention to test
him. But the letter giving word of the assignation?
Written by *Figaro*. He then shall be punished.
Forgiveness is deserved only by those willing to
forgive. All is well, and the *Countess* gives her
hand to be kissed by her lord. Enters *Figaro*
with joyous music to announce that all's ready for
the wedding; trumpets sounding, pipes tootling,
peasants singing and dancing. The *Count* throws
a damper upon his exuberant spirits. How about
that letter? In spite of the efforts of the *Countess*
and *Susanna* to make him confess its authorship,
Figaro stoutly insists that he knows nothing of it.
The *Count* summons *Marcellina*, but before she
arrives, the drunken gardener *Antonio* appears to
tell the *Count* that some one had leaped out of the
salon window and damaged his plants and pots.
Confusion overwhelms the women. But *Figaro's*
wits are at work. He laughs loudly and accuses
Antonio of being too tipsy to know what had happened. The gardener sticks to his story and is
about to describe the man who came like a bolt
from the window, when *Figaro* says it was he made
the leap. He was waiting in the salon to see *Susanna*,
he explains, when he heard the *Count's* footsteps,
and, fearing to meet him because of the decoy letter,
he had jumped from the window and got a sprained
ankle, which he offers in evidence. The orchestra

changes key and tempo, and begins a new inquisition
with pitiless reiteration : —

Antonio produces *Cherubino's* commission, "These,
then, are your papers?" The *Count* takes the commission, opens it, and the *Countess* recognizes it.
With whispers and signs the women let *Figaro* know
what it is, and he is ready with the explanation that
the page had left the paper with him. Why? It
lacked — the women come again to his rescue — it
lacked the seal. The *Count* tears up the paper in
his rage at being foiled again. But his allies are at
hand, in the persons of *Marcellina, Bartolo,* and
Basilio, who appear with the accusing contract,
signed by *Figaro.* The *Count* takes the case under
advisement, and the act ends with *Figaro's* enemies
sure of triumph and his friends dismayed.

The third act plays in a large hall of the palace
decorated for the wedding. In a duet ("Crudel!
perche finora") the *Count* renews his addresses to
Susanna. She, to help along the plot to unmask
him, consents to meet him in the garden. A wonderful grace rests upon the music of the duet, which
Mozart's genius makes more illuminative than the
words. Is it *Susanna's* native candor, or goodness,
or mischievousness, or her embarrassment which
prompts her to answer "yes" when "no" was expected and "no" when the *Count* had already received an affirmative? We can think as we please;

the musical effect is delicious. *Figaro's* coming
interrupts further conversation, and as *Susanna*
leaves the room with her, she drops a remark to
Figaro, which the *Count* overhears: "Hush! We
have won our case without a lawyer." What does
it mean? Treachery, of course. Possibly *Marcellina's* silence has been purchased. But whence the
money? The *Count's amour propre* is deeply wounded
at the thought that his menials should outwit him
and he fail of his conquest. He swears that he will
be avenged upon both. Apparently he has not long
to wait, for *Marcellina, Don Curzio,* and *Bartolo*
enter, followed by *Figaro. Don Curzio* announces
the decision of the court in the duenna's suit against
Figaro. He must pay or marry, according to the
bond. But *Figaro* refuses to abide by the decision.
He is a gentleman by birth, as proved by the jewels
and costly clothing found upon him when he was
recovered from some robbers who stole him when
a babe, and he must have the consent of his parents.
He has diligently sought them and will prove his
identity by a mark upon his arm. "A spatula on
the right elbow?" anxiously inquires *Marcellina.*
"Yes." And now *Bartolo* and the duenna, who a
moment ago would fain have made him an Œdipus,
recognize in *Figaro* their own son, born out of wedlock. He rushes to their arms and is found em-
bracing his mother most tenderly by *Susanna,*
who comes with a purse to repay the loan. She
flies into a passion and boxes *Figaro's* ears before
the situation is explained, and she is made as happy

by the unexpected dénouement as the *Count* and
Don Curzio are miserable. *Bartolo* resolves that
there shall be a double wedding; he will do tardy
justice to *Marcellina*. Now we see the *Countess*
again in her lamentable mood, mourning the loss
of her husband's love. (Aria: "Dove sono.")
Susanna comes to tell of her appointment with the
Count. The place, "in the garden," seems to be
lacking in clearness, and the *Countess* proposes that
it be made more definite and certain (as the lawyers
say), by means of a letter which shall take the form
of a "Song to the Zephyr." This is the occasion of
the exquisite duet which was surely in the mind of
the composer's father when, writing to his daughter
from Vienna after the third performance of the opera,
he said: "One little duet had to be sung three times."
Was there ever such exquisite dictation and transcription? Can any one say, after hearing this
"Canzonetta sull' aria," that it is unnatural to
melodize conversation? With what gracious tact
the orchestra gives time to *Susanna* to set down
the words of her mistress! How perfect is the
musical reproduction of inquiry and repetition
when a phrase escapes the memory of the writer!

sotto i pi-ni? Sotto i pi-ni del bos-chet-to.

sotto i pi-ni del bos-chet-to.

The letter is written, read over phrase by phrase, and sealed with a pin which the *Count* is to return as proof that he has received the note.

The wedding festivities begin with a presentation of flowers to the *Countess* by the village maidens, among whom in disguise is the rogue *Cherubino* — so fair in hat and gown that the *Countess* singles him out of the throng to present his nosegay in person. *Antonio*, who had suspected that he was still about the palace, exposes him to the *Count*, who threatens the most rigorous punishment, but is obliged to grant *Barberina's* petition that he give his consent to her marriage to the page. Had he not often told her to ask him what she pleased, when kissing her in secret? Under the circumstances he can only grant the little maid's wish. During the dance which follows (it is a Spanish fandango which seems to have been popular in Vienna at the time, for Gluck had already made use of the same melody in his ballet "Don Juan"), *Susanna* kneels before the *Count* to have him place the wreath (or veil) upon her head, and slyly slips the "Canzonetta sull' aria" into his hands. He pricks his finger with the pin, drops it. but, on reading the postscript, picks it up, so that he may return it to the writer as a sign of understanding. In the evening *Barberina*, who has been commissioned to carry the pin to her cousin *Susanna*, loses it again, and her lamentation "L'ho perdita," with its childish sobs while hunting it, is one of the little gems of the opera. From her *Figaro* learns that the letter which he had seen the

Count read during the dance was from *Susanna*, and becomes furiously jealous. In an air (which has already been described), he rails against man's credulity and woman's faithlessness. The time is come to unmask the *Count*. The *Countess* and *Susanna* have exchanged dresses, and now come into the garden. Left alone, *Susanna* gives voice to her longing and love (for *Figaro*, though the situation makes it seem to be for the *Count*) in the air which has won great favor in the concert-room: "Deh vieni non tardar." Here some of Otto Jahn's words are again appropriate: —

Mozart was right to let the feelings of the loving maiden shine forth in all their depth and purity, for *Susanna* has none but her *Figaro* in her mind, and the sentiments she expresses are her true ones. *Figaro*, in his hiding-place, listening and suspecting her of awaiting the *Count's* arrival, throws a cross-light on the situation, which, however, only receives its full dramatic signification by reason of the truth of *Susanna's* expression of feeling. *Susanna*, without her sensual charm, is inconceivable, and a tinge of sensuality is an essential element of her nature; but Mozart has transfigured it into a noble purity which may fitly be compared with the grandest achievements of Greek sculpture.

Cherubino, watched from different places of concealment by the *Count*, *Figaro*, and *Susanna*, appears, and, seeing the *Countess*, whom he takes for *Susanna*, confounds not her alone, but also the *Count* and *Figaro*, by his ardent addresses to her. He attempts to kiss her, but the *Count* steps forward and interposes his cheek. The *Count* attempts to box *Cherubino's* ears, but *Figaro*, slipping forward at the moment, receives the blow instead. Confusion is at its height. The *Count* makes love to his wife, thinking she is *Susanna*, promises her a dowry, and places a ring on her finger. Seeing torches approaching, they withdraw into deeper darkness. *Susanna* shows herself, and *Figaro*, who takes her for the Countess, acquaints her of the *Count's* doings which he has just witnessed. *Susanna* betrays herself, and *Figaro* resolves to punish her for her masquerading. He makes love to her with extravagant pathos until interrupted by a slap in the face. *Susanna's* patience had become exhausted, and her temper got the better of her judgment. *Figaro* laughs at her ill-humor and confesses his trick, but renews his sham love-making when he sees the *Count* returning. The latter calls for lights, and seizes *Figaro* and his retainers. In the presence of all he is put to shame by the disclosures of the personality of the *Countess* and *Susanna*. He falls on his knees, asks forgiveness, receives it, and all ends happily.

CHAPTER III

"DIE ZAUBERFLÖTE"

MOZART'S "Zauberflöte" — "The Magic Flute" —
is the oldest German opera holding a place on the
American stage, though not quite 118 years old; but
so far as my memory and records go, it has had
but four performances in the original tongue in New
York in a whole generation. There have been a few
representations in English within this time and a
considerable number in Italian, our operatic institutions being quick, as a rule, to put it upon the stage
whenever they have at command a *soprano leggiero*
with a voice of sufficient range and flexibility to
meet the demands of the extraordinary music
which Mozart wrote for the *Queen of Night* to oblige
his voluble-throated sister-in-law, Mme. Hofer,
who was the original representative of that character. The same operatic conditions having prevailed in New York and London for many years,
it is not strange that English-speaking people have
come to associate "The Magic Flute" with the
Italian rather than the German repertory. Yet we
have the dictum of Beethoven that it is Mozart's
greatest opera, because in it his genius showed

42

itself in so large a variety of musical forms, rang-
ing from ditties in the folk-song style to figurated
chorale and fugue, and more particularly because
in it Mozart first disclosed himself as a German
composer. By this Beethoven did not mean that
Mozart had not written music before for a German
libretto, but that he had never written German
music before in an opera. The distinction is one
more easily observed by Germans and critical historians than by the ordinary frequenters of our
opera-houses. "Die Zauberflöte" has a special
charm for people of German blood, which is both
admirable and amiable. Its magnificent choruses
are sung by men, and Germany is the home of the
Männergesang; among the opera's songs are echoes
of the *Volkslied* — ditties which seem to have been
caught up in the German nurseries or plucked off
the lips of the itinerant German balladist; its emotional music is heartfelt, warm, ingenuous, and in
form and spirit free from the artificiality of Italian
opera as it was in Mozart's day and as it continued
to be for a long time thereafter. It was this last
virtue which gave the opera its largest importance
in the eyes of Otto Jahn, Mozart's biographer. In
it, he said, for the first time all the resources of
cultivated art were brought to bear with the freedom
of genius upon a genuine German opera. In his
Italian operas, Mozart had adopted the traditions
of a long period of development, and by virtue
of his original genius had brought them to a
climax and a conclusion; but in "Die Zauberflöte"

he "stepped across the threshold of the future and unlocked the sanctuary of national art for his countrymen."

In this view every critical historian can concur, no matter what his tastes or where his home. But it is less easy for an English, French, or Italian critic than a German to pardon the incongruities, incoherences, and silly buffooneries which mar the opera. Some of the disturbing elements are dear to the Teutonic heart. *Papageno*, for instance, is but a slightly metamorphosed Kasperl, a Jack Pudding (Hanswurst) twice removed; and Kasperl is as intimately bound up in the German nature as his cousin Punch in the English. Kasperl is, indeed, directly responsible for "Die Zauberflöte." At the end of the eighteenth century there was in Vienna a singular individual named Emmanuel Schikaneder, a Jack-of-all-trades so far as public amusements were concerned — musician, singer, actor, playwright, and manager. There can be no doubt but that he was a sad scalawag and ribald rogue, with as few moral scruples as ever burdened a purveyor of popular amusements. But he had some personal traits which endeared him to Mozart, and a degree of intellectuality which won him a fairly respectable place among the writers for the stage at the turn of the century. Moreover, when he had become prosperous enough to build a new theatre with the proceeds of "Die Zauberflöte," he was wise enough to give a generous commission, unhampered by his customary meddle

some restrictions, to Beethoven; and discreet enough
to approve of the highly virtuous book of "Fidelio."
At the beginning of the last decade of the eighteenth
century, however, his theatre had fallen on evil
days, and in dire straits he went to Mozart, whose
friendship he had enjoyed from the latter's Salzburg days, and begged him to undertake the composition of an opera for which he had written the
book, in conjunction with one of his actors and
choristers, named Gieseke (though this fact never
received public acknowledgment at his hands).
Wieland's "Oberon" had filled the popular mind
with a great fondness for fantastic and Oriental
subjects, and a rival manager had been successful
with musical pieces in which the principal character
was the popular Kasperl. Casting about for an
operatic subject which should appeal to the general
liking for romanticism and buffoonery at once,
Schikaneder hit upon a tale called "Lulu; oder,
Die Zauberflöte," written by Liebeskind, but published by W eland in a volume of Orientalia entitled
"Dschinnistan." He had got pretty deep in his
work when a rival manager brought out an adaptation of the same story, with music by Wenzel Müller.
The farcical character of the piece is indicated by
its title, which was "Kasper, der Fagottist; oder,
Die Zauberzither"; but it made so striking a success
that Schikaneder feared to enter the lists against it
with an opera drawn from the same source. He
was either too lazy, too much in a hurry, or too indifferent to the principles of art to remodel the

completed portion, but finished his book on lines
far different from those originally contemplated.
The transformation thus accomplished brought
about all the blemishes of "Die Zauberflöte," but
also gave occasion for the sublime music with which
Mozart transfigured some of the scenes. This will
be understood better if an outline of Liebeskind's
tale is made to precede the story of the opera as it
came from Mozart's hand.

A wicked magician, *Dilsenghuin*, has robbed the
"radiant fairy" *Perifirime* of her daughter, *Sidi*,
and carried off a magic talisman. The magician
keeps the damsel in confinement and persecutes
her with amatory advances which she is able to
resist through a power which is to support her so
long as her heart is untouched by love. *Perifirime*
promises the hand of her daughter, whose father
is the King of Cashmere, to *Prince Lulu*, son of
the King of Chorassan, if he regain the stolen
talisman for her. To do this, however, is given only
to one who has never felt the divine passion. *Lulu*
undertakes the adventure, and as aids the fairy
gives him a magic flute and a ring. The tone of
the flute will win the hearts of all who hear it; by
turning the ring, the wearer is enabled to assume
any form desired at will; by throwing it away he
may summon the fairy herself to his aid. The
Prince assumes the form of an old man, and, like
Orpheus, softens the nature of the wild beasts that
he meets in the forest. He even melts the heart of
the magician himself, who admits him to his castle.

Once he is within its walls, the inmates all yield to the charm of his magical music, not excepting the lovely prisoner. At a banquet he throws the magician and his companions into a deep sleep, and possesses himself of the talisman. It is a gold fire-steel, every spark struck from which becomes a powerful spirit whose service is at the command of the possessor. With the help of genii, struck from the magical implement, and the fairy whom he summons at the last, *Prince Lulu* overcomes all the obstacles placed in his way. Discomfited, the magician flies away as an owl. *Perifirime* destroys the castle and carries the lovers in a cloud chariot to her own palace. Their royal fathers give their blessings, and *Prince Lulu* and *Princess Sidi* are joined in wedlock.

Following in a general way the lines of this story, but supplying the comic element by the creation of *Papageno* (who is Kasperl in a habiliment of feathers), Schikaneder had already got his hero into the castle of the wicked magician in quest of the daughter of the *Queen of Night* (in whose character there was not yet a trace of maleficence), when the success of his rival's earlier presentation of the story gave him pause. Now there came to him (or to his literary colleague) a conceit which fired the imagination of Mozart and added an element to the play which was bound at once to dignify it and create a popular stir that might lead to a triumph. Whence the suggestion came is not known, but its execution, so far as the libretto was concerned, was left to Gieseke. Under the Emperor Leopold II the Austrian government had adopted a reactionary policy toward the order of Freemasons, which was suspected of making propaganda for liberal ideas in politics and religion. Both Schikaneder and Mozart belonged to the order, Mozart, indeed, being so enthusiastic a devotee that he once confessed to his father his gratitude to God that through Freemasonry he had learned to look upon death as the gateway to true happiness. In continuing the book of the opera, Schikaneder (or Gieseke for him) abruptly transformed the wicked magician into a virtuous sage who had carried off the daughter of a wicked sorceress, the *Queen of Night*, to save the maiden from the baleful influence of her mother. Instead of seeking to frustrate the efforts of the prince who comes to rescue her, the sage initiates him into the mysteries of Isis, leads him into the paths of virtue and wisdom, tests him by trials, and rewards him at the last by blessing his union with the maiden. The trials of silence, secrecy, and hardihood in passing through the dread elements of fire and water were ancient literary materials; they may be found in the account of the initiation of a neophyte into the mysteries of Isis in Apuleius's "Metamorphoses; or, The Golden Ass," a romance written in the second century. By placing the scene of the opera in Egypt, the belief of Freemasons that their order originated in that unspeakably ancient land was humored, while the use of some of its symbolism (such as the conflict

between light and darkness) and the proclamation
of what were believed to be some of its ethical
principles could safely be relied upon to delight
the knowing and irritate the curiosity of the unin-
itiated. The change also led to the shabby treatment which woman receives in the opera, while
Schikaneder's failure to rewrite the first part accounts
for such inconsistencies as the genii who are sent to
guide the prince appearing first in the service of
the evil principle and afterward as agents of the
good.

The overture to "Die Zauberflöte," because of its
firm establishment in our concert-rooms, is more
widely known than the opera. Two of its salient
features have also made it the subject of large
discussion among musical analysts; namely, the
reiterated chords, three times three, which introduce the second part of the overture.[1]

[1] These chords, played by all the wind instruments of the
band, are the chords of the introduction raised to a higher
power.

and the fugued *allegro*, constructed with a skill that will never cease to be a wonder to the knowing, built up on the following subject:—

In the chords (which are heard again in the temple scene, at which the hero is admitted as a novice and permitted to begin his probation), the analysts who seek to find as much symbolism as possible in the opera, see an allusion to the signals given by knocking at the door of the lodge-room. Some such purpose may been have in the mind of Mozart when he chose the device, but it was not unique when he applied it. I have found it used in an almost identical manner in the overture to "Günther von Schwarzburg," by Ignaz Holzbauer, a German opera produced in Mannheim fifteen years before "Die Zauberflöte" saw the light of the stage lamps. Mozart knew Holzbauer, who was a really great musician, and admired his music. Connected with the fugue theme there is a more familiar story. In 1781 Clementi, the great pianist and composer, visited Vienna. He made the acquaintance of Haydn, was introduced at court, and Emperor Joseph II brought him and Mozart together in a trial of skill at playing and improvising. Among other things Clementi played his own sonata in B-flat, the first movement of which begins thus: —

The resemblance between this theme and Mozart's fugal subject is too plain to need pointing out. Such likenesses were more common in Mozart's day than they were a century ago; they were more common in Handel's day than in Mozart's; they are almost as common in our day as they were in Handel's, but now we explain them as being the products of "unconscious cerebration," whereas in the eighteenth century they were frank borrowings in which there was no moral obliquity; for originality then lay as much in treatment as in thematic invention, if not more.

Come we now to a description of the action of the opera. *Tamino,* — strange to say, a "Japanese" prince, — hunting far, very far, from home, is pursued, after his last arrow has been sped, by a great serpent. He flees, cries for help, and seeing himself already in the clutch of death, falls in a swoon. At the moment of his greatest danger three veiled ladies appear on the scene and melodiously and harmoniously unite in slaying the monster. They are smitten, in unison, with the beauty of the unconscious youth whom they have saved, and quarrel prettily among themselves for the privilege of remaining beside him while information of the incident is bearing to the *Queen of Night,* who lives hard by in a castle. No two being willing that the third shall stay, all three go to the *Queen,* who is their mistress. *Tamino's* consciousness returning, he discovers that the serpent has been slain, and hails *Papageno,* who comes upon the scene, as his deliverer. *Papageno* is a bird-catcher by trade and in the service of the *Queen of Night* — a happy-go-lucky, talkative fellow, whose thoughts do not go beyond creature comforts. He publishes his nature (and incidentally illustrates what has been said above about the naïve character of some of the music of the opera) by trolling a ditty with an opening strain as follows:—

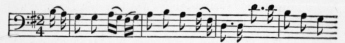

Papageno has no scruples about accepting credit and gratitude for the deed performed by the ladies, and, though he is the veriest poltroon, he boasts inordinately about the gigantic strength which had enabled him to strangle the serpent. He is punished for his mendacity when the ladies return and place a padlock upon his mouth, closing his lips to the things of which he is most fond — speech and food. To *Tamino* they give a miniature portrait, which excites him to rapturous song ("Dies Bildniss ist bezaubernd schön," or "Oh! cara immagine," as

the case may be). Then he learns that the original
of the portrait is *Pamina,* daughter of the *Queen*
of Night, stolen from her mother by a "wicked
demon," *Sarastro.* In the true spirit of knight-
errantry he vows that he will restore the maid to
her mother's arms. There is a burst of thunder,
and the *Queen* appears in such apparel and manner
as the exchequer at the theatre and the ingenuity
of the stage mechanic are able to provide. (When
last I saw her her robe was black, bespangled with
stars and glittering gems, and she rode upon the
crescent moon.) She knows the merits and virtues
of the youth, and promises that he shall have *Pamina*
to wife if he succeeds in his adventure. *Papageno*
is commanded to accompany him, and as aids the
ladies give to *Tamino* a magic flute, whose tones
shall protect him from every danger, and to *Papageno*
a bell-chime of equal potency. (These talismans
have hundreds of prototypes in the folk-lore of all
peoples.) *Papageno* is loath to accompany the prince,
because the magician had once threatened to spit
and roast him like the bird he resembled if ever
he was caught in his domain, but the magical bells
give him comfort and assurance. Meanwhile the
padlock has been removed from his lips, with ad-
monitions not to lie more. In the quintet which
accompanies these sayings and doings, there is exquisite music, which, it is said, Mozart conceived
while playing at billiards. Finally the ladies announce that three boys, "young, beautiful, pure, and
wise," shall guide the pair to the castle of *Sarastro.*

We are next in a room of the castle before the would-be rescuers arrive. *Pamina* has tried to escape, and is put in chains by her keeper, the Moor *Monostatos*. She weeps because of her misery, and repulses the protestations of love with which her jailer plagues her. *Papageno* enters the room, and he and the jailer run in opposite directions at sight of each other — *Papageno* frightened by the complexion of the blackamoor, *Monostatos* terror-stricken at the sight of a man in feathers. Returning, *Papageno* convinces himself of the identity of *Pamina* with the daughter of the *Queen of Night*, tells her of *Tamino*, who is coming for her with a heart full of love, and promptly they sing of the divine dignity of the marital state. It is the duet, "Bei Männern welche Liebe fühlen," or "Là dove prende, amor ricetto," familiar to concert-rooms, and the melody to some hymnals. A story goes that Mozart had to write this duet three or five times before it would pass muster in the censorious eyes of Schikaneder. After the opera had made good its success, the duet as we have it to-day alternated at the performance with a more ornate version — in all likelihood one of the earlier forms in which Mozart cast it.

The three boys — genii they are, and if I were stage-manager they should fly like Peter Pan — lead *Tamino* into a grove wherein stand three temples dedicated respectively to Wisdom, Nature, and Reason. The precinct is sacred; the music tells us that — the halo streaming from sustained notes of flutes and clarinets, the muted trumpets, the solemn trombones in softest monotone, the placid undulations of the song sung by the violins, the muffled, admonitory beats of the kettledrums. The genii leave *Tamino* after admonishing him to be "steadfast, patient, and silent." Conscious of a noble purpose, the hero boldly approaches the Temple of Reason, but, before he can enter its portals, is stopped by an imperative injunction from within: "Back!" He essays the Temple of Nature, and is turned away again by the ominous word. Out of the Temple of Wisdom steps an aged priest, from whom he learns that *Sarastro* is master within, and that no one is privileged to enter whose heart, like his, harbors hatred and vengeful thoughts. *Tamino* thinks *Sarastro* fully deserving of hatred and revenge, and is informed that he had been deceived by a woman — one of the sex "that does little, chatters much." *Tamino* asks if *Pamina* lives, but the priest is bound by an oath to say nothing on that subject until "the hand of friendship shall lead him to an eternal union within the sanctuary." When shall night vanish and the light appear? Oracular voices answer, "Soon, youth, or never!" Does *Pamina* live? The voices: "*Pamina* still lives!" Thus comforted, he sings his happiness, filling the pauses in his song with interludes on the flute, bringing to his feet the wild beasts and forest creatures of all sorts. He hears *Papageno's* syrinx, and at length finds the fowler with *Monostatos;* but before their joy can have expression *Pamina* and the slaves

appear and capture them. *Papageno* recollects
him of his magic bells; he plays upon them, and the
slaves, willy-nilly, dance themselves out of sight.
Scarcely are the lovers free when a solemn strain
announces the approach of *Sarastro*. He comes in
a chariot drawn by lions and surrounded by a brave
retinue. *Pamina* kneels to him, confesses her
attempt to escape, but explains that it was to free
herself from the odious attentions of *Monostatos*.
The latter, asking his reward for having thwarted the
plan of *Papageno*, receives it from *Sarastro* in the shape
of a bastinado. *Pamina* pleads for restoration to her
mother, but the sage refuses to free her, saying that
her mother is a haughty woman, adding the ungallant
reflection that woman's heart should be directed by
man lest she step outside her sphere. He commands
that *Tamino* and *Papageno* be veiled and led into
the Temple of Probation. The first act is ended.

The initiation of *Tamino* and *Papageno* into the
mysteries, their trials, failures, triumph, and reward,
form the contents of the second act. At a conclave
of the elect, *Sarastro* announces that *Tamino* stands
at the door of the Temple of Wisdom, desirous to gaze
upon the "great light" of the sanctuary. He prays
Isis and Osiris to give strength to the neophytes:—

O I-sis und O si-ris . schen-ket Der

Weis-heit Geist dem neu - en Paar.

To the impressiveness of this prayer the orchestra contributes as potent a factor as the stately melody or the solemn harmonies. All the bright-voiced instruments are excluded, and the music assigned to three groups of sombre color, composed, respectively, (1) of divided violas and violoncellos; (2) of three trombones, and (3) of two basset horns and two bassoons. The assent of the sacerdotal assembly is indicated by the three trumpet blasts which have been described in connection with the overture, and *Tamino* and *Papageno* are admitted to the Temple, instructed, and begin their probationary trials. True to the notion of the order, two priests warn the neophytes against the wiles of woman. *Papageno* has little inclination to seek wisdom, but enters upon the trials in the hope of winning a wife who shall be like himself in appearance. In the first trial, which is that of silence, the value of the priestly warning just received is at once made apparent. *Tamino* and *Papageno* have scarcely been left alone, when the three female attendants of the *Queen of Night* appear and attempt to terrify them with tales of the false nature of the priests, whose recruits, say they, are carried to hell, body and breeches (literally "mit Haut und Haar," *i.e.* "with skin and hair"). *Papageno* becomes terror-stricken and falls to the floor, when voices within proclaim that the sanctity of the temple has been profaned by woman's presence. The ladies flee.

The scene changes. *Pamina* is seen asleep in a bower of roses, silvered over by the light of the moon

Monostatos, deploring the fact that love should be
denied him because of his color, though enjoyed by
everything else in nature, attempts to steal a kiss.
A peal of thunder, and the *Queen of Night* rises from
the ground. She importunes *Pamina* to free herself and avenge her mother's wrongs by killing
Sarastro. To this end she hands her a dagger and
pours out the "hellish rage" which "boils" in her
heart in a flood of scintillant *staccati* in the tonal
regions where few soprano voices move:—

Monostatos has overheard all. He wrenches the
dagger from *Pamina,* urges her again to accept his
love, threatens her with death, and is about to put
his threat into execution when *Sarastro* enters, dis-
misses the slave, and announces that his revenge
upon the *Queen of Night* shall lie in promoting the
happiness of the daughter by securing her union
with *Tamino.*

The probationary trials of *Tamino* and *Papageno*
are continued. The two are led into a hall and ad-
monished to remain silent till they hear a trumpet-
call. *Papageno* falls to chattering with an old
woman, is terrified beyond measure by a thunder-
clap, and recovers his composure only when the genii

bring back the flute and bells and a table of food.
Tamino, however, remains steadfast, though *Pamina*
herself comes to him and pleads for a word of love.
Papageno boasts of his own hardihood, but stops
to eat, though the trumpet has called. A lion appears; *Tamino* plays his flute, and the beast returns
to his cage.   The youth is prepared for the final trial;
he is to wander for a space through flood and flame,
and *Pamina* is brought to say her tearful farewells.
The courage and will of the neophyte remain unshaken, though the maiden gives way to despair
and seeks to take her own life.   The genii stay her
hand, and assure her that *Tamino* shall be restored
to her.   Two men in armor guard the gates of a
subterranean cavern.   They sing of the rewards to
be won by him who shall walk the path of danger;
water, fire, air, and earth shall purify him; and if
he withstand death's terrors, heaven shall receive
__m and he be enlightened and fitted to consecrate
himself wholly to the mysteries of Isis: —

A marvellous piece of music is consorted with
this oracular utterance.   The words are set to an
old German church melody — "Ach Gott, vom Him-
mel sieh darein" — around which the orchestral instruments weave a contrapuntal web of wondrous

beauty. At the gates *Pamina* joins her lover and accompanies him on his journey, which is happily achieved with the help of the flute. Meanwhile *Papageno* is pardoned his loquacity, but told that he shall never feel the joy of the elect. He thinks he can make shift with a pretty wife instead. The old woman of the trial chamber appears and discloses herself as the charming, youthful *Papageno*, but only for an instant. He calls after her in vain, and is about to hang himself when the genii remind him of his magic bells. He rings and sings; his feathered mate comes to him. *Monostatos* aids the *Queen of Night* and her companions in an assault upon the sanctuary; but a storm confounds them, and *Sarastro* blesses the union of *Tamino* and *Pamina*, amidst joyful hymning by the elect.

An extraordinary hodgepodge, truly, yet, taken all in all, an effective stage piece. Goethe was so impressed with the ingenuity shown by Schikanede: in treating the device of contrast that he seriously contemplated writing a second part, the music of which was to be composed by Wranitzky, who set Gieseke's operatic version of "Oberon." German critics and managers have deplored its absurdities and contradictions, but have found no way to obviate them which can be said to be generally acceptable. The buffooneries cannot be separated from the sublimities without disrupting the piece, nor can its doggerel be turned into dignified verse. It were best, I fancy, that managers should treat the opera, and audiences receive it, as a sort of Christmas pantomime which Mozart has glorified by his music. The tendency of German critics has been to view it with too much seriousness. It is difficult to avoid this while one is under the magic spell of its music, but the only way to become reconciled to it on reflection is to take it as the story of its creation shows that its creators intended it to be taken; namely, as a piece designed to suit the tastes of the uncultivated and careless masses. This will explain the singular sacrifice of principle which Mozart made in permitting a mountebank like Schikaneder to pass judgment on his music while he was composing it, to exact that one duet should be composed over five times before he would accept it, and even to suggest melodies for some of the numbers. Jahn would have us believe that Mozart was so concerned at the failure of the first act to win applause at the first performance that he came behind the scenes pale as death to receive comfort and encouragement from Schikaneder; I prefer to believe another story, which is to the effect that Mozart almost died with laughing when he found that the public went into ecstasies over his opera. Certain it is that his pleasure in it was divided. Schikaneder had told him that he might occasionally consult the taste of connoisseurs, and he did so, finding profound satisfaction in the music written for *Sarastro* and the priests, and doubtless also in the fine ensembles; but the enthusiasm inspired by what he knew to be concessions to the vulgar only excited his hilarity. The beautiful in the score is amply explained by Mozart's genius and his marvellous command of the technique of composition. The dignity of the simple idea of a celebration of the mysteries of Isis would have been enough, without the composer's reverence for Freemasonry and its principles, to inspire him for a great achievement when it came to providing a setting for the scenes in which the priests figure. The rest of the music he seems to have written with little regard to coherency or unity of character. His sister-in-law had a voice of extraordinary range and elasticity; hence the two display airs; *Papageno* had to have music in keeping in his character, and Mozart doubtless wrote it with as little serious thought as he did the "Piece for an Organ in a Clock, in F minor, 4-4," and "Andante to a Waltz for a Little Organ," which can be found entered in his autograph catalogue for the last year of his life. In the overture, one of the finest of his instrumental compositions, he returned to a form that had not been in use since the time of Hasse and Graum; in the scene with the two men in armor he made use of a German chorale sung in octaves as a *canto firmo*, with counterpoint in the orchestra — a recondite idea which it is difficult to imagine him inventing for this opera. I fancy (not without evidence) that he made the number out of material found in his sketchbook. These things indicate that the depth which the critics with deep-diving and bottom-scraping proclivities affect to see in the work is rather the product of imagination than real.

CHAPTER IV

"DON GIOVANNI"

IN the preceding chapter it was remarked that Mozart's "Zauberflöte" was the oldest German opera in the current American repertory. Accepting the lists of the last two decades as a criterion, "Don Giovanni" is the oldest Italian opera, save one. That one is "Le Nozze di Figaro," and it may, therefore, be said that Mozart's operas mark the beginning of the repertory as it exists at the present time in America. Twenty-five years ago it was possible to hear a few performances of Gluck's "Orfeo" in English and Italian, and its name has continued to figure occasionally ever since in the lists of works put forth by managers when inviting subscriptions for operatic seasons; but that fact can scarcely be said to have kept the opera in the repertory.

Our oldest Italian opera is less than 125 years old, and "Don Giovanni" only 122 — an inconsiderable age for a first-class work of art compared with its companion pieces in literature, painting, and sculpture, yet a highly respectable one for an opera. Music has undergone a greater revolution within the last century than any other art in thrice

the period, yet "Don Giovanni" is as much admired
now as it was in the last decade of the eighteenth
century, and, indeed, has less prejudice to contend
with in the minds of musicians and critics than it
had when it was in its infancy, and I confidently
believe that to its score and that of "Le Nozze di
Figaro" opera writers will soon be turning to learn
the methods of dramatic characterization. Pure
beauty lives in angelic wedlock with psychological
expression in Mozart's dramatic music, and these
factors will act as powerful loadstones in bringing
composers who are now laboriously and vainly seeking devices for characterization in tricks and devices
based on arbitrary formulas back to the gospel of
truth and beauty. Wagner has had no successful
imitator. His scheme of thematic identification
and development, in its union of calculation, reflection, and musical inspiration, is beyond the capaci-
ties of those who have come after him. The bow
of Ulysses is still unbent; but he will be a great
musician indeed who shall use the resources of the
new art with such large ease, freedom, power, and
effectiveness as Mozart used those of the comparatively ingenuous art of his day. And yet the
great opera composer who is to come in great likelihood will be a disciple of Gluck, Mozart, and the
Wagner who wrote "Tristan und Isolde" and "Die
Meistersinger" rather than one of the tribe of
Debussy.

The great opera composers of the nineteenth
century were of one mind touching the greatness

of "Don Giovanni." Beethoven was horrified by its licentious libretto, but tradition says that he kept before him on his writing-table a transcript of the music for the trombones in the second finale of the opera. Shortly after Mme. Viardot-Garcia came into possession of the autograph score of the masterpiece, Rossini called upon her and asked for the privilege of looking at it, adding, "I want to bow the knee before this sacred relic." After poring over a few pages, he placed his hands on the book and said, solemnly: "He is the greatest, the master of them all; the only composer who had as much science as he had genius, and as much genius as he had science." On another occasion he said to a questioner: "Vous voulez connaître celui de mes ouvrages que j'aime le mieux; eh bien, c'est 'Don Giovanni.'" Gounod celebrated the centenary of the opera by writing a commentary on it which he dedicated to young composers and artists called upon to take part in performances of the opera. In the preface of his book he characterizes it as " an unequalled and immortal masterpiece," the " apogee of the lyrical drama," a "wondrous example of truth, beauty of form, appropriateness of characterization, deep insight into the drama, purity of style, richness and restraint in instrumentation, charm and tenderness in the love passages, and power in pathos" — in one word, a "finished model of dramatic music." And then he added: "The score of 'Don Giovanni' has exercised the influence of a revelation upon the whole of my life; it has been

F

and remains for me a kind of incarnation of dramatic and musical impeccability. I regard it as a work without blemish, of uninterrupted perfection, and this commentary is but the humble testimony of my veneration and gratitude for the genius to whom I owe the purest and most permanent joys of my life as a musician." In his "Autobiographical Sketch" Wagner confesses that as a lad he cared only for "Die Zauberflöte," and that "Don Giovanni" was distasteful to him on account of the Italian text, which seemed to him rubbish. But in "Oper und Drama" he says: "Is it possible to find anything more perfect than every piece in 'Don Juan'? ... Oh, how doubly dear and above all honor is Mozart to me that it was not possible for him to invent music for 'Tito' like that of 'Don Giovanni,' for 'Cosi fan tutte' like that of 'Figaro'! How shamefully would it have desecrated music!" And again: "Where else has music won so infinitely rich an individuality, been able to characterize so surely, so definitely, and in such exuberant plenitude, as here?"[1]

Mozart composed "Don Giovanni" for the Italian Opera at Prague, which had been saved from ruin in the season 1786–1787 by the phenomenal success of "Le Nozze di Figaro." He chose the subject and commissioned Lorenzo da Ponte, then official poet to the imperial theatres of Austria, to write the book of words. In doing so, the latter made

[1] See my preface to "Don Giovanni" in the Schirmer Collection of Operas.

free use of a version of the same story made by
an Italian theatrical poet named Bertati, and Dr.
Chrysander (who in 1886 gave me a copy of this
libretto, which Mozart's biographer, Otto Jahn, had
not succeeded in finding, despite diligent search)
has pointed out that Mozart also took as a model
some of the music to which the composer Gazzaniga had set it. The title of the opera by Bertati and Gazzaniga was "Il Convitato di Pietra."
It had been brought forward with great success
in Venice and won wide vogue in Italy before Mozart
hit upon it. It lived many years after Mozart
brought out his opera, and, indeed, was performed
in London twenty-three years before Mozart's
opera got a hearing. It is doubtful, however, if
the London representation did justice to the work.
Da Ponte was poet to the opera there when "Il
Convitato" was chosen for performance, and it fell
to him to prepare the book to suit the taste of the
English people. He tried to persuade the management to give Mozart's opera instead, and, failing in
that, had the malicious satisfaction of helping to
turn the work of Bertati and Gazzaniga into a sort
of literary and musical pasticcio, inserting portions
of his own paraphrase of Bertati's book in place of
the original scenes and preparing occasion for the
insertion of musical pieces by Sarti, Frederici, and
Guglielmi.

Mozart wrote the music to "Don Giovanni" in
the summer of 1787. Judging by the circumstance
that there is no entry in his autograph catalogue

between June 24 and August 10 in that year, it would seem that he had devoted the intervening seven weeks chiefly, if not wholly, to the work. When he went to Prague in September he carried the unfinished score with him, and worked on it there largely in the summer house of his friends, the Duscheks, who lived in the suburbs of the city. Under date of October 28 he entered the overture in his catalogue. As a matter of fact, it was not finished till the early morn of the next day, which was the day of the first production of the opera. Thereby hangs the familiar tale of how it was composed. On the evening of the day before the performance, pen had not been touched to the overture. Nevertheless, Mozart sat with a group of merry friends until a late hour of the night. Then he went to his hotel and prepared to work. On the table was a glass of punch, and his wife sat beside him to keep him awake by telling him stories. In spite of all, sleep overcame him, and he was obliged to interrupt his work for several hours; yet at 7 o'clock in the morning the copyist was sent for and the overture was ready for him. The tardy work delayed the representation in the evening, and the orchestra had to play the overture at sight; but it was a capital band, and Mozart, who conducted, complimented it before starting into the introduction to the first air. The performance was completely successful, and floated buoyantly on a tide of enthusiasm which set in when Mozart entered the orchestra, and rose higher and higher as the music went on.

On May 7, 1788, the opera was given in Vienna, where at first it made a fiasco, though Mozart had inserted new pieces and made other alterations to humor the singers and add to its attractiveness. London heard it first on April 12, 1817, at the King's Theatre, whose finances, which were almost in an exhausted state, it restored to a flourishing condition. In the company which Manuel Garcia brought to New York in 1825 were Carlo Angrisani, who was the *Masetto* of the first London representation, and Domenico Crivelli, son of the tenor Gaetano Crivelli, who had been the *Don Ottavio*. Garcia was a tenor with a voice sufficiently deep to enable him to sing the barytone part of *Don Giovanni* in Paris and at subsequent performances in London. It does not appear that he had contemplated a performance of the opera in New York, but here he met Da Ponte, who had been a resident of the city for twenty years and recently been appointed professor of Italian literature at Columbia College. Da Ponte, as may be imagined, lost no time in calling on Garcia and setting on foot a scheme for bringing forward "my 'Don Giovanni,'" as he always called it. Crivelli was a second-rate tenor, and could not be trusted with the part of *Don Ottavio*, and a Frenchman named Milon, whom I conclude to have been a violoncello player, afterward identified with the organization of the Philharmonic Society, was engaged for that part. A Mme. Barbieri was cast for the part of *Donna Anna*, Mme. Garcia for that of *Donna Elvira*, Manuel Garcia, Jr. (who died in

1906 at the age of 101 years) for that of *Leporello*, Angrisani for his old rôle of *Masetto*, and Maria Garcia, afterward the famous Malibran, for that of *Zerlina*. The first performance took place on May 23, 1826, in the Park Theatre, and the opera was given eleven times in the season. This success, coupled with the speedily acquired popularity of Garcia's gifted daughter, was probably the reason why an English version of the opera which dominated the New York stage for nearly a quarter of a century soon appeared at the Chatham Theatre. In this version the part of the dissolute *Don* was played by H. Wallack, uncle of the Lester Wallack so long a theatrical favorite in the American metropolis. As Malibran the Signorina Garcia took part in many of the English performances of the work, which kept the Italian off the local stage till 1850, when it was revived by Max Maretzek at the Astor Place Opera-house.

I have intimated that Bertati's opera-book was the prototype of Da Ponte's, but the story is centuries older than either. The Spanish tale of Don Juan Tenorio, who killed an enemy in a duel, insulted his memory by inviting his statue to dinner, and was sent to hell because of his refusal to repent him of his sins, was but a literary form of a legend of considerable antiquity. It seems likely that it was moulded into dramatic shape by monks in the Middle Ages; it certainly occupied industriously the minds of playwrights in the seventeenth and eighteenth centuries in Spain, Italy, Germany, and

England. The most eminent men who treated
it at various times were the Spaniard known as Tirza
di Molina, the Frenchman Molière, the Italian
Goldoni, and the Englishman Thomas Shadwell,
whose "Libertine Destroyed" was brought forward
in 1676. Before Mozart, Le Tellier had used it for
a French comic opera, Righini and Gazzaniga for
Italian operas, and Gluck for a ballet.

But we are concerned now only with the play as
Da Ponte and Mozart gave it to us. In the dramatic terminology of the eighteenth century "Don
Giovanni" was a *dramma giocoso;* in the better
sense of the phrase, a playful drama — a lyric comedy. Da Ponte conceived it as such, but Mozart
gave it so tragical a turn by the awful solemnity
with which he infused the scene of the libertine's
punishment that already in his day it was felt that
the last scene as written and composed to suit the
conventional type of a comic opera was an intolerable
anticlimax. Mozart sounds a deeply tragical note
at the outset of his overture. The introduction
is an *Andante,* which he drew from the scene of the
opera in which the ghostly statue of the murdered
Commandant appears to *Don Giovanni* while he is
enjoying the pleasures of the table. Two groups
of solemn chords command attention and "estab-
lish at once the majestic and formidable authority
of divine justice, the avenger of crime." [1] They
are followed by a series of solemn progressions in
stern, sinister, unyielding, merciless, implacable har-

[1] Gounod.

monies. They are like the colossal strides of approaching Fate, and this awfulness is twice raised to a higher power, first by a searching, syncopated phrase in the violins which hovers loweringly over them, and next by a succession of affrighted minor scales ascending *crescendo* and descending *piano*, the change in dynamics beginning abruptly as the crest of each terrifying wave is reached. These wonderful scales begin thus:—

in the last scene of the opera. They were an afterthought of the composer's. They did not appear in the original score of the scene, as the autograph shows, but were written in after the music had once been completed. They are crowded into the staves in tiny notes which sometimes extend from one measure into the next. This circumstance and the other, that they are all fairly written out in the autograph of the overture, indicate that they were conceived either at one of the rehearsals or while Mozart was writing the overture. They could not have been suggested at the first performance, as Jahn seems to imply.[1] The introduction is only thirty measures long, and the *Allegro* which follows

[1] "The Life of Mozart," by Otto Jahn, Vol. III, p. 169.

is made up of new material. I quote again from Gounod: "But suddenly, and with feverish audacity, the *Allegro* breaks out in the major key, an *Allegro* full of passion and delirium, deaf to the warnings of Heaven, regardless of remorse, enraptured of pleasure, madly inconstant and daring, rapid and impetuous as a torrent, flashing and swift as a sword, overleaping all obstacles, scaling balconies, and bewildering the alguazils." [1] From the tragic introduction through the impetuous main section we are led to a peaceful night scene in the garden before the house of *Donna Anna.* There *Leporello*, the servant of *Don Giovanni*, is awaiting in discontented mood for the return of his master, who has entered the house in quest of amatory adventure. *Leporello* is weary of the service in which he is engaged, and contrasts his state with that of the *Don.* (Air: "Notte e giorno faticar.") He will throw off the yoke and be a gentleman himself. He has just inflated himself with pride at the thought, when he hears footsteps, and the poltroon in his nature asserts itself. He hides behind the shrubbery. *Don Giovanni* hurries from the house, concealing his features with his cloak and impeded by *Donna Anna*, who clings to him, trying to get a look into his face and calling for help. *Don Giovanni* commands silence and threatens. The *Commandant, Donna Anna's* father, appears with drawn sword and challenges the intruder. *Don Giovanni* hesitates to draw against so old a man, but the *Commandant* will not parley,

[1] " Mozart's Don Giovanni," by Charles Gounod, p. 3.

They fight. At first the attacks and defences are deliberate (the music depicts it all with wonderful vividness), but at the last it is thrust and parry, thrust and parry, swiftly, mercilessly. The *Commandant* is no match for his powerful young opponent, and falls, dying. A few broken ejaculations, and all is ended. The orchestra sings a slow descending chromatic phrase "as if exhausted by the blood which oozes from the wound," says Gounod. How simple the means of expression! But let the modern composer, with all his apparatus of new harmonies and his multitude of instruments, point out a scene to match it in the entire domain of the lyric drama! *Don Giovanni* and his lumpish servant, who, with all his coward instincts, cannot help trying his wit at the outcome of the adventure, though his master is in little mood for sportiveness, steal away as they see lights and hear a commotion in the palace. *Donna Anna* comes back to the garden, bringing her affianced lover, *Don Ottavio*, whom she had called to the help of her father. She finds the *Commandant* dead, and breaks into agonizing cries and tears. Only an accompanied recitative, but every ejaculation a cry of nature! Gounod is wrought up to an ecstasy by Mozart's declamation and harmonies. He suspends his analysis to make this comment:—

But that which one cannot too often remark nor too often endeavor to make understood, that which renders Mozart an absolutely unique genius, is the constant and indissoluble union of beauty of form with truth of expression. By this truth he is human, by this beauty he is divine. By truth he teaches us, he moves us; we recognize each other in him, and we proclaim thereby that he indeed knows human nature thoroughly, not only in its different passions, but also in the varieties of form and character that those passions may assume. By beauty the real is transfigured, although at the same time it is left entirely recognizable; he elevates it by the magic of a superior language and transports it to that region of serenity and light which constitutes Art, wherein Intelligence repeats with a tranquillity of vision what the heart has experienced in the trouble of passion. Now the union of truth with beauty is Art itself.

Don Ottavio attempts to console his love, but she is insane with grief and at first repulses him, then pours out her grief and calls upon him to avenge the death of her father. Together they register a vow and call on heaven for retribution.

It is morning. *Don Giovanni* and *Leporello* are in the highway near Seville. As usual, *Leporello* is dissatisfied with his service and accuses the *Don* with being a rascal. Threats of punishment bring back his servile manner, and *Don Giovanni* is about to acquaint him of a new conquest, when a lady, *Donna Elvira,* comes upon the scene. She utters woful complaints of unhappiness and resentment against one who had won her love, then deceived and deserted her. (Air: "Ah! chi mi dice mai.") *Don Giovanni* ("aflame already," as *Leporello* remarks) steps forward to console her. He salutes her with soft blandishment in his voice, but to his dismay discovers that she is a noble lady of Burgos and one of the "thousand and three" Spanish victims recorded in the list which *Leporello* mockingly reads

to her after *Don Giovanni*, having turned her over
to his servant, for an explanation of his conduct in
leaving Burgos, has departed unperceived. *Leporello*
is worthy of his master in some things. In danger he
is the veriest coward, and his teeth chatter like cas-
tanets; but confronted by a mere woman in distress
he becomes voluble and spares her nothing in a description of the number of his master's amours,
their place, the quality and station of his victims,
and his methods of beguilement. The curious and
also the emulous may be pleased to learn that the
number is 2065, geographically distributed as follows:
Italy, 240; Germany, 231; France, 100; Turkey,
91; and Spain, 1003. Among them are ladies from
the city and rustic damsels, countesses, baronesses,
marchionesses, and princesses. If blond, he praises
her dainty beauty; brunette, her constancy; pale,
her sweetness. In cold weather his preferences go
toward the buxom, in summer, svelte. Even old
ladies serve to swell his list. Rich or poor, homely
or beautiful, all's one to him so long as the being
is inside a petticoat. "But why go on? Lady,
you know his ways." The air, "Madamina," is
a marvel of malicious humor and musical delineation. "E la grande maestoso" — the music rises
and inflates itself most pompously; "la piccina" —
it sinks in quick iteration lower and lower just as the
Italians in describing small things lower their hands
toward the ground. The final words, "Voi sapete,
quel che fa," scarcely to be interpreted for polite
readers, as given by bass singers who have pre-

served the Italian traditions (with a final "hm" through the nose), go to the extreme of allowable suggestiveness, if not a trifle beyond. The insult throws *Elvira* into a rage, and she resolves to forego her love and seek vengeance instead.

Don Giovanni comes upon a party of rustics who are celebrating in advance the wedding of *Zerlina* and *Masetto*. The damsel is a somewhat vain, forward, capricious, flirtatious miss, and cannot long withstand such blandishments as the handsome nobleman bestows upon her. *Don Giovanni* sends the merrymakers to his palace for entertainment, cajoles and threatens *Masetto* into leaving him alone with *Zerlina*, and begins his courtship of her. (Duet: "Là ci darem la mano.") He has about succeeded in his conquest, when *Elvira* intervenes, warns the maiden, leads her away, and, returning, finds *Donna Anna* and *Don Ottavio* in conversation with *Don Giovanni*, whose help in the discovery of the *Commandant's* murderer they are soliciting. *Elvira* breaks out with denunciations, and *Don Giovanni*, in a whisper to his companions, proclaims her mad, and leads her off. Departing, he says a word of farewell, and from the tone of his voice *Donna Anna* recognizes her father's murderer. She tells her lover how the assassin stole into her room at night, attempted her dishonor, and slew her father. She demands his punishment at *Don Ottavio's* hands, and he, though doubting that a nobleman and a friend could be guilty of such crimes, yet resolves to find out the truth and deliver the guilty man to justice.

The *Don* commands a grand entertainment for *Zerlina's* wedding party, for, though temporarily foiled, he has not given up the chase. *Masetto* comes with pretty *Zerlina* holding on to the sleeve of his coat. The boor is jealous, and *Zerlina* knows well that he has cause. She protests, she cajoles; he is no match for her. She confesses to having been pleased at my lord's flattery, but he had not touched "even the tips of her fingers." If her fault deserves it, he may beat her if he wants to, but then let there be peace between them. The artful minx! Her wheedling is irresistible. Listen to it:—

The most insinuating of melodies floating over an obbligato of the solo violoncello "like a love charm," as Gounod says. Then the celebration of her victory when she captures one of his hands and knows that he is yielding:—

A new melody, blither, happier, but always the violoncello murmuring in blissful harmony with the seductive voice and rejoicing in the cunning witcheries which lull *Masetto's* suspicions to sleep. Now all go into *Don Giovanni's* palace, from which the sounds of dance music and revelry are floating out. *Donna Elvira, Donna Anna,* and *Don Ottavio,* who come to confront him who has wronged them all, are specially bidden, as was the custom, because they appeared in masks. Within gayety is supreme. A royal host, this *Don Giovanni!* Not only are there refreshments for all, but he has humored both classes of guests in the arrangement of the programme of dances. Let there be a minuet, a country-dance, and an allemande, he had said to *Leporello* in that dizzying song of instruction which whirls past our senses like a mad wind: "Finch' han dal vino." No one so happy as Mozart when it came to providing the music for these dances. Would you connoisseurs in music like counterpoint? We shall give it you; — three dances shall proceed at once and together, despite their warring duple and triple rhythms:—

Louis Viardot, who wrote a little book describing the autograph of "Don Giovanni," says that Mozart wrote in the score where the three bands play thus simultaneously the word *accordano* as a direction to the stage musicians to imitate the action of tuning their instruments before falling in with their music. Of this fact the reprint of the libretto as used at Prague and Vienna contains no mention, but a foot-note gives other stage directions which indicate how desirous Mozart was that his ingenious and humorous conceit should not be overlooked. At the point where the minuet, which was the dance of people of quality, is played, he remarked, "*Don Ottavio* dances the minuet with *Donna Anna*"; at the contra-dance in 2–4 time, "*Don Giovanni* begins to dance a contra-dance with *Zerlina*"; at the entrance of the waltz, "*Leporello* dances a 'Teitsch' with *Masetto*." The proper execution of Mozart's elaborate scheme puts the resources of an opera-house to a pretty severe test, but there is ample reward in the result. Pity that, as a rule, so little intelligence is shown by the ballet master in arranging the dances! There is a special significance in Mozart's direction that the cavalier humor the peasant girl by stepping a country-dance with her, which is all lost when he attempts to lead her into the aristocratic minuet, as is usually done.

At the height of the festivities, *Don Giovanni* succeeds in leading *Zerlina* into an inner room, from which comes a piercing shriek a moment later. Anticipating trouble, *Leporello* hastens to his master

to warn him. *Don Ottavio* and his friends storm
the door of the anteroom, out of which now comes
Don Giovanni dragging *Leporello* and uttering
threats of punishment against him. The trick does
not succeed. *Don Ottavio* removes his mask and
draws his sword; *Donna Anna* and *Donna Elvira*
confront the villain. The musicians, servants, and
rustics run away in affright. For a moment *Don
Giovanni* loses presence of mind, but, his wits and
courage returning, he beats down the sword of *Don
Ottavio*, and, with *Leporello*, makes good his escape.

The incidents of the second act move with less
rapidity, and, until the fateful dénouement is reached,
on a lower plane of interest than those of the first,
which have been narrated. *Don Giovanni* turns
his attentions to the handsome waiting-maid of
Donna Elvira. To get the mistress out of the way
he persuades *Leporello* to exchange cloaks and hats
with him and station himself before her balcony
window, while he utters words of tenderness and
feigned repentance. The lady listens and descends
to the garden, where *Leporello* receives her with
effusive protestations; but *Don Giovanni* rudely
disturbs them, and they run away. Then the libertine,
in the habit of his valet, serenades his new charmer.
The song, "Deh vieni alla finestra," is of melting
tenderness and gallantry; words and music float
graciously on the evening air in company with a
delightfully piquant tune picked out on a mandolin.
The maid is drawn to the window, and *Don Giovanni*
is in full expectation of another triumph, when

G

Masetto confronts him with a rabble of peasants, all armed. They are in search of the miscreant who had attempted to outrage *Zerlina*. *Don Giovanni* is protected by his disguise. He feigns willingness to help in the hunt, and rids himself of *Masetto's* companions by sending them on a fool's errand to distant parts of the garden. Then he cunningly possesses himself of *Masetto's* weapons and belabors him stoutly with his own cudgel. He makes off, and *Zerlina*, hearing *Masetto's* cries, hurries in to heal his hurts with pretty endearments. (Air: "Vedrai carino.") Most unaccountably, as it will seem to those who seek for consistency and reason in all parts of the play, all of its actors except *Don Giovanni* find themselves together in a courtyard (or room, according to the notions of the stage manager). *Leporello* is trying to escape from *Elvira*, who still thinks him *Don Giovanni*, and is first confronted by *Masetto* and *Zerlina* and then by *Ottavio* and *Anna*. He is still in his master's hat and cloak, and is taken vigorously to task, but discloses his identity when it becomes necessary in order to escape a beating. Convinced at last that *Don Giovanni* is the murderer of the *Commandant*, *Don Ottavio* commends his love to the care of her friends and goes to denounce the libertine to the officers of the law.

The last scene is reached. *Don Giovanni*, seated at his table, eats, drinks, indulges in badinage with his servant, and listens to the music of his private band. The musicians play melodies from popular

operas of the period in which Mozart wrote — not
Spanish melodies of the unfixed time in which the
veritable Don Juan may have lived:—

From MARTIN'S "Una cosa rara."

From "Fra i due litiganti," by SARTI.

etc.

From "Nozze di Figaro."

etc.

Mozart feared anachronisms as little as Shakespeare. His *Don Giovanni* was contemporary with
himself and familiar with the repertory of the Vienna
Opera. The autograph discloses that the ingenious
conceit was wholly Mozart's. It was he who wrote
the words with which *Leporello* greets the melodies
from "Una cosa rara," "I due Litiganti," and "Le
Nozze di Figaro," and when *Leporello* hailed the
tune "Non piu andrai" from the last opera with
the words "Questo poi la conosco pur troppo"
("This we know but too well"), he doubtless scored
a point with his first audience in Prague which the

German translator of the opera never dreamed of.
Even the German critics of to-day seem dense in
their unwillingness to credit Mozart with a purely
amiable purpose in quoting the operas of his rivals,
Martin and Sarti. The latter showed himself un-
grateful for kindnesses received at Mozart's hands
by publicly denouncing an harmonic progression
in one of the famous six quartets dedicated to Haydn
as a barbarism, but there was no ill-will in the use
of the air from "I due Litiganti" as supper music
for the delectation of the *Don*. Mozart liked the
melody, and had written variations on it for the
pianoforte.

The supper is interrupted by *Donna Elvira*, who
comes to plead on her knees with *Don Giovanni*
to change his mode of life. He mocks at er solicitude and invites her to sit with him av table.
She leaves the room in despair, but sends back
a piercing shriek from the corridor. *Leporello* is
sent out to report on the cause of the cry, and returns trembling as with an ague and mumbling
that he has seen a ghost — a ghost of stone, whose
footsteps, "Ta, ta, ta," sounded like a mighty hammer on the floor. *Don Giovanni* himself goes to
learn the cause of the disturbance, and *Leporello*
hides under the table. The intrepid *Don* opens the
door. There is a clap of thunder, and there enters
the ghost of the *Commandant* in the form of his
statue as seen in the churchyard. The music which
has been described in connection with the overture
accompanies the conversation of the spectre and

his amazed host. *Don Giovanni's* repeated offer of
hospitality is rejected, but in turn he is asked if
he will return the visit. He will. "Your hand as
a pledge," says the spectre. All unabashed, the
doomed man places his hand in that of the statue,
which closes upon it like a vise. Then an awful
fear shakes the body of *Don Giovanni,* and a cry of
horror is forced out of his lips. "Repent, while
there is yet time," admonishes the visitor again
and again, and still again. *Don Giovanni* remains
unshaken in his wicked fortitude. At length he
wrests his hand out of the stony grasp and at the
moment hears his doom from the stony lips, "Ah!
the time for you is past!" Darkness enwraps him;
the earth trembles; supernatural voices proclaim
his punishment in chorus; a pit opens before him,
from which demons emerge and drag him down to
hell.

Here the opera ends for us; but originally, after
the catastrophe the persons of the play, all but the
reprobate whom divine justice has visited, returned
to the scene to hear a description of the awful happenings he had witnessed from the buffoon who
had hidden under the table, to dispose their plans
for the future (for *Ottavio* and *Anna,* marriage in a
year; for *Masetto* and *Zerlina,* a wedding instanter;
for *Elvira,* a nunnery), and platitudinously to mor-
alize that, the perfidious wretch having been carried to the realm of Pluto and Proserpine, naught
remained to do save to sing the old song, "Thus do
the wicked find their end, dying as they had lived."

CHAPTER V

IT was the scalawag Schikaneder who had put together the singular dramatic phantasmagoria known
as Mozart's "Magic Flute," and acted the part of
the buffoon in it, who, having donned the garb of
respectability, commissioned Beethoven to compose
the only opera which that supreme master gave to
the world. The opera is "Fidelio," and it occupies
a unique place in operatic history not only because it
is the only work of its kind by the greatest tone-
poet that ever lived, but also because of its subject.
The lyric drama has dealt with the universal passion ever since the art-form was invented, but
"Fidelio" is the only living opera which occurs to me
now, except Gluck's "Orfeo" and "Alceste," which
hymns the pure love of married lovers. The bond
between the story of *Alcestis*, who goes down to
death to save the life of *Admetus*, and that of
Leonore, who ventures her life to save *Florestan*, is
closer than that of the Orphic myth, for though
the alloy only serves to heighten the sheen of Eury-
dice's virtue, there is yet a grossness in the story of
Aristæus's unlicensed passion which led to her
death, that strongly differentiates it from the modern tale of wifely love and devotion. Beethoven was

Ludwig van Beethoven

(After the engraving by Blasius Höfel)

no ascetic, but he was as sincere and severe a moralist in life as he was in art. In that most melancholy of human documents, written at Heiligenstadt in October, 1802, commonly known as his will, he says to his brothers: "Recommend to your children *virtue;* it alone can bring happiness, not money. I speak from experience. It was virtue which bore me up in time of trouble; to her, next to my art, I owe thanks for my not having laid violent hands on myself."

That Mozart had been able to compose music to such libretti as those of "Don Giovanni" and "Così fan tutte" filled him with pained wonder. Moreover, he had serious views of the dignity of music and of the uses to which it might be put in the drama, and more advanced notions than he has generally been credited with as to how music and the drama ought to be consorted. Like all composers, he longed to write an opera, and it is not at all unlikely that, like Mendelssohn after him, he was deterred by the general tendency of the opera books of his day. Certain it is that though he received a commission for an opera early in the year 1803, it was not until an opera on the story which is also that of "Fidelio" had been brought out at Dresden that he made a definitive choice of a subject. The production which may have influenced him was that of Ferdinando Paër's "Leonora, ossia l'Amore conjugale," which was brought forward at Dresden, where its composer was conductor of the opera, on October 3, 1804. This opera was the

immediate predecessor of Beethoven's, but it also
had a predecessor in a French opera, "Léonore, ou
l'Amour conjugal," of which the music was composed by Pierre Gaveaux, a musician of small but
graceful gifts, who had been a tenor singer before
he became a composer. This opera had its first
performance on February 19, 1798, and may also
have been known to Beethoven, or have been brought
to his notice while he was casting about for a subject.
At any rate, though it was known as early as June,
1803, that Beethoven intended to compose an opera
for the Theater an der Wien, and had taken lodgings
with his brother Caspar in the theatre building more
than two months before, it was not until the winter
of 1804 that the libretto of "Fidelio" was placed in
his hands. It was a German version of the French
book by Bouilly, which had been made by Joseph
Sonnleithner, an intimate friend of Schubert, founder
of the Gesellschaft der Musikfreunde, who had
recently been appointed secretary of the Austrian
court theatres as successor of Kotzebue. Beethoven
had gone to live in the theatre building for the purpose of working on the opera for Schikaneder, but
early in 1804 the Theater an der Wien passed out
of his hands into those of Baron von Braun. The
intervening summer had been passed by the composer at Baden and Unter Döbling in work upon the
"Eroica" symphony. The check upon the operatic
project was but temporary. Baron von Braun
took Schikaneder into his service and renewed the
contract with Beethoven. This accomplished, the

composer resumed his lodgings in the theatre and began energetically to work upon the opera. Let two facts be instanced here to show how energetically and how painstakingly he labored. When he went into the country in the early summer, as was his custom, he carried with him 346 pages of sketches for the opera, sixteen staves on a page; and among these sketches were sixteen openings of *Florestan's* great air, which may be said to mark the beginning of the dramatic action in the opera.

For the rest of the history of the opera I shall draw upon the preface to "Fidelio," which I wrote some years ago for the vocal score in the Schirmer collection. The score was finished, including the orchestration, in the summer of 1805, and on Beethoven's return to Vienna, rehearsals were begun. It was the beginning of a series of trials which made the opera a child of sorrow to the composer. The style of the music was new to the singers, and they pronounced it unsingable. They begged him to make changes, but Beethoven was adamant. The rehearsals became a grievous labor to all concerned. The production was set down for November 20, but when the momentous day came, it found Vienna occupied by the French troops, Bonaparte at Schönbrunn and the capital deserted by the Emperor, the nobility, and most of the wealthy patrons of art. The performance was a failure. Besides the French occupation, two things were recognized as militating against the opera's success: — the music was not to the taste of the people, and the work was too long.

Repetitions followed on November 21 and 22, but the first verdict was upheld.

Beethoven's distress over the failure was scarcely greater than that of his friends, though he was, perhaps, less willing than they to recognize the causes that lay in the work itself. A meeting was promptly held in the house of Prince Lichnowsky and the opera taken in hand for revision. Number by number it was played on the pianoforte, sung, discussed. Beethoven opposed vehemently nearly every suggestion made by his well-meaning friends to remedy the defects of the book and score, but yielded at last and consented to the sacrifice of some of the music and a remodelling of the book for the sake of condensation, this part of the task being intrusted to Stephan von Breuning, who undertook to reduce the original three acts to two.[1] When once Beethoven had been brought to give his consent to the proposed changes, he accepted the result with the greatest good humor; it should be noted, however, that when the opera was put upon the stage again, on March 29, 1806, he was so dilatory with his musical corrections that there was time for only one rehearsal with orchestra. In the curtailed form "Fidelio" (as the opera was called, though Beethoven had fought strenuously from the begin-

[1] As the opera is performed nowadays it is in three acts, but this division is the work of stage managers or directors who treat each of the three scenes as an act. At the Metropolitan Opera House, in New York, Mr. Mahler introduced a division of the first scene into two for what can be said to be merely picturesque effect, since the division is not demanded by the dramatic situation.

ning for the retention of the original title, "Leonore") made a distinctly better impression than it
had four months before, and this grew deeper with
the subsequent repetitions; but Beethoven quarrelled
with Baron von Braun, and the opera was withdrawn. An attempt was made to secure a production in Berlin, but it failed, and the fate of
"Fidelio" seemed to be sealed. It was left to slumber
for more than seven years; then, in the spring of
1814, it was taken up again. Naturally, another
revision was the first thing thought of, but this
time the work was intrusted to a more practised
writer than Beethoven's childhood friend. Georg
Friedrich Treitschke was manager and librettist
for Baron von Braun, and he became Beethoven's
collaborator. The revision of the book was completed by March, 1814, and Beethoven wrote to
Treitschke: "I have read your revision of the opera
with great satisfaction. It has decided me to re-
build the desolate ruins of an ancient fortress."
Treitschke rewrote much of the libretto, and Beethoven made considerable changes in the music,
restoring some of the pages that had been elided
at the first overhauling. In its new form "Fidelio"
was produced at the Theater am Kärnthnerthor on
May 23, 1814. It was a successful reawakening.
On July 18 the opera had a performance for Beethoven's benefit; Moscheles made a pianoforte score
under the direction of the composer, who dedicated
it to his august pupil, the Archduke Rudolph, and
it was published in August by Artaria.

The history of "Fidelio," interesting as it is, need not be pursued here further than to chronicle its first performances in the English and American metropoles. London heard it first from Chelard's German company at the King's Theatre on May 18, 1832. It was first given in English at Covent Garden on June 12, 1835, with Malibran as *Leonore*, and in Italian at Her Majesty's on May 20, 1851, when the dialogue was sung in recitative written by Balfe. There has scarcely ever been a German opera company in New York whose repertory did not include "Fidelio," but the only performances for many years after it came were in English. A company of singers brought from England by Miss Inverarity to the Park Theatre produced it first on September 19, 1839. The parts were distributed as follows: *Leonore*, Mrs. Martyn (Miss Inverarity); *Marcellina*, Miss Poole; *Florestan*, Mr. Manvers; *Pizarro*, Mr. Giubilei; and *Rocco*, Mr. Martyn. The opera was performed every night for a fortnight. Such a thing would be impossible now, but lest some one be tempted to rail against the decadent taste of to-day, let it quickly be recorded that somewhere in the opera — I hope not in the dungeon scene — Mme. Giubilei danced a *pas de deux* with Paul Taglioni.

Beethoven composed four overtures for "Fidelio," but a description of them will best follow comment on the drama and its music. Some two years before the incident which marks the beginning of the action, *Don Pizarro*, governor of a state prison in

Spain, not far from Seville, has secretly seized *Florestan*, a political opponent, whose fearless honesty threatened to frustrate his wicked designs, and immured him in a subterranean cell in the prison. His presence there is known only to *Pizarro* and the jailer *Rocco*, who, however, knows neither the name nor the rank of the man whom, under strict command, he keeps in fetters and chained to a stone in the dimly lighted dungeon, which he alone is permitted to visit. *Florestan's* wife, *Leonore*, suspecting the truth, has disguised herself in man's attire and, under the name of *Fidelio*, secured employment in the prison. To win the confidence of *Rocco*, she has displayed so much zeal and industry in his interests that the old man, whose one weakness is a too great love of money, gives the supposed youth a full measure of admiration and affection. *Fidelio's* beauty and gentleness have worked havoc with the heart of *Marcellina*, the jailer's pretty daughter, who is disposed to cast off *Jaquino*, the turnkey, upon whose suit she had smiled till her love for *Fidelio* came between. *Rocco* looks with auspicious eye upon the prospect of having so industrious and thrifty a son-in-law as *Fidelio* promises to be to comfort his old age. The action now begins in the courtyard of the prison, where, before the jailer's lodge, *Marcellina* is performing her household duties — ironing the linen, to be specific. *Jaquino*, who has been watching for an opportunity to speak to her alone (no doubt alarmed at the new posture which his love affair is assuming),

resolves to ask her to marry him. The duet, quite
in the Mozartian vein, breathes simplicity throughout; plain people, with plain manners, these, who
express simple thoughts in simple language. *Jaquino*
begins eagerly:—

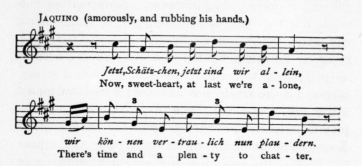

But *Marcellina* affects to be annoyed and urges
him to come to the point at once. Quite delicious
is the manner in which Beethoven delineates *Jaquino's* timid hesitation:—

Jaquino's wooing is interrupted by a knocking at
the door (realistically reproduced in the music)

and when he goes to open the wicket, *Marcellina*
expresses no sympathy for his sufferings, but ecstatically proclaims her love for *Fidelio* as the reason
why she must needs say nay. And this she does,
not amiably or sympathetically, but pettishly and
with an impatient reiteration of "No, no, no, no!"
in which the bassoon drolly supports her. A second
knocking at the door, then a third, and finally she is
relieved of her tormentor by *Rocco*, who calls him
out into the garden. Left alone, *Marcellina* sings
her longing for *Fidelio* and pictures the domestic
bliss which shall follow her union with him. *Rocco*
and *Jaquino* enter, and close after them *Leonore*,
wearied by the weight of some chains which she had
carried to the smith for repairs. She renders an
account for purchases of supplies, and her thrift rejoices the heart of *Rocco*, who praises her zeal in his
behalf and promises her a reward. Her reply, that
she does not do her duty merely for the sake of wage,
he interprets as an allusion to love for his daughter.
The four now give expression to their thoughts and
emotions. *Marcellina* indulges her day-dream of
love; *Leonore* reflects upon the dangerous position
in which her disguise has placed her; *Jaquino* ob-

serves with trepidation the disposition of *Rocco* to bring about a marriage between his daughter and *Fidelio*. Varied and contrasting emotions, these, yet Beethoven has cast their expression in the mould of a canon built on the following melody, which is sung in turn by each of the four personages:—

From a strictly musical point of view the fundamental mood of the four personages has thus the same expression, and this Beethoven justifies by making the original utterance profoundly contemplative, not only by the beautiful subject of the canon, but by the exalted instrumental introduction — one of those uplifting, spiritualized slow movements which are typical of the composer. This feeling he enhances by his orchestration — violas and violoncellos divided, and basses—in a way copying the solemn color with more simple means which Mozart uses in his invocation of the Egyptian deities in "The Magic Flute." Having thus established this fundamental mood, he gives liberty of individual utterance in the counterpoint melodies with which each personage embroiders the original theme when sung by the others. Neither *Rocco* nor *Marcellina* seems to think it necessary to consult *Leonore* in the matter, taking her acquiescence for granted. Between themselves they arrange that the wedding shall take place when next *Pizarro* makes his monthly visit to Seville to give an account of his stewardship, and the jailer admonishes the youthful pair to put money in their purses in a song of little distinction, but containing some delineative music in the orchestra suggesting the rolling and jingling of coins. Having been made seemingly to agree to the way of the maid and her father, *Leonore* seeks now to turn it to the advantage of her mission. She asks and obtains the jailer's permission to visit with him the cells in which political prisoners are kept — all but one, in which is confined one who is either a great criminal or a man with powerful enemies ("much the same thing," comments *Rocco*). Of him even the jailer knows nothing, having resolutely declined to hear his story. However, his sufferings cannot last much longer, for by *Pizarro's* orders his rations are being reduced daily; he has been all but deprived of light, and even the straw which had served as a couch has been taken from him. And how long has he been imprisoned? Over two years. "Two years!" *Leonore* almost loses control of her feelings. Now she urges that she must help the jailer wait upon him. "I have strength and courage." The old man is won over. He will ask the governor for permission to take *Fidelio* with him to the secret cells, for he is growing old, and death will soon claim him. The dramatic nerve has been touched with the first allusion to the mysterious

H

prisoner who is being slowly tortured to death, and
it is thrilling to note how Beethoven's genius (so
often said to be purely epical) responds. In the trio
which follows, the dialogue which has been outlined
first intones a *motif* which speaks merely of com-

Gut, Söhn- chen, gut,   hab' im - mer
Well said, my son,   for half is

Wind.

Viol.

placency. No sooner does it reach the lips of *Leonore*, however, than it becomes the utterance of
proud resolve: —

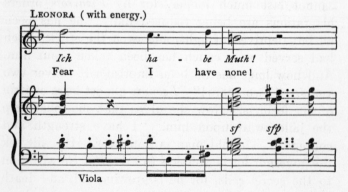

LEONORA (with energy.)

Ich   ha - be Muth !
Fear   I   have none !

Viola

and out of it grows a hymn of heroic daring.
Marcellina's utterances are all concerned with her

self, with an admixture of solicitude for her father, whose lugubrious reflections on his own impending dissolution are gloomily echoed in the music:—

Ich bin ja bald des Gra - bes Beu - te,
Death soon will claim me as his prey, now,

A march accompanies the entrance of *Pizarro.*[1] *Pizarro* receives his despatches from *Rocco,* and from one of the letters learns that the *Minister of Justice,* having been informed that several victims of arbitrary power are confined in the prisons of which he is governor, is about to set out upon a tour of inspection. Such a visit might disclose the wrong done to *Florestan,* who is the *Minister's* friend and believed by him to be dead, and *Pizarro* resolves to shield himself against the consequences of such a discovery by compassing his death. He publishes his resolution in a furious air, "Ha! welch' ein Augenblick!" in which he gloats over the culmination of his revenge upon his ancient enemy. It is a terrible outpouring of bloodthirsty rage, and I have yet to hear the singer who can cope with its awful accents. Here, surely, Beethoven asks more of the human voice than it is capable of giving. Quick action is necessary. The officer of the guard is ordered to post a

[1] In Mr. Mahler's arrangement this march becomes *entr'acte* music to permit of a change of scene from the interior of the jailer's lodge to the courtyard of the prison prescribed in the book.

trumpeter in the watch-tower, with instructions to
give a signal the moment a carriage with outriders
is seen approaching from Seville. *Rocco* is summoned, and *Pizarro*, praising his courage and fidelity
to duty, gives him a purse as earnest of riches which
are to follow obedience. The old man is ready
enough until he learns that what is expected of
him is

whereupon he revolts, nor is he moved by *Pizarro's*
argument that the deed is demanded by the welfare
of the state. Foiled in his plan of hiring an assassin, *Pizarro* announces that he will deal the blow
himself, and commands that a disused cistern be
opened to receive the corpse of his victim. The
duet which is concerned with these transactions is
full of striking effects. The orchestra accompanies
Rocco's description of the victim as "one who scarcely
lives, but seems to float like a shadow" with chords
which spread a cold, cadaverous sheen over the
words, while the declamation of "A blow!—and he is
dumb," makes illustrative pantomime unnecessary

Leonore has overheard all, and rushes forward on the
departure of the men to express her horror at the
wicked plot, and proclaim her trust in the guidance
and help of love as well as her courageous resolve
to follow its impulses and achieve the rescue of the
doomed man.   The scene and air in which she does
this ("Abscheulicher! wo eilst du hin?") is now
a favorite concert-piece of all dramatic singers; but
when it was written its difficulties seemed appalling
to Fräulein Milder (afterward the famous Frau
Milder-Hauptmann), who was the original *Leonore*.
A few years before Haydn had said to her, "My
dear child, you have a voice as big as a house," and
a few years later she made some of her finest successes
with the part; but in the rehearsals she quarrelled
violently with Beethoven because of the unsingable-
ness of passages in the *Adagio*, of which, no doubt,
this was one:—

sie wird's er - rei - - - - - chen

and when called upon, in 1814, to re-create the part
which had been written expressly for her, she refused until Beethoven had consented to modify
it.   Everything is marvellous in the *scena* — the
mild glow of orchestral color delineating the bow
of promise in the recitative, the heart-searching,
transfigurating, prayerful loveliness of the slow

melody, the *obbligato* horn parts, the sweep of the final *Allegro*, all stand apart in operatic literature.

At *Leonore's* request, and presuming upon the request which *Pizarro* had made of him, *Rocco* permits the prisoners whose cells are above ground to enjoy the light and air of the garden, defending his action later, when taken to task by *Pizarro*, on the plea that he was obeying established custom in allowing the prisoners a bit of liberty on the name-day of the king. In an undertone he begs his master to save his anger for the man who is doomed to die. Meanwhile *Leonore* convinces herself that her husband is not among the prisoners who are enjoying the brief respite, and is overjoyed to learn that she is to accompany *Rocco* that very day to the mysterious subterranean dungeon. With the return of the prisoners to their cells, the first act ends.

An instrumental introduction ushers in the second act. It is a musical delineation of *Florestan's* surroundings, sufferings, and mental anguish. The darkness is rent by shrieks of pain; harsh, hollow, and threatening sound the throbs of the kettle-drums. The parting of the curtain discloses the prisoner chained to his rocky couch. He declaims against the gloom, the silence, the deathly void surrounding him, but comforts himself with the thought that his sufferings are but the undeserved punishment inflicted by an enemy for righteous duty done. The melody of the slow part of his air, which begins thus,

In   des   Le - bens Früh - lings - ta - gen

ist   das   Glück von   mir   ge-floh'n.

will find mention again when the overtures come
under discussion. His sufferings have overheated
his fancy, and, borne upon cool and roseate breezes,
he sees a vision of his wife, *Leonore*, come to comfort and rescue him. His exaltation reaches a
frenzy which leaves him sunk in exhaustion on his
couch. *Rocco* and *Leonore* come to dig his grave.
Melodramatic music accompanies their preparation,
and their conversation while at work forms a duet.
Sustained trombone tones spread a portentous atmosphere, and a contra-bassoon adds weight and
solemnity to the *motif* which describes the labor
of digging:—

They have stopped to rest and refresh themselves, when *Florestan* becomes conscious and addresses *Rocco*. *Leonore* recognizes his voice as
that of her husband, and when he pleads for a drink
of water, she gives him, with *Rocco's* permission,
the wine left in her pitcher, then a bit of bread.
A world of pathos informs his song of gratitude.

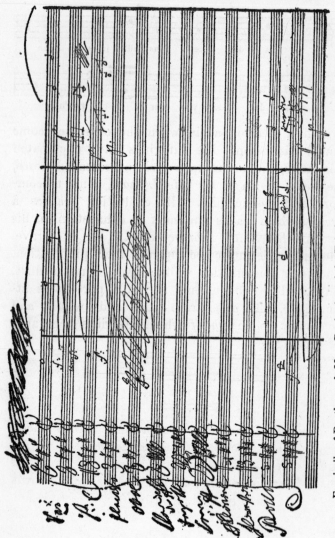

Facsimile of Beethoven's Ms.   Beginning of the Trio in the Dungeon Scene of "Fidelio."

Pizarro comes to commit the murder, but first he commands that the boy be sent away, and confesses his purpose to make way with both *Fidelio* and *Rocco* when once the deed is done. He cannot resist the temptation to disclose his identity to *Florestan,* who, though released from the stone, is still fettered. The latter confronts death calmly, but as *Pizarro* is about to plunge the dagger into his breast, *Leonore* (who had concealed herself in the darkness) throws herself as a protecting shield before him. *Pizarro,* taken aback for a moment, now attempts to thrust *Leonore* aside, but is again made to pause by her cry, "First kill his wife!" Consternation and amazement seize all and speak out of their ejaculations. Determined to kill both husband and wife, *Pizarro* rushes forward again, only to see a pistol thrust into his face, hear a shriek, "Another word, and you are dead!" and immediately after the trumpet signal which, by his own command, announces the coming of the *Minister of Justice:*—

(The trumpet sounds from the tower.)

Pizarro is escorted out of the dungeon by *Rocco* and attendants with torches, and the reunited lovers are left to themselves and their frenetic rejoicings. Surrounded by his guard, the populace attracted by his coming, and the prisoners into whose condition he had come to inquire, *Don Fernando* metes out punishment to the wicked *Pizarro*, welcomes his old friend back to liberty and honor, and bids *Leonore* remove his fetters as the only person worthy of such a task. The populace hymn wifely love and fidelity.

Mention has been made of the fact that Beethoven wrote four overtures for his opera. Three of these are known as Overtures "Leonore No. 1," "Leonore No. 2," and "Leonore No. 3" — "Leonore" being the title by which the opera was known at the unfortunate first performance. The composer was never contented with the change to "Fidelio" which was made, because of the identity of the story with the "Leonore" operas, of Gaveaux and Paër. Much confusion has existed in the books (and still exists, for that matter) touching the order in which the four overtures were composed. The early biographers were mistaken on that point, and the blunder was perpetuated by the numbering when the scores were published. The true "Leonore No. 1" is the overture known in the concert-room, where it is occasionally heard, as "Leonore No. 2." This was the original overture to the opera, and was performed at the three representations in 1805. The overture called "Leonore No. 3" was the result of the revision undertaken by Beethoven and his friends after the failure. . In May, 1807, the German opera at Prague was established and "Fidelio" selected as one of the works to be given. Evidently Beethoven was dissatisfied both with the original overture and its revision, for he wrote a new one, in which he retained the theme from *Florestan's* air, but none of the other themes used in Nos. 2 and 3. The performances at Prague did not take place, and nobody knows what became of the autograph score of the overture. When Beethoven's effects were sold at auction after his death, Tobias Haslinger bought a parcel of dances and other things in manuscript. Among them were a score and parts of an overture in C, not in Beethoven's handwriting, but containing corrections made by him. It bore no date, and on a violin part Beethoven had written first "Overtura, Violino Imo." Later he had added words in red crayon to make it read, "Overtura in C, charakteristische Overture, Violino Imo." On February 7, 1828, the composition was played at a concert in Vienna, but notwithstanding the reminiscence of *Florestan's* air, it does not seem to have been associated with the opera, either by Haslinger or the critics. Before 1832, when Haslinger published the overture as Op. 138, however, it had been identified, and, not unnaturally, the conclusion was jumped at that it was the original overture. That known as "Leonore No. 2" having been withdrawn for revision by Beethoven himself, was not heard of till 1840, when it was performed at a Gewandhaus concert in Leipsic. For the revival of the opera in 1814 Beethoven composed the overture in E major, now called the "Fidelio" overture, and generally played as an introduction to the opera, the much greater "Leonore No. 3" being played either between the acts, or, as by Mahler in New York and Vienna, between the two scenes of the second act, where it may be said it distinctly has the effect of an anticlimax. The thematic material of the "Leonore" overtures Nos. 2 and 3 being practically the same, careless listeners may easily confound one with the other. Nevertheless, the differences between the two works are many and great, and a deep insight into the workings of Beethoven's mind would be vouchsafed students if they were brought into juxtaposition in the concert-room. The reason commonly given for the revision of No. 2 (the real No. 1) is that at the performance it was found that some of the passages for wind instruments troubled the players; but among the changes made by Beethoven, all of which tend to heighten the intensity of the overture which presents the drama *in nuce*, may be mentioned the elision of a recurrence to material drawn from his principal theme between the two trumpet-calls, and the abridgment of the development or free fantasia portion. Finally, it may be stated that though the "Fidelio" overture was written for the revival of 1814, it was not heard at the first performance in that year. It was not ready, and the overture to "The Ruins of Athens" was played in its stead.

CHAPTER VI

"FAUST"

MM. MICHEL CARRÉ and Jules Barbier, who made the book for Gounod's opera "Faust," went for their subject to Goethe's dramatic poem. Out of that great work, which had occupied the mind of the German poet for an ordinary lifetime, the French librettists extracted the romance which sufficed them — the story of *Gretchen's* love for the rejuvenated philosopher, her seduction and death. This romance is wholly the creation of Goethe; it has no place in any of the old legends which are at the bottom of the history of Dr. Faust, or Faustus. Those legends deal with the doings of a magician who has sold his soul to the devil for the accomplishment of some end on which his ambition is set. There are many such legends in mediæval literature, and their fundamental thought is older than Christianity. In a sense, the idea is a product of ignorance and superstition combined. In all ages men whose learning and achievements were beyond the comprehension of simple folk were thought to have derived their powers from the practice of necromancy. The list is a long one, and includes some of the great names of antiquity. The imagination of the Middle Ages made bondsmen of the infernal powers out of such men as Zoroaster, Democritus, Empedocles, Apollonius, Virgil, Albertus Magnus, Merlin, and Paracelsus. In the sixth century Theophilus of Syracuse was said to have sold himself to the devil and to have been saved from damnation only by the miraculous intervention of the Virgin Mary, who visited hell and bore away the damnable compact. So far as his bond was concerned, Theophilus was said to have had eight successors among the Popes of Rome.

Architects of cathedrals and engineers of bridges were wont, if we believe popular tales, to barter their souls in order to realize their great conceptions. How do such notions get into the minds of the people? I attempted not an answer but an explanation in a preface to Gounod's opera published by Schirmer some years ago, which is serving me a good turn now. For the incomprehensible the supernatural is the only accounting. These things are products of man's myth-making capacity and desire. With the advancement of knowledge this capacity and desire become atrophied, but spring into life again in the presence of a popular stimulant. The superstitious peasantry of Bavaria beheld a man in league with the devil in the engineer who ran the first locomotive engine through that country. More recently, I am told, the same people conceived the notion that the Prussian needle-gun, which had wrought destruction among their soldiery in the war of 1866, was an infernal machine for which Bismarck had given the immortal part of himself.

When printing was invented, it was looked upon in a double sense as a black art, and it was long and widely believed that Johann Fust, or Faust, of Mayence, the partner of Gutenberg, was the original Dr. Johann Faustus (the prototype of Goethe's *Faust*), who practised magic toward the end of the fifteenth and at the beginning of the sixteenth century, made a compact with Mephistopheles, performed many miraculous feats, and died horribly at the last. But Fust, or Faust, was a rich and reputable merchant of Mayence who provided capital to promote the art of Gutenberg and Schöffer, and Mr. H. Sutherland Edwards, who gossips pleasantly and at great length about the Faust legends in Volume I of his book, "The Lyrical Drama," indulges a rather wild fancy when he considers it probable that he was the father of the real mediæval incarnation of the ancient superstition. The real Faust had been a poor lad, but money inherited from a rich uncle enabled him to attend lectures at the University of Cracow, where he seems to have devoted himself with particular assiduity to the study of magic, which had at that period a respectable place in the curriculum. Having obtained his doctorial hat, he travelled through Europe practising necromancy and acquiring a thoroughly bad reputation. To the fact that this man actually lived, and lived such a life as has been described, we have the testimony of a physician, Philip Begardi; a theologian, Johann Gast, and no less a witness than Philip Melanchthon, the reformer. Martin Luther refers to Faust in his "Table Talk" as a man lost beyond all hope of redemption; Melanchthon, who says that he talked with him, adds: "This sorcerer Faust, an abominable beast, a common sewer of many devils (*turpissima bestia et cloaca multorum diabolvrum*), boasted that he had enabled the imperial armies to win their victories in Italy."

The literary history of Faust is much too long to be even outlined here; a few points must suffice us. In a book published in Frankfort in 1587 by a German writer named Spiess, the legend received its first printed form. An English ballad on the subject appeared within a year. In 1590 there came a translation of the entire story, which was the source from which Marlowe drew his "Tragical History of the Life and Death of Dr. Faustus," brought forward on the stage in 1593 and printed in 1604. New versions of the legend followed each other rapidly, and Faust became a favorite character with playwrights, romancers, and poets. Toward the end of the eighteenth century, when Goethe conceived the idea of utilizing the subject for publishing his comprehensive philosophy of human life, it seems to have held possession of a large portion of literary Germany. All together, it was in the mind of the great poet from his adolescence till his death; but while he was working on his original plan, literary versions of the legend were published by twenty-eight German authors, including Lessing, whose manuscript, unhappily, was lost. Goethe had known the legend from

DR. FAUSTUS

(After a painting by Rembrandt)

childhood, when he had seen puppet-plays based
on it — these plays being the vulgar progeny of
Marlowe's powerful tragedy, which is still an ornament of English literature. Music was a part of
these puppet-plays. In the first one that fell into
my hands I find the influence of opera manifest in
recitatives and airs put into the mouth of *Mephistopheles*, and comic songs sung by *Kasperle*, the
Punch of the German marionette fraternity.

The love tale which furnished forth the entire
opera book of MM. Carré and Barbier is, as I have
said, wholly the invention of Goethe. There is the
shadowy form of a maiden in some of the versions
of the legend, but not a hint of the romantic sentiment so powerfully and pathetically set forth by
the poet. Nor did the passion either for good or evil
play a part in the agreement between Faust and
the devil. That agreement covered five points only:
Faust pledged himself to deny God, hate the human race, despise the clergy, never set foot in a
church, and never get married. So far from being
a love episode in the story, when Faustus, in the
old book by Spiess, once expressed a wish to abro-
gate the last condition, Mephistopheles refused him
permission on the ground that marriage is something pleasing to God, and for that reason in con-
travention of the contract. "Hast thou," quoth
Mephistopheles, "sworn thyself an enemy to God
and to all creatures? To this I answer thee, thou
canst not marry; thou canst not serve two masters, God and thy prince. For wedlock is a chief

institution ordained of God, and that thou hast promised to defy as we do all, and that thou hast not only done, but, moreover, thou hast confirmed it with thy blood. Persuade thyself that what thou hast done in contempt of wedlock, it is all to thine own delight. Therefore, Faustus, look well about thee and bethink thyself better, and I wish thee to change thy mind, for if thou keep not what thou hast promised in thy writing, we will tear thee in pieces, like the dust under thy feet. Therefore, sweet Faustus, think with what unquiet life, anger, strife, and debate thou shalt live in when thou takest a wife. Therefore, change thy mind." Faustus abandons his purpose for the time being, but within two hours summons his spirit again and demands his consent to marriage; whereupon up there comes a whirlwind, which fills the house with fire and smoke and hurls Faustus about until he is unable to stir hand or foot. Also there appears an ugly devil, so dreadful and monstrous to behold that Faustus dares not look upon him. This devil is in a mood for jesting. "How likest thou thy wedding?" he asks of Faustus, who promises not to mention marriage more, and is well content when Mephistopheles engages to bring him any woman, dead or alive, whom he may desire to possess. It is in obedience to this promise that Helen of Troy is brought back from the world of shades to be Faustus's paramour. By her he has a son, whom he calls Justus Faustus, but in the end, when Faustus loses his life, mother and child vanish. Goethe uses the

scene of the amour between Faust and the ancient
beauty in the second part of his poem as does Boito
in his "Mefistofele," charging it with the beautiful
symbolism which was in the German poet's mind.
In the Polish tale of Pan Twardowsky, built on the
lines of the old legend, there is a more amusing
fling at marriage. In return for the help which he
is to receive, the Polish wizard has the privilege of
demanding three duties of the devil. After enjoying to the full the benefits conferred by two, he commands the devil to marry Mme. Twardowska. This
is more than the devil had bargained for, or is willing to perform. He refuses; the contract is broken,
and Twardowsky is saved. The story may have
inspired Thackeray's amusing tale in "The Paris
Sketch-book," entitled "The Painter's Bargain."

For the facts in the story of the composition and
production of Gounod's opera, we have the authority
of the composer in his autobiography. In 1856 he
made the acquaintance of Jules Barbier and Michel
Carré, and asked them to collaborate with him in
an opera. They assenting, he proposed Goethe's
"Faust" as a subject, and it met with their approval. Together they went to see M. Carvalho
who was then director of the Théâtre Lyrique. He,
too, liked the idea of the opera, and the librettists
went to work. The composer had written nearly
half of the score, when M. Carvalho brought the
disconcerting intelligence that a grand melodrama
treating the subject was in preparation at the Théâtre de la Porte Saint-Martin. Carvalho said that

it would be impossible to get the opera ready before
the appearance of the melodrama, and unwise to
enter into competition with a theatre the luxury of
whose stage mounting would have attracted all
Paris before the opera could be produced. Carvalho
therefore advised a change of subject, which was
such a blow to Gounod that he was incapable of
applying himself to work for a week. Finally,
Carvalho came to the rescue with a request for a
lyric comedy based on one of Molière's plays.
Gounod chose "Le Médecin malgré lui," and the
opera had its production at the Théâtre Lyrique
on the anniversary of Molière's birth, January 15,
1858. The melodrama at the Porte Saint-Martin
turned out to be a failure in spite of its beautiful
pictures, and Carvalho recurred to the opera, which
had been laid aside, and Gounod had it ready by
July. He read it to the director in the greenroom
of the theatre in that month, and Mme. Carvalho,
wife of the director, who was present, was so deeply
impressed with the rôle of *Marguerite* that M. Carvalho asked the composer's permission to assign it
to her. "This was agreed upon," says Gounod,
"and the future proved the choice to be a veritable
inspiration."

Rehearsals began in September, 1858, and soon
developed difficulties. Gounod had set his heart
upon a handsome young tenor named Guardi for the
titular rôle, but he was found to be unequal to its
demands. This caused such embarrassment that,
it is said, Gounod, who had a pretty voice and was

rather fond of showing it, seriously pondered the feasibility of singing it himself. He does not tell us this in his autobiography, but neither does he tell us that he had chosen Mme. Ugalde for the part of *Marguerite*, and that he yielded to M. Carvalho in giving it to the director's wife because Mme. Ugalde had quarrelled with him (as prima donnas will), about Massé's opera, "La Fée Carabosse," which preceded "Faust" at the Lyrique. The difficulty about the tenor rôle was overcome by the enlistment of M. Barbot, an artist who had been a companion of Carvalho's when he sang small parts at the Opéra Comique. He was now far past his prime, and a pensioned teacher at the Conservatoire, but Gounod bears witness that he "showed himself a great musician in the part of *Faust*." Of Belanqué, who created the part of *Méphistophélès*, Gounod says that "he was an intelligent comedian whose play, physique, and voice lent themselves wonderfully to this fantastic and Satanic personage." As for Mme. Carvalho, it was the opinion of the composer that, though her masterly qualities of execution and style had already placed her in the front rank of contemporary singers, no rôle, till *Marguerite* fell to her lot, had afforded her opportunity to show in such measure "the superior phases of her talent, so sure, so refined, so steady, so tranquil — its lyric and pathetic qualities."

It was a distinguished audience that listened to the first performance of "Faust" on March 19, 1859. Auber, Berlioz, Reyer, Jules Janin, Perrin,

Émile Ollivier, and many other men who had made
their mark in literature, art, or politics sat in the
boxes, and full as many more of equal distinction
in the stalls. Among these latter were Delacroix,
Vernet, Eugène Giraud, Pasdeloup, Scudo, Heugel,
and Jules Lévy. The criticism of the journals
which followed was, as usual, a blending of censure
and praise. Berlioz was favorably inclined toward
the work, and, with real discrimination, put his
finger' on the monologue at the close of the third
act ("Il m'aime! Quel trouble en mon cœur") as the
best thing in the score. Scudo gave expression to
what was long the burden of the critical song in
Germany; namely, the failure of the authors to
grasp the large conception of Goethe's poem; but,
with true Gallic inconsistency, he set down the
soldiers' chorus as a masterpiece. The garden
scene, with its sublimated mood, its ecstasy of feeling, does not seem to have moved him; he thought
the third act monotonous and too long. There was
no demand for the score on the part of the French
publishers, but at length Choudens was persuaded
to adventure 10,000 francs, one-half of an inherit-
ance, in it. He was at that time an *éditeur* on a
small scale, as well as a postal official, and the
venture put him on the road to fortune. For the
English rights Gounod is said to have received only
forty pounds sterling, and this only after the energetic championship of Chorley, who made the English translation. The opera was given thirty-seven
times at the Théâtre Lyrique. Ten years after its

first performance it was revised to fit the schemes of the Grand Opéra, and brought forward under the new auspices on March 3, 1869. Mlle. Christine Nilsson was the new *Marguerite*. No opera has since equalled the popularity of "Faust" in Paris. Twenty-eight years after its first performance, Gounod was privileged to join his friends in a celebration of its 500th representation. That was in 1887. Eight years after, the 1000 mark was reached, and the 1250th Parisian representation took place in 1902.

Two years before "Faust" reached London, it was given in Germany, where it still enjoys great popularity, though it is called "Margarethe," in deference to the *manes* of Goethe. Within a few weeks in 1863 the opera had possession of two rival establishments in London. At Her Majesty's Theatre it was given for the first time on June 11, and at the Royal Italian Opera on July 2. On January 23, 1864, it was brought forward in Mr. Chorley's English version at Her Majesty's. The first American representation took place at the Academy of usic, New York, on November 25, 1863, the parts being distributed as follows: *Margherita*, Miss Clara Louise Kellogg; *Siebel*, Miss Henrietta Sulzer; *Martha*, Miss Fanny Stockton; *Faust*, Francesco Mazzoleni; *Mephistopheles*, Hanibal Biachi; *Valentine*, G. Yppolito; *Wagner*, D. Coletti. It was sung in Italian, won immediate popularity, and made money for Max Maretzek, who was at once the manager and the conductor of the company. Forty years before an English version of Goethe's tragedy (the first part, of course) had been produced at the Bowery Theatre, with the younger Wallack as *Faust* and Charles Hill as *Mephistopheles*.

The opera begins, like Goethe's dramatic poem, after the prologue, with the scene in *Faust's* study. The aged philosopher has grown weary of fruitless inquiry into the mystery of nature and its Creator, and longs for death. He has just passed a night in study, and as the morning breaks he salutes it as his last on earth and pledges it in a cup of poison. As he is about to put the cup to his lips, the song of a company of maidens floats in at the window. It tells of the joy of living and loving and the beauty of nature and its inspirations. *Faust's* hand trembles, strangely, unaccountably; again he lifts the cup, but only to pause again to listen to a song sung by a company of reapers repairing to the fields, chanting their gratitude to God for the loveliness surrounding them, and invoking His blessing. The sounds madden the despairing philosopher. What would prayer avail him? Would it bring back youth and love and faith? No. Accursed, therefore, be all things good — earth's pleasures, riches, allurements of every sort; the dreams of love; the wild joy of combat; happiness itself; science, religion, prayers, belief above all, a curse upon the patience with which he had so long endured! He summons Satan to his aid. *Méphistophélès* answers the call, in the garb of a cavalier. His tone and bearing irritate *Faust*, who bids him begone. The fiend would know his will, his desires. Gold, glory, power? — all shall be his for the asking. But these things are not the heart's desire of *Faust*. He craves youthfulness, with its desires and delights, its passions and puissance. *Méphistophélès* promises all, and, when he hesitates, inflames his ardor with a vision of the lovely *Marguerite* seated at her spinning-wheel. Eagerly *Faust* signs the compact — the devil will serve *Faust* here, but below the relations shall be reversed. *Faust* drinks a pledge to the vision, which fades away. In a twinkling the life-weary sage is transformed into a young man, full of eager and impatient strength.

Méphistophélès loses no time in launching *Faust* upon his career of adventures. First, he leads him to a fair in a mediæval town. Students are there who sing the pleasures of drinking; soldiers, too, bent on conquest — of maidens or fortresses, all's one to them; old burghers, who find delight in creature comforts; maids and matrons, flirtatious and envious. All join in the merriest of musical hubbubs. *Valentin*, a soldier who is about to go to the wars, commends his sister *Marguerite* to the care of *Siebel*, a gentle youth who loves her. *Wagner*, a student, begins a song, but is interrupted by *Méphistophélès*, who has entered the circle of merry-makers with *Faust*, and who now volunteers to sing a better song than the one just begun. He sings of the Calf of Gold ("Le veau d'or est toujours debout"), and the crowd delightedly shouts the refrain. The singer accepts a cup of wine, but, finding it not at all to his taste, he causes vintages to the taste of every one to flow from the cask which serves as a tavern sign.   He offers the company a toast, "To *Marguerite!*" and when *Valentin* attempts to resent the insult to his sister with his sword, it breaks in his hand as he tries to penetrate a magic circle which *Méphistophélès* draws around himself. The men now suspect the true character of their singular visitor, and turn the cruciform hilts of their swords against him, to his intense discomfort. With the return of the women the merrymaking is resumed. All join in a dance, tripping it gayly to one waltz sung by the spectators and another which rises simultaneously from the instruments. *Marguerite* crosses the market-place on her way home from church. *Faust* offers her his arm, but she declines his escort — not quite so rudely as Goethe's *Gretchen* does in the corresponding situation. *Faust* becomes more than ever enamoured of the maiden, whom he had seen in the vision conjured up in the philosopher's study.

Méphistophélès is a bit amused at *Faust's* first attempt at wooing, and undertakes to point the way for him. He leads him into the garden surrounding the cottage in which *Marguerite* dwells. *Siebel* had just been there and had plucked a nosegay for the maiden of his heart, first dipping his fingers in holy water to protect them from the curse which *Méphistophélès* had pronounced against them while parading as a fortune-teller at the fair. *Faust* is lost in admiration at sight of the humble abode of loveliness and innocence, and lauds it in a romance ("Salut! demeure chaste et pure"), but is taken aside by *Méphistophélès*, who gives warning of the approach of *Marguerite*, and places a casket of jewels beside the modest bouquet left by *Siebel*. *Marguerite*, seated at her spinning-wheel, alternately sings a stanza of a ballad ("Il était un Roi de Thule") and speaks her amazed curiosity concerning the handsome stranger who had addressed her in the market-place. She finds the jewels, ornaments herself with them, carolling her delight the while, and admiring the regal appearance which the gems lend her.

Here I should like to be pardoned a brief digression. Years ago, while the German critics were resenting the spoliation of the masterpiece of their greatest poet by the French librettists, they fell upon this so-called Jewel Song ("Air des bijoux," the French call it), and condemned its brilliant and ingratiating waltz measures as being out of keeping with the character of *Gretchen*. In this they forgot that *Marguerite* and *Gretchen* are very different characters indeed. There is much of the tender grace of the unfortunate German maiden in the creation of the French authors, but none of her simple, almost rude, rusticity. As created by, let me say, Mme. Carvalho and perpetuated by Christine Nilsson and the painter Ary Scheffer, *Marguerite* is a good deal of a *grande dame*, and against the German critics it might appositely be pleaded that there are more traces of childish ingenuousness in her rejoicing over the casket of jewels than in any of her other utterances. The episode is poetically justified, of course, by the eighth scene of Goethe's drama, and there was not wanting one German writer who boldly came to the defence of *Marguerite* on the ground that she moved on a higher moral plane than *Gretchen*. The French librettists, while they emptied the character of much of its poetical contents, nevertheless made it in a sense more gentle, and Gounod refined it still more by breathing an ecstasy into all of its music. Goethe's *Gretchen*, though she rejects *Faust's* first advances curtly enough to be called impolite, nevertheless ardently returns *Faust's* kiss on her first meeting with him in the garden, and already at the second (presumably) offers to leave her window open, and accepts the sleeping potion for her mother. It is a sudden, uncontrollable rush of passion to which *Marguerite* succumbs. *Gretchen* remains in simple amaze that such a fine gentleman as *Faust* should find anything to admire in her, even after she has received and returned his first kiss; but *Marguerite* is exalted, transfigured by the new feelings surging within her.

> Il m'aime! quel trouble en mon cœur!
> L'oiseau chante! Le vent murmure!
> Toutes les voix de la nature
> Semblent me répéter en chœur:
> Il t'aime!

I resume the story. *Martha*, the neighborhood gossip, comes to encourage *Marguerite* in a belief which she scarcely dares cherish, that the jewels had been left for her by some noble admirer, and

her innocent pleasure is interrupted by the entrance
of *Faust* and *Méphistophélès*. The latter draws
Martha away, and *Faust* wooes the maiden with
successful ardor. They have indulged in their first
embrace, and said their farewells till to-morrow:
Faust is about to depart, when *Méphistophélès* detains him and points to *Marguerite*, who is burdening the perfumed air with her new ecstasy. He
rushes to her, and, with a cry of delight, she falls
into his arms.

Goethe's scene at the fountain becomes, in the
hands of the French librettists, a scene in the chamber of *Marguerite*. The deceived maiden is cast down
by the jeers and mockings of her erstwhile companions, and comforted by *Siebel*. It is now generally
omitted. *Marguerite* has become the talk of the
town, and evil reports reach the ear of her brother
Valentin on his return from the wars with the victorious soldiery. *Valentin* confronts *Faust* and
Méphistophélès while the latter is singing a ribald
serenade at *Marguerite's* door. The men fight, and,
through the machinations of *Méphistophélès*, *Valentin* is mortally wounded. He dies denouncing the
conduct of *Marguerite*, and cursing her for having
brought death upon him. *Marguerite* seeks conso-
lation in religious worship; but the fiend is at her
elbow even in the holy fane, and his taunts and the
accusing chant of a choir of demons interrupt her
prayers. The devil reveals himself in his proper
(or improper) person at the end, and *Marguerite*
falls in a swoon.

The Walpurgis night scene of Goethe furnished the suggestion for the ballet which fills the first three scenes of the fifth act, and which was added to the opera when it was remodelled for the Grand Opéra in 1869. The scene holds its place in Paris, but is seldom performed elsewhere. A wild scene in the Harz Mountains gives way to an enchanted hall in which are seen the most famous courtesans of ancient history — Phryne, Laïs, Aspasia, Cleopatra, and Helen of Troy. The apparition of *Marguerite* appears to *Faust,* a red line encircling her neck, like the mark of a headsman's axe. We reach the end. The distraught maiden has slain her child, and now lies in prison upon her pallet of straw, awaiting death. *Faust* enters and tries to persuade her to fly with him. Her poor mind is all awry and occupies itself only with the scenes of her first meeting and the love-making in the garden. She turns with horror from her lover when she sees his companion, and in an agony of supplication, which rises higher and higher with each reiteration, she implores Heaven for pardon. She sinks lifeless to the floor. *Méphistophélès* pronounces her damned, but a voice from on high proclaims her saved. Celestial voices chant the Easter hymn, "Christ is risen!" while a band of angels bear her soul heavenward.

CHAPTER VII

"MEFISTOFELE"

THERE is no reason to question Gounod's state‐ ment that it was he who conceived the idea of writing a Faust opera in collaboration with MM. Barbier and Carré. There was nothing novel in the notion. Music was an integral part of the old puppet-plays which dealt with the legend of Dr. Faustus, and Goethe's tragedy calls for musical aid imperatively. A musical pantomime, "Harle‐ quin Faustus," was performed in London as early as 1715, and there were Faust operas long before even the first part of Goethe's poem was printed, which was a hundred and one years ago. A com‐ poser named Phanty brought out an opera entitled "Dr. Faust's Zaubergürtel" in 1790; C. Hanke used the same material and title at Flushing in 1794, and Ignaz Walter produced a "Faust" in Hanover in 1797. Goethe's First Part had been five years in print when Spohr composed his "Faust," but it is based not on the great German poet's version of the legend, but on the old sources. This opera has still life, though it is fitful and feeble, in Germany, and was produced in London by a German company in 1840 and by an Italian in 1852, when the com‐

poser conducted it; but I have never heard of a representation in America. Between Spohr's "Faust,"
written in 1813 and performed in 1818, and Boito's
"Mefistofele," produced in 1868, many French,
German, English, Italian, Russian, and Polish Faust
operas have come into existence, lived their little
lives, and died. Rietz produced a German "Faust,"
founded on Goethe, at Düsseldorf, in 1836; Lind-
painter in Berlin, in 1854; Henry Rowley Bishop's
English "Faustus" was heard in London, in 1827;
French versions were Mlle. Angélique Bertin's
"Faust" (Paris, 1831), and M. de Pellaert's (Brussels,
1834); Italian versions were "Fausta," by Donizetti (Mme. Pasta and Signor Donzelli sang in it in
Naples in 1832), "Fausto," by Gordigiano (Florence,
1837), and "Il Fausto arrivo," by Raimondi (Naples,
1837); the Polish Faust, Twardowsky, is the hero
of a Russian opera by Verstowsky (Moscow, 1831),
and of a Polish opera by J. von Zaitz (Agram, 1880).
How often the subject has served for operettas,
cantatas, overtures, symphonies, etc., need not be
discussed here. Berlioz's "Dramatic Legend," entitled "La Damnation de Faust," tricked out with
stage pictures by Raoul Gunsbourg, was performed
as an opera at Monte Carlo in 1903, and in New
York at the Metropolitan and Manhattan opera-
houses in the seasons 1906–1907 and 1907–1908, respectively; but the experiment was unsuccessful,
both artistically and financially.

I have said that there is no reason to question
Gounod's statement that it was he who conceived

the idea of writing the opera whose popularity is without parallel in the musical history of the Faust legend; but, if I could do so without reflecting upon his character, I should like to believe a story which says that it was Barbier who proposed the subject to Gounod after Meyerbeer, to whom he first suggested it, had declined the collaboration. I should like to believe this, because it is highly honorable to Meyerbeer's artistic character, which has been much maligned by critics and historians of music since Wagner set an example in that direction. "'Faust,'" Meyerbeer is reported to have replied to Barbier's invitation, "is the ark of the covenant, a sanctuary not to be approached with profane music." For the composer who did not hesitate to make an opera out of the massacre of St. Bartholomew, this answer is more than creditable. The Germans, who have either felt or affected great indignation at the want of reverence for their great poet shown by the authors of "Faust" and "Mignon," ought to admire Meyerbeer in a special degree for the moral loftiness of his determination and the dignified beauty of its expression. Composers like Kreutzer, Reissiger, Pierson, Lassen, and Prince Radziwill have written incidental music for Goethe's tragedy without reflecting that possibly they were profaning the sanctuary; but Meyerbeer, compared with whom they were pygmies, withheld his hand, and thereby brought himself into sympathetic association with the only musician that ever lived who was completely equipped for so magnifi-

K

cent a task. That musician was Beethoven, to whom Rochlitz bore a commission for music to "Faust" from Breitkopf and Härtel in 1822. The Titan read the proposition and cried out: "Ha! that would be a piece of work! Something might come of that!" but declined the task because he had the choral symphony and other large plans on his mind.

Boito is not a Beethoven nor yet a Meyerbeer; but, though he did what neither of them would venture upon when he wrote a Faust opera, he did it with complete and lovely reverence for the creation of the German poet. It is likely that had he had less reverence for his model and more of the stagecraft of his French predecessors, his opera would have had a quicker and greater success than fell to its lot. Of necessity it has suffered by comparison with the opera of Barbier, Carré, and Gounod, though it was far from Boito's intentions that it should ever be subjected to such a comparison. Boito is rather more poet and dramatist than he is musician. He made the book not only of "Mefistofele," but also of "Otello" and "Falstaff," which Verdi composed, "La Gioconda," for which Ponchielli wrote the music, and "Ero e Leandro," which he turned over to Bottesini, who set it with no success, and to Mancinelli, who set it with little. One of the musical pieces which the poet composed for this last opera found its way into "Mefistofele," for which work "Ero e Leandro" seems to have been abandoned. He also translated Wagner's "Tristan und

Isolde" into Italian. Being a poet in the first instance, and having the blood of the Northern bar-
barians as well as the Southern Romans in his veins,
he was unwilling to treat Goethe's tragedy as the
Frenchman had treated it. The tearful tale of
the love of the rejuvenated philosopher, and the
village maiden, with its woful outcome, did not
suffice him. Though he called his opera "Mefistofele," not "Faust," he drew its scenes, of which
only two have to do with *Marguerite* (or *Gretchen*),
from both parts of Goethe's allegorical and philosophical phantasmagoria. Because he did this
he failed from one point of view. Attempting too
much, he accomplished too little. His opera is not
a well-knit and consistently developed drama, but
a series of episodes, which do not hold together
and have significance only for those who know
Goethe's dramatic poem in its entirety. It is very
likely that, as originally produced, "Mefistofele"
was not such a thing of shreds and patches as it
now is. No doubt, it held together better in 1868,
when it was ridiculed, whistled, howled, and hissed
off the stage of the Teatro la Scala, than it did when
it won the admiration of the Italians in Bologna
twelve years later. In the interval it had been
subjected to a revision, and, the first version never
having been printed, the critical fraternity became
exceedingly voluble after the success in Bologna,
one of the debated questions being whether Boito
had bettered his work by his voluminous excisions,
interpolations, and changes (*Faust*, now a tenor,

was originally a barytone), or had weakly surrendered his better judgment to the taste of the *hoi polloi*, for the sake of a popular success. It was pretty fighting ground; it is yet, and will remain such so long as the means of comparison remain hidden and sentimental hero-worship is fed by the notion that Boito has refused to permit the opera or operas which he has written since to be either published or performed because the world once refused to recognize his genius. This notion, equally conven- ient to an indolent man or a colossal egoist — I do not believe that Boito is either — has been nurtured by many pretty stories; but, unhappily, we have had nothing to help us to form an opinion of Boito as a creative artist since "Mefistofele" appeared, except the opera books written for Verdi and Pon- chielli and the libretto of "Ero e Leandro."

Boito's father was an Italian, his mother a Pole. From either one or both he might have inherited the intensity of expression which marks his works, both poetical and musical; but the tendency to philosophical contemplation which characterizes "Mefistofele," even in the stunted form in which it is now presented, is surely the fruit of his maternal heritage and his studies in Germany. After com- pleting the routine of the conservatory in Milan, he spent a great deal of time in Paris and the larger German cities, engrossed quite as much in the study of literature as of music. Had he followed his inclinations and the advice of Victor Hugo, who gave him a letter of introduction to Émile de Girardin,

he would have become a journalist in Paris instead
of the composer of "Mefistofele" and the poet of
"Otello," "Falstaff," "La Gioconda," and "Ero e
Leandro." But Girardin was too much occupied
with his own affairs to attend to him when Boito
presented himself, and after waiting wearily, vainly,
and long, he went to Poland, where, for want of
something else to do, he sketched the opera "Mefistofele," which made its memorable fiasco at Milan
in March, 1868.

To show that it is impossible to think of "Mefistofele" except as a series of disconnected episodes,
it suffices to point out that its prologue, epilogue,
and four acts embrace a fantastic parody or per
version of Goethe's Prologue in Heaven, a fragment of his Easter scene, a smaller fragment of
the scene in *Faust's* study, a bit of the garden scene,
the scene of the witches' gathering on the Brocken,
the prison scene, the classical Sabbath in which
Faust is discovered in an amour with *Helen of Troy*,
and the death and salvation of *Faust* as an old man.
Can any one who knows that music, even of the
modern dramatic type, in which strictly musical
forms have given way to as persistent an onward
flow as the text itself, must of necessity act as a clog
on dramatic action, imagine that such a number
and variety of scenes could be combined into a logical,
consistent whole, compassed by four hours in performance? Certainly not. But Boito is not content to emulate Goethe in his effort to carry his
listeners "from heaven through the earth to hell".

he must needs ask them to follow him in his ex position of Goethe's philosophy and symbolism. Of course, that is impossible during a stage representation, and therefore he exposes the workings of his mind in an essay and notes to his score. From these we may learn, among other things, that the poet-composer conceives Faust as the type of man athirst for knowledge, of whom Solomon was the Biblical prototype, Prometheus the mythological, Manfred and Don Quixote the predecessors in modern literature. Also that Mephistopheles is as inexhaustible as a type of evil as Faust is as a type of virtue, and therefore that this picturesque stage devil, with all his conventionality, is akin to the serpent which tempted Eve, the Thersites of Homer, and — *mirabile dictu!* — the Falstaff of Shakespeare!

The device with which Boito tried to link the scenes of his opera together is musical as well as philosophical. In the book which Barbier and Carré wrote for Gounod, *Faust* sells his soul to the devil for a period of sensual pleasure of indefinite duration, and, so far as the hero is concerned, the story is left unfinished. All that has been accomplished is the physical ruin of *Marguerite*. *Méphistophélès* exults for a moment in contemplation of the destruction, also, of the immortal part of her, but the angelic choir proclaims her salvation. *Faust* departs hurriedly with *Méphistophélès*, but whether to his death or in search of new adventures, we do not know. The Germans are, therefore, not so wrong, after all, in calling the opera after the name of the heroine instead of that of the hero. In Boito's book the love story is but an incident. *Faust's* compact with *Mefistofele*, as in Goethe's dramatic poem, is the outcome of a wager between *Mefistofele* and God, under the terms of which the Spirit of Evil is to be permitted to seduce *Faust* from righteousness, if he can. *Faust's* demand of *Mefistofele* is rest from his unquiet, inquisitive mind; a solution of the dark problem of his own existence and that of the world; finally, one moment of which he can say, "Stay, for thou art lovely!" The amour with *Margherita* does not accomplish this, and so Boito follows Goethe into the conclusion of the second part of his drama, and shows *Faust*, at the end, an old man about to die. He recalls the loves of *Margherita* and *Helen*, but they were insufficient to give him the desired moment of happiness. He sees a vision of a people governed by him and made happy by wise laws of his creation. He goes into an ecstasy. *Mefistofele* summons sirens to tempt him, and spreads his cloak for another flight. But the chant of celestial beings falls into *Faust's* ear, and he speaks the words which terminate the compact. He dies. *Mefistofele* attempts to seize upon him, but is driven back by a shower of roses dropped by cherubim. The celestial choir chants redeeming love.

Thus much for the dramatic exposition. Boito's musical exposition rests on the employment of typical phrases, not in the manner of Wagner,

indeed, but with the fundamental purpose of Wag
ner. A theme:—

which begins the prologue, ends the epilogue. The
reader may label it as he pleases. Its significance
is obvious from the circumstances of its employment. It rings out *fortissimo* when the mystic
chorus, which stands for the Divine Voice, puts the
question, "Knowest thou *Faust?*" An angelic
ascription of praise to the Creator of the Universe
and to Divine Love is the first vocal utterance and
the last. In his notes Boito observes: "Goethe
was a great admirer of form, and his poem ends
as it begins, — the first and last words of 'Faust'
are uttered in Heaven." Then he quotes a remark
from Blaze de Bury's essay on Goethe, which is
apropos, though not strictly accurate: "The glorious
motive which the immortal phalanxes sing in the
introduction to the first part of 'Faust' recurs at the
close, garbed with harmonies and mystical clouds.
In this Goethe has acted like the musicians, — like
Mozart, who recurs in the finale of 'Don Giovanni'
to the imposing phrase of the overture."

M. de Bury refers, of course, to the supernatural
music, which serves as an introduction to the overture to "Don Giovanni," and accompanies the visi-
tation of the ghostly statue and the death of the
libertine. But this is not the end of Mozart's

opera as he wrote it, as readers of this book have been told.

This prologue of "Mefistofele" plays in heaven. "In the heavens," says Theodore Marzials, the English translator of Boito's opera, out of deference to the religious sensibilities of the English people, to spare which he also changes "God" into "sprites," "spirits," "powers of good," and "angels." The effect is vastly diverting, especially when Boito's paraphrase of Goethe's

> Von Zeit zu Zeit seh' ich den Alten gern
> Und hüte mich mit ihm zu brechen.
> Es ist gar hübsch von einem grossen Herrn,
> So menschlich mit dem Teufel selbst zu sprechen.[1]

is turned into: "Now and again 'tis really pleasant thus to chat with the angels, and I'll take good care not to quarrel with them. 'Tis beautiful to hear Good and Evil speak together with such humanity." The picture disclosed by the opening of the curtain is a mass of clouds, with *Mefistofele*, like a dark blot, standing on a corner of his cloak in the shadow. The denizens of the celestial regions are heard but never seen. A trumpet sounds the fundamental theme, which is repeated in full

[1] I like, at times, to hear the Ancient's word,
And have a care to be most civil :
It's really kind of such a noble Lord
So humanly to gossip with the Devil.
— *Bayard Taylor's Translation*

harmony after instruments of gentler voice have
sung a hymn-like phrase, as follows:—

It is the first period of the "Salve Regina" sung
by *Earthly Penitents* in the finale of the prologue.
The canticle is chanted through, its periods separated by reiterations of the fundamental theme.
A double chorus acclaims the Lord of Angels and
Saints. A plan, evidently derived from the symphonic form, underlies the prologue as a whole.
Prelude and chorus are rounded out by the significant trumpet phrase. One movement is completed. There follows a second movement, an Instrumental Scherzo, with a first section beginning
thus:—

and a trio. Over this music *Mefistofele* carries
on converse with God. He begs to disagree with

the sentiments of the angelic hymn. Wandering about the earth, he had observed man and found him in all things contemptible, especially in his vanity begotten by what he called "reason"; he, the miserable little cricket, vaingloriously jumping out of the grass in an effort to poke his nose among the stars, then falling back to chirp, had almost taken away from the devil all desire to tempt him to evil doings. "Knowest thou *Faust?*" asks the Divine Voice; and *Mefistofele* tells of the philosopher's insatiable thirst for wisdom. Then he offers the wager. The scene, though brief, follows Goethe as closely as Goethe follows the author of the Book of Job: —

Now, there was a day when the sons of God came to present themselves before the Lord, and Satan came also among them.

And the Lord said unto Satan, Whence comest thou? Then Satan answered the Lord and said, From going to and fro in the earth and from walking up and down in it.

And the Lord said unto Satan, Hast thou considered my servant Job, that there is none like him in the earth, a perfect and an upright man, one that feareth God and escheweth evil?

Then Satan answered the Lord, and said, Doth Job fear God for nought? . . .

And the Lord said unto Satan, Behold, all that he hath is in thy power; only upon himself put not forth thine hand. So Satan went forth from the presence of the Lord.

Boito treats the interview in what he calls a Dramatic Interlude, which gives way to the third movement, a Vocal Scherzo, starting off with a

chorus of *Cherubim*, who sing in fugacious tnirds
and droning dactyls: —

Tempo di Scherzo velocissimo. ♩ = 176.

Siam nim - bi   vo - lan - ti   dai lim - bi, nei san - ti
We're flames ev - er fly - ing And voi - ces re - ply - ing

It is well to note particularly Boito's metrical
device. He seemingly counted much on the effect
of incessantly reiterated dactyls. Not only do his
Cherubim adhere to the form without deviation, but
Helen and *Pantalis* use it also in the scene imitated
from Goethe's Classical Walpurgis Night, — use it
for an especial purpose, as we shall see presently.
Rapid syllabication is also a characteristic of the
song of the witches in the scene on the Brocken;
but the witches sing in octaves and fifths except
when they kneel to do homage to *Mefistofele;* then
their chant sounds like the responses to *John of
Leyden's* prayer by the mutinous soldiers brought
to their knees in "Le Prophète." Not at all ineptly,
Mefistofele, who does not admire the *Cherubs*, likens
their monotonous cantillation to the hum of bees.
A fourth movement consists of a concluding
psalmody, in which the *Cherubs* twitter, *Earthly
Penitents* supplicate the Virgin, and the combined
choirs, celestial and terrestrial, hymn the Creator.

The tragedy now begins. Boito changes the order
of the scenes which he borrows from Goethe, presenting first the merrymaking of the populace out

side the walls of Frankfort-on-the-Main, and then
the interview between *Faust* and *Mefistofele*, in
which, as in the opening scene of Gounod's opera,
the infernal compact is agreed upon. There is
some mediæval pageantry in the first scene,
— a cavalcade headed by the Elector, and including dignitaries, pages, falconers, the court fool,
and ladies of the court. Students, townspeople,
huntsmen, lads, and lasses pursue their pleasures,
and up and down, through the motley groups, there
wanders a gray friar, whose strange conduct repels
some of the people, and whose pious garb attracts
others. *Faust* and *Wagner*, his pupil, come upon the
scene, conversing seriously, and stop to comment on
the actions of the friar, who is approaching them,
supposedly in narrowing circles. *Wagner* sees nothing in him except a mendicant friar, but *Faust* calls
attention to the fact that to his eye, flames blaze
up from his footprints. This friar is the "poodle"
of Goethe's poem, and *Mefistofele* in disguise. It is
thus that the devil presented himself to Faustus
in the old versions of the legend, and as a friar he
is a more practicable dramatic figure than he would
have been as a dog; but it cannot but provoke a
smile from those familiar with Goethe's poem to hear
(as we do in the opera a few moments later) the
familiar lines:—

> Das also war des Pudels Kern!
> Ein fahrender Scolast?

turned into: "This, then, was the kernel of the
friar! A cavalier?" The music of the score is

characterized by frequent changes from triple to
double time, as illustrated in the opening measures:

The rhythmical energy and propulsiveness thus
imparted to the music of the merrymaking is heightened by the dance.   Peasants rush upon the scene
with shouts of "Juhé!" and make preparations to
trip it while singing what, at first, promises to be
a waltz-song:—

The dance, however, is not a waltz, but an obertass — the most popular of the rustic dances of
Poland.   Why should Boito have made his Rhine-
landers dance a step which is characteristically
that of the Poles? Sticklers for historical verity
could easily convict him of a most unpardonable

anachronism, if they were so disposed, by pointing out that even if German peasants were in the
habit of dancing the obertass now (which they are
not), they could not have done it in the sixteenth
century, which is the period of the drama, for the
sufficient reason that the Polish dance was not introduced in North Germany till near the middle of
the eighteenth century. But we need not inquire
too curiously into details like this when it comes
to so arbitrary an art-form as the opera. Yet
Boito was his own poet, master of the situation so
far as all parts of his work were concerned, and
might have consulted historical accuracy in a de-
partment in which Gluck once found that he was
the slave of his ballet master. Gluck refused to
introduce a chaconne into "Iphigénie en Aulide."
"A chaconne?" cried the composer. "When did
the Greeks ever dance a chaconne?" "Didn't
they?" replied Vestris ; "then so much the worse
for the Greeks!" A quarrel ensued, and Gluck, becoming incensed, withdrew his opera and would
have left Paris had not Marie Antoinette come to
the rescue. But Vestris got his chaconne. In all
likelihood Boito put the obertass into "Mefistofele"
because he knew that musically and as a spectacle
the Polish dance would be particularly effective in
the joyous hurly-burly of the scene. A secondary
meaning of the Polish word is said to be "confusion," and Boito doubtless had this in mind when
he made his peasants sing with an orderly disorder
which is delightful:—

Tutti vanno alla rinfusa
Sulla musica confusa,

or, as one English translation has it:—

All is going to dire confusion
With the music in collusion.

Perhaps, too, Boito had inherited a love for the vigorous dance from his Polish mother.

Night falls, and *Faust* is returned to his laboratory. The gray friar has followed him (like Goethe's poodle) and slips into an alcove unobserved. The philosopher turns to the Bible, which lies upon a lectern, and falls into a meditation, which is interrupted by a shriek. He turns and sees the friar standing motionless and wordless before him. He conjures the apparition with the seal of Solomon, and the friar, doffing cowl and gown, steps forward as a cavalier (an itinerant scholar in Goethe). He introduces himself as a part of the power that, always thinking evil, as persistently accomplishes good — the spirit of negation. The speech ("Son fo Spirito che nega sempre") is one of the striking numbers of Boito's score, and the grim humor of its "No!" seems to have inspired the similar effect in *Falstaff's* discourse on honor in Verdi's opera. The pair quickly come to an understanding on the terms already set forth.

Act II carries us first into the garden of *Dame Martha*, where we find *Margherita* strolling arm in arm with *Faust*, and *Martha* with *Mefistofele*. The gossip is trying to seduce the devil into an avowal of love; *Margherita* and *Faust* are discussing their first meeting and the passion which they already feel for each other. Boito's *Margherita* has more of Goethe's *Gretchen* than Gounod's *Marguerite*. Like the former, she wonders what a cavalier can find to admire in her simple self, and protests in embarrassment when *Faust* (or *Enrico*, as he calls himself) kisses her rough hand. Like Goethe's maiden, too, she is concerned about the religious beliefs of her lover, and Boito's *Faust* answers, like Goethe's *Faust*, that a sincere man dares protest neither belief nor unbelief in God. Nature, Love, Mystery, Life, God — all are one, all to be experienced, not labelled with a name. Then he turns the talk on herself and her domestic surroundings, and presses the sleeping potion for her mother upon her. The scene ends with the four people scurrying about in a double chase among the flowers, for which Boito found exquisitely dainty music.

L.

There is a change from the pretty garden of the first scene, with its idyllic music, to the gathering place of witches and warlocks, high up in the Brocken, in the second. We witness the vile orgies of the bestial crew into whose circles *Faust* is introduced, and see how *Mefistofele* is acclaimed king and receives the homage. Here Boito borrows a poetical conceit from Goethe's scene in the witches' kitchen, and makes it a vehicle for a further exposition of the character and philosophy of the devil. *Mefistofele* has seated himself upon a rocky throne and been vested with the robe and symbols of state by the witches. Now they bring to him a crystal globe, which he takes and discourses upon to the following effect (the translation is Theodore T. Barker's):—

> Lo, here is the world!
>   A bright sphere rising,
> Setting, whirling, glancing,
> Round the sun in circles dancing;
>   Trembling, toiling,
>   Yielding, spoiling,
> Want and plenty by turn enfold it —
> This world, behold it!
> On its surface, by time abraded,
> Dwelleth a vile race, defiled, degraded;
>   Abject, haughty,
>   Cunning, naughty,
> Carrying war and desolation
> From the top to the foundation
>   Of creation.
> For them Satan has no being;
>   They scorn with laughter
>   A hell hereafter.

　　　And heavenly glory
　　　As idle story.
Powers eternal!　I'll join their laugh infernal
Thinking o'er their deeds diurnal.　Ha!　Ha!
　　　Behold the world!

He dashes the globe to pieces on the ground and
thereby sets the witches to dancing.　To the antics
of the vile crew *Faust* gives no heed; his eyes are
fixed upon a vision of *Margherita*, her feet in
fetters, her body emaciated, and a crimson line
encircling her throat.　His love has come under
the headsman's axe!　In the Ride to Hell, which
concludes Berlioz's "Damnation de Faust," the
infernal horsemen are greeted with shouts in a
language which the mystical Swedenborg says is
the speech of the lower regions.　Boito also uses
an infernal vocabulary.　His witches screech "Saboé
har Sabbah!" on the authority of Le Loyer's "Les
Spectres."

From the bestiality of the Brocken we are plunged
at the beginning of the third act into the pathos
of *Margherita's* death.　The episode follows the
lines laid down by Barbier and Carré in their paraphrase of Goethe, except that for the sake of the
beautiful music of the duet (which Boito borrowed
from his unfinished "Ero e Leandro"), we learn that
Margherita had drowned her child.　*Faust* urges
her to fly, but her poor mind is all awry.　She recalls
the scene of their first meeting and of the love-
making in *Dame Martha's* garden, and the earlier
music returns, as it does in Gounod's score, and

as it was bound to do. At the end she draws back in horror from *Faust*, after uttering a prayer above the music of the celestial choir, just as the executioner appears. *Mefistofele* pronounces her damned, but voices from on high proclaim her salvation.

The story of *Faust* and *Margherita* is ended, but, in pursuance of his larger plan, already outlined here, Boito makes use of two scenes from the second part of Goethe's drama to fill a fourth act and epilogue. They tell of the adventure of *Faust* with *Helen of Troy*, and of his death and the demon's defeat. The "Night of the Classical Sabbath" serves a dramatic purpose even less than the scene on the Brocken, but as an intermezzo it has many elements of beauty, and its scheme is profoundly poetical. Unfortunately we can only attain to a knowledge of the mission of the scene in the study with Goethe's poem in hand and commentaries and Boito's prefatory notes within reach. The picture is full of serene loveliness. We are on the shore of Peneus, in the Vale of Tempe. The moon at its zenith sheds its light over the thicket of laurel and oleanders, and floods a Doric temple on the left. *Helen of Troy* and *Pantalis*, surrounded by a group of sirens, praise the beauty of nature in an exquisite duet, which flows on as placidly as the burnished stream. *Faust* lies sleeping upon a flowery bank, and in his dreams calls upon *Helen* in the intervals of her song. *Helen* and *Pantalis* depart, and *Faust* is ushered in by *Mefistofele*. He is clad in his proper mediæval garb, in strong contrast to the classic robes of the denizens of the valley in Thessaly. *Mefistofele* suggests to *Faust* that they now separate; the land of antique fable has no charm for him. *Faust* is breathing in the idiom of *Helen's* song like a delicate perfume which inspires him with love; *Mefistofele* longs for the strong, resinous odors of the Harz Mountains, where dominion over the Northern hags belongs to him. *Faust* is already gone, and he is about to depart when there approaches a band of *Choretids*. With gentle grace they move through a Grecian dance, and *Mefistofele* retires in disgust. *Helen* returns profoundly disquieted by a vision of the destruction of Troy, of which she was the cause. The *Choretids* seek to calm her in vain, but the tortures of conscience cease when she sees *Faust* before her. He kneels and praises her beauty, and she confesses herself enamoured of his speech, in which sound answers sound like a soft echo. "What," she asks, "must I do to learn so sweet and gentle an idiom?" "Love me, as I love you," replies *Faust*, in effect, as they disappear through the bowers. Now let us turn to Goethe, his commentators, and Boito's explanatory notes to learn the deeper significance of the episode, which, with all its gracious charm, must still appear dramatically impertinent and disturbing. Rhyme was unknown to the Greeks, the music of whose verse came from syllabic quantity. *Helen* and her companions sing in classic strain, as witness the opening duet: —

La luna immobile innonda l' etere d'un raggio pallido.
Callido balsamo stillan le ramora dai cespi roridi;
Doridi e silfidi, cigni e nereidi vagan sul l' alighi.

Faust addresses *Helen* in rhyme, the discovery of
the Romantic poets: —

> Forma ideal purissima
> Della bellezza eterna!
> Un uom ti si prosterna
>   Innamorato al suolo
> Volgi ver me la cruna
> Di tua pupilla bruna,
> Vaga come la luna,
>   Ardente come il sole.

"Here," says Boito, "is a myth both beautiful
and deep. *Helen* and *Faust* represent Classic and
Romantic art gloriously wedded, Greek beauty
and Germanic beauty gleaming under the same
aureole, glorified in one embrace, and generating
an ideal poesy, eclectic, new, and powerful."

The contents of the last act, which shows us
Faust's death and salvation, have been set forth
in the explanation of Boito's philosophical purpose.
An expository note may, however, profitably be
added in the poet-composer's own words: "Goethe
places around *Faust* at the beginning of the scene
four ghostly figures, who utter strange and obscure
words. What Goethe has placed on the stage we
place in the orchestra, submitting sounds instead
of words, in order to render more incorporeal and
impalpable the hallucinations that trouble *Faust*

on the brink of death." The ghostly figures referred to by Boito are the four "Gray Women" of
Goethe — *Want, Guilt, Care,* and *Necessity.* Boito
thinks like a symphonist, and his purpose is profoundly poetical, but its appreciation asks more
than the ordinary opera-goer is willing or able to
give.[1]

[1] "Mefistofele" had its first performance in New York at the
Academy of Music on November 24, 1880. Mlle. Valleria was
the *Margherita* and *Elena,* Miss Annie Louise Cary the *Marta* and
Pantalis, Signor Campanini *Faust,* and Signor Novara *Mefistofele.*
Signor Arditi conducted. The first representation of the opera
at the Metropolitan Opera-house took place on December 5, 1883,
when, with one exception, the cast was the same as at the first
performance in London, at Her Majesty's Theatre, on July 6,
1880 — namely, Nilsson as *Margherita* and *Elena,* Trebelli as
Marta and *Pantalis,* Campanini as *Faust* and Mirabella as *Mefistofele.* (In London Nannetti enacted the demon.) Cleofonte Campanini, then *maestro di cembalo* at the Metropolitan Opera-house,
conducted the performance.

CHAPTER VIII

"LA DAMNATION DE FAUST"

In an operatic form Berlioz's "Damnation de Faust" had its first representation in New York at the Metropolitan Opera-house on December 7, 1906. Despite its high imagination, its melodic charm, its vivid and varied colors, its frequent flights toward ideal realms, its accents of passion, its splendid picturesqueness, it presented itself as a "thing of shreds and patches." It was, indeed, conceived as such, and though Berlioz tried by various devices to give it entity, he failed. When he gave it to the world, he called it a "Dramatic Legend," a term which may mean much or little as one chooses to consider it; but I can recall no word of his which indicates that he ever thought that it was fit for the stage. It was Raoul Gunsbourg, director of the opera at Monte Carlo, who, in 1903, conceived the notion of a theatrical representation of the legend and tricked it out with pictures and a few attempts at action. Most of these attempts are futile and work injury to the music, as will presently appear, but in a few instances they were successful, indeed very successful. Of course, if Berlioz had wanted to make an opera out of Goethe's

152

drama, he could have done so. He would then have anticipated Gounod and Boïto and, possibly, have achieved one of those popular successes for which he hungered. But he was in his soul a poet, in his heart a symphonist, and intellectually (as many futile efforts proved) incapable of producing a piece for the boards. When the Faust subject first seized upon his imagination, he knew it only in a prose translation of Goethe's poem made by Gerald de Nerval. In his "Memoirs" he tells us how it fascinated him. He carried it about with him, reading it incessantly and eagerly at dinner, in the streets, in the theatre. In the prose translation there were a few fragments of songs. These he set to music and published under the title "Huit Scènes de Faust," at his own expense. Marx, the Berlin critic, saw the music and wrote the composer a letter full of encouragement. But Berlioz soon saw grave defects in his work and withdrew it from circulation, destroying all the copies which he could lay hands on. What was good in it, however, he laid away for future use. The opportunity came twenty years later, when he was fired anew with a desire to write music for Goethe's poem.

Though he had planned the work before starting out on his memorable artistic travels, he seems to have found inspiration in the circumstance that he was amongst a people who were more appreciative of his genius than his own countrymen, and whose language was that employed by the poet. Not more than one-sixth of his "Eight Scenes" had con-

sisted of settings of the translations of M. de Nerval.
A few scenes had been prepared by M. Gaudonnière
from notes provided by the composer. The rest
of the book Berlioz wrote himself, now paraphrasing
the original poet, now going to him only for a suggestion. As was the case with Wagner, words and
music frequently presented themselves to him si‹
multaneously. Travelling from town to town, conducting rehearsals and concerts, he wrote whenever
and wherever he could — one number in an inn at
Passau, the Elbe scene and the Dance of the Sylphs
at Vienna, the peasants' song by gaslight in a shop
one night when he had lost his way in Pesth, the
angels' chorus in *Marguerite's* apotheosis at Prague
(getting up in the middle of the night to write it
down), the song of the students, "Jam nox stellata
velamina pandit" (of which the words are also
Berlioz's), at Breslau. He finished the work in
Rouen and Paris, at home, at his café, in the gardens
of the Tuilleries, even on a stone in the Boulevard du
Temple. While in Vienna he made an orchestral
transcription of the famous Rakoczy march (in one
night, he says, though this is scarcely credible, since
the time would hardly suffice to write down the
notes alone). The march made an extraordinary
stir at the concert in Pesth when he produced it,
and this led him to incorporate it, with an introduction, into his Legend — a proceeding which he
justified as a piece of poetical license; he thought
that he was entitled to put his hero in any part of
the world and in any situation that he pleased.

This incident serves to indicate how lightly all dramatic fetters sat upon Berlioz while "La Damnation" was in his mind, and how little it occurred to him that any one would ever make the attempt to place his scenes upon the stage. In the case of the Hungarian march, this has been done only at the sacrifice of Berlioz's poetical conceit to which the introductory text and music were fitted; but of this more presently. As Berlioz constructed the "Dramatic Legend," it belonged to no musical category. It was neither a symphony with vocal parts like his "Roméo et Juliette" (which has symphonic elements in some of its sections), nor a cantata, nor an oratorio. It is possible that this fact was long an obstacle to its production. Even in New York where, on its introduction, it created the profoundest sensation ever witnessed in a local concert-room, it was performed fourteen times with the choral parts sung by the Oratorio Society before that organization admitted it into its lists.

And now to tell how the work was fitted to the uses of the lyric theatre. Nothing can be plainer to persons familiar with the work in its original form than that no amount of ingenuity can ever give the scenes of the "Dramatic Legend" continuity or coherency. Boito, in his opera, was unwilling to content himself with the episode of the amour between *Faust* and *Marguerite;* he wanted to bring out the fundamental ethical idea of the poet, and he went so far as to attempt the Prologue in Heaven, the Classical Sabbath, and the death of *Faust* with the contest for his soul. Berlioz had no scruples of any kind. He chose his scenes from Goethe's poem, changed them at will, and interpolated an incident simply to account for the Hungarian march. Connection with each other the scenes have not, and some of the best music belongs wholly in the realm of the ideal. At the outset Berlioz conceived *Faust* alone on a vast field in Hungary in spring. He comments on the beauties of nature and praises the benison of solitude. His ruminations are interrupted by a dance of peasants and the passage of an army to the music of the Rakoczy march. This scene M. Gunsbourg changes to a picture of a mediæval interior in which *Faust* soliloquizes, and a view through the window of a castle with a sally-port. Under the windows the peasants dance, and out of the huge gateway come the soldiery and march off to battle. At the climax of the music which drove the people of Pesth wild at its first performance, so that Berlioz confessed that he himself shuddered and felt the hair bristling on his head — when in a long *crescendo* fugued fragments of the march theme keep reappearing, interrupted by drumbeats like distant cannonading, Gunsbourg's battalions halt, and there is a solemn benediction of the standards. Then, to the peroration, the soldiers run, not as if eager to get into battle, but as if in inglorious retreat.

The second scene reproduces the corresponding incident in Gounod's opera — *Faust* in his study, life-weary and despondent. He is about to drink a cup of poison when the rear wall of the study rolls up and discloses the interior of a church with a kneeling congregation which chants the Easter canticle, "Christ is risen!" Here is one of the fine choral numbers of the work for which concert, not operatic, conditions are essential. The next scene, however, is of the opera operatic, and from that point of view the most perfect in the work. It discloses the revel of students, citizens, and soldiers in Auerbach's cellar. *Brander* sings the song of the rat which by good living had developed a paunch "like Dr. Luther's," but died of poison laid by the cook. The drinkers shout a boisterous refrain after each stanza, and supplement the last with a mock-solemn "Requiescat in pace, Amen." The phrase suggests new merriment to *Brander*, who calls for a fugue on the "Amen," and the roisterers improvise one on the theme of the rat song, which calls out hearty commendation from *Méphistophélès*, and a reward in the shape of the song of the flea — a delightful piece of grotesquerie with its accompaniment suggestive of the skipping of the pestiferous little insect which is the subject of the song.

The next scene is the triumph of M. Gunsbourg, though for it he is indebted to Miss Loie Fuller and the inventor of the aërial ballet. In the conceit of Berlioz, *Faust* lies asleep on the bushy banks of the Elbe. *Méphistophélès* summons gnomes and sylphs to fill his mind with lovely fancies. They do their work so well as to entrance, not only *Faust*, but all who hear their strains. The instrumental ballet is a fairy waltz, a filmy musical fabric, seemingly woven of moonbeams and dewy cobwebs, over a pedal-point on the muted violoncellos, ending with drum taps and harmonics from the harp — one of the daintiest and most original orchestral effects imaginable. So dainty is the device, indeed, that one would think that nothing could come between it and the ears of the transported listeners without ruining the ethereal creation. But M. Gunsbourg's fancy has accomplished the miraculous. Out of the river bank he constructs a floral bower rich as the magical garden of *Klingsor*. Sylphs circle around the sleeper and throw themselves into graceful attitudes while the song is sounding. Then to the music of the elfin waltz, others enter who have, seemingly, cast off the gross weight which holds mortals in contact with the earth. With robes a-flutter like wings, they dart upwards and remain suspended in mid-air at will or float in and out of the transporting picture. To *Faust* is also presented a vision of *Marguerite*.

The next five scenes in Berlioz's score are connected by M. Gunsbourg and forced to act in sequence for the sake of the stage set, in which a picture of *Marguerite's* chamber is presented in the conventional fashion made necessary by the exigency of showing an exterior and interior at the same time, as in the last act of "Rigoletto." For a reason at which I cannot even guess, M. Gunsbourg goes farther and transforms the chamber of *Marguerite* into a sort of semi-enclosed arbor, and places a lantern in her hand instead of the lamp, so that she may enter in safety from the street. In this street there walk soldiers, followed by students, singing their songs. Through them *Faust* finds his way and into the trellised enclosure. The strains of the songs are heard at the last blended in a single harmony. *Marguerite* enters through the street with her lantern and sings the romance of the King of Thule, which Berlioz calls a *Chanson Gothique*, one of the most original of his creations and, like the song in the next scene, "L'amour l'ardente flamme," which takes the place of Goethe's "Meine Ruh' ist hin," is steeped in a mood of mystical tenderness quite beyond description. *Méphistophélès* summons will-o'-the-wisps to aid in the bewilderment of the troubled mind of *Marguerite*. Here realism sadly disturbs the scene as Berlioz asks that the fancy shall create it. The customary dancing lights of the stage are supplemented with electrical effects which are beautiful, if not new. They do not mar if they do not help the grotesque minuet. But when M. Gunsbourg materializes the ghostly flames and presents them as a mob of hopping figures, he throws douches of cold water on the imagination of the listeners. Later he spoils enjoyment of the music utterly by making it the accompaniment of some utterly irrelevant pantomime by *Marguerite*, who goes into the street and is seen writhing between the conflicting emotions of love and duty, symbolized by a vision of *Faust* and the glowing of a cross on the façade of a church. To learn the meaning of this, one must go to the libretto, where he may read that it is all a dream dreamed by *Marguerite* after she had fallen asleep in her arm-chair. But we see her awake, not asleep, and it is all foolish and disturbing stuff put in to fill time and connect two of Berlioz's scenes. *Marguerite* returns to the room which she had left only in her dream, *Faust* discovers himself, and there follows the inevitable love-duet which *Méphistophélès* changes into a trio when he enters to urge *Faust* to depart. Meanwhile, *Marguerite's* neighbors gather in the street and warn *Dame Martha* of the misdeeds of *Marguerite*. The next scene seems to have been devised only to give an environment to Berlioz's paraphrase of Goethe's immortal song at the spinning-wheel. From the distance is heard the fading song of the students and the last echo of drums and trumpets sounding the retreat. *Marguerite* rushes to the window, and, overcome, rather unaccountably, with remorse and grief, falls in a swoon.

The last scene. A mountain gorge, a rock in the foreground surmounted by a cross. *Faust's* soliloquy, "Nature, immense, impénétrable et fière," was inspired by Goethe's exalted invocation to nature. *Faust* signs the compact, *Méphistophélès* summons the infernal steeds, *Vortex* and *Giaour*, and the ride to hell begins. Women and children at the foot of the cross supplicate the prayers of Mary, Magdalen, and Margaret. The cross disappears in a fearful crash of sound, the supplicants flee, and a moving panorama shows the visions which are supposed to meet the gaze of the riders — birds of night, dangling skeletons, a hideous and bestial phantasmagoria at the end of which *Faust* is delivered to the flames. The picture changes, and above the roofs of the sleeping town appears a vision of angels welcoming *Marguerite*.

CHAPTER IX

"LA TRAVIATA"

IN music the saying that "familiarity breeds contempt," is true only of compositions of a low order. In the case of compositions of the highest order, familiarity generally breeds ever growing admiration. In this category new compositions are slowly received; they make their way to popular appreciation only by repeated performances. It is true that the people like best the songs as well as the symphonies which they know best; but even this rule has its exceptions. It is possible to grow indifferent to even high excellence because of constant association with it. Especially is this true when the form — that is, the manner of expression — has grown antiquated; then, not expecting to find the kind of quality to which our tastes are inclined, we do not look for it, and though it may be present, it frequently passes unnoticed. The meritorious old is, therefore, just as much subject to non-appreciation as the meritorious new. Let me cite an instance.

Once upon a time duty called me to the two opera-houses of New York on the same evening. At the first I listened to some of the hot-blooded music of an Italian composer of the so-called school of *verismo*. Thence I went to the second. Verdi's "Traviata" was performing. I entered the room just as the orchestra began the prelude to the last act. As one can see without observing, so one can hear without listening — a wise provision which nature has made for the critic, and a kind one; I had heard that music so often during a generation of time devoted to musical journalism that I had long since quit listening to it. But now my jaded faculties were arrested by a new quality in the prelude. I had always admired the composer of "Rigoletto," "Il Trovatore," and "Traviata," and I loved and revered the author of "Aïda," "Otello," and "Falstaff." I had toddled along breathlessly in the trail made by his seven-league boots during the last thirty-five years of his career; but as I listened I found myself wondering that I had not noticed before that his modernity had begun before I had commenced to realize even what maternity meant — more than half a century ago, for "La Traviata" was composed in 1853. The quivering atmosphere of *Violetta's* sick-room seemed almost visible as the pathetic bit of hymnlike music rose upward from the divided viols of the orchestra like a cloud of incense which gathered itself together and floated along with the pathetic song of the solo violin. The work of palliating the character of the courtesan had begun, and on it went with each recurrence of the sad, sweet phrase as it punctuated the conversation between *Violetta* and her maid, until memory of her moral grossness was swallowed up in pity for her suffering. Conventional song-forms returned when poet and composer gave voice to the dying woman's lament for the happiness that was past and her agony of fear when she felt the touch of Death's icy hand, but where is melody more truthfully eloquent than in "Addio, del passato," and "Gran Dio! morir so giovane"? Is it within the power of instruments, no matter how great their number, or harmony with all the poignancy which it has acquired through the ingenious use of dissonance, or of broken phrase floating on an instrumental flood, to be more dramatically expressive than are these songs? Yet they are, in a way, uncompromisingly formal, architectural, strophic, and conventionally Verdian in their repetition of rhythmical motives and their melodic formularies. This introduction to the third act recalls the introduction to the first, which also begins with the hymnlike phrase, and sets the key-note of pathos which is sounded at every dramatic climax, though pages of hurdy-gurdy tune and unmeaning music intervene. Recall "Ah, fors' è lui che l' anima," with its passionate second section, "A quell' amor," and that most moving song of resignation, "Dite all' giovine." These things outweigh a thousand times the glittering tinsel of the opera and give "Traviata" a merited place, not only beside the later creations of the composer, but among those latter-day works which we call lyric dramas to distinguish them from those which we still call opera, with commiserating emphasis on the word.

That evening I realized the appositeness of Dr. von Bülow's remark to Mascagni when the world seemed inclined to hail that young man as the continuator of Verdi's operatic evangel: "I have found your successor in your predecessor, Verdi," but it did not seem necessary to think of "Otello" and "Falstaff" in connection with the utterance; "La Traviata" alone justifies it. Also it was made plain what Verdi meant, when after the first performance of his opera, and its monumental fiasco, he reproached his singers with want of understanding of his music. The story of that fiasco and the origin of the opera deserve a place here. "La Traviata," as all the world knows, is based upon the book and drama, "La Dame aux Camélias," by the younger Dumas, known to Americans and Englishmen as "Camille." The original book appeared in 1848, the play in 1852. Verdi witnessed a performance of the play when it was new. He was writing "Il Trovatore" at the time, but the drama took so strong a hold upon him that he made up his mind at once to turn it into an opera. As was his custom, he drafted a plan of the work, and this he sent to Piave, who for a long time had been his librettist in ordinary. Francesco Maria Piave was little more than a hack-writer of verse, but he knew how to put Verdi's ideas into practicable shape, and he deserves to be remembered with kindly interest as the great composer's collaborator in the creation of "I due Foscari," "Ernani," "Macbetto," "Il Corsaro," "Stiffelio," "Simon Boc-

canegra," "Aroldo" (a version of "Stiffelio"), and
"La Forza del Destino."   His artistic relations with
Verdi lasted from 1844 to 1862, but the friendship of
the men endured till the distressful end of Piave's
life, which came in 1876.   He was born three years
earlier than Verdi (in 1810), in Durano, of which
town his father had been the last podesta under
the Venetian republic.   He went mad some years
before he died, and thenceforward lived off Verdi's
bounty, the warm-hearted composer not only giving
him a pension, but also caring for his daughter
after his death.   In 1853 Verdi's creative genius was
.. ˉood-tide.   Four months was the time which he
usually devoted to the composition of an opera,
but he wrote "La Traviata" within four weeks,
and much of the music was composed concurrently
with that of "Il Trovatore."   This is proved by the
autograph, owned by his publishers, the Ricordis,
and there is evidence of the association in fraternity
of phrase in some of the uninteresting pages of the
score.   (See "Morrò! la mia memoria" for instance,
and the dance measures with their trills.)   "Il
Trovatore" was produced at Rome on January 19,
1853, and "La Traviata" on March 6 of the same
year at the Fenice Theatre in Venice.   "Il Trovatore" was stupendously successful; "La Traviata" made a woful failure.   Verdi seems to have
been fully cognizant of the causes which worked together to produce the fiasco, though he was disin-
clined at the time to discuss them.   Immediately
after the first representation he wrote to Muzio

" 'La Traviata' last night a failure. Was the fault mine or the singers'? Time will tell." To Vincenzo Luccardi, sculptor, professor at the Academy of San Luca in Rome, one of his most intimate friends, he wrote after the second performance: "The success was a fiasco — a complete fiasco! I do not know whose fault it was; it is best not to talk about it. I shall tell you nothing about the music, and permit me to say nothing about the performers." Plainly, he did not hold the singers guiltless. Varesi, the barytone, who was intrusted with the part of the elder *Germont,* had been disaffected, because he thought it beneath his dignity. Nevertheless, he went to the composer and offered his condolences at the fiasco. Verdi wanted none of his sympathy. "Condole with yourself and your companions who have not understood my music," was his somewhat ungracious rejoinder. No doubt the singers felt some embarrassment in the presence of music which to them seemed new and strange in a degree which we cannot appreciate now. Abramo Basevi, an Italian critic, who wrote a book of studies on Verdi's operas, following the fashion set by Lenz in his book on Beethoven, divides the operas which he had written up to the critic's time into examples of three styles, the early operas marking his first manner and "Luisa Miller" the beginning of his second. In "La Traviata" he says Verdi discovered a third manner, resembling in some things the style of French *opéra comique.* "This style of music," he says, "although it has not been tried on the stage in Italy, is, however, not unknown in private circles. In these latter years we have seen Luigi Gordigiani and Fabio Campana making themselves known principally in this style of music, called *da camera*. Verdi, with his 'Traviata,' has transported this chamber-music on to the stage, to which the subject he has chosen still lends itself, and with happy success. We meet with more simplicity in this work than in the others of the same composer, especially as regards the orchestra, where the quartet of stringed instruments is almost always predominant; the *parlanti* occupy a great part of the score; we meet with several of those airs which repeat under the form of verses; and, finally, the principal vocal subjects are for the most part developed in short binary and ternary movements, and have not, in general, the extension which the Italian style demands." Campana and Gordigiani were prolific composers of romanzas and canzonettas of a popular type. Their works are drawing-room music, very innocuous, very sentimental, very insignificant, and very far from the conception of chamber-music generally prevalent now. How they could have been thought to have influenced so virile a composer as Verdi, it is difficult to see. But musical critics enjoy a wide latitude of observation. In all likelihood there was nothing more in Dr. Basevi's mind than the strophic structure of "Di Provenza," the song style of some of the other arias to which attention has been called and the circumstance that these, the most striking numbers in the score,

GIUSEPPE VERDI

mark the points of deepest feeling. In this respect, indeed, there is some relationship between "La Traviata" and "Der Freischütz" — though this is an observation which will probably appear as far-fetched to some of my critics as Dr. Basevi's does to me.

There were other reasons of a more obvious and external nature for the failure of "La Traviata" on its first production. Lodovico Graziani, the tenor, who filled the rôle of *Alfredo*, was hoarse, and could not do justice to the music; Signora Salvini-Donatelli, the *Violetta* of the occasion, was afflicted with an amplitude of person which destroyed the illusion of the death scene and turned its pathos into absurdity. The spectacle of a lady of mature years and more than generous integumental upholstery dying of consumption was more than the Venetian sense of humor could endure with equanimity. The opera ended with shrieks of laughter instead of the lachrymal flood which the music and the dramatic situation called for. This spirit of irreverence had been promoted, moreover, by the fact that the people of the play wore conventional modern clothes. The lure of realism was not strong in the lyric theatres half a century ago, when laces and frills, top-boots and plumed hats, helped to confine the fancy to the realm of idealism in which it was believed opera ought to move. The first result of the fiasco was a revision of the costumes and stage furniture, by which simple expedient Mr. Dumas's *Marguerite Gauthier* was

changed from a courtesan of the time of Louis
Philippe to one of the period of Louis XIV. It is
an amusing illustration of how the whirligig of time
brings its revenges that the spirit of *verismo*, masquerading as a desire for historical accuracy, has
restored the period of the Dumas book, — that is,
restored it in name, but not in fact, — with the result,
in New York and London at least, of making the
dress of the opera more absurd than ever. *Violetta*,
exercising the right which was conquered by the
prima donna generations ago, appears always garbed
in the very latest style, whether she be wearing one
of her two ball dresses or her simple afternoon gown.
For aught that I know, the latest fad in woman's
dress may also be hidden in the dainty folds of the
robe de chambre in which she dies. The elder
Germont has for two years appeared before the New
York public as a well-to-do country gentleman of
Provence might have appeared sixty years ago, but
his son has thrown all sartorial scruples to the wind,
and wears the white waistcoat and swallowtail of
to-day.

The Venetians were allowed a year to get over
the effects of the first representations of "La Traviata," and then the opera was brought forward
again with the new costumes. Now it succeeded
and set out upon the conquest of the world. It
reached London on May 24, St. Petersburg on November 1, New York on December 3, and Paris on
December 6 — all in the same year, 1856. The first
Violetta in New York was Mme. Anna La Grange,

the first *Alfredo* Signor Brignoli, and the first *Germont père* Signor Amodio. There had been a destructive competition between Max Maretzek's Italian company at the Academy of Music and a German company at Niblo's Garden. The regular Italian season had come to an end with a quarrel between Maretzek and the directors of the Academy. The troupe prepared to embark for Havana, but before doing so gave a brief season under the style of the La Grange Opera Company, and brought forward the new opera on December 3, three days before the Parisians were privileged to hear it. The musical critic of the *Tribune* at the time was Mr. W. H. Fry, who was not only a writer on political and musical subjects, but a composer, who wrote an opera, "Leonora," in which Mme. La Grange sang at the Academy about a year and a half later. His review of the first performance of "La Traviata," which appeared in the *Tribune* of December 5, 1856, is worth reading for more reasons than one:—

The plot of "La Traviata" we have already given to our readers. It is simply "Camille." The first scene affords us some waltzing music, appropriate in its place, on which a (musical) dialogue takes place. The waltz is not specially good, nor is there any masterly outworking of detail. A fair drinking song is afforded, which pleased, but was not encored. A pretty duet by Mme. de la Grange and Signor Brignoli may be noticed also in this act; and the final air, by Madame de la Grange, "Ah! fors' e lui che l' anima," contained a brilliant, florid close which brought down the house, and the curtain had to be reraised to admit of a repetition. Act II admits of more intensified music than Act I. A brief air by *Alfred* (Brignoli) is followed by an air by *Germont* (Amodio), and by a duet, *Violetta* (La Grange) and *Germont*. The duet is well worked up and is rousing, passionate music. Verdi's mastery of dramatic accent — of the modern school of declamation — is here evident. Some dramatic work, the orchestra leading, follows — bringing an air by *Germont*, "Di Provenza il mar." This is a 2-4 travesty of a waltz known as Weber's Last Waltz (which, however, Weber never wrote); and is too uniform in the length of its notes to have dramatic breadth or eloquence. A good hit is the sudden exit of *Alfred* thereupon, not stopping to make an andiamo duet as is so often done. The next scene introduces us to a masquerade where are choruses of quasi-gypsies, matadors, and picadors, — sufficiently characteristic. The scene after the card-playing, which is so fine in the play, is inefficient in music. Act III in the book (though it was made Act IV on this occasion by subdividing the second) reveals the sick-room of *Traviata*. A sweet air, minor and major by turns, with some hautboy wailing, paints the sufferer's sorrows. A duet by the lovers, "Parigi, O cara," is especially original in its peroration. The closing trio has due culmination and anguish, though we would have preferred a quiet ending to a hectic shriek and a doubly loud force in the orchestra.

Goldsmith's rule in "The Vicar" for criticising a painting was always to say that "the picture would have been better if the painter had taken more pains." Perhaps the same might be said about "La Traviata"; but whether it would have pleased the public more is another question. Some of the airs certainly would bear substitution by others in the author's happier vein. The opera was well received. Three times the singers were called before the curtain. The piece was well put on the stage. Madame La Grange never looked so well. Her toilet was charming.

The principal incidents of Dumas's play are reproduced with general fidelity in the opera. In the first act there are scenes of gayety in the house of *Violetta*—dancing, feasting, and love-making. Among the devotees of the courtesan is *Alfredo Germont*, a young man of respectable Provençal family. He joins in the merriment, singing a drinking song with *Violetta*, but his devotion to her is unlike that of his companions. He loves her sincerely, passionately, and his protestations awaken in her sensations never felt before. For a moment, she indulges in a day-dream of honest affection, but banishes it with the reflection that the only life for which she is fitted is one devoted to the pleasures of the moment, the mad revels rounding out each day, and asking no care of the moment. But at the last the voice of *Alfredo* floats in at the window, burdening the air and her heart with an echo of the longing to which she had given expression in her brief moment of thoughtfulness. She yields to *Alfredo's* solicitations and a strangely new emotion, and abandons her dissolute life to live with him alone.

In the second act the pair are found housed in a country villa not far from Paris. From the maid *Alfredo* learns that *Violetta* has sold her property in the city — house, horses, carriages, and all — in order to meet the expenses of the rural establishment. Conscience-smitten, he hurries to Paris to prevent the sacrifice, but in his absence *Violetta* is called upon to make a much greater. *Giorgio Ger-*

mont, the father of her lover, visits her, and, by appealing to her love for his son and picturing the ruin which is threatening him and the barrier which his illicit association with her is placing in the way of the happy marriage of his sister, persuades her to give him up. She abandons home and lover, and returns to her old life in the gay city, making a favored companion of the *Baron Duphol*. In Paris, at a masked ball in the house of *Flora*, one of her associates, *Alfredo* finds her again, overwhelms her with reproaches, and ends a scene of excitement by denouncing her publicly and throwing his gambling gains at her feet.

Baron Duphol challenges *Alfredo* to fight a duel. The baron is wounded. The elder *Germont* sends intelligence of *Alfredo's* safety to *Violetta*, and informs her that he has told his son of the great sacrifice which she had made for love of him. *Violetta* dies in the arms of her lover, who had hurried to her on learning the truth, only to find her suffering the last agonies of disease.

In the preface to his novel, Dumas says that the principal incidents of the story are true. It has also been said that Dickens was familiar with them, and at one time purposed to make a novel on the subject; but this statement scarcely seems credible. Such a novel would have been un-English in spirit and not at all in harmony with the ideals of the author of "David Copperfield" and "Dombey and Son." Play and opera at the time of their first production raised questions of taste and morals which have remained open ever since. Whether the anathema periodically pronounced against them by private and official censorship helps or hinders the growth of such works in popularity, there is no need of discussing here. There can scarcely be a doubt, however, but that many theatrical managers of to-day would hail with pleasure and expectation of profit such a controversy over one of their new productions as greeted "La Traviata" in London. The Lord Chamberlain had refused to sanction the English adaptations of "La Dame aux Camélias," and when the opera was brought forward (performance being allowed because it was sung in a foreign language), pulpit and press thundered in denunciation of it. Mr. Lumley, the manager of Her Majesty's Theatre, came to the defence of the work in a letter to the *Times*, but it was more his purpose to encourage popular excitement and irritate curiosity than to shield the opera from condemnation. He had every reason to be satisfied with the outcome. "La Traviata" had made a complete fiasco, on its production in Italy, where no one dreamed of objecting to the subject-matter of its story; in London there was a loud outcry against the "foul and hideous horrors of the book," and the critics found little to praise in the music; yet the opera scored a tremendous popular success, and helped to rescue Her Majesty's from impending ruin.

CHAPTER X

"AÏDA"

Two erroneous impressions concerning Verdi's "Aïda" may as well as not be corrected at the beginning of a study of that opera: it was not written to celebrate the completion of the Suez Canal, nor to open the Italian Opera-house at Cairo, though the completion of the canal and the inauguration of the theatre were practically contemporaneous with the conception of the plan which gave the world one of Verdi's finest and also most popular operas. It is more difficult to recall a season in any of the great lyric theatres of the world within the last thirty-five years in which "Aïda" was not given than to enumerate a score of productions with particularly fine singers and imposing *mise en scène*. With it Verdi ought to have won a large measure of gratitude from singers and impresarios as well as the fortune which it brought him; for though, like all really fine works, it rewards effort and money bestowed upon it with corresponding and proportionate generosity, it does not depend for its effectiveness on extraordinary vocal outfit or scenic apparel. Fairly well sung and acted and respectably dressed, it always wins the sympathies and warms the enthusiasm of an audience the world over. It is seldom thought of as a conventional opera, and yet it is full of conventionalities which do not obtrude themselves simply because there is so much that is individual about its music and its pictures — particularly its pictures. Save for the features of its score which differentiate it from the music of Verdi's other operas and the works of his predecessors and contemporaries, "Aïda" is a companion of all the operas for which Meyerbeer set a model when he wrote his works for the Académie Nationale in Paris— the great pageant operas like "Le Prophète," "Lohengrin," and Goldmark's "Queen of Sheba." With the last it shares one element which brings it into relationship also with a number of much younger and less significant works — operas like Mascagni's "Iris," Puccini's "Madama Butterfly," and Giordano's "Siberia." In the score of "Aïda" there is a slight infusion of that local color which is lavishly employed in decorating its externals. The pomp and pageantry of the drama are Egyptian and ancient; the play's natural and artificial environment is Egyptian and ancient; two bits of its music are Oriental, possibly Egyptian, and not impossibly ancient. But in everything else "Aïda" is an Italian opera. The story plays in ancient Egypt, and its inventor was an archæologist deeply versed in Egyptian antiquities, but I have yet to hear that Mariette Bey, who wrote the *scenario* of the drama, ever claimed an historical foundation for it or pretended that anything in its story was characteris-

tically Egyptian. Circumstances wholly fortuitous
give a strong tinge of antiquity and nationalism to
the last scene; but, if the ancient Egyptians were
more addicted than any other people to burying
malefactors alive, the fact is not of record; and the
picture as we have it in the opera was not conceived
by Mariette Bey, but by Verdi while working hand
in hand with the original author of the libretto, which,
though designed for an Italian performance, was
first written in French prose.

The Italian Theatre in Cairo was built by the
khedive, Ismaïl Pacha, and opened in November,
1869. It is extremely likely that the thought of the
advantage which would accrue to the house, could it
be opened with a new piece by the greatest of living
Italian opera composers, had entered the mind of
the khedive or his advisers; but it does not seem
to have occurred to them in time to insure such a
work for the opening. Nevertheless, long before
the inauguration of the theatre a letter was sent
to Verdi asking him if he would write an opera on
an Egyptian subject, and if so, on what terms. The
opportunity was a rare one, and appealed to the
composer, who had written "Les Vêpres Siciliennes"
and "Don Carlos" for Paris, "La Forza del Destino"
for St. Petersburg, and had not honored an Italian
stage with a new work for ten years. But the suggestion that he state his terms embarrassed him.
So he wrote to his friend Muzio and asked him what
to do. Muzio had acquired much more worldly
wisdom than ever came to the share of the great

genius, and he replied sententiously: "Demand 4000 pounds sterling for your score. If they ask you to go and mount the piece and direct the rehearsals, fix the sum at 6000 pounds."

Verdi followed his friend's advice, and the khedive accepted the terms. At first the opera people in Cairo thought they wanted only the score which carried with it the right of performance, but soon they concluded that they wanted also the presence of the composer, and made him, in vain, munificent offers of money, distinctions, and titles. His real reason for not going to prepare the opera and direct the first performance was a dread of the voyage. To a friend he wrote that he feared that if he went to Cairo they would make a mummy of him. Under the terms of the agreement the khedive sent him 50,000 francs at once, and deposited the balance of 50,000 francs in a bank, to be paid over to the composer on delivery of the score.

The story of "Aïda" came from Mariette Bey, who was then director of the Egyptian Museum at Boulak. Auguste Édouard Mariette was a Frenchman who, while an attaché of the Louvre, in 1850, had gone on a scientific expedition to Egypt for the French government and had discovered the temple of Serapis at Memphis. It was an "enormous structure of granite and alabaster, containing within its enclosure the sarcophagi of the bulls of Apis, from the nineteenth dynasty to the time of the Roman supremacy." After his return to Paris, he was appointed in 1855 assistant conservator of the

Egyptian Museum in the Louvre, and after some further years of service, he went to Egypt again, where
he received the title of Bey and an appointment as
director of the museum at Boulak. Bayard Taylor
visited him in 1851 and 1874, and wrote an account
of his explorations and the marvellous collection
of antiquities which he had in his care.

Mariette wrote the plot of "Aïda," which was sent
to Verdi, and at once excited his liveliest interest.
Camille du Locle, who had had a hand in making
the books of "Les Vêpres Siciliennes" and "Don
Carlos" (and who is also the librettist of Reyer's
"Salammbô"), went to Verdi's home in Italy, and
under the eye of the composer wrote out the drama
in French prose. It was he who gave the world
the information that the idea of the double scene
in the last act was conceived by Verdi, who, he
says, "took a large share in the work." The drama,
thus completed, was translated into Italian verse
by Antonio Ghislanzoni, who, at the time, was editor
of the *Gazetta Musicale*, a journal published in
Milan. In his early life Ghislanzoni was a barytone
singer. He was a devoted friend and admirer of
Verdi's, to whom he paid a glowing tribute in his
book entitled "Reminiscenze Artistiche." He died
some fifteen or sixteen years ago, and some of his
last verses were translations of Tennyson's poems.

The khedive expected to hear his opera by the
end of 1870, but there came an extraordinary disturbance of the plan, the cause being nothing less
than the war between France and Germany. The

scenery and costumes, which had been made after designs by French artists, were shut up in Paris. At length, on December 24, 1871, the opera had its first performance at Cairo. Considering the sensation which the work created, it seems strange that it remained the exclusive possession of Cairo and a few Italian cities so long as it did, but a personal equation stood in the way of a performance at the Grand Opéra, where it properly belonged. The conduct of the conductor and musicians at the production of "Les Vêpres Siciliennes" had angered Verdi; and when M. Halanzier, the director of the Académie Nationale, asked for the opera in 1873, his request was refused. Thus it happened that the Théâtre Italien secured the right of first performance in Paris. It was brought out there on April 22, 1876, and had sixty-eight representations within three years. The original *King* in the French performance was Édouard de Reszke. It was not until March 22, 1880, that "Aïda" reached the Grand Opéra. M. Vaucorbeil, the successor of Halanzier, visited Verdi at his home and succeeded in persuading him not only to give the performing rights to the national institution, but also to assist in its production. Maurel was the *Amonasro* of the occasion. The composer was greatly fêted, and at a dinner given in his honor by President Grévy was made a Grand Officer of the National Order of the Legion of Honor.

The opening scene of the opera is laid at Memphis, a fact which justifies the utmost grandeur in the stage furniture, and is explained by Mariette's interest in that place. It was he who helped moderns to realize the ancient magnificence of the city described by Diodorus. It was the first capital of the united kingdom of upper and lower Egypt, the chief seat of religion and learning, the site of the temples of Ptah, Isis, Serapis, Phra, and the sacred bull Apis. Mariette here, on his first visit to Egypt, unearthed an entire avenue of sphinxes leading to the Serapeum, over four thousand statues, reliefs, and inscriptions, eight gigantic sculptures, and many other evidences of a supremely great city. He chose his scenes with a view to an exhibition of the ancient grandeur. In a hall of the Royal Palace, flanked by a colonnade with statues and flowering shrubs, and commanding a view of the city's palaces and temples and the pyramids, *Radames*, an Egyptian soldier, and *Ramfis*, a high priest, discuss a report that the Ethiopians are in revolt in the valley of the Nile, and that Thebes is threatened. The high priest has consulted Isis, and the goddess has designated who shall be the leader of Egypt's army against the rebels. An inspiring thought comes into the mind of *Radames*. What if he should be the leader singled out to crush the rebellion, and be received in triumph on his return? A consummation devoutly to be wished, not for his own glory alone, but for the sake of his love, *Aïda*, whose beauty he sings in a romance ("Celeste Aïda") of exquisite loveliness and exaltation. *Amneris*, the daughter of the King of Egypt (Ma-

riette gives him no name, and so avoids possible
historical complications), enters. She is in love with
Radames, and eager to know what it is that has
so illumined his visage with joy. He tells her of
his ambition, but hesitates when she asks him if
no gentler dream had tenanted his heart. *Aïda*
approaches, and the perturbation of her lover is
observed by *Amneris,* who affects love for her slave
(for such *Aïda* is), welcomes her as a sister, and bids
her tell the cause of her grief. *Aïda* is the daughter
of Ethiopia's king; but she would have the princess
believe that her tears are caused by anxiety for
Egypt's safety. The *King* appears with *Ramfis*
and a royal retinue, and learns from a messenger
that the Ethiopians have invaded Egypt and, under
their king, *Amonasro,* are marching on Thebes.
The *King* announces that Isis has chosen *Radames*
to be the leader of Egypt's hosts. *Amneris* places
the royal banner in his eager hand, and to the sounds
of a patriotic march he is led away to the temple
of Ptah (the Egyptian Vulcan), there to receive his
consecrated armor and arms. "Return a victor!"
shout the hosts, and *Aïda,* carried away by her love,
joins in the cry; but, left alone, she reproaches herself for impiousness in uttering words which imply
a wish for the destruction of her country, her father,
and her kinsmen. (*Scena:* "Ritorna vincitor.")
Yet could she wish for the defeat and the death of the
man she loves? She prays the gods to pity her sufferings ("Numi, pieta"). Before a colossal figure
of the god in the temple of Ptah, while the sacred

fires rise upward from the tripods, and priestesses
move through the figures of the sacred dance or
chant a hymn to the Creator, Preserver, Giver, of
Life and Light, the consecrated sword is placed in
the hands of *Radames*.

It is in this scene that the local color is not confined to externals alone, but infuses the music as well.
Very skilfully Verdi makes use of two melodies which
are saturated with the languorous spirit of the East.
The first is the invocation of Ptah, chanted by an invisible priestess to the accompaniment of a harp: —

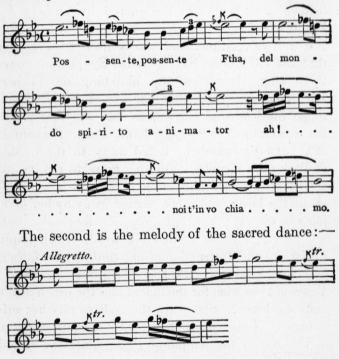

The second is the melody of the sacred dance: —

The tunes are said to be veritable Oriental strains which some antiquary (perhaps Mariette himself) put into the hands of Verdi. The fact that their characteristic elements were nowhere else employed by the composer, though he had numerous opportunities for doing so, would seem to indicate that Verdi was chary about venturing far into the territory of musical nationalism. Perhaps he felt that his powers were limited in this direction, or that he might better trust to native expression of the mood into which the book had wrought him. The limitation of local color in his music is not mentioned as a defect in the opera, for it is replaced at the supreme moments, especially that at the opening of the third act, with qualities far more entrancing than were likely to have come from the use of popular idioms. Yet, the two Oriental melodies having been mentioned, it is well to look at their structure to discover the source of their singular charm. There is no mystery as to the cause in the minds of students of folk-song. The tunes are evolved from a scale so prevalent among peoples of Eastern origin that it has come to be called the Oriental scale. Its distinguishing characteristic is an interval, which contains three semitones: —

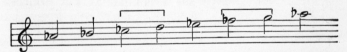

The interval occurring twice in this scale is enclosed in brackets. Its characteristic effect is most

obvious when the scale is played downward. A
beautiful instance of its artistic use is in Rubinstein's song "Der Asra." The ancient synagogal
songs of the Jews are full of it, and it is one of the
distinguishing marks of the folk-songs of Hungary
(the other being rhythmical), as witness the "Rakoczy March." In some of the Eastern songs it
occurs once, in some twice (as in the case of the
melodies printed above), and there are instances of
a triple use in the folk-songs of the modern Greeks.

Act II. News of the success of the Egyptian expedition against the Ethiopians has reached *Amneris*, whose slaves attire her for the scene of
Radames's triumph. The slaves sing of Egypt's
victory and of love, the princess of her longing,
and Moorish slaves dance before her to dispel her
melancholy. *Aïda* comes, weighed down by grief.
Amneris lavishes words of sympathy upon her, and
succeeds in making her betray her love for *Radames*
by saying that he had been killed in battle. Then
she confesses the falsehood and proclaims her own
passion and purpose to crush her rival, who shall
appear at the triumph of *Radames* as her slave.
Aïda's pride rebels for the moment, and she almost
betrays her own exalted station as the daughter of
a king. As a slave she accompanies the princess
to the entrance gate of Thebes, where the *King*, the
priests, and a vast concourse of people are to welcome
Radames and witness his triumphal entry. *Radames*, with his troops and a horde of Ethiopian
prisoners, comes into the city in a gorgeous pageant.

The procession is headed by two groups of trumpeters, who play a march melody, the stirring effect of which is greatly enhanced by the characteristic tone quality of the long, straight instruments which they use : —

A word about these trumpets. In shape, they recall antique instruments, and the brilliancy of their tone is due partly to the calibre of their straight tubes and partly to the fact that nearly all the tones used are open — that is, natural harmonics of the fundamental tones of the tubes. There is an anachronism in the circumstance that they are provided with valves (which were not invented until some thousands of years after the period of the drama), but only one of the valves is used. The first trumpets are in the key of A-flat and the second B-natural, a peculiarly stirring effect being produced by the sudden shifting of the key of the march when the second group of trumpeters enters on the scene.

The *King* greets *Radames* with an embrace, bids him receive the wreath of victory from the hands of his daughter and ask whatever boon he will as a reward for his services. He asks, first, that the prisoners be brought before the *King*. Among them *Aïda* recognizes her father, who is disguised as an officer of the Ethiopian army. The two are in each other's arms in a moment, but only long

enough for *Amonasro* to caution his daughter not
to betray him. He bravely confesses that he had
fought for king and country, and pleads for clemency
for the prisoners. They join in the petition, as does
Aïda, and though the priests warn and protest,
Radames asks the boon of their lives and freedom,
and the *King* grants it. Also, without the asking,
he bestows the hand of his daughter upon the victorious general, who receives the undesired honor
with consternation.

Transporting beauty rests upon the scene which
opens the third act. The moon shines brightly on
the rippling surface of the Nile and illumines a temple
of Isis, perched amongst the tropical foliage which
crowns a rocky height. The silvery sheen is spread
also over the music, which arises from the orchestra
like a light mist burdened with sweet odors. *Amneris* enters the temple to ask the blessing of the
goddess upon her marriage, and the pious canticle
of the servitors within floats out on the windless air.
A tone of tender pathos breathes through the music
which comes with *Aïda*, who is to hold secret converse with her lover. Will he come? And if so, will
he speak a cruel farewell and doom her to death
within the waters of the river? A vision of her
native land, its azure skies, verdant vales, perfumed breezes, rises before her. Shall she never
see them more? Her father comes upon her. He
knows of her passion for *Radames*, but also of her
love for home and kindred. He puts added hues
into the picture with which her heavy fancy had

dallied, and then beclouds it all with an account of
homes and temples profaned, maidens ravished,
grandsires, mothers, children, slain by the oppressor.
Will she aid in the deliverance? She can by learning from her lover by which path the Egyptians will
march against the Ethiopians, who are still in the
field, though their king is taken. That she will
not do. But *Amonasro* breaks down her resolution.
Hers will be the responsibility for torrents of blood,
the destruction of cities, the devastation of her
country. No longer his daughter she, but a slave
of the Pharaohs! Her lover comes. She affects
to repulse him because of his betrothal to *Amneris*,
but he protests his fidelity and discloses his plan.
The Ethiopians are in revolt again. Again he will
defeat them, and, returning again in triumph, he
will tell the *King* of his love for her and thereafter
live in the walks of peace. But *Aïda* tells him that
the vengeance of *Amneris* will pursue her, and urges
him to fly with her. Reluctantly he consents, and
she, with apparent innocence, asks by which path
they shall escape the soldiery. Through the gorge
of Napata; 'twill be unpeopled till to-morrow, for
it has been chosen as the route by which the Egyptian
advance shall be made. Exulting, *Amonasro* rushes
from his place of concealment. At the gorge of
Napata will he place his troops — he the King of
Ethiopia! *Radames* has betrayed his country.
Amneris comes out of the temple, and *Amonasro* is
about to poignard her when *Radames* throws himself
between. To the high priest, *Ramfis*, he yields him-

self and his sword. *Amonasro* drags *Aïda* away
with him.

We reach the last act of the drama. *Radames*
is to be tried for treason in having betrayed a secret
of war to his country's enemy. *Amneris* fain would
save him were he to renounce *Aïda* and accept her
love. She offers on such terms to intercede for him
with her father, the king. From her *Radames*
learns that *Aïda* escaped the guards who slew her
father. He is resolute to die rather than prove
faithless to her, and is led away to the subterranean
trial chamber. *Amneris*, crouched without, hears
the accusing voices of the priests and the awful
silence which follows each accusation; for *Radames* refuses to answer the charges. The priests
pronounce sentence:—Burial alive! *Amneris* hurls
curses after them, but they depart, muttering,
"Death to the traitor!"

Radames is immured in a vault beneath the
temple of Vulcan, whose sacred priestesses move in
solemn steps above, while he gropes in the darkness below. Never again shall light greet his eyes,
nor sight of *Aïda*. A groan. A phantom rises before him, and *Aïda* is at his side. She had foreseen the doom of her lover, and entered the tomb
before him to die in his arms. Together they say
their farewell to the vale of tears, and their streaming eyes have a prevision of heaven. Above in
the temple a figure, shrouded in black, kneels upon
the stone which seals the vault and implores Isis
to cease her resentment and give her adored one
peace. It is *Amneris*.

CHAPTER XI

A DESCRIPTION of Carl Maria von Weber's opera, "Der Freischütz," ought to begin with a study of the overture, since that marvellous composition has lived on and on in the concert-rooms of the world without loss of popularity for nearly a century, while the opera which it introduces has periodically come and gone according to popular whim or the artistic convictions or caprices of managers in all the countries which cultivate opera, except Germany. Why Germany forms an exception to the rule will find an explanation when the character of the opera and its history come under investigation. The overture, notwithstanding its extraordinary charm, is only an exalted example of the *pot-pourri* class of introductions (though in the classic sonata form), which composers were in the habit of writing when this opera came into existence, and which is still imitated in an ignoble way by composers of ephemeral operettas. It is constructed on a conventional model, and its thematic material is drawn from the music of the opera; but, like the prelude to Wagner's lyric comedy, "Die Meistersinger von Nürnberg," it presents the contents of the play in the form of what many years after its composition came to be called a symphonic poem, and illustrates the ideal which was in Gluck's mind

191

when, in the preface to "Alceste," he said, "I imag
ined that the overture ought to prepare the audience
for the action of the piece, and serve as a kind of
argument to it." The atmosphere of the opera is
that which pervades the sylvan life of Germany —
its actualities and its mysteries, the two elements
having equal potency. Into the peacefulness of
the woods the French horns ("Forest horns," the
Germans call them) usher us at once with the hymn
which they sing after a few introductory measures.

But no sooner do we yield to the caress of this mood
than there enters the supernatural element which
invests the tragical portion of the story. Ominous
drum beats under a dissonant *tremolo* of the strings
and deep tones of the clarinets, a plangent declamatory phrase of the violoncellos: —

tell us of the emotions of the hero when he feels
himself deserted by Heaven; the agitated principal subject of the main body of the overture
(*Molto vivace*):—

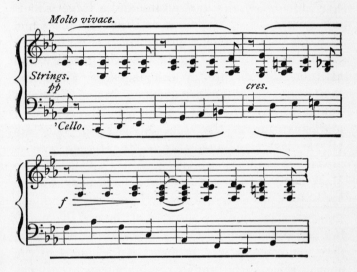

proclaims his terror at the thought that he has fallen
into the power of the Evil One, while the jubilant
second theme:—

o

gives voice to the happiness of the heroine and the triumph of love and virtue which is the outcome of the drama.

The first glimpse of the opera reveals an open space in a forest and in it an inn and a target-shooting range. *Max*, a young assistant to the Chief Forester of a Bohemian principality, is seated at a table with a mug of beer before him, his face and attitude the picture of despondency. Hard by, huntsmen and others are grouped around *Kilian*, a young peasant who fires the last shot in a contest of marksmanship as the scene is disclosed. He hits off the last remaining star on the target, and is noisily acclaimed as *Schützenkönig* (King of the Marksmen), and celebrated in a lusty song by the spectators, who decorate the victor, and forming a procession bearing the trophies of the match, march around the glade. As they pass *Max* they point their fingers and jeer at him. *Kilian* joins in the sport until *Max's* fuming ill-humor can brook the humiliation no longer; he leaps up, seizes the lapel of *Kilian's* coat, and draws his hunting-knife. A deadly quarrel seems imminent, but is averted by the coming of *Cuno*, Chief Forester, and *Caspar*, who, like *Max*, is one of his assistants. To the reproaches of *Cuno*, who sees the mob surging around *Max*, *Kilian* explains that there was no ill-will in the mockery of him, the crowd only following an old custom which permitted the people to make sport of a contestant who failed to hit the target, and thus forfeited the right to make trial for the king-

ship. *Cuno* is amazed that a mere peasant should
have defeated one of his foresters, and that one the
affianced lover of his daughter, *Agathe,* and who, as
his son-in-law, would inherit his office, provided he
could prove his fitness for it by a trial shot on the
wedding day. That day had been set for the morrow. How the custom of thus providing for the
successorship originated, *Cuno* now relates in answer to the questions of one of the party. His
great-grandfather, also bearer of the name Cuno, had
been one of the rangers of the prince who ruled the
dominion in his day. Once upon a time, in the
course of a hunt, the dogs started a stag who bounded
toward the party with a man tied to his back.
It was thus that poachers were sometimes punished. The Prince's pity was stirred, and he promised that whoever should shoot the stag without
harming the man should receive the office of Chief
Forester, to be hereditary in the family, and the
tenancy of a hunting lodge near by. Cuno, moved
more by pity than hope of reward, attempted the
feat and succeeded. The Prince kept his promise,
but on a suggestion that the old hunter may have
used a charmed bullet, he made the hereditary succession contingent upon the success of a trial shot.
Before telling the tale, *Cuno* had warned *Max* to
have a care, for should he fail in the trial shot on the
morrow, his consent to the marriage between him
and *Agathe* would be withdrawn. *Max* had suspected that his ill luck for a month past, during
which time he had brought home not a single trophy

of bird or beast, was due to some malign influence, the cause of which he was unable to fathom. He sings of the prowess and joys that once were his (Aria: "Durch die Wälder, durch die Auen"), but falls into a moody dread at the thought that Heaven has forsaken him and given him over to the powers of darkness. It is here that the sinister music, mentioned in the outline of the overture, enters the drama. It accompanies the appearance of *Samiel* (the Wild Huntsman, or Black Hunter, — in short, the Devil), and we have thus in Von Weber's opera a pre-Wagnerian example of the *Leitmotif* of the Wagnerian commentators. *Caspar* returns to the scene, which all the other personages have left to join in a dance, and finds his associate in the depths of despair. He plies *Max* with wine, and, affecting sympathy with him in his misfortunes, gradually insinuates that there is a means of insuring success on the morrow. *Max* remains sceptical until *Caspar* hands him his rifle and bids him shoot at an eagle flying overhead. The bird is plainly out of rifle range, a mere black dot against the twilight sky; but *Max*, scarcely aiming, touches the trigger and an eagle of gigantic size comes hurtling through the air and falls at his feet. *Max* is convinced that there is a sure way to win his bride on the morrow. He asks *Caspar* if he has more bullets like the one just spent. No; that was the hunter's last; but more might be obtained, provided the effort be made that very night. The moment was propitious. It was the second of three days in which the sun was in the constellation of the Archer; at midnight there would occur an eclipse of the moon. What a fortunate coincidence that all the omens should be fair at so momentous a juncture of *Max's* affairs! The fear of losing his bride overcomes *Max's* scruples, he agrees to meet the tempter in the Wolf's Glen, a spot of evil repute, at midnight, and at least witness the casting of more of the charmed bullets.

At the moment when *Max's* shot brought down the eagle, a portrait of the original Cuno fell from the wall of the cottage occupied by his descendant; and when the second act begins, we see *Aennchen*, a cousin of *Agathe's*, putting it back in its place. *Aennchen* is inclined to be playful and roguish, and serves as a pretty foil to the sentimental *Agathe*. She playfully scolds the nail which she is hammering into the wall again for so rudely dropping the old ranger to the floor, and seeks to dispel the melancholy which has obsessed her cousin by singing songs about the bad companionship of the blues and the humors of courtship. She succeeds, in a measure, and *Agathe* confesses that she had felt a premonition of danger ever since a pious *Hermit*, to whom she had gone for counsel in the course of the day, had warned her of the imminency of a calamity which he could not describe. The prediction seemed to have been fulfilled in the falling of the picture, which had slightly hurt her, but might easily have killed her. *Aennchen* urges her to go to bed, but she refuses, saying she shall not retire for sleep until *Max* has come. *Agathe* sings the *scena* which has clung to our concert-rooms as persistently as the overture. The slow portion of the aria ("Leise, leise, fromme Weise"), like the horn music at the beginning of the overture, has found its way into the Protestant hymn-books of England and America, and its *Allegro* furnishes forth the jubilant music of the instrumental introduction to the opera. Berlioz in his book "A Travers Chants" writes in a fine burst of enthusiasm of this *scena:* "It is impossible for any listener to fail to hear the sighs of the orchestra during the prayer of the virtuous maiden who awaits the coming of her affianced lover; or the strange hum in which the alert ear imagines it hears the rustling of the tree-tops. It even seems as if the darkness grew deeper and colder at that magical modulation to C major. What a sympathetic shudder comes over one at the cry ''Tis he! 'tis he!' No, no. It must be confessed, there is no other aria as beautiful as this. No master, whether German, Italian, or French, was ever able to delineate, as is done here in a single scene, holy prayer, melancholy, disquiet, pensiveness, the slumber of nature, the mysterious harmony of the starry skies, the torture of expectation, hope, uncertainty, joy, frenzy, delight, love delirious! And what an orchestra to accompany these noble song melodies! What inventiveness! What ingenious discoveries! What treasures of sudden inspiration! These flutes in the depths, this quartet of violins; these passages in sixths between violas and 'cellos; this *crescendo* bursting into refulgence at the close;

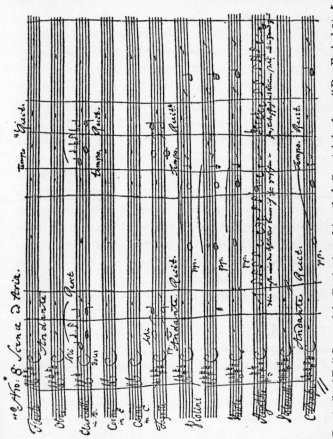

Facsimile of Full Score of the Beginning of Agatha's Great Aria, from "Der Freischütz."

these pauses during which the passions seem to be gathering themselves together in order to launch their forces anew with greater vehemence! No, this piece has not its fellow! Here is an art that is divine! This is poetry; this is love itself!"

Max comes at last, but he is preoccupied, and his words and acts do little to reassure *Agathe*. She wants to know what luck he had at the shooting-match, and he replies that he did not participate in the target-shooting, but had nevertheless been marvellously lucky, pointing to the eagle's feather in his hat as proof. At the same moment he notices the blood upon his sweetheart's hair, and her explanation of the falling of the portrait of her ancestor just as the clock struck seven greatly disturbs him. *Agathe*, too, lapses into gloomy brooding; she has fears for the morrow, and the thought of the monstrous eagle terrifies her. And now *Max*, scarcely come, announces that he must go; he had shot, he says, a stag deep in the woods near the Wolf's Glen, indeed, and must bring it in lest the peasants steal it. In a trio *Aennchen* recalls the uncanny nature of the spot, *Agathe* warns against the sin of tempting Providence and begs him to stay; but *Max* protests his fearlessness and the call of duty, and hurries away to meet *Caspar*, at the appointed time in the appointed place. We see him again in the Wolf's Glen, but *Caspar* is there before him. The glen lies deep in the mountains. A cascade tumbles down the side of a mighty crag on the one hand: on the other sits a monstrous owl

on the branch of a blasted tree, blinking evilly.   A
path leads steeply down to a great cave.   The
moon throws a lurid light on the scene and shows us
Caspar in his shirt-sleeves preparing for his infernal
work.   He arranges black stones in a circle around
ı skull.   His tools lie beside him: a ladle, bullet-
mould, and eagle's-wing fan.   The high voices of
an invisible chorus utter the cry of the owl, which
the orchestra mixes with gruesome sounds, while
bass voices monotonously chant: —

> Poisoned dew the moon hath shed,
> Spider's web is dyed with red;
> Ere to-morrow's sun hath died
> Death will wed another bride.
> Ere the moon her course has run
> Deeds of darkness will be done.[1]

On the last stroke of a distant bell which rings
midnight, *Caspar* thrusts his hunting-knife into the
skull, raises it on high, turns around three times,
and summons his familiar: —

> By th' enchanter's skull, oh, hear,
> *Samiel, Samiel*, appear !

The demon answers in person, and the reason of
Caspar's temptation of *Max* is made plain.   He has
sold himself to the devil for the charmed bullets, the
last of which had brought down the eagle, and the
time for the delivery of his soul is to come on the
morrow.   He asks a respite on the promise to deliver
another victim into the demon's hands, — his com-

[1] Natalia Macfarren's translation.

panion *Max*.   What, asks the *Black Huntsman*, is
the proffered victim's desire?   The magical bullets.

> Sechse treffen,
> Sieben äffen !

warns *Samiel*, and *Caspar* suggests that the seventh
bullet be directed to the heart of the bride; her death
would drive both lover and father to despair.   But
Samiel says that as yet he has no power over the
maiden; he will claim his victim on the morrow,
Max or him who is already his bondsman.   *Caspar*
prepares for the moulding.   The skull disappears, and
in its place rises a small furnace in which fagots
are aglow.   Ghostly birds, perched on the trees
round about in the unhallowed spot, fan the fire with
their wings.   *Max* appears on a crag on one side of
the glen and gazes down.   The sights and sounds
below affright him; but he summons up his courage
and descends part way.   Suddenly his steps are
arrested by a vision of his dead mother, who appears
on the opposite side of the gulch and raises her
hand warningly.   *Caspar* mutters a prayer for help
to the fiend and bids *Max* look again.   Now the
figure is that of *Agathe*, who seems about to throw
herself into the mountain torrent.   The sight
nerves him and he hurries down.   The moon enters
into an eclipse, and *Caspar* begins his infernal work
after cautioning *Max* not to enter the circle nor
utter a word, no matter what he sees or who comes
to join them.   Into the melting-pot *Caspar* now puts
the ingredients of the charm: some lead, bits of

broken glass from a church window, a bit of mer-
cury, three bullets that have already hit their mark,
the right eye of a lapwing, the left of a lynx; then
speaks the conjuration formula: —

> Thou who roamst at midnight hour,
> *Samiel, Samiel,* thy pow'r !
> Spirit dread, be near this night
> And complete the mystic rite.
> By the shade of murderer's dead,
> Do thou bless the charmèd lead.
> Seven the number we revere;
> *Samiel, Samiel,* appear !

The contents of the ladle commence to hiss and
burn with a greenish flame; a cloud obscures the
moon wholly, and the scene is lighted only by
the fire under the melting-pot, the owl's eyes, and the
phosphorescent glow of the decaying oaks. As he
casts the bullets, *Caspar* calls out their number,
which the echoes repeat. Strange phenomena accompany each moulding; night-birds come flying
from the dark woods and gather around the fire; a
black boar crashes through the bushes and rushes
through the glen; a hurricane hurtles through the
trees, breaking their tops and scattering the sparks
from the furnace; four fiery wheels roll by; the Wild
Hunt dashes through the air; thunder, lightning,
and hail fill the air, flames dart from the earth, and
meteors fall from the sky; at the last the *Black
Hunter* himself appears and grasps at *Max's* hand;
the forester crosses himself and falls to the earth,
where *Caspar* already lies stretched out uncon-

scious. *Samiel* disappears, and the tempest abates.
Max raises himself convulsively and finds his companion still lying on the ground face downward.

At the beginning of the third act the wedding day
has dawned. It finds *Agathe* kneeling in prayer
robed for the wedding. She sings a cavatina ("Und
ob die Wolken sie verhülle") which proclaims her
trust in Providence. *Aennchen* twits her for having
wept; but "bride's tears and morning rain—neither
does for long remain." *Agathe* has been tortured by
a dream, and *Aennchen* volunteers to interpret it.
The bride had dreamt that she had been transformed
into a white dove and was flying from tree to tree
when *Max* discharged his gun at her. She fell
stricken, but immediately afterward was her own
proper self again and saw a monstrous black bird of
prey wallowing in its blood. *Aennchen* explains all
as reflexes of the incidents of the previous night —
the work on the white bridal dress, the terrible
black feather on *Max's* hat; and merrily tells a
ghostly tale of a nocturnal visitor to her sainted
aunt which turned out to be the watch-dog. Enter
the bridesmaids with their song: —

Wir win - den dir den Jung - fern-kranz mit
The bri - dal wreath for thee we bind, **With**

veil - chen - blau - er Sei - de,
silk - en thread of a - zure,

etc.

Nearly three generations of Germans have sung this song; it has accompanied them literally from the cradle to the grave. When Ludwig Geyer, Richard Wagner's stepfather, lay dying, the lad, then seven years old, was told to play the little piece in a room adjoining the sick chamber. The dying man had been concerned about the future of his stepson. He listened. "What if he should have talent for music?" Long years after the mother told this story, and the son, when he became famous as a composer, repeated it in one of his autobiographical writings, and told with what awe his childish eyes had looked on the composer as he passed by the door on the way to and from the theatre.

Evil omens pursue *Agathe* even on her bridal morn. The bridesmaids are still singing to her when *Aennchen* brings a box which she thinks contains the bridal wreath. All fall back in dismay when out comes a funeral wreath of black. Even *Aennchen's* high spirits are checked for a moment, but she finds an explanation. Old Cuno has tumbled from the wall a second time; but she herself assumes the blame: the nail was rusty and she not an adept with the hammer. The action now hastens to its close. *Prince Ottokar*, with his retainers, is present at the festival at which *Max* is to justify *Cuno's* choice of him as a son-in-law. The choice meets with the *Prince's* approval. The moment approaches for the trial shot, and *Max* stands looking at the last of his charmed bullets, which seems to weigh with ominous heaviness in his hand. He had taken four of the seven and *Caspar* three. Of the four he had spent three in unnecessary shots, but he hopes that *Caspar* has kept his. Of course *Caspar* has done nothing of the kind. It is suggested that *Max* shoot at once, not awaiting the arrival of his betrothed, lest the sight of her make him nervous. The *Prince* points to a white dove as the mark, and *Max* lifts his gun. At the moment *Agathe* rushes forward, crying, "Do not shoot; I am the dove!" The bird flies toward a tree which *Caspar*, impatient for the coming of his purposed victim, had climbed. *Max* follows it with his gun and pulls the trigger. *Agathe* and *Caspar* both fall to the ground. The holy man of the woods raises *Agathe*, who is unhurt; but *Caspar* dies with curses for everything upon his lips. The devil has cared for his own and claimed his forfeit. *Ottokar* orders his corpse thrown amongst the carrion in the Wolf's Glen and turns to *Max* for an explanation. He confesses his wrong and is ordered out of the *Prince's* dominion; but on the intercession of *Cuno*, *Agathe*, and the *Hermit* the sentence is commuted to a year of probation, at the end of which time he shall marry his love. But the traditional trial shot is abolished.

* * *

Though there are a dozen different points of view from which Weber's opera "Der Freischütz" is of fascinating interest, it is almost impossible for any one except a German to understand fully what the

opera means now to the people from whose loins
the composer sprung, and quite impossible to realize
what it meant to them at the time of its production.
"Der Freischütz" is spoken of in all the handbooks
as a "national" opera. There are others to which
the term might correctly and appropriately be
applied — German, French, Italian, Bohemian, Hungarian, Russian; but there never was an opera,
and there is no likelihood that there ever will be
one, so intimately bound up with the loves, feelings,
sentiments, emotions, superstitions, social customs,
and racial characteristics of a people as this is with
the loves, feelings, sentiments, emotions, superstitions, social customs, and racial characteristics of
the Germans. In all its elements as well as in its
history it is inextricably intertwined with the fibres
of German nationality. It could not have been
written at another time than it was; it could not
have been written by any other composer living at
that time; it could not have been conceived by
any artist not saturated with Germanism. It is possible to argue one's self into a belief of these things,
but only the German can feel them. Yet there is
no investigator of comparative mythology and religion who ought not to go to the story of the opera to
find an illustration of one of the pervasive laws of
his science; there is no folklorist who ought not to
be drawn to its subject; no student of politics and
sociology who cannot find valuable teachings in its
history; no critic who can afford to ignore its significance in connection with the evolution of musical

styles and schools; no biographer who can fail to
observe the kinship which the opera establishes
between the first operatic romanticist and him who
brought the romantic movement to its culmination;
that is, between Carl Maria von Weber and Richard
Wagner. It is even a fair subject for the study of
the scientific psychologist, for, though the story of
the opera is generally supposed to be a fanciful
structure reared on a legendary foundation, it was
a veritable happening which gave it currency a century ago and brought it to the notice of the composer; and this happening may have an explanation
in some of the psychical phenomena to which modern science is again directing attention, such as
hypnotism, animal magnetism, and the like.

I am here not at all fanciful. Some thirty years
ago I came across a pamphlet published by Dr.
J. G. Th. Grässe, a Saxon Court Councillor, in which
he traced the origin of the story at the base of "Der
Freischütz" to a confession made in open court in
a Bohemian town in 1710. Grässe found the story
in a book entitled "Monathliche Unterredungen aus
dem Reich der Geister," published in Leipsic in
1730, the author of which stated that he had drawn
the following statement of facts from judicial records: In 1710 in a town in Bohemia, George Schmid,
a clerk, eighteen years old, who was a passionate
lover of target-shooting, was persuaded by a hunter
to join in an enterprise for moulding charmed bullets
on July 30, the same being St. Abdon's Day. The
hunter promised to aid the young man in casting

sixty-three bullets, of which sixty were to hit in-
fallibly and three to miss just as certainly. The two
men provided themselves with coals, moulds, etc.,
and betook themselves at nightfall to a cross-roads.
There the hunter drew a circle with his knife and
placed mysterious characters, the meaning of which
his companion did not know, around the edge. This
done, he told the clerk to step within the ring, take
off his clothing, and make denial of God and the Holy
Trinity. The bullets, said the hunter, must all be
cast between eleven o'clock and midnight, or the
clerk would fall into the clutches of the devil. At
eleven o'clock the dead coals began to glow of their
own accord, and the two men began the moulding,
although all manner of ghostly apparitions tried to
hinder them. At last there came a horseman in
black, who demanded the bullets which had been
cast. The hunter refused to yield them up, and in
revenge the horseman threw something into the fire
which sent out so noisome an odor that the two
venturesome men fell half dead within the circle.
The hunter escaped, and, as it turned out subse-
quently, betook himself to the Salzkammergut, near
Salzburg; but the clerk was found lying at the cross-
roads and carried into town. There he made a
complete confession in court, and because he had
had intercourse with the Evil One, doubtless, was
condemned to be burned to death. In consideration
of his youth, however, the sentence was commuted
to imprisonment at hard labor for six years.

In the legend of the Wild Huntsman, who under

the name of Samiel purchases the souls of men with his magic bullets, the folklorist and student of the evolution of religions sees one of many evidences of ancient mythology perverted to bring it into the service of Christianity. Originally the Wild Huntsman was Odin (or Wotan). The missionaries to the Germans, finding it difficult to root out belief in the ancient deities, gave their attributes to saints in a few cases, but for the greater part transformed them into creatures of evil. It was thus that Frau Holle (or Holda) became a wicked Venus, as we shall see in the next chapter. The little spotted beetle which English and American children call ladybug or lady-bird (that is, the bug or bird of our Lady), the Germans *Marienkäferchen*, and the French *La bête du bon Dieu*, was sacred to Holda; and though the name of the Virgin Mary was bestowed upon it in the long ago, it still remains a love oracle, as the little ones know who bid it —

> Fly to the East,
> And fly to the West,
> And fly to the one that I love best !

It was the noise of Wotan's hunting train which the ancient Germans heard when the storms of winter howled and whistled through the deep woods of the Northland; but in time it came to be the noise of the Wild Hunt. In Thuringia the rout headed by Frau Holda and the Wild Huntsman issues in the Yuletide from the cave in the Hörselberg, which is the scene of *Tannhäuser's* adventure with *Venus* in Wagner's opera, and Holda is the mother of many of the uncanny creatures which strike terror to the souls of the unlucky huntsmen who chance to espy them.

From the story drawn from the records of the Bohemian law court, it is plain that to make a compact with the Wild Huntsman was a much more gruesome and ceremonious proceeding than that which took place between *Faust* and the Evil One in the operas of Gounod and Boito. In both these instances a scratch of the pen sufficed, and the deliberations which preceded the agreement were conducted in a decorous and businesslike manner. But to invoke Samiel and obtain his gifts was a body, mind, and nerve-racking business. In some particulars the details differed a little from those testified to by the Bohemian clerk. In the first place, the Devil's customer had to repair to a crossroads of a Friday between midnight and one o'clock when the moon was in an eclipse and the sun in Sagittarius. If in such a place and at such a time he drew a circle around himself with his hunting-spear and called "Samiel!" three times, that worthy would appear, and a bargain might be driven with him for his wares, which consisted of seven magical bullets ("free bullets," they were called), which were then cast under the eye of the Evil One and received his "blessing." The course of six of them rested with the "free shooter," but the seventh belonged to Samiel, who might direct it wheresoever he wished. The price of these bullets was the soul of the man who moulded them, at the end of three years; but it was the privilege of the bondsman to purchase a respite before the expiration of the period by delivering another soul into the clutches of the demon.

Weber used all these details in his opera, and added to them the fantastic terrors of the Wild Hunt and the Wolf's Glen. Of this favored abode of the Evil One, Wagner gave a vivid description in an essay on "Der Freischütz" which he wrote for the *Gazette musicale* in May, 1841, when the opera was preparing, under the hand of Berlioz, for representation at the Grand Opéra in Paris. Wagner's purpose in writing the essay was to acquaint the Parisians with the contents and spirit of the piece, make them understand its naïve Teutonism, and also to s we it from the maltreatment and mutilation which he knew it would have to suffer if it were to be made to conform to the conventions of the Académie. He wanted to preserve the spoken dialogue and keep out the regulation ballet, for the sake of which he had to make changes in his "Tannhäuser" twenty years later. He failed in both efforts, and afterward wrote an account of the performance for a German newspaper, which is one of the best specimens of the feuilleton style which his sojourn in Paris provoked. There was no need of telling his countrymen what the Wolf's Glen was, for it had been the most familiar of all scenes in the lyric theatres of Germany for a score of years, but for the Parisians he pictured the place in which Weber's hero meets *Samiel* very graphically indeed: —

The Wolf's Glen Scene in "Der Freischütz"
As represented at the Metropolitan Opera-House, New York

"In the heart of the Bohemian Forest, old as the world, lies the Wolf's Glen. Its legend lingered till the Thirty Years' War, which destroyed the last traces of German grandeur; but now, like many another boding memory, it has died out from the folk. Even at that time most men only knew the gulch by hearsay. They would relate how some gamekeeper, straying on indeterminable paths through wild, untrodden thickets, scarce knowing how, had come to the brink of the Wolf's Gulch. Returning, he had told of gruesome sights he had there seen, at which the hearer crossed himself and prayed the saints to shield him from ever wandering to that region. Even on his approach the keeper had heard an eerie sound; though the wind was still, a muffled moaning filled the branches of the ancient pines, which bowed their dark heads to and fro unbidden. Arrived at the verge, he had looked down into an abyss whose depths his eye could never plumb. Jagged reefs of rock stood high in shape of human limbs and terribly distorted faces. Beside them heaps of pitch-black stones in form of giant toads and lizards; they moved and crept and rolled in heavy ragged masses; but under them the ground could no more be distinguished. From thence foul vapors rose incessantly and spread a pestilential stench around. Here and there they would divide and range themselves in ranks that took the form of human beings with faces all convulsed. Upon a rotting tree-trunk in the midst of all these horrors sat an enormous owl, torpid in its daytime roost; behind it a frowning cavern, guarded by two monsters direly blent of snake and toad and lizard. These, with all the other seeming life the chasm harbored, lay in deathlike slumber, and any movement visible was that of one plunged in deep dreams; so that the forester had dismal fears of what this odious crew might wake into at midnight.

"But still more horrible than what he saw, was what he heard. A storm that stirred nothing, and whose gusts he himself could not feel, howled over the glen, paused suddenly, as if listening to itself, and then broke out again with added fury. Atrocious cries thronged from the pit; then a flock of countless birds of prey ascended from its bowels, spread like a pitch-black pall across the gulf, and fell back again into night. The screeches sounded to the huntsman like the groans of souls condemned, and tore his heart with anguish never felt before. Never had he heard such cries, compared to which the croak of ravens was as the song of nightingales. And now again deep silence; all motion ceased; only in the depths there seemed a sluggish writhing, and the owl flapped its wings as though in a dream. The most undaunted huntsman, the best acquainted with the wood's nocturnal terrors, fled like a timid roe in speechless agony, and, heedless where his footsteps bore him, ran breathless to the nearest hut, the nearest cabin, to meet some human soul to whom to tell his horrible adventure, yet ne'er could find words in which to frame it." [1]

[1] "Richard Wagner's Prose Works," translated by William Ashton Ellis, Vol. VII, p. 169

So much for the folklore and mythology of "Der Freischütz," the element which makes it not only a national but also the chiefest of romantic operas. We are grown careless in our use of musical terms, or else it would not be necessary to devote words to an explanation of what is meant by romantic in this case. We hear a great deal about romanticism as contradistinguished from classicism, but it is seldom that we have the line of demarcation between the two tendencies or schools drawn for us. Classical composers, I am inclined to think, are composers of the first rank who have developed music to its highest perfection on its formal side in obedience to long and widely accepted laws, preferring æsthetic beauty over emotional content, or, at any rate, refusing to sacrifice form to characteristic expression. Romantic composers would then be those who have sought their ideals in other directions and striven to give them expression irrespective of the restrictions and limitations of form — composers who, in short, prefer content to manner. In the sense of these definitions, Weber's opera is a classic work, for in it the old forms which Wagner's influence destroyed are preserved. Nevertheless, "Der Freischütz" is romantic in a very particular sense, and it is in this romanticism that its political significance to which I have referred lies. It is romantic in subject and the source of its inspiration. This source is the same to which the creators of the romantic school of literature went for its subjects — the fantastical stories of chivalry and knighthood, of which the principal elements were the marvellous and supernatural. The literary romanticists did a great deal to encourage patriotism among the Germans in the beginning of the nineteenth century by disclosing to the German people the wealth of their legendary lore and the beauty of their folk-songs. The circumstances which established the artistic kinship between Von Weber and Wagner, to which I have alluded, was a direct fruit of this patriotism. In 1813 Von Weber went to Prague to organize a German opera. A part of the following summer he spent in Berlin. Prussia was leading Europe in the effort to throw off the yoke of Bonaparte, and the youths of the Prussian capital, especially the students, were drunken with the wine of Körner's "Lyre and Sword." While returning to Prague Von Weber stopped for a while at the castle Gräfen-Tonna, where he composed some of Körner's poems, among them "Lützow's wilde Jagd" and the "Schwertlied." These songs were soon in everybody's mouth and acted like sparks flung into the powder-magazine of national feeling. Naturally they reacted upon the composer himself, and under their influence and the spirit which they did so much to foster Weber's Germanism developed from an emotion into a religion. He worked with redoubled zeal in behalf of German opera at Prague, and when he was called to be Court Music Director in Dresden in 1817, he entered upon his duties as if consecrated to a holy task. He had found

the conditions more favorable to German opera
in the Bohemian capital than in the Saxon. In
Prague he had sloth and indifference to overcome,
in Dresden the obstacles were hatred of Prussia, the
tastes of a court and people long accustomed to
Italian traditions, and the intrigues of his colleagues
in the Italian opera and the church. What I wrote
some eighteen years ago [1] of Weber's labors in Dresden may serve again to make plain how the militant Germanism of the composer achieved its great
triumph.

The Italian régime was maintained in Dresden
through the efforts of the conductor of the Italian
opera, Morlacchi; the concert master, Poledro;
the church composer, Schubert, and Count von
Einsiedel, Cabinet Minister. The efforts of these
men placed innumerable obstacles in Weber's path,
and their influence heaped humiliations upon him.
Confidence alone in the ultimate success of his efforts
to regenerate the lyric drama sustained him in his
trials. Against the merely sensuous charm of suave
melody and lovely singing he opposed truthfulness
of feeling and conscientious endeavor for the attainment of a perfect ensemble. Here his powers
of organization, trained by his experiences in Prague,
his perfect knowledge of the stage, imbibed with his
mother's milk, and his unquenchable zeal, gave him
amazing puissance. Thoroughness was his watch-
word. He put aside the old custom of conducting
while seated at the pianoforte, and appeared before

[1] "Famous Composers and their Works," Vol. I, p. 396

his players with a bâton. He was an inspiration, not a figurehead. His mind and his emotions dominated theirs, and were published in the performance. He raised the standard of the chorus, stimulated the actors, inspected the stage furnishings and costumes, and stamped harmony of feeling, harmony of understanding, and harmony of effort upon the first work undertaken — a performance of Méhul's "Joseph in Egypt." Nor did he confine his educational efforts to the people of the theatre. He continued in Dresden the plan first put into practice by him in Prague of printing articles about new operas in the newspapers to stimulate public appreciation of their characteristics and beauties. For a while the work of organization checked his creative energies, but when his duties touching new music for court or church functions gave him the opportunity, he wrote with undiminished energy.

In 1810 Apel's "Gespensterbuch" had fallen into his hands and he had marked the story of "Der Freischütz" for treatment. His mind reverted to it again in the spring of 1817. Friedrich Kind agreed to write the book, and placed it complete in his hands on March 1, nine days after he had undertaken the commission. Weber's enthusiasm was great, but circumstances prevented him from devoting much time to the composition of the opera. He wrote the first of its music in July, 1817, but did not complete it till May 13, 1820. It was in his mind during all this period, however, and would doubtless have been finished much earlier had he received an order to write an opera from the Saxon court. In this expectation he was disappointed, and the honor of having encouraged the production of the most national opera ever written went to Berlin, where the patriotism which had been warmed by Weber's setting of Körner's songs was still ablaze, and where Count Brühl's plans were discussing to bring him to the Prussian capital as Capellmeister. The opera was given on June 18, 1821, under circumstances that produced intense excitement in the minds of Weber's friends. The sympathies of the musical areopagus of Berlin were not with Weber or his work — neither before nor after the first performance; but Weber spoke to the popular heart, and its quick, responsive throb lifted him at once to the crest of the wave which soon deluged all Germany. The overture had to be repeated to still the applause that followed its first performance, and when the curtain fell on the las scene, a new chapter in German art had been opened.[1]

[1] As I write it is nearly eighty-five years since "Der Freischütz" was first heard in New York. The place was the Park Theatre and the date March 2, 1825. The opera was only four years old at the time, and, in conformity with the custom of the period, the representation, which was in English, no doubt was a very different affair from that to which the public has become accustomed since. But it is interesting to know that there is at least one opera in the Metropolitan list which antedates the first Italian performance ever given in America. Even at that early day the scene in the Wolf's Glen created a sensation. The world over "Der Freischütz" is looked upon as peculiarly the property of the Germans, but a German performance of it was not heard in New York till 1856, when the opera was brought out under the direction of Carl Bergmann, at the old Broadway Theatre.

CHAPTER XII

"TANNHÄUSER"

NOTHING could have demonstrated more perfectly the righteousness of Wagner's claim to the title of poet than his acceptance of the Greek theory that a people's legends and myths are the fittest subjects for dramatic treatment, unless it be the manner in which he has reshaped his material in order to infuse it with that deep ethical principle to which reference has several times been made. In "The Flying Dutchman," "The Nibelung's Ring," and "Tannhäuser" the idea is practically his creation. In the last of these dramas it is evolved out of the simple episode in the parent-legend of the death of Lisaura, whose heart broke when her knight went to kiss the Queen of Love and Beauty. The dissolute knight of the old story Wagner in turn metamorphoses into a type of manhood "in its passionate desires and ideal aspirations" — the *Faust* of Goethe. All the magnificent energy of our ideal man is brought forward in the poet's conception, but it is an energy which is shattered in its fluctuation between sensual delights and ideal aspirations, respectively typified in the *Venus* and *Elizabeth* of the play. Here is the contradiction against which he was shattered as the heroes of Greek tragedy were shattered on the rock of implacable Fate. But the transcendent beauty of the modern drama is lent by the ethical idea of salvation through the love of pure woman — a salvation touching which no one can be in doubt when *Tannhäuser* sinks lifeless beside the bier of the atoning saint, and

Venus's cries of woe are swallowed up by the pious canticle of the returning pilgrims.[1]

It will be necessary in the expositions of the
lyric dramas of Wagner, which I shall attempt in
these chapters, to choose only such material as
will serve directly to help to an understanding of
them as they move by the senses in the theatre,
leaving the reader to consult the commentaries,
which are plentiful, for deeper study of the composer's methods and philosophical purposes. Such
study is not to be despised; but, unless it be wisely
conducted, it is likely to be a hindrance rather
than a help to enjoyment. It is a too common
error of musical amateurs to devote their attention
to the forms and names of the phrases out of which
Wagner constructs his musical fabric, especially
that of his later dramas. This tendency has been
humored, even in the case of the earlier operas, by
pedants, who have given names to the themes which
the composer used, though he had not yet begun
to apply the system of symbolization which marks
his works beginning with "Tristan und Isolde."
It has been done with "Tannhäuser," though it
is, to all intents and purposes, an opera of the conventional type, and not what is called a "music-
drama." The reminiscent use of themes is much
older than Wagner. It is well to familiarize one's

[1] "Studies in the Wagnerian Drama," by H. E. Krehbiel.
pp. 35, 36.

self with the characteristic elements of a score,
but, as I have urged in the book quoted above,
if we confine our study of Wagner to the forms of
the musical motives and the names which have
arbitrarily been given to them, we shall at the last
have enriched our minds with a thematic catalogue,
and nothing else. It is better to know nothing
about these names, and content ourselves with
simple, sensuous enjoyment, than to spend our time
at the theatre answering the baldest of all the riddles
of Wagner's orchestra: "What am I playing now?"
In the studies of Wagner's works I shall point to
some of the most significant phrases in the music
in connection with significant occurrences in the
play, but I shall seldom, if ever, analyze the motival
construction in the style of the Wolzogen handbooks.

* * *

There are texts in the prefatory excerpt for a
discussion of "Tannhäuser" from all the points
of view which might make such a discussion interesting and profitable. There is no doubt in my
mind that it is the poet-composer's noblest tragedy
and, from a literary point of view, his most artistic.
It is laid out on such a broad, simple, and symmetri-
cal plan that its dramatic contents can be set forth
in a few paragraphs, and we can easily forego a de-
tailed description of its scenes. A knightly minstrel,
who has taken part in one of the tournaments of
song which tradition says used to be held at the
court of the Landgrave of Thuringia in the early

part of the thirteenth century, has, by his song and bearing, won the heart of *Elizabeth*, niece of the *Landgrave*. Unmindful of his great good fortune, he has found his way to the court held by the God dess of Love within the hollow of the Hörselberg, which lies across the valley and over against the Wartburg. *Dame Venus* herself becomes enamoured of the knight, who calls himself *Tannhäuser*, and for a year and a day he remains at her side and in her arms. At length, mind and senses surfeited, a longing seizes him for the world which he has abandoned, for the refreshing sights and sounds of earth, and even for its pains. *Dame Venus* seeks to detain him, but he is resolute to leave her and her realm. Like a true knight, however, he promises to sing her praises wherever he may go; but when she offers to welcome him again if he should weary and sicken of the world and seek redemption from its hypocrisies, he replies that for him redemption rests only in the Virgin Mary. The invocation breaks the bonds of enchantment which have held him. The scenes of allurement which have so long surrounded him melt away, and he finds himself in an attitude of prayer in a blooming valley below the Wartburg. It is spring, and a shepherd lad, seated on a rock, trolls a lay to spring's goddess. A troop of pilgrims passing by on their way to Rome suggest by their canticle the need of absolution from the burden of sin which rests upon him, but before he can join them, the *Landgrave* and a hunting party come upon him. He is recognized by his erstwhile companions in song, and consents to return to the castle on being told by one of the minstrels, *Wolfram von Eschenbach*, that his song had vanquished not only them, but the heart of the saintly *Elizabeth* as well.

In the Wartburg *Tannhäuser* meets the maiden whose heart he has won just after she has apostrophized the walls which had echoed his voice; and from him she learns the meaning of the strange emotion which fills her in his presence. Again minstrels gather before a company of great nobles for a contest in the Hall of Song. Love is to be the theme, and the hand of *Elizabeth* the reward of the victor. Spiritual love is hymned by *Tannhäuser's* companions. *Wolfram von Eschenbach* likens it to a pure fountain from which only high and sacred feelings can flow. *Tannhäuser* questions the right of those who have not experienced the passion as he has felt it to define the nature of love. Goaded by the taunts and threats of rude *Biterolf*, he bursts forth in a praise of Venus. The assembly is in commotion. Swords are drawn. Sacrilege must be punished. Death confronts the impiously daring minstrel. But *Elizabeth*, whose heart has been mortally pierced by his words, interposes to save him. She has been stricken, but what is that to his danger of everlasting damnation? Would they rob his soul of its eternal welfare? The knight, indifferent to a score of swords, is crushed by such unselfish devotion, and humbly accepts the *Landgrave's* clemency, which spares his life that he may join a younger band of pilgrims and seek absolution at Rome. He goes to the Holy City, mortifying his flesh at every step, and humbles himself in self-abasement and accusation before the Pope; but only to hear from the hard lips of the Keeper of the Keys that for such sin as his there is as little hope of deliverance as for the rebudding of the papal staff.

The elder pilgrims return in the fall of the year, and *Elizabeth* eagerly seeks among them for the face of the knight whose soul and body she had tried to save. He is not among them. Gently she puts aside the proffered help of *Wolfram,* whose unselfish love is ever with her, climbs the hill to the castle, and dies. Famished and footsore, *Tannhäuser* staggers after the band of pilgrims who have returned to their homes with sins forgiven. His greeting of *Wolfram* is harsh, but the good minstrel's sympathy constrains him to tell the story of his vain pilgrimage. Salvation forfeited, naught is left for him but to seek surcease of suffering in the arms of *Venus.* Again he sees her grotto streaming with roseate light and hears her alluring voice. He rushes forward toward the scene of enchantment, but *Wolfram* utters again the name of her who is now pleading for him before the judgment seat of God Himself; and he reels back. A funeral cortège descends from the castle. With an agonized cry: "Holy *Elizabeth,* pray for me!" *Tannhäuser* sinks lifeless beside the bier just as the band of younger pilgrims comes from Rome bearing the crozier of the Pope clothed in fresh verdure. They hymn the miracle of redemption.

Wagner has himself told us what fancies he is willing shall flit through the minds of listeners to the overture to his opera. It was performed at a concert under his direction while he was a political refugee at Zurich, and for the programme of the concert he wrote a synopsis of its musical and poetical contents which I shall give here in the translation made by William Ashton Ellis, but with the beginnings of the themes which are referred to reproduced in musical notes: —

To begin with, the orchestra leads before us the pilgrims' chant alone: —

it draws near, then swells into a mighty outpour and passes, finally, away. Evenfall; last echo of the chant. As night breaks, magic sights and sounds appear, the whirlings of a fearsomely voluptuous dance are seen: —

These are the Venusberg's seductive spells that show
themselves at dead of night to those whose breasts are
fired by daring of the senses. Attracted by the tempting
show, a shapely human form draws nigh; 'tis *Tannhäuser*,
love's minstrel. He sounds his jubilant song of love

in joyous challenge, as though to force the wanton witch-
ery to do his bidding. Wild cries of riot answer him; the
rosy cloud grows denser round him; entrancing perfumes
hem him in and steal away his senses. In the most
seductive of half-lights his wonder-seeing eye beholds
a female form indicible; he hears a voice that sweetly
murmurs out the siren call, which promises contentment
of the darer's wildest wishes: —

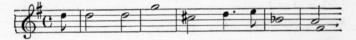

Venus herself it is, this woman who appears to him.
Then the heart and senses burn within him; a fierce, de-
vouring passion fires the blood in all his veins; with
irresistible constraint it thrusts him nearer; before the
goddess's self he steps with that canticle of love triumphant,
and now he sings it in ecstatic praise of her. As though
at wizard spell of his, the wonders of the Venusberg unroll
their brightest fill before him; tumultuous shouts and
savage cries of joy mount up on every hand; in drunken
glee bacchantes drive their raging dance and drag *Tannhäuser* to the warm caresses of love's goddess, who throws
her glowing arms around the mortal, drowned with bliss,
and bears him where no step dare tread, to the realm of
Being-no-more.

A scurry, like the sound of the wild hunt, and speedily
the storm is laid. Merely a wanton whir still pulses in
the breeze, a wave of weird voluptuousness, like the sensuous breath of unblest love, still soughs above the spot
where impious charms had shed their raptures and over
which the night now broods once more. But dawn
begins to break; already from afar is heard again the
pilgrims' chant. As this chant draws closer and closer,
as the day drives farther back the night, that whir and
soughing of the air — which had erewhile sounded like
the eerie cry of souls condemned — now rises to ever
gladder waves, so that when the sun ascends at last in
splendor and the pilgrims' chant proclaims in ecstasy to
all the world, to all that live and move thereon, salvation won, this wave itself swells out the tidings of sub-
limest joy. 'Tis the carol of the Venusberg itself redeemed from curse of impiousness, this cry we hear amid
the hymn of God. So wells and leaps each pulse of life
in chorus of redemption, and both dissevered elements,
both soul and senses, God and nature, unite in the atoning
kiss of hallowed love.

This description of the poetical contents of the
overture to "Tannhäuser" applies to the ordinary
form of the introduction to the opera which was
used (and still is in many cases) until Wagner revised the opera for performance in Paris in 1861.
The traditions of French opera called for a ballet
in the third act. Wagner was willing to yield to
the desire for a ballet, but he could not place it
where the habits of the opera-going public demanded
it. Instead, he remodelled the overture and, sacrificing the *coda* which brought back a return of the
canticle of the pilgrims, he lengthened the middle
portion to fit an extended choreographic scene, and

with it led into the opera without a break. The neglect to provide a ballet in the usual place led to a tremendous disturbance in which the Jockey Club took the lead. Wagner's purpose in the extended portion of the overture now called the "Bacchanale" may be read in his stage-directions for the scene.

The scene represents the interior of the Venusberg (Hörselberg), in the neighborhood of Eisenach. A large cave seems to extend to an invisible distance at a turn to the right. From a cleft through which the pale light of day penetrates, a green waterfall tumbles foaming over rocks the entire length of the cave. From the basin which receives the water, a brook flows toward the background, where it spreads out into a lake, in which naiads are seen bathing and on the banks of which sirens are reclining. On both sides of the grotto are rocky projections of irregular form, overgrown with singular, coral-like tropical plants. Before an opening extending upward on the left, from which a rosy twilight enters, *Venus* lies upon a rich couch; before her, his head upon her lap, his harp by his side, half kneeling, reclines *Tannhäuser*. Surrounding the couch in fascinating embrace are the *Three Graces;* beside and behind the couch innumerable sleeping amorettes, in attitudes of wild disorder, like children who had fallen asleep wearied with the exertions of a struggle. The entire foreground is illumined by a magical, ruddy light shining upward from below, through which the emerald green of the waterfall, with its white foam, penetrates. The distant background, with the shores of the lake, seems transfigured by a sort of moonlight. When the curtain rises, youths, reclining on the rocky projections, answering the beckonings of the nymphs, hurry down to them; beside the basin of the waterfall the nymphs have begun the dance designed to lure the

youths to them.   They pair off; flight and chase enliven
the dance.

From the distant background a procession of bacchantes
approach, rushing through the rows of the loving couples
and stimulating them to wilder pleasures.   With gestures
of enthusiastic intoxication they tempt the lovers to growing recklessness.   Satyrs and fauns have appeared from the
cleft of the rocks and, dancing the while, force their way
between the bacchantes and lovers, increasing the disorder by chasing the nymphs.   The tumult reaches its
height, whereupon the *Graces* rise in horror and seek
to put a stop to the wild conduct of the dancing rout and
drive the mad roisterers from the scene.   Fearful that
they themselves might be drawn into the whirlpool, they
turn to the sleeping amorettes and drive them aloft.
They flutter about, then gather into ranks on high, filling
the upper spaces of the cave, whence they send down a
hail of arrows upon the wild revellers.   These, wounded
by the arrows, filled with a mighty love-longing, cease
their dance and sink down exhausted.   The *Graces*
capture the wounded and seek, while separating the in-
toxicated ones into pairs, to scatter them in the background.   Then, still pursued by the flying amorettes, the
bacchantes. fauns, satyrs, nymphs, and youths depart
in various directions.   A rosy mist, growing more and
more dense, sinks down, hiding first the amorettes and
then the entire background, so that finally only *Venus*,
Tannhäuser, and the *Graces* remain visible.   The *Graces*
now turn their faces to the foreground; gracefully intertwined, they approach *Venus*, seemingly informing her of
the victory they have won over the mad passions of her
subjects.

The dense mist in the background is dissipated, and
a tableau, a cloud picture, shows the rape of Europa, who,
sitting on the back of a bull decorated with flowers and
led by tritons and nereids, sails across the blue lake.

Fac-simile of Wagner's Autograph of a Page of the Bacchanale in "Tannhäuser," arranged for Two Violins for the Ballet Master at the Paris Grand Opéra.

Song of the Sirens:—

The rosy mist shuts down, the picture disappears, and
the *Graces* suggest by an ingratiating dance the secret
significance that it was an achievement of love. Again
the mists move about. In the pale moonlight Leda is
discovered reclining by the side of the forest lake; the
swan swims toward her and caressingly lays his head
upon her breast. Gradually this picture also disappears
and, the mist blown away, discloses the grotto deserted
and silent. The *Graces* courtesy mischievously to *Venus*
and slowly leave the grotto of love. Deepest silence.
(The duet between *Venus* and *Tannhäuser* begins.)

The work which Wagner accomplished in behalf
of the legend of Tannhäuser is fairly comparable
with the tales which have been woven around the
figure of King Arthur. The stories of the Knights
of the Round Table are in the mouths of all English-
speaking peoples because of the "Idylls of the King";
the legend of Tannhäuser was saved from becoming
the exclusive property of German literary students

by Wagner's opera. Like many folk-tales, the
story touches historical circumstance in part, and
for the rest reaches far into the shadowy realm of
legendary lore. The historical element is compassed
by the fact that the principal human characters
involved in it once had existence. There was a
Landgrave Hermann of Thuringia whose court was
held in the Wartburg — that noble castle which in
a later century gave shelter to Martin Luther while
he endowed the German people with a reformed
religion, their version of the Bible and a literary
language. The minstrel knights, which in the opera
meet in a contest of song, also belong to history.
Wolfram von Eschenbach wrote the version of the
Quest of tne Holy Grail which inspired Wagner's
"Parsifal" and which is morally the most exalted
epical form which that legend ever received. His
companions also existed. Tannhäuser is not an
invention, though it is to Wagner alone that we
owe his association with the famous contest of
minstrelsy which is the middle picture in Wagner's
drama. Of the veritable Tannhäuser, we know extremely little. He was a knight and minstrel at
the court of Duke Frederick II of Austria in the first
decades of the thirteenth century, who, it is said,
led a dissolute life, squandered his fortune, and
wrecked his health, but did timely penance at the
end and failed not of the consolations of Holy Church.
After he had lost his estate near Vienna he found
protection with Otto II of Bavaria, who was Stadt-
holder of Austria from A.D. 1246 till his death in

THE CONTEST OF MINSTRELS IN THE WARTBURG
(From the Manessian Ms. in Heidelberg)

(Above, from left to right: Landgravine Sophia and Landgrave
Hermann of Thuringia.

Below: Herr Biterolf, Wolfram von Eschenbach, Heinrich von
Ofterdingen, Klingesor von Ungarland, Reinmar der Alte, Walther
von der Vogelweide, Heinrich von Rispach.)

234

1253. He sang the praises of Otto's son-in-law, Conrad IV, who was father of Conradin, the last heir of the Hohenstaufens. Tannhäuser was therefore a Ghibelline, as was plainly the folk-poet who made him the hero of the ballad which tells of his adventure with Venus. Tannhäuser's extant poems, when not in praise of princes, are gay in character, with the exception of a penitential hymn — a circumstance which may have had some weight with the ballad-makers. There is a picture labelled with his name in a famous collection of minnesongs called the Manessian Manuscript, which shows him with the Crusaders' cross upon his cloak. This may be looked upon as evidence that he took part in one of the crusades, probably that of A.D. 1228. There is no evidence that the contest of minstrelsy at the Wartburg ever took place. It seems to have been an invention of mediæval poets. The Manessian Manuscript is embellished with a picture of the principal personages connected with the story. They are Landgrave Hermann, the Landgravine Sophia, Wolfram von Eschenbach, Reinmar der Alte, Heinrich von Rispach, Biterolf, Heinrich von Ofterdingen, and Klingesor. The subject discussed by the minstrels was scholastic, and Ofterdingen, to save his life, sought help of Klingesor, who was a magician and the reputed nephew of Virgilius of Naples; and the Landgravine threw her cloak around him when he was hardest pressed. This incident, its ethical significance marvellously enhanced, is the culmination of Wagner's second act.

Instead of the historical Sophia, however, we have
in the opera Hermann's niece, Elizabeth, a creation of the poet's, though modelled apparently after
the sainted Elizabeth of Hungary, who, however,
had scarcely opened her eyes upon the world in
the Wartburg at the date ascribed to the contest,
i.e. A.D. 1206. Wagner has given the rôle played
by Heinrich von Ofterdingen (also Effterdingen) to
Tannhäuser apparently on the strength of an essay
which appeared about the time that he took up the
study of the mediæval legends of Germany, which
identified the two men. Ofterdingen himself is
now thought to be a creation of some poet's fancy;
but the large part devoted to his adventure in the
old poem which tells of the contest of minstrelsy
led the mediæval poets to attribute many great
literary deeds to him, one of them nothing less than
the authorship of the "Nibelungenlied."

Wagner seems to have been under the impression
that there was an old book of folk-tales (a so-called
Volksbuch) devoted to the story of Tannhäuser and
his adventure with Dame Venus. This is a mistake.
The legend came down to modern times by way of
popular ballads. One of these, which was printed
by Uhland, consists largely of the dialogue between
Tannhäuser and his enslaver, as does also the carnival
play which Hans Sachs wrote on the subject. The
writer of the ballad was so energetic an enemy of
the Papal power that he condemns Urban IV to
eternal torment because of his severe judgment of
the penitent sinner: —

Do was er widrumb in den berg
und het sein lieb erkoren,
des muoss der vierde babst Urban
auch ewig sein verloren.

A ballad which was sung in one Swiss district as
late as the third decade of the nineteenth century
gives the story of the knight and his temptress in
fuller detail, though it knows as little of the episode of Elizabeth's love as it does of the tournament of song. In this ballad Tannhäuser (or "Tan-
huser") is a goodly knight who goes out into the
forest to seek adventures, or "see wonders." He
finds a party of maidens engaged in a bewildering
dance, and tarries to enjoy the spectacle. Frau
Frene, or, as we would write it now, Freya (the
Norse Venus whose memory we perpetuate in our
Friday), seeks to persuade him to remain with her,
promising to give him her youngest daughter to
wife. The knight remains, but will not mate with
the maiden, for he has seen the devil lurking in
her brown eyes and learned that once in her toils
he will be lost forever. Lying under Frau Frene's
fig tree, at length, he dreams that he must quit his
sinful life. He tears himself loose from the enchantment and journeys to Rome, where he falls at the
feet of the Pope and asks absolution. The Pope
holds in his hand a staff so dry that it has split.
"Your sins are as little likely to be forgiven as this
staff is to green," is his harsh judgment. Tannhäuser kneels before the altar, extends his arms, and
asks mercy of Christ; then leaves the church in

despair and is lost to view. On the third day after
this the Pope's staff is found to be covered with
fresh leaves. He sends out messengers to find
Tannhäuser, but he has returned to Frau Frene.
Then comes the moral of the tale expressed with a
naïve forcefulness to which a translation cannot do
justice: —

> Drum soll kein Pfaff, kein Kardinal,
> Kein Sünder nie verdammen;
> Der Sünder mag sein so gross er will,
> Kann Gottes Gnad erlangen.

Two other sources supplied Wagner with material for as many effective scenes in his drama.
From E. T. A. Hofmann's "Der Kampf der Sänger"
he got the second scene of the first act, the hunt
and the gathering in the valley below Wartburg;
from Ludwig Tieck's "Der getreue Eckhart und
der Tannhäuser" the narrative of the minstrel's
pilgrimage to Rome.

Students of comparative mythology and folklore
will have no difficulty in seeing in the legend of
Tannhäuser one of the many tales of the association during a period of enchantment of men and
elves. Parallels between the theatre and apparatus
of these tales extend back into remote antiquity.
The grotto of Venus, in which Tannhäuser steeps
himself with sensuality, is but a German variant
of the Garden of Delight, in which the heroes of
antiquity met their fair enslavers. It is Ogygia,
the Delightful Island, where Ulysses met Calypso.
It is that Avalon in which King Arthur was healed

TANNHÄUSER AT THE BIER OF ELIZABETH

(After a painting by von Kaulbach)

of his wounds by his fairy sister Morgain. The crozier which bursts into green in token of Tannhäuser's forgiveness has prototypes in the lances which, when planted in the ground by Charlemagne's warriors, were transformed overnight into a leafy forest; in the javelins of Polydore, of which Virgil tells us in the "Æneid"; in the staff of St. Christopher, which grew into a tree after he had carried the Christ Child across the river; in the staff which put on leaves in the hands of Joseph, wherefore the Virgin Mary gave him her hand in marriage; in the rod of Aaron, which, when laid up among others in the tabernacle, "brought forth buds and bloomed blossoms and yielded almonds."

There are many parallels in classic story and folklore of the incident of Tannhäuser's sojourn with Venus. I mention but a few. There are the episodes of Ulysses and Calypso, Ulysses and Circe, Numa and Egeria, Rinaldo and Armida, Prince Ahmed and Peri Banou. Less familiar are the folktales which Mr. Baring-Gould has collected of Helgi's life with the troll Ingibjorg, a Norse story; of James Soideman of Serraade, "who was kept by the spirits in a mountain during the space of seven years, and at length came out, but lived afterwards in great distress and fear lest they should again take him away"; of the young Swede lured away by an elfin woman from the side of his bride into a mountain, where he abode with the siren forty years and thought it but an hour.

There are many Caves of Venus in Europe, but

none around which there clusters such a wealth of
legend as around the grotto in the Hörselberg.
Nineteen years ago the writer of this book visited the
scene and explored the cave.   He found it a decidedly
commonplace hole in the ground, but was richly
rewarded by the results of the literary explorations to which the visit led him.   Before Christianity
came to reconstruct the folk-tales of the Thuringian
peasants, the Hörselberg was the home of Dame
Holda, or Holle, and the horde of weird creatures
which used to go tearing through the German forests
on a wild rout in the Yuletide.   Dame Holle, like
many another character in Teutonic mythology,
was a benignant creature, whose blessing brought
forth fruitfulness to fields and vineyards, before the
Christian priests metamorphosed her into a thing
wholly of evil.   She was the mother of all the fays
and fairies that followed in the train of the Wild
Huntsman, and though she appeared at times as a
seductive siren and tempted men to their destruction,
she appeared oftener as an old woman who rewarded
acts of kindness with endless generosity.   It was
she who had in keeping the souls of unborn children,
and babes who died before they could be christened
were carried by her to the Jordan and baptized in its
waters.   Even after priestly sermons had transformed her into a beauteous she-devil, she still kept
up her residence in the cave, which now, in turn, took
on a new character.   Venturesome persons who got
near its mouth, either purposely or by accident,
told of strange noises which issued from it, like the

rushing of many waters or the voice of a subterranean storm. The priests supplied explanation and etymology to fit the new state of things. The noise was the lamentation of souls in the fires of purgatory, to which place of torment the cave was an opening. This was said to account for the old German name of the mountain — "Hör-Seel-Berg" — that is, "Hear-Souls-Mountain." To this Latin writers added another, viz. "Mons Horrisonus" — "the Mountain of Horrible Sounds." The forbidding appearance of the exterior — in which some fantastic writers avowed they saw a resemblance to a coffin — was no check on the fancy of the mediæval storyteller, however, who pictured the interior of the mountain as a marvellous palace, and filled it with glittering jewels and treasures incalculable. The story of Tannhäuser's sojourn within this magical cavern is only one of many, nor do they all end like that of the minstrel knight. Undeterred by the awful tales told by monks and priests, poets and romancers sang the glories and the pleasures of the cave as well as its gruesome punishments. From them we know many things concerning the appearance of the interior, the cave's inhabitants, and their merrymakings. I cannot resist the temptation to retell one of these old tales.

Adelbert, Knight of Thuringia, was one of those who experienced the delights of the Cave of Venus, yet, unlike Tannhäuser in the original legend, was saved at the last. He met Faithful Eckhart at the mouth of the cave, who warned him not to enter, but entrancing music sounded within and he was powerless to resist. He entered. Three maidens came forward to meet him. They were airily clad, flowers were twisted in their brown locks, and they waved branches before them as they smiled and beckoned and sang a song of spring's awakening. What could Sir Adelbert do but follow when they glanced coyly over their white shoulders and led the way through a narrow passage into a garden surrounded with rose-bushes in bloom, and filled with golden-haired maidens, lovelier than the flowers, who wandered about hand in hand and sang with sirens' voices? In the middle of the rose-hedged garden stood a red gate, which bore in bold letters this legend: —

HERE DAME VENUS HOLDS COURT

The gate-keeper was the fairest of the maidens, and her fingers were busy weaving a garland of roses, but she stopped her work long enough to smile a welcome to Sir Adelbert. He thanked her gallantly and queried: Was the pretty sight a May Day celebration? Replied the winsome gate-keeper: "Here Dame Venus holds court in honor of the noble knight Sir Tannhäuser"; and she opened the gate and Adelbert entered. Within he beheld a gay tent pitched in a grove of flowering shrubs, and out of it emerged a beauteous creature and advanced toward him. Her robe was rose color, adorned with strings of pearls and festooned with fragrant blossoms. A crown which glistened with gems rested lightly on her head. In her right hand — a dainty hand — she carried a tiny kerchief of filmy white stuff embroidered with gold, and in her left a lute. She sate herself down on a golden chair, bent her head over her left shoulder. A dreamy, tender light came into her eyes, and her rosy fingers sought the strings of her lute — strings of gold. Would she sing? Just then one of the maidens approached her, lisped musically into her ear, and pointed to the approaching knight. Almost imperceptibly, but oh, so graciously, the lips of the vision moved. As if in obedience to a command, the maiden approached, and said in rhythmical cadence: "Greetings, Sir Knight, from Dame Venus, who sends you message that all who love gaming and fair women are welcome at her court." She gave him her hand to escort him, and when the knight pressed her fingers in gratitude he felt a gentle pressure in return. The knight approached the dazzling queen of the palace and fell upon his knee; but she gave him her hand and she bade him arise, which he did after he had kissed her fingers. And she called to a maiden, who fetched a golden horn filled to the brim with wine and handed it to the knight. "Empty the goblet, like a true knight, to the health of all fair women who love and are beloved," said the queen. Sir Adelbert smiled obedience: "To love, fair lady," he said and drank the wine at a draught. And thus he became a captive and a slave.

Long did he sojourn within the magic realm, in loving dalliance with Venus and her maidens, until one day a hermit entered the cave in the absence of the queen and bore him back to the outer world, where penance and deeds of piety restored him to moral health and saved him from the fate of Tann-häuser.

CHAPTER XIII

"TRISTAN UND ISOLDE"

A VASSAL is sent to woo a beauteous princess for his
lord. While he is bringing her home the two, by accident,
drink a love potion, and ever thereafter their hearts are
fettered together. In the midday of delirious joy, in the
midnight of deepest woe, their thoughts are only of each
other, for each other. Meanwhile the princess has become the vassal's queen. Then the wicked love of
the pair is discovered, and the knight is obliged to
seek safety in a foreign land. There (strange note this
to our ears) he marries another princess whose name is
like that of his love, save for the addition With the White
Hand; but when wounded unto death he sends across
the water for her who is still his true love, that she come
and be his healer. The ship which is sent to bring her
is to bear white sails on its return if successful in the mission; black, if not. Day after day the knight waits for
the coming of his love while the lamp of his life burns
lower and lower. At length the sails of the ship appear
on the distant horizon. The knight is now himself too
weak to look. "White or black?" he asks of his wife.
"Black," replies she, jealousy prompting the falsehood;
and the knight's heart-strings snap in twain just as his
love steps over the threshold of his chamber. Oh, the
pity of it! for with the lady is her lord, who, having learned
the story of the fateful potion, has come to unite the lovers.
Then the queen, too, dies, and the remorseful king buries
the lovers in a common grave, from whose caressing sod

spring a rose-bush and a vine and intertwine so curiously
that none may separate them.[1]

Upon the ancient legend which has thus been outlined Wagner reared his great tragedy entitled
"Tristan und Isolde." Whence the story came
nobody can tell. It is a part of the great treasure
preserved from remotest antiquity by itinerant
singers and story-tellers, and committed to writing
by poets of the Middle Ages.   The first of these, so
far as unquestioned evidence goes, were French
trouvères. From them the tale passed into the
hands of the German minnesinger. The greatest
of these who treated it was Gottfried von Strasburg
(*circa* A.D. 1210), who, however, left the tale unfinished. His continuators were Ulrich von Türn-
heim and Heinrich von Freiberg, whose denouement
(not, however, original with them) was followed by
Hermann Kurtz when he published a version of
Gottfried's poem in modern German in 1844. This,
unquestionably, was the version which fell into
Wagner's hands when, in the Dresden period (1843–
1849) he devoted himself assiduously to the study of
Teutonic legend and mythology.   In English the
romance has an equally honorable literary record.
In 1804 Sir Walter Scott edited a metrical version
which he fondly believed to be the work of the somewhat mythical Thomas the Rhymer and to afford
evidence that the oldest literary form of the legend was British. The adventures of Tristram of

[1] "Studies in the Wagnerian Drama," by H. E. Krehbiel.

Lyonesse (who is the *Tristan* of Wagner's tragedy) form a large portion of Sir Thomas Malory's thrice glorious "Morte d'Arthur." Of modern poets Tennyson, Matthew Arnold, and Swinburne have sung the passion of the ill-starred lovers.

Elements of the legend can be traced back to the ancient literatures of the Aryan peoples. The courtship by proxy has a prototype in Norse mythology in Skirnir's wooing of Gerd for Van Frey. The incident of the sails belongs to Greek story — the legend of Ægeus and Theseus; the magic potion may be found in ancient Persian romance; the interlocked rose-tree and vine over the grave of the lovers is an example of those floral auguries and testimonies which I have mentioned in connection with the legend of Tannhäuser and the blossoming staff: in token of their innocence flowers spring miraculously from the graves of persons wrongly done to death.

A legend which lives to be retold often is like a mirror which reflects not only the original picture, but also the social and moral surroundings of different relators. So this ancient tale has been varied by the poets who have told it; and of these variants the most significant are those made by Wagner. If the ethical scheme of the poet-composer is to be observed, the chief of these must be kept in mind. In the poems of Gottfried, Arnold, and Swinburne the love potion is drunk accidentally and the passion which leads to the destruction of the lovers is a thing for which they are in nowise responsible. Wagner puts antecedent and conscious guilt at the door of both of his heroic characters; they love each other before the dreadful drinking and do not pay the deference to the passion which in the highest conception it demands. *Tristan* is carried away by love of power and glory before man and *Isolde* is at heart a murderer and suicide. The potion is less the creator of an uncontrollable passion than it is an agency which makes the lovers forget honor, duty, and respect for the laws of society. Tennyson omits all mention of the potion and permits us to imagine *Tristram* and *Iseult* as a couple of ordinary sinners. Swinburne and Arnold follow the old story touching the hero's life in Brittany with the second *Iseult* (she of the White Hand); but while Swinburne preserves her a "maiden wife," Arnold gives her a family of children. Wagner ennobles his hero by omitting the second *Isolde*, thus bringing the story into greater sympathy with modern ideas of love and exalting the passion of the lovers.

The purpose to write a Tristan drama was in Wagner's mind three years before he began its execution. While living in Zurich, in 1854, he had advanced as far as the second act of his "Siegfried" when, in a moment of discouragement, he wrote to Liszt "As I have never in my life enjoyed the true felicity of love, I shall erect to this most beautiful of my dreams" (*i.e.* the drama on which he was working) "a monument in which, from beginning to end, this love shall find fullest gratification.

I have sketched in my head a 'Tristan und Isolde,' the simplest of musical conceptions, but full-blooded; with the 'black flag' which waves at the end I shall then cover myself — to die." Three years later he took up the project, but under an inspiration vastly different from that notified to Liszt. The tragedy was not to be a monument to a mere dream of felicity or to his artistic despair, but a tribute to a consuming passion for Mathilde Wesendonck, wife of a benefactor who had given him an idyllic home at Triebschen, on the Lake of Lucerne. Mme. Wesendonck was the author of the two poems "Im Treibhaus" and "Träume," which, with three others from the same pen, Wagner set to music. The first four were published in the winter of 1857–1858; the last, "Im Treibhaus," on May 1, 1858. The musical theme of "Träume" was the germ of the love-music in the second act of "Tristan und Isolde"; out of "Im Treibhaus" grew some of the introduction to the third act. The tragedy was outlined in prose in August, 1857, and the versification was finished by September 18. The music was complete by July 16, 1859. Wagner gave the pencil sketches of the score to Mme. Wesendonck, who piously went over them with ink so that they might be preserved for posterity.

In 1857 Wagner had been eight years an exile from his native land. Years had passed since he began work on "Der Ring des Nibelungen," and there seemed to him little prospect of that work receiving either publication or performance. In

May of that year he received an invitation from
Dom Pedro, Emperor of Brazil, to write an opera
for Rio de Janeiro and direct its production. Two
and a half years before he had seriously considered
the project of coming to America for a concert tour;
so the invitation did not strike him as so strange
and extraordinary as it might have appeared to
a musician of less worldly wisdom. It is not likely
that he took it seriously into consideration, but
at any rate it turned his thoughts again to the opera
which he had mentioned to Liszt. With it he saw
an opportunity for again establishing a connection
with the theatre. Dom Pedro wanted, of course,
an Italian opera. Wagner's plan contemplated
the writing of "Tristan und Isolde" in German,
its translation into Italian, the dedication of its
score to the Emperor of Brazil, with the privilege
of its performance there and a utilization of the
opportunity, if possible, to secure a production
beforehand of "Tannhäuser." Meanwhile, he would
have the drama produced in its original tongue at
Strasburg, then a French city conveniently near
the German border, with Albert Niemann in the
titular rôle and an orchestra from Karlsruhe, or
some other German city which had an opera-house.
He communicated the plan to Liszt, who approved
of the project heartily, though he was greatly amazed
at the intelligence which he had from another source
that Wagner intended to write the music with an
eye to a performance in Italian. "How in the
name of all the gods are you going to make of it

an opera for Italian singers, as B. tells me you are? Well, since the incredible and impossible have become your elements, perhaps you will achieve this, too," Liszt wrote to him, and promised to go to Strasburg with a Wagnerian coterie to act as a guard of honor for the composer. Nothing came of either plan. Inspired by his love for Mathilde Wesendonck, Wagner wrote the opera and succeeded in selling the score to Breitkopf & Härtel for the equivalent of $800. Then began the hunt for a theatre in which to give the first representation. Eduard Devrient urged Karlsruhe, where he was director, but Wagner wanted to supervise the production, and this was impossible in a theatre of Germany so long as the decree of banishment for participation in the Saxon rebellion hung over his head. The Grand Duke of Baden appealed to the King of Saxony to recall the decree, but in vain. Wagner went to Paris and Brussels, but had to content himself with giving concerts. Weimar, Prague, and Hanover were considered in order, and at length Wagner turned to Vienna. There the opera was accepted for representation at the Court Opera, but after fifty-four rehearsals between November, 1862, and March, 1863, it was abandoned as "impossible."

The next year saw the turning-point in Wagner's career. Ludwig of Bavaria invited him to come to Munich, the political ban was removed, and "Tristan und Isolde" had its first performance, to the joy of the composer and a host of his friends, on June 10,

1865, at the Royal Court Theatre of the Bavarian
capital, under the direction of Hans von Bülow.
The rôles of *Tristan* and *Isolde* were in the hands
of Ludwig Schnorr von Carolsfeld and his wife.
Albert Niemann was prevented by the failure of
the Strasburg plan from being the first representative of the hero, but to him fell the honor of setting
the model for all American representations. The
first performance in the United States took place
in the Metropolitan Opera-house on December 1,
1886, under the direction of Anton Seidl. The cast
was as follows: *Isolde*, Lilli Lehmann; *Brangäne*,
Marianne Brandt; *Tristan*, Albert Niemann; *Kurwenal*, Adolf Robinson; *König Marke*, Emil Fischer;
Melot, Rudolph von Milde; *ein Hirt*, Otto Kemlitz;
ein Steuermann, Emil Saenger; *ein Seemann*, Max
Alvary.

Two circumstances bid us look a little carefully
into the instrumental prelude with which Wagner
has prefaced his drama. One is that it has taken
so prominent a place in the concert-room that even
those whose love for pure music has made them
indifferent to the mixed art-form called the opera
ought to desire acquaintance with its poetical and
musical contents; the other is that the prelude,
like the overture to "Fidelio" known as "Leonore
No. 3," presents the spiritual progress of the tragedy
from beginning to end to the quickened heart and
mind of the listener freed from all material integument. To do this it makes use of the themes which
are most significant in the development of the

psychology of the drama, which is far and away
its most important element, for the pictures are not
many, and the visible action is slight. Listening
to the music without thought of the drama, and,
therefore, with no purpose of associating it with
the specific conceptions which later have exposition
in the text, we can hear in this prelude an expression of an ardent longing, a consuming hunger,

> which doth make
> The meat it feeds on,

a desire that cannot be quenched, yet will not despair. Then, at the lowest ebb of the sweet agony,
an ecstasy of hope, a wildly blissful contemplation
of a promise of reward. If I depart here for a
brief space from my announced purpose not to analyze the music in the manner of the Wagnerian
commentators, it will be only because the themes
of the prelude are the most pregnant of those employed in the working out of the drama, because their
specific significance in the purpose of the composer
is plainly set forth by their association with scenes
and words, and because they are most admirably
fitted by structure and emotional content to express the things attributed to them. The most important of the themes is that with which the prelude begins: —

Note that it is two-voiced and that one voice
ascends chromatically (that is, in half steps), and
the other descends in the same manner. In the as-
piring voice there is an expression of longing; in
the descending, of suffering and dejection. We
therefore may look upon it as a symbol of the lovers
and their passion in a dual aspect. After an exposition of this theme there enters another: —

followed immediately by: —

In the play the first of these two is associated
with the character of the hero; the second with the
glance which *Tristan* cast upon *Isolde* when she
was about to kill him — the glance which inspired
the love of the princess. Two modifications of the
principal theme provide nearly all the rest of the
material used in the building up of the prelude.
The first is a diminution of the *motif* compassed
by the second and third measures, which by reiteration develops the climax of the piece: —

The second is a harmonized inversion of the same short figure, preceded by a jubilantly ascending scale: —

This is the expression of the ecstasy of hope, the wildly blissful contemplation of a promise of reward of which I have spoken. Wagner tells us what the thing hoped for, the joy contemplated in expectation, is, not only in the drama, but also in an exposition of the contents of the prelude made for concert purposes. He deserves that it shall be known, and I reproduce it in the translation of William Ashton Ellis. After rehearsing the legend down to the drinking of the fateful philtre, he says: —

The musician who chose this theme for the prelude to his love drama, as he felt that he was now in the boundless realm of the very element of music, could only have one care: how he should set bounds to his fancy, for the exhaustion of the theme was impossible. Thus he took, once for all, this insatiable desire. In long-drawn accents it surges up, from its first timid confession, its softest attraction, through sobbing sighs, hope and pain, laments and wishes, delight and torment, up to the mightiest onslaught, the most powerful endeavor to find the breach which shall open to the heart the path to the ocean of the endless joy of love. In vain! Its power spent, the heart sinks back to thirst with desire, with desire unfulfilled, as each fruition only brings forth seeds of fresh desire, till, at last, in the depths of its exhaustion, the starting eye sees the glimmering of the highest bliss of attainment. It is the ecstasy of dying, of the surrender of being, of the final redemption into that wondrous realm from which we wander farthest when we strive to take it by force. Shall we call this Death? Is it not rather the wonder world of night, out of which, so says the story, the ivy and the vine sprang forth in tight embrace o'er the tomb of Tristan and Isolde?

If we place ourselves in spirit among the personages of Wagner's play, we shall find ourselves at the parting of the curtain which hangs between the real and the mimic world, on board a mediæval ship, within a few hours' sail of Cornwall, whither *Tristan* is bearing *Isolde* to be the wife of his king *Marke*. The cheery song of a sailor who, unseen, at the masthead, sings to the winds which are blowing him away from his wild Irish sweetheart, floats down to us. It has a refreshing and buoyant lilt, this song, with something of the sea breeze in it, and yet something, as it is sung, which emphasizes the loneliness of the singer:—

Frisch weht der Wind der Hei-mat zu: Mein
i-risch Kind, wo wei-lest Du?

An innocent song, the strain of which, more decorous than any modern chantey, inspires the

sailors as they pull at the ropes, and gives voice
to the delights of the peaceful voyage: —

Yet it stirs up a tempest in the soul of *Isolde.*
She is the daughter of an Irish queen, a sorceress,
and she now deplores the degeneracy of her race
and its former potency. Once her ancestors could
command wind and wave, but now they can brew
only balsamic potions. Wildly she invokes the
elements to dash the ship to pieces, and when her
maid, *Brangäne,* seeks to know the cause of her
tumultuous disquiet, she tells the story of her love
for *Tristan* and of its disgraceful requital. He had
come to Ireland's queen to be healed of a wound
received in battle. He had killed his enemy, and
that enemy was *Morold, Isolde's* betrothed. The
princess, ignorant of that fact, — ignorant, too, of
his name, for he had called himself Tantris, — had
herself nursed him back almost to health, when one
day she found that a splinter of steel, taken from
the head of *Morold,* where he had received the

s

dolorous stroke, fitted into a nick in the sword of
the wounded knight. At her mercy lay the slayer
of her affianced husband. She raised the sword to
take revenge, when his look fell upon her. In a
twinkling her heart was empty of hate and filled
instead with love. Now, instead of requiting her
love, *Tristan* is taking her to Cornwall to deliver
her to a loveless marriage to Cornwall's "weary
king." It will be well to note in this narrative
how the description of *Tristan's* sufferings are set
to a descending chromatic passage, like the second
voice of the principal theme already described: —

Von   ei - nem Kahn,   der klein   und   arm

The thought of her humiliation maddens the high-
spirited woman, and she sends her maid, *Brangäne*,
to summon the knight into her presence. The
knight parleys diplomatically with the messenger.
Duty keeps him at the helm, but once in port he
will suffer no one but himself to escort the exalted
lady into the presence of the king. At the last
the maid is forced to deliver the command in the
imperious words used by her mistress. This touches
the pride of *Tristan's* squire, *Kurwenal*, who asks
permission to frame an answer, and, receiving it,
shouts a ballad of his master's method of paying
tribute to Ireland with the head of his enemy; for
the battle between *Tristan* and *Morold* had grown
out of the effort made by the latter to collect tribute.

money from England. It is a stiff stave, rugged, forceful, and direct, in which the spirit of the political ballad of all times is capitally preserved.

Isolde resolves to wipe out what she conceives to be her disgrace by slaying *Tristan* and herself. *Brangäne* tries to persuade her that the crown of Cornwall will bring her honor, and when *Isolde* answers that it would be intolerable to live in the presence of *Tristan* and not have his love, she hints that her mother had not sent her into a strange land without providing for all contingencies. *Isolde* understands the allusion to her mother's magical lore, and commands that a casket be brought to her. *Brangäne* obeys with alacrity and exhibits its contents: lotions for wounds, antidotes for poisons, and, best of all, — she holds a phial aloft. *Isolde* will not have it so; she herself had marked the phial whose contents were to remedy her ills. "The death draught!" exclaims *Brangäne,* and immediately the "Yo, heave ho!" of the sailors is heard and the shout of "Land!" Throughout this scene a significant phrase is heard — the symbol of death: —

Also the symbol of fate — a downward leap of a seventh, as in the last two notes of the brief figure illustrative of the glance which had inspired *Isolde's* fatal love.

At sight of land *Tristan* leaves the helm and presents himself before *Isolde*. She upbraids him for having avoided her during the voyage; he replies that he had obeyed the commands of honor and custom. She reminds him that a debt of blood is due her — he owes her revenge for the death of *Morold*. *Tristan* offers her his sword and his breast; but she declines to kill the best of all *Marke's* knights, and offers to drink with him a cup of forgiveness. He divines her purpose and takes the cup from her hand and gives this pledge: Fidelity to his honor, defiance to anguish. To his heart's illusion, his scarcely apprehended dream, will he drink the draught which shall bring oblivion. Before he has emptied the cup, *Isolde* snatches it from his hands and drains it to the bottom. Thus they meet their doom, which is not death and surcease of sorrow, as both had believed, but life and misery; for *Brangäne*, who had been commanded to pour the poison in the cup, had followed an amiable prompting and presented the love-potion instead. A moment of bewilderment, and the fated ones are in each other's arms, pouring out an ecstasy of passion. Then her maids robe *Isolde* to receive the king, who is coming on board the ship to greet his bride.

In the introduction to the second act, based upon this restless phrase, —

LILLI LEHMANN

MILKA TERNINA   ROSA SUCHER

we have a picture of the longing and impatience
of the lovers before a meeting. When the curtains
part, we discover a garden before the chamber of
Isolde, who is now Cornwall's queen. It is a lovely
night in summer. A torch burns in a ring beside
the door opening into the chamber at the top of a
stone staircase. The king has gone a-hunting, and
the tones of the hunting-horns, dying away in the
distance, blend entrancingly with an instrumental
song from the orchestra which seems a musical
sublimation of night and nature in their tenderest
moods. *Isolde* appears with *Brangäne* and pleads
with her to extinguish the torch and thus give the
appointed signal to *Tristan*, who is waiting in concealment. But *Brangäne* suspects treachery on the
part of *Melot*, a knight who is jealous of *Tristan*
and himself enamoured of *Isolde*. It was he who
had planned the nocturnal hunt. She warns her
mistress, and begs her to wait. Beauty rests upon
the scene like a benediction. To *Isolde* the horns
are but the rustling of the forest leaves as they are
caressed by the wind, or the purling and laughing
of the brook. Longing has eaten up all patience,
all discretion, all fear. In spite of *Brangäne's*
pleadings she extinguishes the torch, and with wildly
waving scarf beckons on her hurrying lover. Beneath the foliage they sing their love through all
the gamut of hope and despair, of bliss and wretched-
ness. The duet consists largely of detached ejaculations and verbal plays, each paraphrasing or vary-
ing or giving a new turn to the outpouring of the

other, the whole permeated with the symbolism of pessimistic philosophy in which night, death, and oblivion are glorified, and day, life, and memory contemned. In this dialogue lies the key to the philosophy which Wagner has proclaimed in the tragedy. In Wagner's exposition of the prelude we saw that he wishes us to observe "the one glimmering of the highest bliss of attainment" in the "surrender of being," the "final redemption into that wondrous realm from which we wander farthest when we try to take it by force." For this realm he chooses death and night as symbols, but what he means to imply is the nirvana of Buddhistic philosophy, the final deliverance of the soul from transmigration. Such love as that of *Tristan* and *Isolde* presented itself to Wagner as ceaseless struggle and endless contradiction, and for this problem nirvana alone offers a happy outcome; it means quietude and identity.

In vain does *Brangäne* sing her song of warning from the tower; the lovers have been transported beyond all realization of their surroundings; they sing on, dream on in each other's arms, until at the moment of supremest ecstasy there comes a rude interruption. *Kurwenal* dashes in with a sword and a shout: "Save thyself, *Tristan!*" the king, *Melot*, and courtiers at his heels. Day, symbol of all that is fatal to their love, has dawned. *Tristan* is silent, though *Marke* bewails the treachery of his nephew and his friend. From the words of the heart-torn king we learn that he had been forced

into the marriage with *Isolde* by the disturbed
state of his kingdom, and had not consented to it
until *Tristan*, whose purpose it was thus to quiet
the jealous anger of the barons, had threatened to
depart from Cornwall unless the king revoked his
purpose to make him his successor, and took unto
himself a wife. *Tristan's* answer to the sorrowful
upbraidings of his royal uncle is to obtain a promise
from *Isolde* to follow him into the "wondrous realm
of night." Then, seeing that *Marke* does not wield
the sword of retribution, he makes a feint of attacking *Melot*, but permits the treacherous knight to reach
him with his sword. He falls wounded unto death.

The last act has been reached. The dignified, reserved knight of the first act, the impassioned
lover of the second, is now a dream-haunted, longing, despairing, dying man, lying under a lime tree
in the yard of his ancestral castle in Brittany,
wasting his last bit of strength in feverish fancies
and ardent yearnings touching *Isolde*. *Kurwenal* has
sent for her. Will she come? A shepherd tells
of vain watches for the sight of a sail by playing a
mournful melody on his pipe:—

Oh, the heart-hunger of the hero! The longing! Will she never come? The fever is consuming him, and his heated brain breeds fancies which one moment lift him above all memories of pain and the next bring him to the verge of madness. Cooling breezes waft him again toward Ireland, whose princess healed the wound struck by *Morold*, then ripped it up again with the avenging sword with its telltale nick. From her hands he took the drink whose poison sears his heart. Accursed the cup and accursed the hand that brewed it! Will the shepherd never change his doleful strain? Ah, *Isolde*, how beautiful you are! The ship, the ship! It must be in sight. *Kurwenal*, have you no eyes? *Isolde's* ship! A merry tune bursts from the shepherd's pipe: —

It is the ship! What flag flies at the peak? The flag of "All's well!" Now the ship disappears behind a cliff. There the breakers are treacherous. Who is at the helm? Friend or foe? *Melot's* accomplice? Are you, too, a traitor, *Kurwenal?* *Tristan's* strength is unequal to the excitement of the moment. His mind becomes dazed. He hears *Isolde's* voice, and his wandering fancy transforms it into the torch whose extinction once summoned him to her side: "Do I hear the light?" He staggers to his feet and tears the bandages from his wound. "Ha! my blood! flow merrily now! She who opened the wound is here to heal it!" Life endures but for one embrace, one glance, one word: "*Isolde!*" While *Isolde* lies mortally stricken upon *Tristan's* corpse, *Marke* and his train arrive upon a second ship. *Brangäne* has told the secret of the love-draught, and the king has come to unite the lovers. But his purpose is not known, and faithful *Kurwenal* receives his death-blow while trying to hold the castle against *Marke's* men. He dies at *Tristan's* side. *Isolde,* unconscious of all these happenings, sings out her broken heart, and expires.

And ere her ear might hear, her heart had heard,
Nor sought she sign for witness of the word;
But came and stood above him, newly dead,
And felt his death upon her: and her head
Bowed, as to reach the spring that slakes all drouth;
And their four lips became one silent mouth.[1]

[1] Swinburne, "Tristram of Lyonesse."

CHAPTER XIV

"PARSIFAL"

A LAD, hotfoot in pursuit of a wild swan which one of his arrows has pierced, finds himself in a forest glade on the side of a mountain. There he meets a body of knights and esquires in attendance on a king who is suffering from a wound. The knights are a body of men whose mission it is to succor suffering innocence wherever they may find it. They dwell in a magnificent castle on the summit of the mountain, within whose walls they assemble every day to contemplate and adore a miraculous vessel from which they obtain both physical and spiritual sustenance. In order to enjoy the benefits which flow from this talisman, they are required to preserve their bodies in ascetic purity. Their king has fallen from this estate and been grievously wounded in an encounter with a magician, who, having failed in his ambition to enter the order of knighthood, had built a castle over against that of the king, where, by practice of the black art and with the help of sirens and a sorceress, he seeks the ruin of the pure and celestial soldiery. In his hands is a lance which once belonged to the knights, but which he had wrested from their king

266

and with which he had given the dolorous stroke from which the king is suffering.

The healing of the king can be wrought only by a touch of the lance which struck the wound; and this lance can be regained only by one able to withstand the sensual temptations with which the evil-minded sorcerer has surrounded himself in his magical castle. An oracle, that had spoken from a vision, which one day shone about the talisman, had said that this deliverer should be a guileless fool, an innocent simpleton, whom compassionate pity had made knowing:—

THE ORACLE

For this hero king and knights are waiting and longing, since neither lotions nor baths nor ointments can bring relief, though they be of the rarest potency and brought from all the ends of the earth. The lad who thus finds himself in this worshipful but woful company is himself of noble and knightly lineage. This we learn from the recital of his history, but also from the bright, incisive, militant, chivalresque music associated with him:—

THE SYMBOL OF PARSIFAL

But he has been reared in a wilderness, far from courts and the institutions of chivalry and in ignorance of the world lying beyond his forest boundaries. His father died before he was born, and his mother withheld from him all knowledge of knighthood, hoping thus to keep him for herself. One day, however, he saw a cavalcade of horsemen in brilliant trappings. The spectacle stirred the chivalric spirit slumbering within him; he deserted his mother, followed after the knights, and set out in quest of adventure. The mother died: —

THE SYMBOL OF HERZELEIDE

In the domain whither his quarry had led the lad, all animals were held sacred. A knight (*Gurnemanz*) rebukes him for his misdeed in shooting the swan, and rue leads him to break his bow and arrows. From a strange creature (*Kundry*), —

THE PENITENT KUNDRY

in the service of the knights, he learns of the death
of his mother, who had perished for love of him and
grief over his desertion. He is questioned about
himself, but is singularly ignorant of everything,
even of his own name. Hoping that the lad may
prove to be the guileless fool to whom knowledge
was to come through pity, the knight escorts him to
the temple, which is the sanctuary of the talisman
whose adoration is the daily occupation of the
brotherhood. They walk out of the forest and find
themselves in a rocky defile of the mountain. A
natural gateway opens in the face of a cliff, through
which they pass, and are lost to sight for a space.
Then they are seen ascending a sloping passage,
and little by little the rocks lose their ruggedness
and begin to take on rude architectural contours.
They are walking to music which, while merely suggesting their progress and the changing natural
scene in the main, ever and anon breaks into an
expression of the most poignant and lacerating suffering and lamentation :—

SUFFERING AND LAMENTATION

Soon the pealing of bells is heard:—

and the tones blend synchronously and harmoniously with the music of their march:—

FUNDAMENTAL PHRASE OF THE MARCH

At last they arrive in a mighty Byzantine hall,
which loses itself upward in a lofty, vaulted dome,

from which light streams downward and illumines
the interior. Under the dome, within a colonnade,
are two tables, each a segment of a circle. Into the
hall there come in procession knights wearing red
mantles on which the image of a white dove is
embroidered. They chant a pious hymn as they
take their places at the refectory tables: —

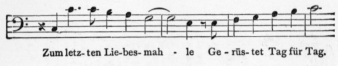

Zum letz- ten Lie-bes- mah - le   Ge - rūs- tet Tag für Tag.

THE EUCHARISTIC HYMN

The king, whom the lad had seen in the glade, is
borne in on a litter, before him a veiled shrine containing the mystical cup which is the object of the
ceremonious worship. It is the duty of the king
to unveil the talisman and hold it up to the adoration of the knights. He is conveyed to a raised
couch and the shrine is placed before him. His
sufferings of mind and body are so poignant that he
would liever die than perform his office; but the
voice of his father (*Titurel*), who had built the
sanctuary, established the order of knighthood, and
now lives on in his grave sustained by the sight of
the talisman, admonishes the king of his duty. At
length he consents to perform the function imposed
upon him by his office. He raises himself painfully
upon his couch. The attendants remove the covering from the shrine and disclose an antique crystal
vessel which they reverently place before the lamen-

table king. Boys' voices come wafted down from
the highest height of the dome, singing a formula
of consecration: "Take ye my body, take my blood
in token of our love": —

THE LOVE-FEAST FORMULA

A dazzling ray of light flashes down from above
and falls into the cup, which now glows with a
reddish purple lustre and sheds a soft radiance
around. The knights have sunk upon their knees.
The king lifts the luminous chalice, moves it gently
from side to side, and thus blesses the bread and
wine provided for the refection of the knights.
Meanwhile, celestial voices proclaim the words of
the oracle to musical strains that are pregnant with
mysterious suggestion.

Another choir sturdily, firmly, ecstatically hymns
the power of faith: —

THE SYMBOL OF FAITH

and, at the end, an impressive antiphon, starting
with the knights, ascends higher and higher, and,
calling in gradually the voices of invisible singers
in the middle height, becomes metamorphosed
into an angelic canticle as it takes its flight to
the summit.   It is the voice of aspiration, the
musical symbol of the talisman which directs the
thoughts and desires of its worshippers ever upward: —

THE SYMBOL OF THE HOLY GRAIL

The lad disappoints his guide. He understands
nothing of the solemn happenings which he has
witnessed, nor does he ask their meaning, though
his own heart had been lacerated with pain at sight
of the king's sufferings. He is driven from the
sanctuary with contumely.

He wanders forth in quest of further adventures
and enters the magical garden surrounding the castle
of the sorcerer. A number of knights who are sent
against him he puts to rout. Now the magician
summons lovely women, clad in the habiliments of
flowers, to seduce him with their charms: —

KLINGSOR'S INCANTATION

They sing and play about him with winsome wheedlings and cajoleries, with insinuating blandishments and dainty flatteries, with pretty petulancies and delectable quarrellings:—

THE SEDUCTIVE SONG OF THE FLOWER MAIDENS

But they fail of their purpose, as does also an unwilling siren whom the magician invokes with powerful conjurations. It is *Kundry*, who is half Magdalen, half wicked sorceress, a messenger in the service of the pious knights, and as such hideous of aspect; a tool in the hands of the magician, and as such supernaturally beautiful. It was to her

charms that the suffering king had yielded. **To**
win the youth she tells him the story of his mother's
death and gives to him her last message and — a
kiss! At the touch of her impure lips a flood of
passion, hitherto unfelt, pours through the veins
of the lad, and in its surge comes understanding
of the suffering and woe which he had witnessed in
the castle on the mountain. Also a sense of his
own remissness. Compassionate pity brings enlightenment; and he thrusts back the woman who
is seeking to destroy him. Finding that the wiles
of his tool have availed him naught, the wicked
magician himself appears to give battle, for he,
too, knows the oracle and fears the coming of the
king's deliverer and the loss of the weapon which
he hopes will yet enable him to achieve the mystical talisman. He hurls the lance at the youth, but
it remains suspended in midair. The lad seizes it,
makes the sign of the cross, speaks some words of
exorcism, and garden, castle, damsels — all the
works of enchantment disappear.

Now the young hero is conscious of a mission.
He must find again the abode of the knights and
their ailing king, and bring to them surcease of
suffering. After long and grievous wanderings he
is again directed to the castle. Grief and despair
have overwhelmed the knights, whose king, unable
longer to endure the torture in which he has lived,
has definitively refused to perform his holy office.
In consequence, his father, no longer the recipient
of supernatural sustenance, has died, and the king

longs to follow him. The hero touches the wound in the side of the king with the sacred spear, ends his dolors, and is hailed as king in his place. The temptress, who has followed him as a penitent, freed from a curse which had rested upon her for ages, goes to a blissful and eternal rest.

* * *

Such is the story of Wagner's "Parsifal." It is the purpose of this book to help the musical layman who loves lyric drama to enjoyment. Criticism might do this, but a purpose of simple exposition has already been proclaimed, and shall be adhered to lest some reader think that he is being led too far afield. In this case the exposition shall take the form of a marshalling of the elements of the story in two aspects — religious and legendary. Careful readers of English literature will have had no difficulty in recognizing in it a story of the quest of the Holy Grail. Tennyson will have taught them that the hero is that

Sir Percivale
Whom Arthur and his knighthood called the Pure;

that the talismanic vessel is

the cup itself from which our Lord
Drank at the last sad supper with His own;

that the lance which struck and healed the grievous wound in the side of the king is the spear with which the side of the Christ was pierced on Calvary. It is also obvious that the king, whose name is

Amfortas, that is, "the powerless one," is a symbol
of humanity suffering from the wounds of slavery
to desire; that the heroic act of *Parsifal*, as Wagner
calls him, which brings release to the king and his
knights, is renunciation of desire, prompted by pity,
compassion, fellow-suffering; and that this gentle
emotion it was that had inspired knowledge simultaneously of a great need and a means of deliverance.   The ethical idea of the drama, as I set forth in
a book entitled "Studies in the Wagnerian Drama"
many years ago, is that it is the enlightenment which
comes through pity which brings salvation.   The
allusion is to the redemption of mankind by the
sufferings and compassionate death of Christ; and
that stupendous tragedy is the prefiguration of the
mimic drama which Wagner has constructed.   The
spectacle to which he invites us, and with which
he hoped to impress us and move us to an acceptance
of the lesson underlying his play, is the adoration of the Holy Grail, cast in the form of a mimicry
of the Last Supper, bedizened with some of the
glittering pageantry of mediæval knighthood and
romance.

In the minds of many persons it is a profanation
to make a stage spectacle out of religious things;
and it has been urged that "Parsifal" is not only
religious but specifically Christian; not only Christian but filled with parodies of elements which are
partly liturgical, partly Biblical.   In narrating the
incidents of the play I have purposely avoided
all allusions to the things which have been matters

of controversy. It is possible to look upon "Parsifal" as a sort of glorified fairy tale, and to this end
I purpose to subject its elements to inquiry, and shall
therefore go a bit more into detail. Throughout
the play *Parsifal* is referred to as a redeemer, and
in the third act scenes in which he plays as the
central figure are borrowed from the life of Christ.
Kundry, the sorceress, who attempts his destruction
at one time and is in the service of the knights of
the Grail at another, anoints his feet and dries them
with her hair, as the Magdalen did the feet of Christ
in the house of Simon the Pharisee. *Parsifal*
baptizes *Kundry* and admonishes her to believe in
the Redeemer:—

Die Taufe nimm
Und glaub' an den Erlöser!

Kundry weeps. Unto the woman who was a sinner and wept at His feet Christ said: "Thy sins are
forgiven. . . . Thy faith hath saved thee. Go
in peace." At the elevation of the grail by *Parsifal*
after the healing of *Amfortas* a dove descends from
the dome and hovers over the new king's head.
What saith the Scripture? "And Jesus, when he
was baptized, went up straightway out of the water;
and lo, the heavens were opened unto him, and
he saw the Spirit of God descending like a dove,
and lighting upon him." (St. Matthew iii. 16.) It
would be idle to argue that these things are not
Biblical, though the reported allusions to *Parsifal*
as a redeemer do not of necessity belong in the

category. We shall see presently that the drama
is permeated with Buddhism, and there were a
multitude of redeemers and saviours in India besides the Buddha.

Let us look at the liturgical elements. The Holy
Grail is a chalice. It is brought into the temple in
solemn procession in a veiled shrine and deposited
on a table. Thus, also, the chalice, within its pall,
is brought in at the sacrament of the mass and
placed on the altar before the celebrant. In the
drama boys' voices sing in the invisible heights : —

> Nehmet hin mein Blut
> Um unserer Liebe willen!
> Nehmet hin meinem Leib
> Auf dass ihr mein gedenkt!

Is there a purposed resemblance here to the words
of consecration in the mass? *Accipite, et mandu-
cate ex hoc omnes. Hoc est enim Corpus meum.
Accipite, et bibite ex eo omnes. Hic est enim Calix
sanguinis mei!* In a moment made wonderfully
impressive by Wagner's music, while *Amfortas*
bends over the grail and the knights are on their
knees, a ray of light illumines the cup and it glows
red. *Amfortas* lifts it high, gently sways it from
side to side, and blesses the bread and wine which
youthful servitors have placed beside each knight
on the table. In the book of the play, as the hall
gradually grows light the cups before the knights
appear filled with red wine, and beside each lies a
small loaf of bread. Now the celestial choristers

sing: "The wine and bread of the Last Supper, once the Lord of the Grail, through pity's love-power, changed into the blood which he shed, into the body which he offered. To-day the Redeemer whom ye laud changes the blood and body of the sacrificial offering into the wine poured out for you, and the bread that you eat!" And the knights respond antiphonally: "Take of the bread; bravely change it anew into strength and power. Faithful unto death, staunch in effort to do the works of the Lord. Take of the blood; change it anew to life's fiery flood. Gladly in communion, faithful as brothers, to fight with blessed courage." Are these words, or are they not, a paraphrase of those which in the canon of the mass follow the first and second ablutions of the celebrant: *Quod ore sumpsimus Domine*, etc., and: *Corpus tuum, Domine*, etc.? He would be but little critical who would deny it.

Nevertheless, it does not necessarily follow that Wagner wished only to parody the eucharistic rite. He wanted to create a ceremonial which should be beautiful, solemn, and moving; which should be an appropriate accompaniment to the adoration of a mystical relic; which should, in a large sense, be neither Catholic, Protestant, nor Buddhistic; which should symbolize a conception of atonement older than Christianity, older than Buddhism, older than all records of the human imagination. Of this more anon. As was his custom, Wagner drew from whatever source seemed to him good and fruitful; and though he doubtless thought himself at liberty to receive suggestions from the Roman Catholic ritual, as well as the German Lutheran, it is even possible that he had also before his mind scenes from Christian Masonry. This possibility was once suggested by Mr. F. C. Burnand, who took the idea from the last scene of the first act only, and does not seem to have known how many connections the Grail legend had with mediæval Freemasonry or Templarism. There are more elements associated with the old Knights Templars and their rites in Wagner's drama than I am able to discuss. To do so I should have to be an initiate and have more space at my disposal than I have here. I can only make a few suggestions: In the old Welsh tale of Peredur, which is a tale of the quest of a magical talisman, the substitute for the grail is a dish containing a bloody head. That head in time, as the legend passed through the imaginations of poets and romances, became the head of John the Baptist, and there was a belief in the Middle Ages that the Knights Templars worshipped a bloody head. The head of John the Baptist enters dimly into Wagner's drama in the conceit that *Kundry* is a reincarnation of Herodias, who is doomed to make atonement, not for having danced the head off the prophet's shoulders, but for having reviled Christ as he was staggering up Calvary under the load of the cross. But this is pursuing speculations into regions that are shadowy and vague. Let it suffice for this branch of our study that Mr. Burnand has given expression to the

theory that the scene of the adoration of the grail
and the Love Feast may also have a relationship
with the ceremony of installation in the Masonic
orders of chivalry, in which a cup of brotherly love
is presented to the Grand Commander, who drinks
and asks the Sir Knights to pledge him in the cup
"in commemoration of the Last Supper of our
Grand Heavenly Captain, with his twelve disciples,
whom he commanded thus to remember him."
Here, says Mr. Burnand, there is no pretence to
sacrifice. Participation in the wine is a symbol of
a particular and peculiarly close intercommunion
of brotherhood.

To get the least offence from "Parsifal" it ought
to be accepted in the spirit of the time in which
Christian symbolism was grafted on the old tales
of the quest of a talisman which lie at the bottom
of it. The time was the last quarter of the twelfth
century and the first quarter of the thirteenth. It
is the period of the third and fourth crusades.
Relic worship was at its height. Less than a hundred years before (in 1101) the Genoese crusaders
had brought back from the Holy Land as a part
of the spoils of Cæsarea, which they were helpful
in capturing under Baldwin, a three-cornered dish,
which was said to be the veritable dish used at the
Last Supper of Christ and his Apostles. The belief
that it was cut out of a solid emerald drew Bonaparte's attention to it, and he carried it away to
Paris in 1806 and had it examined. It proved to be
nothing but glass, and he graciously gave it back to

Genoa in 1814. There it still reposes in the Church of St. John, but it is no longer an object of worship, though it might fairly excite a feeling of veneration.

For 372 years Nuremberg possessed what the devout believed to be the lance of Longinus, with which the side of Christ was opened. The relic, like most objects of its kind (the holy coat, for instance), had a rival which, after inspiring victory at the siege of Antioch, found its way to Paris with the most sacred relics, for which Louis IX built the lovely Sainte Chapelle; now it is in the basilica of the Vatican, at Rome. The Nuremberg relic, however, enjoyed the advantage of historical priority. It is doubly interesting, or rather was so, because it was one of Wagner's historical characters who added it to the imperial treasure of the Holy Roman Empire. This was none other than Henry the Fowler, the king who is righteous in judgment and tuneful of speech in the opera "Lohengrin." Henry, so runs the story, wrested the lance from the Burgundian king, Rudolph III, some time about A.D. 929. After many vicissitudes the relic was given for safe keeping to the imperial city of Nuremberg, in 1424, by the Emperor Sigismund. It was placed in a casket, which was fastened with heavy chains to the walls of the Spitalkirche. There it remained until 1796. One may read about the ceremonies attending its annual exposition, along with other relics, in the old history of Nuremberg, by Wagenseil, which was the source of Wagner's knowledge of the mastersingers. The disruption of the Holy Roman Empire caused a scattering of the jewels and relics in the imperial treasury, and the present whereabouts of this sacred lance is unknown. The casket and chains, however, are preserved in the Germanic Museum at Nuremberg to this day, and there have been seen, doubtless, by many who are reading these lines.

There is nothing in "Parsifal," neither personage nor incident nor thing, no principle of conduct, which did not live in legendary tales and philosophical systems long before Christianity existed as a universal religion. The hero in his first estate was born, bred, went out in search of adventure, rescued the suffering, and righted wrong, just as Krishna, Perseus, Theseus, Œdipus, Romulus, Remus, Siegfried, and Wolf-Dietrich did before him. He is an Aryan legendary and mythical hero-type that has existed for ages. The talismanic cup and spear are equally ancient; they have figured in legend from time immemorial. The incidents of their quest, the agonies wrought by their sight, their mission as inviters of sympathetic interest, and the failure of a hero to achieve a work of succor because of failure to show pity, are all elements in Keltic Quester and Quest stories, which antedate Christianity. *Kundry*, the loathly damsel and siren, has her prototypes in classic fable and romantic tale. Read the old English ballad of "The Marriage of Sir Gawain." So has the magic castle of *Klingsor*, surrounded by its beautiful garden. It is all the things which I enumerated in the chapter devoted to "Tannhäuser." It is also the Underworld, where prevails the law of taboo — "Thou must," or "Thou shalt not;" whither Psyche went on her errand for Venus and came back scot-free; where Peritheus and Theseus remained grown to a rocky seat till Hercules came to release them with mighty wrench and a loss of their bodily integrity. The sacred lance which shines red with blood after it. has by its touch healed the wound of *Amfortas* is the bleeding spear which was a symbol of righteous vengeance unperformed in the old Bardic day of Britain; it became the lance of Longinus which pierced the side of Christ when Christian symbolism was applied to the ancient Arthurian legends; and you may read in Malory's "Morte d'Arthur" how a dolorous stroke dealt with it by Balin opened a wound in the side of King Pellam from which he suffered many years, till Galahad healed him in the quest of the Sangreal by touching the wound with the blood which flowed from the spear.

These are the folklore elements in Wagner's "Parsifal." It is plain that they might have been wrought into a drama substantially like that which was the poet-composer's last gift to art without loss of either dignity or beauty. Then his drama would have been like a glorified fairy play, imposing and of gracious loveliness, and there would have been nothing to quarrel about. But Wagner was a philosopher of a sort, and a sincere believer in the idea that the theatre might be made to occupy the same place in the modern world that it did in the classic. It was to replace the Church and teach by direct preachments as well as allegory the philosophical notions which he thought essential to the salvation of humanity. For the chief of these he went to that system of philosophy which rests on the idea that the world is to be redeemed by negation of the will to live, the conquering of all desire — that the highest happiness is the achievement of nirvana, nothingness. This conception finds its highest expression in the quietism and indifferentism of the old Brahmanic religion (if such it can be called), in which holiness was to be obtained by speculative contemplation, which seems to me the quintessence of selfishness. In the reformed Brahmanism called Buddhism, there appeared along with the old principle of self-erasure a compassionate sympathy for others. Asceticism was not put aside, but regulated and ordered, wrought into a communal system. It was purged of some of its selfishness by appreciation of the loveliness of compassionate love as exemplified in the life of Çakya-Muni and those labors which made him one of the many redeemers and saviours of which Hindu literature is full. Something of this was evidently in the mind of Wagner as long ago as 1857, when, working on "Tristan und Isolde," he for a while harbored the idea of bringing Parzival (as he would have called him then) into the presence of the dying *Tristan* to comfort him with a sermon on the happiness of renunciation. Long before Wagner had sketched a tragedy entitled

"Jesus of Nazareth," the hero of which was to be a human philosopher who preached the saving grace of love and sought to redeem his time and people from the domination of conventional law, the off-spring of selfishness.   His philosophy was socialism imbued by love.   Before Wagner finished "Tristan und Isolde" he had outlined a Hindu play in which hero and heroine were to accept the doctrines of the Buddha, take the vow of chastity, renounce the union toward which love impelled them, and enter into the holy community.   Blending these two schemes, Wagner created "Parsifal."   For this drama he could draw the principle of compassionate pity and fellow-suffering from the stories of both Çakya-Muni and Jesus of Nazareth.   But for the sake of a spectacle, I think, he accepted the Christian doctrine of the Atonement with all its mystical ele-ments; for they alone put the necessary symbolical significance into the principal apparatus of the play — the Holy Grail and the Sacred Lance.[1]

[1] "Parsifal" was performed for the first time at the Wagner Festival Theatre in Bayreuth on July 28, 1882.   The prescription that it should belong exclusively to Bayreuth was respected till December 24, 1903, when Heinrich Conried, taking advantage of the circumstance that there was no copyright on the stage rep resentation of the work in America, brought it out with sensa-tional success at the Metropolitan Opera-house in New York. The principal artists concerned in this and subsequent perform-ances were Milka Ternina (*Kundry*), Alois Burgstaller (*Parsifal*), Anton Van Rooy (*Amfortas*), Robert Blass (*Gurnemanz*), Otto Goritz (*Klingsor*) and Louise Homer (*a voice*).

CHAPTER XV

THE best definition of the true purpose of comedy which I know is that it is to "chastise manners with a smile" (*Ridendo castigat mores*); and it has no better exemplification in the literature of opera than Wagner's "Die Meistersinger von Nürnberg." Wagner's mind dwelt much on Greek things, and as he followed a classical principle in choosing mythological and legendary subjects for his tragedies, so also he followed classical precedent in drawing the line between tragedy and comedy. "Tannhäuser," "Tristan und Isolde," "Der Ring des Nibelungen," "Parsifal," and, in a lesser degree, "Lohengrin," are examples of the old tragedy type. To them the restrictions of time and space do not apply. They deal with large passions, and their heroes are gods or godlike men who are shattered against the rock of immutable law — the "Fate" of the ancient tragedians. His only significant essay in the field of comedy was made in "Die Meistersinger," and this is as faithful to the old conception of comedy as the dramas mentioned are to that of tragedy. It deals with the manners, vices, and follies of the common people; and, therefore, it has local environment and illustrates a period in history.

It was conceived as a satyr-play following a tragedy ("Tannhäuser"), and though there can be no doubt that it was designed to teach a lesson in art, it nevertheless aims primarily to amuse, and only secondarily to instruct and correct. Moreover, even the most cutting of its satirical lashes are administered with a smile.

As a picture of the social life of a quaint German city three and a half centuries ago, its vividness and truthfulness are beyond all praise; it is worthy to stand beside the best dramas of the world, and has no equal in operatic literature. The food for its satire, too, is most admirably chosen, for no feature of the social life of that place and period is more amiably absurd than the efforts of the handicraftsmen and tradespeople, with their prosaic surroundings, to keep alive by dint of pedantic formularies the spirit of minstrelsy, which had a natural stimulus in the chivalric life of the troubadours and minnesingers of whom the mastersingers thought themselves the direct and legitimate successors. In its delineation of the pompous doings of the mastersingers, Wagner is true to the letter. He has vitalized the dry record to be found in old Wagenseil's book on Nuremberg,[1] and intensified the vivid description of a mastersingers' meeting which the curious may read in August Hagen's novel

[1] "Joh. Christophori Wagenseilii De Sacri Rom. Imperii Libera Civitate Noribergensi Commentatio. Accedit, De Germaniæ Phonascorum Von Der Meister-Singer Origine, Præstantia, Utilitate, et Institutis, Sermone Vernaculo Liber. Altdorf Noricorum Typis Impensisque Jodoci Wilhelmi Kohlesii. CIↃ IↃↃ XCVII."

"Norica." His studies have been marvellously exact and careful, and he has put Wagenseil's book under literal and liberal contribution, as will appear after a while. Now it seems best to tell the story of the comedy before discussing it further.

Veit Pogner, a rich silversmith, desiring to honor the craft of the mastersingers, to whose guild he belongs, offers his daughter *Eva* in marriage to the successful competitor at the annual meeting of the mastersingers on the feast of St. John. *Eva* is in love (she declares it in the impetuous manner peculiar to Wagner's heroines) with *Walther von Stolzing*, a young Franconian knight; and the knight with her. After a flirtation in church during divine service, *Walther* meets her before she leaves the building, and asks if she be betrothed. She answers in the affirmative, but it is to the unknown victor at the contest of singing on the morrow. He resolves to enter the guild so as to be qualified for the competition. A trial of candidates takes place in the church of St. Catherine in the afternoon, and *Walther*, knowing nothing of the rules of the mastersingers, some of which have hurriedly been outlined to him by *David*, a youngster who is an apprentice at shoemaking and also songmaking, fails, though *Hans Sachs*, a master in both crafts, recognizes evidences of genius in the knight's song, and espouses his cause as against *Beckmesser*, the town clerk, who aims at acquiring *Pogner's* fortune by winning his daughter. The young people, in despair at *Walther's* failure, are about to elope when they are prevented by the arrival on the scene of *Beck-messer*. It is night, and he wishes to serenade *Eva;* *Sachs* sits cobbling at his bench, while *Eva's* nurse, *Magdalena*, disguised, sits at a window to hear the serenade in her mistress's stead. *Sachs* interrupts the serenader, who is an ill-natured clown, by lustily shouting a song in which he seeks also to give warning of knowledge of her intentions to *Eva*, whose departure with the knight had been interrupted by the cobbler when he came out of his shop to work in the cool of the evening; but he finally agrees to listen to *Beckmesser* on condition that he be permitted to mark each error in the composition by striking his lap-stone. The humorous consequences can be imagined. *Beckmesser* becomes enraged at *Sachs*, sings more and more falsely, until *Sachs* is occupied in beating a veritable tattoo on his lap-stone. To add to *Beckmesser's* discomfiture, *David*, *Sachs's* apprentice and *Magdalena's* sweetheart, thinking the serenade intended for his love, begins to belabor the singer with a club; neighbors join in the brawl, which proceeds right merrily until interrupted by the horn of a night watchman. The dignity and vigor of Wagner's poetical fancy are attested by the marvellous close of the act. The tremendous hubbub of the street brawl is at its height and the business of the act is at an end. The coming of the *Watchman*, who has evidently been aroused by the noise, is foretold by his horn. The crowd is seized with a panic. All the brawlers disappear behind doors. The sleepy *Watchman* stares about him in amazement, rubs his eyes, sings the monotonous chant which publishes the hour of the night, continues on his round, and the moon shines on a quiet street in Nuremberg as the curtain falls.

In the third act *Walther*, who had been taken into his house by *Sachs* and spent the night there, sings a recital of a dream; and *Sachs*, struck by its beauty, transcribes it, punctuating it with bits of comments and advice. *Beckmesser*, entering *Sachs's* shop when the cobbler-poet is out for a moment, finds the song, concludes that it is *Sachs's* own composition, and appropriates it. *Sachs*, discovering the theft, gives the song to *Beckmesser*, who secures a promise from *Sachs* not to betray him, and resolves to sing it at the competition. The festival is celebrated in a meadow on the banks of the Pegnitz River, between Fürth and Nuremberg. It begins with a gathering of all the guilds of Nuremberg, each division in the procession entering to characteristic music — a real masterpiece, whether viewed as spectacle, poetry, or music. The competition begins, and *Beckmesser* makes a monstrously stupid parody of *Walther's* song. He is hooted at and ridiculed, and, becoming enraged, charges the authorship of the song on *Sachs*, who coolly retorts that it is a good song when correctly sung. To prove his words he calls on *Walther* to sing it. The knight complies, the mastersingers are delighted, and *Pogner* rewards the singer with *Eva's* hand. *Sachs*, at the request of the presiding officer of the guild, also offers him the medal as the insignia of membership in the guild of mastersingers. *Walther's* experience with the pedantry which had condemned him the day before, when he had sung as impulse, love, and youthful ardor had prompted, leads him to decline the distinction; but the old poet discourses on the respect due to the masters and their work as the guaranty of the permanence of German art, and persuades him to enter the guild of mastersingers.

"Die Meistersinger" is photographic in many of its scenes, personages, and incidents; but so far as the stage pictures which we are accustomed to see in the opera-houses of New York and the European capitals are concerned, this statement must be taken with a great deal of allowance, owing to the fact that opera directors, stage managers, scene painters, and costumers are blithely indifferent to the verities of history. I have never seen a mimic reproduction of the church of St. Catherine on any stage; yet the church stands to-day with its walls intact as they were at the time in which the comedy is supposed to play. This time is fixed by the fact that its principal character, *Hans Sachs*, is represented as a widower who might himself be a suitor for *Eva's* hand. Now the veritable Sachs was a widower in the summer of the year 1560. I visited Nuremberg in 1886 in search of relics of the mastersingers and had no little difficulty in finding the church. It had not been put to its original purposes for more than a hundred years, and there seemed to be but few people in Nuremberg who knew of its existence. It

has been many things since it became secularized :
a painter's academy, drawing-school, military hos-

THE CHURCH OF ST. CATHERINE IN NUREMBERG
(Sketched for the author by Louis Loeb in 1891)

pital, warehouse, concert-hall, and, no doubt, a score
of other things. When I found it with the aid of

the police it was the paint-shop and scenic store-room of the municipal theatre. It is a small build-ing, utterly unpretentious of exterior and interior, innocent of architectural beauty, hidden away in the middle of a block of lowly buildings used as dwellings, carpenter shops, and the like. That Wagner never visited it is plain from the fact that though he makes it the scene of one act of his comedy (as he had to do to be historically accurate), his stage directions could not possibly be accommodated to its architecture. In 1891 Mr. Louis Loeb, the American artist, whose early death in the summer of 1909 is widely mourned, visited the spot and made drawings for me of the exterior and interior of the church as it looked then. The church was built in the last half decade of the thirteenth century, and on its water-stained walls, when I visited it, there were still to be seen faint traces of the frescoes which once adorned it and were painted in the fourteenth, fifteenth, and six-teenth centuries; but they were ruined beyond hope of restoration. In the Germanic Museum I found a wooden tablet dating back to 1581, painted by one Franz Hein. It preserves portraits of four distinguished members of the mastersingers' guild. There is a middle panel occupied by two pictures, the upper showing King David, the patron saint of the guild, so forgetful of chronology as to be praying before a crucifix, the lower a meeting of the master-singers. Over the heads of the assemblage is a representative of the medallion with which the vic-tor in a contest used to be decorated, as we see in the last scene of Wagner's comedy. One of these decorations was given to the guild by Sachs and was in use for a whole century. At the end of that time it had become so worn that Wagenseil replaced it with another.

Church and tablet are the only relics of the mastersingers left in Nuremberg which may be called personal. I had expected to find autobiographic manuscripts of Sachs, but in this was disappointed. There is a volume of mastersongs in the poet-cobbler's handwriting in the Royal Library of Berlin, and one of these is the composition of the veritable Sixtus Beckmesser; but most of the Sachs manuscripts are in Zwickau. In the Bibliotheca Norica Williana, incorporated with the Municipal Library of Nuremberg, there are several volumes of mastersingers' songs purchased from an old mastersinger some 135 years ago, and from these the students may learn the structure and spirit of the mastersongs of the period of the opera as well as earlier and later periods, though he will find all the instruction he needs in any dozen or twenty of the 4275 mastersongs written by Hans Sachs. The manuscript books known serve to prove one thing which needed not to have called up a doubt. In them are poems from all of the mastersingers who make up the meeting which condemns *Walther* in St. Catherine's church. Wagner has adhered to the record.[1] The most inter-

---

[1] I quote from Wagenseil's book — he is writing about the history of the mastersingers: "Nach der Stadt Mäyntz, hat in den Stätten Nürnberg und Strassburg; die Meister-Singer-Kunst

esting of Sixtus Beckmesser's compositions is "A New Year's Song," preserved in the handwriting of Sachs in the Royal Library at Berlin. This I have translated in order to show the form of the old mastersongs as described by the apprentice, *David*, in Wagner's comedy, and also to prove (so far as a somewhat free translation can) that the veritable Beckmesser was not the stupid dunce that Wagner, for purposes of his own, and tempted, doubtless, by the humor which he found in the name, represented him to be. In fact, I am strongly tempted to believe that with the exception of Sachs himself, Beckmesser was the best of the mastersingers of the Nuremberg school:—

A NEW YEAR'S SONG

By Sixtus Beckmesser

(First "Stoll")

Joy
Christian thoughts employ
This day
Doth say
The Book of old
That we should hold
The faith foretold;
For naught doth doubt afford.
The patriarchs with one accord

sonderlich floriret/ wie dann auchXII. Alte Nürnbergische Meister annoch im Beruff sind; so mit Namen geheissen/ 1. Veit Pogner. 2. Cuntz Vogelgesang. 3. Hermann Ortel. 4. Conrad Nachtigal. 5. Fritz Zorn. 6. Sixtus Beckmesser. 7. Fritz Kohtner. 8. Niclaus Vogel. 9. Augustin Moser. 10. Hannss Schwartz. 11. Ulrich Eisslinger. 12. Hannss Foltz."

Lived hoping that the Lord
Would rout the wicked horde.
 Thus saith the word
 To all believers given.

(*Second* "*Stoll*")

 God
Council held, triune,
When soon
The boon
 The son foresaw:
 Fulfilled the law
 That we might draw
Salvation's prize. God then
An angel sent cross moor and fen,
('Twas Gabriel, heaven's denizen,)
To Mary, purest maid 'mongst men.
 He greeted her
 With blessings sent from heaven.

(*The* "*Abgesang*")

Thus spake the angel graciously:
 " The Lord with thee,
 Thou blessed she;
The Lord's voice saith,
Which breathes thy breath,
That men have earned eternal death.
 Faith
 Saves alone from sin's subjection;
 For while weak Eve God's anger waked,
'Twas, Ave, thine the blest election
To give the world peace and protection,
 Most blessed gift
 To mortals ever given!"

In Nuremberg the veritable Hans Sachs wrote plays on Tännhauser, Tristan, and Siegfried between three and four hundred years before the poet-composer who put the old cobbler-poet into his comedy. Very naïve and very archaic indeed are Hans Sachs's dramas compared with Wagner's; but it is, perhaps, not an exaggeration to say that Sachs was as influential a factor in the dramatic life of his time as Wagner in ours. He was among the earliest of the German poets who took up the miracle plays and mysteries after they had been abandoned by the church and developed them on the lines which ran out into the classic German drama. His immediate predecessors were the writers of the so-called "Fastnacht" (*Mardi-gras*) plays, who flourished in Nuremberg in the fifteenth century. Out of these plays German comedy arose, and among those who rocked its cradle was another of the mastersingers who plays a part in Wagner's opera, — Hans Folz. It was doubtless largely due to the influence of Hans Sachs that the guild of mastersingers built the first German theatre in Nuremberg in 1550. Before then plays with religious subjects were performed in St. Catherine's church, as we have seen, the meeting place of the guild. Secular plays were represented in private houses.

Hans Sachs wrote no less than 208 dramas, which he divided into "Carnival Plays," "Plays," "Comedies," and "Tragedies." He dropped the first designation in his later years, but his first dramatic effort was a *Fastnachtspiel,* and treated the subject of Tannhäuser and Venus. It bears the date February 21, 1517, and was therefore written 296 years before Wagner was born. Of what is now dramatic form and structure, there is not a sign in this play. It is merely a dialogue between *Venus* and various persons who stand for as many classes of society. The title is: "Das Hoffgesindt Veneris," or, as it might be rendered in English, "The Court of Venus." The characters are a *Herald, Faithful Eckhardt, Danheuser* (*sic*), *Dame Venus*, a *Knight, Physician, Citizen, Peasant, Soldier, Gambler, Drunkard, Maid,* and *Wife*. The *Knight, Citizen,* and the others appear in turn before *Venus* and express contempt for her powers, — the *Knight* because of his bravery, the *Physician* because of his learning, the *Maid* because of her virtue, the *Wife* because of her honor. *Faithful Eckhardt,* a character that figures in many Thuringian legends, especially in tales of the Wild Hunt, warns each person in turn to beware of *Venus*. The latter listens to each boast and lets loose an arrow. Each boaster succumbs with a short lamentation. When the play opens, *Danheuser* is already a prisoner of the goddess. After all the rest have fallen victims, he begs for his release, and they join in his petition. Venus rejects the prayer, speaks in praise of her powers, and calls on a piper for music. A general dance follows, whereupon the company go with the enchantress into the Venusberg. The last speech of *Venus* ends with the line: —

So says Hans Sachs of Nuremberg.

There is but a single scene in "The Court of
Venus." In other plays written in after years, no
matter how often the action demanded it, there is
neither change of scenes nor division into acts; and the
personages, whether Biblical or classical, talk in the
manner of the simple folk of the sixteenth century.
Sachs's tragedy, "Von der strengen Lieb' Herrn Tristrant mit der schönen Königin Isalden" ("Of the
strong love of Lord Tristram and the beautiful
Queen Iseult"), contains seven acts, as is specified in
the continuation of the title "und hat sieben Akte."
It was written thirty-six years later than the carnival play and three years after the establishment
of a theatre in Nuremberg by the mastersingers.
Each act ends with a triple rhyme. Though Sachs
uses stage directions somewhat freely compared
with the other dramatists of the period, the personages all speak in the same manner, and time and
space are annihilated in the action most bewilderingly. Thus, no sooner does *Herr Tristrant* volun-
teer to meet *Morhold der Held* to settle the question
of "Curnewelshland's" tribute to "Irland" than the
two are at it hammer and tongs on an island in
the ocean. All the other incidents of the old legends
follow as fast as they are mentioned. *Tristrant*
saves his head in Ireland when discovered as the
slayer of *Morhold* by ridding the country of a dragon,
and is repeatedly convicted of treachery and taken
back into confidence by *König Marx*, as one may
read in Sir Thomas Malory's "Morte d'Arthur."
Sachs follows an old conclusion of the story and

gives *Tristrant* a second *Iseult* to wife, and she tells
the lie about the sails. The first *Iseult* dies of a
broken heart at the sight of her lover's bier, and
the *Herald* in a speech draws the moral of the tale:—

.Aus dem so lass dich treulich warnen,
O Mensch, vor solcher Liebe Garnen,
Und spar dein Lieb' bis in die Eh',
Dann hab' Ein lieb' und keine meh.
Diesselb' Lieb' ist mit Gott und Ehren,
Die Welt damit fruchtbar zu mehren.
Dazu giebt Gott selbst allewegen
Sein' Gnad' Gedeihen und milden Segen.
Dass stete Lieb' und Treu' aufwachs'
Im ehlich'n Stand', das wünscht Hans Sachs.

One of the most thrilling scenes in "Die Meistersinger" is the greeting of *Hans Sachs* by the populace when the hero enters with the mastersingers'
guild at the festival of St. John (the chorus, "Wach
auf! es nahet gen den Tag"). Here there is another
illustration of Wagner's adherence to the verities
of history, or rather, of his employment of them.
The words of the uplifting choral song are not Wagner's, but were written by the old cobbler-poet himself. Wagner's stage people apply them to their
idol, but Sachs uttered them in praise of Martin
Luther; they form the beginning of his poem entitled "The Wittenberg Nightingale," which was
printed in 1523.

To the old history of Nuremberg written by Wagenseil, Wagner went for other things besides the
theatre and personages of his play. From it he got

the rules which governed the meeting of the mastersingers, like that which follows the religious service
in the church of St. Catherine in the first act, and
the singular names of the melodies to which, according to *David*, the candidates for mastersingers'
honors were in the habit of improvising their songs.
In one instance he made a draft on an authentic
mastersinger melody. The march which is used
throughout the comedy to symbolize the guild begins as follows: —

Here we have an exact quotation from the beginning of the first *Gesetz* in the "Long Tone" of Heinrich Müglin, which was a tune that every candidate
for membership in the guild had to be able to sing.
The old song is given in full in Wagenseil's book, and
on the next page I have reproduced a portion of
this song in *fac-simile*, so that my readers can observe the accuracy of Wagner's quotation and
form an idea of the nature of the poetic frenzy
which used to fill the mastersingers, as well as enjoy the ornamental passages (called "Blumen"
in the old regulations) and compare them with the
fiorituri of *Beckmesser's* serenade.

There is no doubt in my mind but that Wagner's
purpose in "Die Meistersinger" was to celebrate
the triumph of the natural, poetical impulse, stimulated by healthy emotion and communion with

Part of the "Meisterliche Hort" in Wagenseil's book on the Nuremberg Mastersingers, printed in 1697.

nature, over pedantry and hide-bound conservatism. In the larger study of the opera made in another place, I have attempted to show that the contest is in reality the one which is always waging between the principles of romanticism and classicism, a contest which is essentially friendly and necessary to progress. The hero of the comedy is not *Walther*, but *Sachs*, who represents in himself both principles, who stands between the combatants and checks the extravagances of both parties.[1]

Like Beethoven in his "Leonore" overtures written for the opera "Fidelio," Wagner constructs the symphonic introduction to his comedy so as to indicate the elements of his dramatic story, their progress in the development of the play, and, finally, the outcome. The melodies are of two sorts conforming to the two parties into which the personages

[1] "In the musical contest it is only the perverted idea of Classicism which is treated with contumely and routed; the glorification of the triumph of Romanticism is found in the stupendously pompous and brilliant setting given to the mastersingers' music at the end. You see already in this prelude that Wagner is a true comedian. He administers chastisement with a smile and chooses for its subject only things which are temporary aberrations from the good. What is strong, and true, and pure, and wholesome in the art of the mastersingers he permits to pass through his satirical fires unscathed. Classicism, in its original sense as the conservator of that which is highest and best in art, he leaves unharmed, presenting her after her trial, as Tennyson presents his Princess at the close of his corrective poem, when

"All
Her falser self slipt from her like a robe,
And left her woman, lovelier in her mood
Than in her mould that other, when she came
From barren deeps to conquer all with love."

"Studies in the Wagnerian Drama," by H. E. KREHBIEL, p. 95.

of the play can be divided; and, like those parties, the melodies are broadly distinguished by external physiognomy and emotional essence. Most easily recognized are the two broad march tunes typical of the mastersingers and their pageantry. One of them has already been presented. Like its companion, —

which opens the prelude, it is a strong, simple melody, made on the intervals of the diatonic scale, square-cut in rhythm, firm and dignified, and, like the mastersingers, complacent and a trifle pompous in stride. The three melodies which are presented in opposition to the spirit represented by the mastersingers and their typical music, are disclosed by a study of the comedy to be associated with the passion of the young lovers, *Walther* and *Eva*. They differ in every respect — melodic, rhythmic, and harmonic, — from those which stand for the old guildsmen and their rule-of-thumb notions. They are chromatic, as see this: —

and this (which is the melody which in a broadened form becomes that of *Walther's* prize song): —

and this, which is peculiarly the symbol of youthful ardor: —

Their rhythms are less regular and more eager (note
the influence of syncopation upon them); they are
harmonized with greater warmth and infused with
greater passion. In the development of the prelude
these melodies are presented at first consecutively,
then as in conflict (first one, then another pushing
forward for expression), finally in harmonious and
contented union. The middle part of the prelude,
in which the opening march tune is heard in short,
quick notes (in diminution, as the theoreticians
say) may be looked upon as caricaturing the mastersingers, not in their fair estate, but as they are satirized in the comedy in the person of *Beckmesser.*

CHAPTER XVI

In the last hundred lines of the last book of his epic poem to which Wagner went for the fundamental incidents, not principles, of his "Parsifal," Wolfram von Eschenbach tells the story of one of the Grail King's sons whom he calls Loherangrin. This son was a lad when Parzival (thus Wolfram spells the name) became King of the Holy Grail and the knights who were in its service. When he had grown to manhood, there lived in Brabant a queen who was equally gifted in beauty, wealth, and gentleness. Many princes sought her hand in marriage, but she refused them all, and waited for the coming of one whom God had disclosed to her in a vision. One day a knight of great beauty and nobley, as Sir Thomas Mallory would have said, came to Antwerp in a boat drawn by a swan. To him the queen at once gave greeting as lord of her dominions; but in the presence of the assembled folk he said to her: "If I am to become ruler of this land, know that it will be at great sacrifice to myself. Should you nevertheless wish me to remain with you, you must never ask who I am; otherwise I must leave you forever." The queen made solemn protestation that

309

she would never do aught against his will. Then her marriage with the stranger knight was celebrated, and they abode together long in happiness and honor. But at the last the queen was led to put the fatal question. Then the swan appeared with the boat, and Loherangrin, for it was he, was drawn back to Montsalvat, whence he had come. But to those whom he left behind he gave his sword, horn, and ring.

There are other mediæval poems which deal with the story of Lohengrin, more, indeed, than can or need be discussed here. Some, however, deserve consideration because they supply elements which Wagner used in his opera but did not find in Wolfram's poem. Wagner went, very naturally, to a poem of the thirteenth century, entitled "Lohengrin," for the majority of the incidents of the drama. Thence he may have drawn the motive for the curiosity of *Elsa* touching the personality of her husband. Of course, it lies in human nature, as stories which are hundreds if not thousands of years older attest; but I am trying, as I have been in preceding chapters in this book, to account for the presence of certain important elements in Wagner's opera, and so this poem must also be considered. In it Lohengrin rescues Elsa, the Duchess of Brabant, from the false accusations of Telramund, the knight having been summoned from Montsalvat (or "Monsalväsch," to be accurate) by the ringing of a bell which Elsa had taken from a falcon's leg. The knight marries her, but first exacts a promise that she will never seek of him

knowledge of his race or country. After the happy
domestic life of the pair has been described, it is told
how Lohengrin overthrew the Duke of Cleves at a
tournament in Cologne and broke his arm. The
Duchess of Cleves felt humiliated at the overthrow
of her husband by a knight of whom nothing was
known, and wickedly insinuated that it was a pity
that so puissant a jouster should not be of noble
birth, thereby instilling a fatal curiosity into the
mind of the Lady of Brabant, which led to questions
which Lohengrin answered before the emperor's
court and then disappeared from view. From "Der
jüngere Titurel," another mediæval poem, came the
suggestion that the mysterious knight's prowess was
due to sorcery and might be set at naught if his bodily
integrity were destroyed even in the slightest degree.
In the French tale of "Le Chevalier au Cygne," as
told in the "Chansons de geste," you may read the
story of Helyas, who was one of seven children of
King Oriant and Queen Beatrix, who were born with
silver chains around their necks. The chains being
removed with evil purpose, the children turned
into swans and flew away — all but one, Helyas,
who was absent at the time. But Helyas got
possession of all the chains but one, which had
been wrought into a cup, and one day, when he heard
the sound of wings, and six swans let themselves
down into the water, he threw the chains around
their necks, and they at once assumed the forms of
his brothers. Also how, one day, Helyas, from the
window of his palace, saw a swan drawing a boat,

and how he donned his armor, took a golden horn, and was drawn away to Nimwegen, where Emperor Otto was holding court. There he found that the Count of Blankenbourg had accused his sister-in-law, the Duchess of Bouillon, of having poisoned her husband, and had laid claim to the duchy. There was to be a trial by ordeal of battle, and while the duchess waited for the coming of a champion, lo! there was the sound of a horn, and Helyas came down the river in a boat drawn by a swan, undertook the cause of the innocent lady, slew her accuser, and married her daughter. For long she was a good and faithful wife, and bore him a child who became the mother of Godfrey de Bouillon, Baldwin de Sebourg, and Eustace de Boulogne. But one day she asked of her lord his name and race. Then he bade her repair to Nimwegen, and commending her and her daughter to the care of the emperor, he departed thence in a swan-drawn boat and was never seen more.

Here we have the essentials of the story which Wagner wrought into his opera "Lohengrin." Only a few details need be added to make the plot complete. The meeting of *Lohengrin* and *Elsa* takes place on the banks of the river Scheldt in Brabant. The *King* has come to ask the help of the Brabantians against the Huns, who are invading Germany. He finds Brabant in a disturbed state. The throne is vacant; *Count Frederick of Telramund,* who has his eyes upon it, had offered his hand in marriage to *Elsa,* who, with her brother, *Gottfried,* had been left in his care on the death of their father, but had met with a refusal. He had then married *Ortrud*, a Frisian princess. She is the last of a royal line, but a pagan, and practises sorcery. To promote the ambition of herself and her husband, she has changed *Gottfried* into a swan by throwing a magical chain about his neck, and persuaded *Telramund* to accuse *Elsa* of having murdered the boy in the hope of enjoying the throne together with a secret lover. The *King* summons *Elsa* to answer the charge and decrees trial by ordeal of battle. Commanded to name her champion, she tells of a knight seen in a dream: upon him alone will she rely. Not until the second call of the *Herald* has gone out and *Elsa* has fallen to her knees in prayer does the champion appear. He is a knight in shining white armor who comes in a boat drawn by a swan. He accepts the gage of battle, after asking *Elsa* whether or not she wants him to be her husband if victorious in the combat, and exacting a promise never to ask of him whence he came or what his name or race. He overcomes *Telramund*, but gives him his life; the *King*, however, banishes the false accuser and sets the stranger over the people of Brabant with the title of Protector. *Telramund* is overwhelmed by his misfortunes, but *Ortrud* urges him to make another trial to regain what he has lost. The knight, she says, had won by witchcraft, and if but the smallest joint of his body could be taken from him, he would be impotent. Together they instil disquiet and suspicion into the mind of *Elsa* as she is about to enter the minster to be married. After the wedding guests have departed, her newly found happiness is disturbed by doubt, and a painful curiosity manifests itself in her speech. *Lohengrin* admonishes, reproves, and warns in words of tenderest love. He had given up greater glories than his new life had to offer out of love for her. A horrible fear seizes her: he who had so mysteriously come would as mysteriously depart. Cost what it may, she must know who he is. She asks the question, but before he can reply *Telramund* rushes into the room with drawn weapon. *Elsa* has but time to hand *Lohengrin* his sword, with which he stretches the would-be assassin dead on the chamber floor. Then he commands that the body be carried before the *King*, whither he also directs her maids to escort his wife. There is another conclave of *King* and nobles. *Lohengrin* asks if he had acted within his right in slaying *Telramund*, and his deed is approved by all. Then he gives public answer to *Elsa's* question:

> In distant lands, where ye can never enter,
> A castle stands and Montsalvat its name;
> A radiant temple rises from its centre
> More glorious far than aught of earthly fame.
> And there a vessel of most wondrous splendor,
> A shrine, most holy, guarded well doth rest,
> To which but mortals purest service render —
> 'Twas brought to earth by hosts of angels blest!
> Once every year a dove from heaven descendeth
> To strengthen then its wondrous powers anew:
> 'Tis called the Grail — and purest faith it lendeth
> To those good knights who are its chosen few.
> To serve the Grail whoe'er is once elected
> Receives from it a supernatural might;
> From baneful harm and fraud is he protected,

Away from him flees death and gloom of night!
Yea, whom by it to distant lands is bidden
As champion to some virtuous cause maintain,
Well knows its powers are from him never hidden,
If, as its knight, he unrevealed remain.
Such wondrous nature is the Grail's great blessing,
Reveal'd must then the knight from mortals flee:
Let not rest in your hearts a doubt oppressing, —
If known to you he saileth o'er the sea.
Now list what he to you in troth declareth:
The Grail obeying here to you I came.
My father Parzival, a crown he weareth,
His knight am I and Lohengrin my name![1]

A prohibition which rests upon all who are served
by a Knight of the Grail having been violated, he
must depart from thence; but before going he gives
his sword, horn, and ring to *Elsa*, and tells her that
had he been permitted to live but one year at her
side, her brother would have returned in conduct of
the Grail. The swan appears to convey him back to
his resplendent home. *Ortrud* recognizes the chain
around its neck and gloats over her triumph; but
Lohengrin hears her shout. He sinks on his knees
in silent prayer. As he rises, a white dove floats
downward toward the boat. *Lohengrin* detaches the
chain from the neck of the swan. The bird disappears, and in its place stands *Gottfried*, released from
the spell put upon him by the sorceress. The dove
draws the boat with its celestial passenger away, and
Elsa sinks lifeless into the arms of her brother.

In this story of *Lohengrin* there is an admixture of

[1] John P. Jackson's translation.

several elements which once had no association. It is the story of an adventure of a Knight of the Holy Grail; also a story involving the old principle of taboo; and one of many stories of the transformation of a human being into a swan, or a swan into a human being. This swan myth is one of the most widely spread of all transformation tales; it may even be found in the folk-stories of the American Indians. To discuss this feature would carry one too far afield, and I have a different purpose in view.

* * *

The two Figaro operas, the discussion of which opened this book, were composed by different men, and a generation of time separated their production. The opera which deals with the second chapter of the adventures of Seville's factotum was composed first, and is the greater work of the two; yet we have seen how pleasantly they can be associated with each other, and, no doubt, many who admire them have felt with me the wish that some musician with sufficient skill and the needful reverence would try the experiment of remodelling the two and knitting their bonds closer by giving identity of voice to the personages who figure in both. The Wagnerian list presents something like a parallel, and it would be a pleasant thing if two of the modern poet-composer's dramas which have community of subject could be brought into similar association, so that one might be performed as a sequel to the other. The operas are "Lohengrin" and "Parsifal." A generation also lies between them, and they ought to bear a relation-ship to each other something like that existing between "Le Nozze di Figaro" and "Il Barbiere di Siviglia." Indeed, the bond ought to be closer, for one man wrote books and music as well of the Grail dramas, whereas different librettists and different composers created the Figaro comedies. But it will never be possible to bring Wagner's most popular opera and his "stage-consecrating play" into logical union, notwithstanding that both deal with the legend of the Holy Grail and that the hero of one proclaims himself to be the son of the hero of the other. Wagner cast a loving glance at the older child of his brain when he quoted some of the "swan music" of "Lohengrin" in "Parsifal"; but he built an insurmountable wall between them when he forsook the sane and simple ideas which inspired him in writing "Lohengrin" for the complicated fabric of mediæval Christianity and Buddhism which he strove to set forth in "Parsifal." In 1847 Wagner was willing to look at the hero of the quest of the Holy Grail whom we call Percival through the eyes of his later guide, Wolfram von Eschenbach. To Wolfram Parzival was a married man; more than that — a married lover, clinging with devotion to the memory of the wife from whose arms he had torn himself to undertake the quest, and losing himself in tender brooding for days when the sight of blood-spots on the snow suggested to his fancy the red and white of fair Konwiramur's cheeks. Thirty years later Wagner could only conceive of his

Grail hero as a celibate and an ascetic. *Lohengrin* glories in the fact that he is the son of him who wears the crown of the Grail; but *Parsifal* disowns his son.

This is one instance of the incoherency of the two Grail dramas. There is another, and by this second departure from the old legends which furnished forth his subject, Wagner made "Lohengrin" and "Parsifal" forever irreconcilable. The whole fabric of the older opera rests on the forbidden question: —

> Nie sollst du mich befragen,
> noch Wissen's Sorge tragen,
> woher ich kam der Fahrt,
> noch wie mein Nam' und Art.[1]

So impressed was Wagner with the significance of this dramatic motive sixty years ago, that he gave it a musical setting which still stands as the finest of all his many illustrations of the principle of fundamental or typical phrases in dramatic music: —

Nie   sollst   du   mich   be - fra - gen

And no wonder. No matter where he turned in his studies of the Grail legend, he was confronted by the fact that it was by asking a question that the seeker

[1] In Mr. John P. Jackson's translation: —

> Ne'er with thy fears shalt task me,
> Nor questions idly ask me:
> The land and from whence I came,
> Nor yet my race and name.

after the Grail was to release the ailing king, whom he found in the castle in which the talismans were preserved, from his sufferings. In the Welsh tale of Peredur and the French romances the question went only to the meaning of the talismans; but this did not suffice Wolfram von Eschenbach, who in many ways raised the ethical standard of the Grail legend. He changed the question so as to make it a sign of affectionate and compassionate interest on the part of the questioner; it was no longer, "What mean the bloody head and the bleeding lance?" but "What ails thee, uncle?"

Wagner was fond, a little overfond, indeed, of appealing to the public over the heads of the critics, of going to the jury rather than the judge, when asking for appreciation of his dramas; but nothing is plainer to the close student than that he was never wholly willing to credit the public with possession of that high imaginativeness to which his dramas more than those of any other composer make appeal. His first conception of the finale of "Tannhäuser," for instance, was beautiful, poetical, and reasonable, for the sake of a spectacle he reconstructed it after the original production and plunged it into indefensible confusion and absurdity.

A desire to abstain as much as possible from criticism (that not being the purpose of this book) led me to avoid mention of this circumstance in the exposition of "Tannhäuser"; but I find that I must now set it forth, though briefly. In the original form of the opera there was no funeral procession

and no death of the hero beside the bier of the atoning
saint.　The scene between *Tannhäuser* and *Wolfram*
was interrupted by the tolling of a bell in the castle to
indicate the death of *Elizabeth* and the appearance
of a glow of rose-colored light across the valley to
suggest the presence of *Venus*.　By bringing the
corpse of *Elizabeth* on the stage so that *Tannhäuser* might die by its side, Wagner was guilty
of worse than an anachronism.　The time which
elapses in the drama between *Elizabeth's* departure
from the scene and her return as a corpse is just as
long as the song which *Wolfram* sings in which he
apostrophizes her as his "holder Abendstern" —
just as long and not a moment longer.　There is no
question here of poetical license, for *Wolfram* sings
the apostrophe after her retreating figure, and the
last chord of his postlude is interrupted by *Tannhäuser's* words, "Ich hörte Harfenschlag!"　Yet
we are asked to assume that in the brief interim
Elizabeth has ascended the mountain to the Wartburg, died, been prepared for burial, and brought
back to the valley as the central object of a stately
funeral.

It would have been much wiser to have left the
death of *Elizabeth* to the imagination of the public
than to have made the scene ridiculous.　But Wagner was afraid to do that, lest his purpose be overlooked.　He was a master of theatrical craft, and
though he could write a tragedy like "Tristan und
Isolde," with little regard for external action, he was
quite unwilling to miss so effective a theatrical effect

RICHARD WAGNER

(From a drawing by Franz von Lenbach)

as the death of *Tannhäuser* beside *Elizabeth's* bier. After all, he did not trust the public, whose judgment he affected to place above that of his critics, and for this reason, while he was willing to call up memories of his earlier opera by quoting some of its music in "Parsifal," he ignored the question which plays so important a rôle in "Lohengrin," and made the healing of *Amfortas* depend upon a touch of the talismanic spear — a device which came into the Grail story from pagan sources, as I have already pointed out.

Now, why was the questioning of *Lohengrin* forbidden? Wolfram von Eschenbach tells us, and his explanation sufficed Wagner when he made his first studies of the Grail legends as a preparation for "Lohengrin." It was the Holy Grail itself which pronounced the taboo. An inscription appeared on the talisman one day commanding that whenever a Knight of the Grail went into foreign lands to assume rule over a people, he was to admonish them not to question him concerning his name and race; should the question be put, he was to leave them at once. And the reason?

> Weil der gute Amfortas
> So lang in bittern Schmerzen lag,
> Und ihn die Frage lange mied,
> Ist ihnen alles Fragen leid;
> All des Grales Dienstgesellen
> Wollen sich nicht mehr fragen lassen.

The same explanation is made in the mediæval poem "Lohengrin." We are not called upon to admire the logic of Wolfram and the Knights of the Grail, but nothing could be plainer than this: The sufferings of Amfortas having been wofully prolonged by Parzival's failure to ask the healing question, the Knights of the Grail were thereafter required by their oracular guide to prohibit all questioning of themselves under penalty of forfeiture of their puissant help. When Wagner wrote his last drama, he was presented with a dilemma: should he remain consistent and adhere to the question as a dramatic motive, or dare the charge of inconsistency for the sake of that bit of spectacular apparatus, the sacred lance? He chose inconsistency and the show, and emphasized the element of relic worship to such a degree as to make his drama foreign to the intellectual and religious habits of the time in which he wrote. But this did not disturb him; for he knew that beauty addresses itself to the emotions rather than the intellect, and that his philosophical message of the redeeming power of loving compassion would find entrance to the hearts of the people over all the obstacles that reason might interpose. Yet he destroyed all the poetical bonds which ought or might have existed between "Parsifal" and "Lohengrin."

It was Wagner who created the contradiction which puts his operas in opposition by his substitution of the sacred lance as a dramatic motive for the question. But poets had long before taken the privilege of juggling with two elements of ancient myths and folk-tales which are blended in the story of Lohengrin. Originally there was no relationship between the Knight of the Holy Grail and the Swan Knight, and there is no telling when the fusion of the tales was made. But the element of the forbidden question is of unspeakable antiquity and survives in the law of taboo which exists among savages to-day. When Wagner discussed his opera in his "Communication to My Friends" he pointed out the resemblance between the story of Lohengrin and the myth of Zeus and Semele. Its philosophical essence he proclaimed to be humanity's feeling of the necessity of love. Elsa was "the woman who drew Lohengrin from the sunny heights to the depths of earth's warm heart. . . . Thus yearned he for woman — for the human heart. And thus did he step down from out his loneliness of sterile bliss when he heard this woman's cry for succor, this heart cry from humanity below." This is all very well, and it would be churlish to say that it is not beautifully reflected in Wagner's drama; but it does not explain the need of the prohibition. A woman who loves must have unquestioning faith in her husband — that is all. But there are two ancient myths which show that the taboo was conceived as a necessary ingredient of the association of divine men with human women. Let both be recalled, for both have plainly gone over into the mediæval story.

The first is the one to which Wagner made allusion: Jupiter has given his love to Semele. Wickedly prompted by the jealous Juno, Semele asks her august lover to grant her a wish. He promises that she shall have her desire, and confirms his words with the irrevocable oath, swearing by the Stygian flood. Semele asks him then to appear to her in all his celestial splendor. The god would have stopped her when he realized her purpose, but it was too late. Sorrowfully he returned to the celestial abode and fearfully he put on his lesser panoply. Arrayed in this he entered the chamber of Semele, but though he had left behind him the greater splendors, the immortal radiance consumed her to ashes.

That is one story; the other is the beautiful fable, freighted with ethical symbolism, which Apuleius gave to literature in the second century of the Christian era, though, no doubt, his exquisite story is only the elaboration of a much older conceit. Psyche, the daughter of a king, arouses the envy of Venus because of her beauty, and the goddess's anger because of the feeling which that beauty inspires among men. She resolves to punish her presumptuous mortal rival, and sends Cupid as her messenger of vengeance. But the God of Love falls himself a victim to the maiden's charms. The spell which he puts upon her he cannot wholly dissipate. Hosts of admirers still follow Psyche, but no worthy man offers her marriage. Her parents consult the oracle of Apollo, who tells him that she is doomed to become the wife of a monster who lives upon a high mountain. The maiden sees in this a punishment meted out by Venus and offers herself as a propitiatory sacrifice. Left alone by parents and friends, she climbs the rocky steeps and falls asleep in the wilderness. Thither come the Zephyrs and carry her to a beautiful garden, where unseen hands serve her sumptuously in a magnificent palace and the voices of invisible singers ravish her ears with music. Every night she is visited by a mysterious being who lavishes loving gifts upon her, but forbids her to look upon his face, and disappears before dawn. Psyche's sisters, envious of her good fortune and great happiness, fill her mind with wicked doubt and distrust. A fatal curiosity seizes upon her, and one night she uncovers her lamp to look upon the form of her doting companion. Instead of the monster spoken of by the oracle, she sees the loveliest of the immortals. It is Cupid who lies sleeping before her, with snowy wings folded, and golden ringlets clustering about his shoulders. Anxious for a closer view, Psyche leans over him, but a drop of hot oil falls from the lamp upon his shining skin. The god awakes, and without a word flies out of the window. Palace and garden disappear, and Psyche is left alone to suffer the consequences of her foolish curiosity. After wandering long in search of the lost one, she wins the sympathy of Ceres, who advises her to seek out Venus and offer reparation. She becomes the slave of the goddess, who imposes cruel tasks upon her. But at length Cupid can no longer endure to be separated from her, and goes to Jupiter, who intercedes with Venus and wins her forgiveness for Psyche. Then the supreme god gives her immortality, and she becomes forever the wife of Cupid.

There are two other points, one legendary, one

historical, which ought to be mentioned for the sake of those who like to know the sources of stories like that of Lohengrin. The ancient Angles had a saga which told of the arrival in their country of a boat, evidently sailless, oarless, and rudderless, containing only a child surrounded by arms and treasure. They brought him up and called him Skéaf (from which word our "sheaf"), because he lay upon a bundle of grain. He became king of the people, and, when he felt death upon him, commanded to be carried back to the shore where he had been found. There lay the boat in which he had come, and when his dead body was placed in it, it moved away of its own accord. From him descended a race of kings. Here, I am inclined to see a survival of the story of Danaë and her child Perseus found floating on the sea in a chest, as sung by Simonides. The historical element in "Lohengrin" is compassed by the figure of the king, who metes out justice melodiously in the opening and closing scenes. It is King Henry I of Germany, called the Fowler, who reigned from A.D. 918 to 936. He was a wise, brave, and righteous king, who fought the savage Huns, and for his sake the management of the festival performances at Bayreuth, in 1894, introduced costumes of the tenth century.

CHAPTER XVII

"HÄNSEL UND GRETEL"

In many respects "Hänsel und Gretel" is the most interesting opera composed since "Parsifal," and, by being an exception, proves the rule to which I directed some remarks in the chapter on "Don Giovanni." For a quarter of a century the minds of musical critics and historians have been occupied at intervals with the question whether or not progress in operatic composition is possible on the lines laid down by Wagner. Of his influence upon all the works composed within a period twice as long there never was a doubt; but this influence manifested itself for the greater part in modifications of old methods rather than the invention of new. In Germany attempts have been made over and over again to follow Wagner's system, but though a few operas thus produced have had a temporary success, in the end it has been found that the experiments have all ended in failures. It was but natural that the fact should provoke discussion. If no one could write successfully in Wagner's manner, was there a future for the lyric drama outside of a return to the style which he had striven to overthrow? If there was no such future, was the fact not proof of the failure of the Wagnerian movement as a creative force? The question was frequently answered in a spirit antagonistic to Wagner; but many of the answers were overhasty and short-sighted. It needed only that one should come who had thoroughly assimilated Wagner's methods and had the genius to apply them in a spirit of individuality, to demonstrate that it was possible to continue the production of lyric dramas without returning to the hackneyed manner of the opposing school. The composer who did this was Engelbert Humperdinck, and it is particularly noteworthy that his demonstration acquired its most convincing force from the circumstance that instead of seeking his material in the myths of antiquity, as Wagner did, he found them in the nursery.

While emphasizing this fact, however, it is well not to forget that in turning to the literature of folklore for an operatic subject Humperdinck was only carrying out one of the principles for which Wagner contended. The *Mährchen* of a people are quite as much a reflex of their intellectual, moral, and emotional life as their heroic legends and myths. In fact, they are frequently only the fragments of stories which, when they were created, were embodiments of the most profound and impressive religious conceptions of which the people were capable. The degeneration of the sun god of our Teutonic forefathers into the Hans of Grimm's tale, who could not learn to shiver and shake, through the Sinfiotle of the "Volsunga Saga" and the Siegfried of the "Nibelungenlied," is so obvious that it needs no commentary. Neither should the translation of Brynhild into Dornröschen, the Sleeping Beauty of our children's tales. The progress illustrated in these examples is that from myth to *Mährchen*, and Humperdinck in writing his fairy opera, or nursery opera if you will, paid tribute to German nationality in the same coin that Wagner did when he created his "Ring of the Nibelung." Everything about "Hänsel und Gretel" is charming to those who can feel their hearts warm toward the family life and folklore of Germany, of which we are, or ought to be, inheritors. The opera originated, like Thackeray's delightful fireside pantomime for great and small children, "The Rose and the Ring." The composer has a sister, Frau Adelheid Wette, wife of a physician in Cologne. She, without any particular thought of literary activity, had been in the habit of writing little plays for production within the family circle. For these plays her brother provided the music. In this way grew the first dramatic version of the story of Hänsel and Gretel, which, everybody who has had a German nurse or has read Grimm's fairy tales knows, tells the adventures of two children, a brother and sister, who, driven into the woods, fell into the toils of the Crust Witch (*Knusperhexe*), who enticed little boys and girls into her house, built of gingerbread and sweetmeats, and there ate them up. The original performers of the principal characters in the play were the daughters of Frau Wette. Charmed

with the effect of the fanciful little comedy, Herr
Humperdinck suggested its expansion into a piece
of theatrical dimensions; and the opera was the
result. It was brought forward for the first time
in public on December 23, 1893, in Weimar, and
created so profound an impression that it speedily
took possession of all the principal theatres of Germany, crossed the channel into England, made its
way into Holland, Belgium, and Italy, and reached
America within two years. Its first performance
in New York was in an English version at Daly's
Theatre on October 8, 1895. There were drawbacks
in the representation which prevented a success,
but after it had been incorporated in the German
repertory of the Metropolitan Opera-house in the
season of 1895–1896 it became as much of a perma-
nency as any opera in the list.

Humperdinck has built up the musical structure
of "Hänsel und Gretel" in the Wagnerian manner
but has done it with so much fluency and deftness
that a musical layman might listen to it from beginning to end without suspecting the fact, save from
the occasional employment of what may be called
Wagnerian idioms. The little work is replete with
melodies which, though original, bear a strong
family resemblance to two little songs which the
children sing at the beginning of the first and second
acts, and which are veritable nursery songs in Germany. These ditties and the principal melodies
consorted with them contribute characteristic *motifs*
out of which the orchestral part is constructed;

and these *motifs* are developed in accordance with an interrelated scheme every bit as logical and consistent as the scheme at the bottom of "Tristan und Isolde." As in that stupendous musical tragedy, the orchestra takes the part played by the chorus in Greek tragedy, so in "Hänsel und Gretel" it unfolds the thoughts, motives, and purposes of the personages of the play and lays bare the simple mysteries of the plot and counterplot. The careless happiness of the children, the apprehension of the parents, promise and fulfilment, enchantment and disenchantment — all these things are expounded by the orchestra in a fine flood of music, highly ingenious in contrapuntal texture, rich in instrumental color, full of rhythmical life, on the surface of which the idyllic play floats buoyantly, like a water-lily which

> starts and slides
> Upon the level in little puffs of wind,
> Tho' anchored to the bottom.

It is necessary, because the music is so beautiful and also because the piece, like the "Leonore" overtures of Beethoven and the "Meistersinger" prelude of Wagner (of which, indeed, it is a pretty frank imitation) is a sort of epitome of the play, to spend some time with the prelude to " Hänsel und Gretel." After I have done this I shall say what I have to say about the typical phrases of the score as they are reached, and shall leave to the reader the agreeable labor of discovering the logical scheme underlying their introduction and development.

The prelude is built out of a few themes which are associated with some of the most significant elements of the play. Not one of them is a personal label, as is widely, but erroneously, supposed to be the case in Wagner's dramas. They stand for dramatic ideas and agencies, and when these are passed in review, as it is purposed shall be done presently, it will be found that not the sinister but the amiable features of the story have been chosen for celebration in the overture. Here, too, in what may be called the ethical meaning of the prelude, Humperdinck has followed the example of Wagner in the prelude to his comedy. Simply for the sake of identification hereafter names will be attached to the themes out of which the prelude is constructed and which come from the chief melodic factors of the opera. The most important of these is the melody sung by the horns at the beginning:—

Let it be called the "Prayer Theme," for the melody is that of the prayer which the little ones utter before laying themselves down to sleep in the wood. The melody seems to be associated throughout the opera with the idea of divine guardianship, and is first heard in the first scene, when *Hänsel*, having complained of hunger, *Gretel* gently chides him and holds out comfort in the words (here I use the English version of the opera): —

> When past bearing is our grief
> God, the Lord, will send relief.

Humperdinck's splendid contrapuntal skill shows itself in a most varied use of this theme. Once in the prelude it appears in three different forms simultaneously, and in an augmented shape it forms the substratum of the prelude, while other themes are cunningly woven above it. The second theme is an exceedingly bright and energetic little phrase with which the rapid portion of the prelude begins. It shall be called the "Counter-Charm" theme, because it is the melodic phrase which serves as a formula with which the spell which the witch puts upon her victims is released by her as well as by the children who overhear it. When it occurs in the play it has this form: —

Ho - cus po - cus el - der bush!

Words and music come from the mouth of *Gretel* when she releases *Hänsel* from the spell in the third act, and from that of *Hänsel* when he performs the same office for the gingerbread children. After two phrases of minor significance there comes the "Theme of Fulfilment," so called because of its association with the answer to the prayer for pro-

tection in the woods. Thus it forms part of the
dawn music at the beginning of the third act when
the children are awakened by the *Dewman*. It
makes up the original part of the song of this *Dawn
Fairy* and is the melody to which *Hänsel* and *Gretel*
sing their explanation to the wondering gingerbread
children : —

The angels whispered in dreams to us in silent night
What this happy day has brought to light.

There is a fourth theme, the "Theme of Rejoicing,"
which is the inspiration of the dance which the
gingerbread children execute around *Hänsel* and
Gretel to celebrate their release from the enchantment put upon them by the wicked *Witch*.

At the parting of the curtain we see the interior
of the hut of a poor broom-maker. Specimens of
his handiwork hang upon the walls. A tiny window beside the door in the background shows a
glimpse of the forest beyond. *Hänsel* and *Gretel*
are at work, he making brooms, she knitting. *Gretel*
sings an old German folk-song, beginning thus : —

Su - se lie - be su - se was rasch - elt   im Stroh ?

All the melodies in this act have a strong family
resemblance, but this song, a cradle song of the
long ago, is the only one not composed by Hum-

perdinck. Miss Constance Bache has failed, in her English translation, to reproduce the quaint sentiment of the old song, which calls attention to the fact that all geese are shoeless. It is not for want of leather, — the shoemaker has that in plenty, — but he has no lasts, and so the poor things must needs go barefoot. The song invites a curious historical note. "Suse" and "Sause" were common expressions in the cradle songs which used to be sung to the Christ-child in the German churches at Christmas when the decadent nativity plays (now dwarfed to a mere tableau of the manger, the holy parents, and the adoring shepherds and magi) were still cultivated. From the old custom termed *Kindelwiegen,* which remained in the German Protestant Church centuries after the Reformation, Luther borrowed the refrain, "Susaninne" for one of his Christmas chorales. The beginning of the little song which *Gretel* sings used to be "Sause liebe Ninne," which, of course, is Luther's "Susaninne." The song dominates the whole of the first act. Out of portions of its melody grows a large part of the instrumental accompaniment to the melodious recitative in which the dialogue is carried on. Through expressive changes, not only in this act, but later also, it provides a medium for much dramatic expression. A little *motif* with which the orchestra introduces it develops into a song, with which *Hänsel* greets his sister's announcement that a neighbor has sent in some milk, and when *Gretel,* as soon as she does, attempts to teach *Hänsel* how to dance, the delightful little polka tune which the two sing is almost a twin brother to the cradle song.

It is the gift of milk which directly brings the sinister element into the play. The mother comes home weary, hungry, and out of humor. She finds that the children have neglected their work, and while attempting to punish them she overturns the milk jug. It is the last straw, and, with threats of a terrible beating if they do not bring home a heaping basket of berries for supper, she drives the little ones out into the forest. Exhausted, she falls asleep beside the hearth. From the distance comes the voice of the broom-maker trolling a song which is now merry, now sad. He enters his hut in great good humor, however, for he has sold all his wares and comes with his basket loaded with good things to eat and no inconsiderable quantity of kümmel in his stomach. Till now, save for the few moments which followed the entrance of the mother, the music has echoed nothing but childish joy. All this is changed, however, when the father, inquiring after his children, learns that they have gone into the woods. He tells his wife the legend of the *Witch* of the Ilsenstein and her dreadful practices, while the orchestra builds up a gruesome picture out of fragments from the innocent song which had opened the act. Fearful for the fate of her children, the mother dashes into the forest, followed by the broom-maker.

A musical delineation of a witch's ride separates the first and second acts. It is a garishly colored composition beginning with a pompous proclamation of the "Theme of the Witch":—

This is interwoven with echoes from the song of the broom-maker, and, as might be expected, a great deal of chromatic material, such as seems indispensable in musical pictures of the supernatural. Towards the close the weird elements gradually disappear and give way to a peaceful forest mood, pervaded by a long-drawn melody from the trumpet, accompanied by sounds suggestive of the murmuring of trees. The parting of the curtain discovers a scene in the depths of the woods. *Gretel* sits under a large tree weaving a garland of flowers. *Hänsel* is picking strawberries. The sun is setting. *Gretel* sings another folk-song, the meaning of which is lost to those who are unfamiliar with the song in the original. It is a riddle of the German nursery: "A little man stands in the forest, silent and alone, wearing a purplish red mantle. He stands on one leg, and wears a little black cap. Who is the little man?" Answer:— the *Hagebutte; i.e.* the rose apple, fruit of the rose tree. After the *Witch's* ride, nothing could be more effective in restoring the ingenuous mood essential to the play than this song, which is as graceful and pretty in melody as it is arch in sentiment. With the dialogue which follows, a variation of the closing

z

cadence of the song is sweetly blended by the orchestra. *Hänsel* crowns *Gretel* Queen of the Woods
with the floral wreath, and is doing mock reverence
to her when a cuckoo calls from a distance. The
children mimic the cry, then playfully twit the bird
with allusions to its bad practice of eating the eggs
of other birds and neglecting its own offspring.
Then they play at cuckoo, eating the strawberries
in lieu of eggs, until the basket is empty. They remember the threat of their mother, and want to fill
the basket again, but darkness is settling around
them. They lose their way, and their agitated
fancy sees spectres and goblins all around them.
Hänsel tries to reassure his sister by hallooing, and
scores of voices send back echoes, while the cuckoo
continues its lonely cry. *Gretel* is overcome by fear
for a moment, and *Hänsel*, too, succumbs to fright
when he sees a figure approaching through the mist.
But it is not a goblin, as the children think — only
the *Sandman*, a little gray, stoop-shouldered old
man, carrying a bag. He smiles reassuringly and
sings a song of his love for children, while he sprinkles
sleep-sand in the eyes of the pair. The second part
of his song introduces another significant phrase
into the score; it is the "Theme of Promise," to
which the Sleep Fairy sings the assurance that the
angels give protection and send sweet dreams to
good children while they are asleep:—

"*Sandman* has been here," says *Hänsel*, sleepily; "let us say our evening blessing." They kneel and repeat the prayer to the melody which has been called the "Prayer Theme," then go to sleep in each other's arms. All has been dark. Now a bright light pierces the mist, which gathers itself into a cloud that gradually takes the shape of a staircase reaching apparently from heaven to earth. The orchestra plays a beautiful and extended piece of music, of which the principal melodic material is derived from the themes of "Prayer" and "Promise," while seven pairs of angels descend the cloud-stairs and group themselves about the little sleepers, and a golden host extends upward to the celestial abode. By this time the scene is filled with a glory of light, and the curtain closes.

The greater part of the dramatic story is told in the third act. The opening of the curtain is preceded by a brief instrumental number, the principal elements of which are a new theme: —

and the "Theme of Fulfilment." The significance of the latter in this place is obvious: the promised benison to the children has been received. The former theme is a pretty illustration of what has already been said of Humperdinck's consistent devotion to the folk-song spirit in his choice of melodies. The phrase has an interrogatory turn and

is, in fact, the melody of the mysterious question
which comes from the house of the *Witch* a few
minutes later, when the children help themselves
to some of the toothsome material out of which the
magic structure is built: —

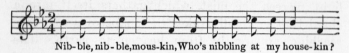

Nib-ble, nib-ble, mous-kin, Who's nibbling at my house-kin?

Simple as this little phrase is, it is yet a draught
from a song-game that comes nigh to being universal.   No phrase is more prevalent among nursery
songs than that made up of the first six notes.
The original German song itself has come down to
American and English children, and enthusiastic
folklorists see in it a relic of the ancient tree worship and an invocation of Frau Holda, the goddess
of love and spring of our Teutonic ancestors.   It is
the first phrase of the German, "Ringel, ringel, reihe,"
which our children know as "Ring around a rosy."
It was an amiable conceit of the composer's to put
such a tune into the mouth of the *Witch* at a moment of terror in the play.   By it he publishes his
intention not to be too utterly gruesome in his
treatment of the hag.   This intention, moreover,
he fulfils in the succeeding scene.   The *Witch* appears weird and wicked enough in appearance, in
her discordant laugh, and the instrumental delineation of her, but when she sings to the children, she
is almost ingratiating.   Of course, she is seeking
to lure them to a horrible fate, but though she

does not deceive them for even a moment, her musical manner is much like theirs, except when she is whirling through the air on a broomstick.

When the curtain opens on the third act the scene is the same as at the close of the second, except that morning is breaking and the background is filled with mist, which is slowly dissipated during the song of the *Dewman* (Dawn Fairy), who sprinkles dew on the sleeping children as he sings. The beginning of his song is like that of the *Sandman*, but its second part consists of the melody of "Fulfilment" instead of that of "Promise." *Gretel* is the first to awake, and she wakes *Hänsel* by imitating the song of the lark. He springs up with the cry of chanticleer, and lark's trill and cock's crow are mingled in a most winsome duet, which runs out into a description of the dream. They look about them to point out the spot where the angels had been. By this time the last veil of mist has withdrawn from the background, and in the place of the forest of firs the gingerbread house stands glistening with barley sugar in the sunshine. To the left is the *Witch's* oven, to the right a cage, all inside a fence of gingerbread children. A duet of admiration and amazement follows in a new, undulatory melody. *Hänsel* wants to enter the house, but *Gretel* holds him back. Finally they decide to venture so far as to nibble a bit. *Hänsel* stealthily breaks a piece of gingerbread off the corner, and at once the voice of the *Witch* is heard in the phrase already quoted : —

> Nibble, nibble, mousekin,
> Who's nibbling at my housekin?

After a moment of alarm *Gretel* picks up a bit of the gingerbread which had fallen from *Hänsel's* hand at the sound of the *Witch's* voice, and the duet of enjoyment is resumed in a higher key. Then a second piece of gingerbread is stolen and munched, and the weird voice is heard again; but this time without alarm. The *Witch* stealthily approaches and throws a noose about *Hänsel's* neck. They have fallen into her clutches, and in a luring song she tells of the sweetmeats which she keeps in the house for children of whom she is fond. *Hänsel* and *Gretel* are not won over, however, by her blandishments, and try to run away. The *Witch* extends her magic wand and chants the charm which deprives her victims of the power of motion, beginning:—

Ho - cus po - cus witch - es' charm

This phrase stands in the score as the antithesis of the "Counter-Charm" mentioned in the analysis of the prelude. It illustrates an ingenious constructive device. Desiring to send *Gretel* on an errand a moment later, the *Witch* disenchants her with the formula,

Hocus, pocus, elderbush,

Fac-simile of Humperdinck's Autograph. The *Knusperwalzer*,
Act II, "Hänsel und Gretel."[A]

already described as the first theme of the *Allegro* in the prelude. It is an inversion of the theme of enchantment, a proceeding analogous to reversing the rod, or spelling the charm backward. Wagner makes use of the same device in "Götterdäm-merung" when he symbolizes the end of things by inverting the symbol of the original elements in "Das Rheingold." The *Witch* now discloses her true character, and in the exuberance of her de-moniac glee indulges in a ride on a broom, first repeating some jargon in imitation of the cabalistic formulas common to mediæval necromancy. Frau Wette's lines are partly a copy of the *Witch's* mul-tiplication table in Goethe's "Faust." The play hurries to its catastrophe. *Gretel* gives *Hänsel* power of motion by repeating the "Counter-Charm," which she has overheard from the *Witch,* and the children push the hag into her own oven while she is heating it to roast *Hänsel.* The two then break into a jubilant waltz, which the composer desig-nates the *Knusperwalzer, i.e.* the "Crust Waltz." A frightful explosion destroys the *Witch's* oven, and with the crash the gingerbread covering falls from the children, who formed the fence around the house. They are unable to move, being still partly under a spell, but when *Hänsel* repeats the "Counter-Charm," they crowd around their deliverers and sing their gratitude. The parents of *Hänsel* and *Gretel,* who have been hunting them, appear on the scene. Out of the ruins of the oven the happy children drag the figure of the *Witch* baked into a

monstrous gingerbread, and dance around it hand
in hand. At the last all join in a swelling utterance of the "Prayer Theme" to the words, "When
need is greatest God is nearest."

proportions ... with ... band around it, a band
in black. ... just ... in a swelling circum-
ance of the ... out to the world. When
need is greatest, God is nearest.

CHALIAPINE AS CZAR BORIS.

A SECOND BOOK OF OPERAS

CONTENTS AND INDEX

CHAPTER I

BIBLICAL OPERAS

CHAPTER II

BIBLE STORIES IN OPERA AND ORATORIO

CHAPTER III

RUBINSTEIN AND HIS "GEISTLICHE OPER"

CHAPTER IV

"SAMSON ET DALILA"

CHAPTER V

"DIE KÖNIGIN VON SABA"

CHAPTER VI
"HÉRODIADE"

CHAPTER VII
"LAKMÉ"

CHAPTER VIII
"PAGLIACCI"

CHAPTER IX

"CAVALLERIA RUSTICANA"

CHAPTER X

THE CAREER OF MASCAGNI

CHAPTER XI

"IRIS"

CHAPTER XII
"MADAMA BUTTERFLY"

CHAPTER XIII
"DER ROSENKAVALIER"

CHAPTER XVII

TWO OPERAS BY WOLF-FERRARI

A SECOND BOOK OF OPERAS

CHAPTER I

BIBLICAL OPERAS

WHETHER or not the English owe a grudge to their Lord Chamberlain for depriving them of the pleasure of seeing operas based on Biblical stories I do not know. If they do, the grudge cannot be a deep one, for it is a long time since Biblical operas were in vogue, and in the case of the very few survivals it has been easy to solve the difficulty and salve the conscience of the public censor by the simple device of changing the names of the characters and the scene of action if the works are to be presented on the stage, or omitting scenery, costumes and action and performing them as oratorios. In either case, whenever this has been done, however, it has been the habit of critics to make merry at the expense of my Lord Chamberlain and the puritanicalness of the popular spirit of which he is supposed to be the official embodiment, and to discourse lugubriously and mayhap profoundly on the perversion of composers' purposes and the loss of things essential to the lyric drama.

It may be heretical to say so, but is it not possible that Lord Chamberlain and Critic have both taken too serious a view of the matter? There is a vast amount of admirable material in the Bible (historical, legendary or mythical, as one happens to regard it), which would not necessarily be degraded by dramatic treatment, and which might be made entertaining as well as edifying, as it has been made in the past, by stage representation. Reverence for this material is neither inculcated nor preserved by shifting the scene and throwing a veil over names too transparent to effect a disguise. Moreover, when this is done, there is always danger that the process may involve a sacrifice of the respect to which a work of art is entitled on its merits as such. Gounod, in collaboration with Barbier and Carré, wrote an opera entitled "La Reine de Saba." The plot had nothing to do with the Bible beyond the name of Sheba's Queen and King Solomon. Mr. Farnie, who used to make comic operetta books in London, adapted the French libretto for performance in English and called the opera "Irene." What a title for a grand opera! Why not "Blanche" or "Arabella"? No doubt such a thought flitted through many a careless mind unconscious that an Irene was a Byzantine Empress of the eighth century, who, by her devotion to its tenets, won beatification after death from the Greek Church. The opera failed on the Continent as well as in London, but if it had not been given a comic operetta flavor by its title and association with the name of the excellent Mr. Farnie, would the change in supposed time, place and people have harmed it?

A few years ago I read (with amusement, of course) of the metamorphosis to which Massenet's "Hérodiade" was subjected so that it might masquerade for a brief space on the London stage; but when I saw the opera in New York "in the original package" (to speak commercially), I could well believe that the music sounded the same in London, though John the Baptist sang under an alias and the painted scenes were supposed to delineate Ethiopia instead of Palestine.

There is a good deal of nonsensical affectation in the talk about the intimate association in the minds of composers of music, text, incident, and original purpose. "Un Ballo in Maschera," as we see it most often nowadays, plays in Nomansland; but I fancy that its music would sound pretty much the same if the theatre of action were transplanted back to Sweden, whence it came originally, or left in Naples, whither it emigrated, or in Boston, to which highly inappropriate place it was banished to oblige the Neapolitan censor. So long as composers have the habit of plucking feathers out of their dead birds to make wings for their new, we are likely to remain in happy and contented ignorance of *mésalliances* between music and score, until they are pointed out by too curious critics or confessed by the author. What is present habit was former custom to which no kind or degree of stigma attached. Bach did it; Handel did it; nor was either of these worthies always scrupulous in distinguishing between *meum* and *tuum* when it came to appropriating existing thematic material. In their day the merit of individuality and the right of property lay more in the manner in which ideas were presented than in the ideas themselves.

In 1886 I spent a delightful day with Dr. Chrysander at his home in Bergedorf, near Hamburg, and he told me the story of how on one occasion, when Keiser was incapacitated by the vice to which he was habitually prone, Handel, who sat in his orchestra, was asked by him to write the necessary opera. Handel complied, and his success was too great to leave Keiser's mind in peace. So he reset the book. Before Keiser's setting was ready for production Handel had gone to Italy. Hearing of Keiser's act, he secured a copy of the new setting from a member of the orchestra and sent back to Hamburg a composition based on Keiser's melodies "to show how such themes ought to be treated." Dr. Chrysander, also, when he gave me a copy of Bertati's "Don Giovanni" libretto, for which Gazzaniga composed the music, told me that Mozart had been only a little less free than the poet in appropriating ideas from the older work.

One of the best pieces in the final scene of "Fidelio" was taken from a cantata on the death of the emperor of Austria, composed by Beethoven before he left Bonn. The melody originally conceived for the last movement of the Symphony in D minor was developed into the finale of one of the last string quartets. In fact the instances in which composers have put their pieces to widely divergent purposes are innumerable and sometimes amusing, in view of the fantastic belief that they are guided by plenary inspiration. The overture which Rossini wrote for his "Barber of Seville" was lost soon after the first production of the opera. The composer did not take the trouble to write another, but appropriated one which had served its purpose in an earlier work. Persons ignorant of that fact, but with lively imaginations, as I have said in one of my books,[1] have rhapsodized on its appositeness, and professed to hear in it the whispered plottings of the lovers and the merry raillery of *Rosina* contrasted with the futile ragings of her grouty guardian ; but when Rossini composed this piece of music its mission was to introduce an adventure of the Emperor Aurelianus in Palmyra in the third century of the Christian era. Having served that purpose it became the prelude to another opera which dealt with Queen Elizabeth of England, a monarch who reigned some twelve hundred years after Aurelianus. Again, before the melody now known as that of *Almaviva's* cavatina had burst into the efflorescence which now distinguishes it, it came as a chorus from the mouths of Cyrus and his Persians in ancient Babylon.

[1] "A Book of Operas," p. 9.

When Mr. Lumley desired to produce Verdi's "Nabucodonosor" (called "Nabucco" for short) in London in 1846 he deferred to English tradition and brought out the opera as "Nino, Rè d'Assyria." I confess that I cannot conceive how changing a king of Babylon to a king of Assyria could possibly have brought about a change one way or the other in the effectiveness of Verdi's Italian music, but Mr. Lumley professed to have found in the transformation reason for the English failure. At any rate, he commented, in his "Reminiscences of the Opera," "That the opera thus lost much of its original character, especially in the scene where the captive Israelites became very uninteresting Babylonians, and was thereby shorn of one element of success present on the Continent, is undeniable."

There is another case even more to the purpose of this present discussion. In 1818 Rossini produced his opera "Mosè in Egitto" in Naples. The strength of the work lay in its choruses; yet two of them were borrowed from the composer's "Armida." In 1822 Bochsa performed it as an oratorio at Covent Garden, but, says John Ebers in his "Seven Years of the King's Theatre," published in 1828, "the audience accustomed to the weighty metal and pearls of price of Handel's compositions found the 'Moses' as dust in the balance in comparison." "The oratorio having failed as completely as erst did Pharaoh's host," Ebers continues, "the ashes of 'Mosè in Egitto' revived in

the form of an opera entitled 'Pietro l'Eremita.'
Moses was transformed into *Peter*. In this form
the opera was as successful as it had been unfortunate as an oratorio. . . . 'Mosè in Egitto' was
condemned as cold, dull, and heavy. 'Pietro
l'Eremita,' Lord Sefton, one of the most competent judges of the day, pronounced to be the most
effective opera produced within his recollection;
and the public confirmed the justice of the remark,
for no opera during my management had such un-
equivocal success." [1] This was not the end of the
opera's vicissitudes, to some of which I shall recur
presently; let this suffice now:

Rossini rewrote it in 1827, adding some new music
for the Académie Royal in Paris, and called it
"Moïse"; when it was revived for the Covent
Garden oratorios, London, in 1833, it was not only
performed with scenery and dresses, but recruited
with music from Handel's oratorio and renamed
"The Israelites in Egypt; or the Passage of the
Red Sea"; when the French "Moïse" reached
the Royal Italian Opera, Covent Garden, in April,
1850, it had still another name, "Zora," though
Chorley does not mention the fact in his "Thirty
Years' Musical Recollections," probably because
the failure of the opera which he loved grieved
him too deeply. For a long time "Moses" occupied a prominent place among oratorios. The

---

[1] "Seven Years of the King's Theatre," by John Ebers,
pp. 157, 158.

Handel and Haydn Society of Boston adopted it in 1845, and between then and 1878 performed it forty-five times.

In all the years of my intimate association with the lyric drama (considerably more than the number of which Mr. Chorley has left us a record) I have seen but one opera in which the plot adheres to the Biblical story indicated by its title. That opera is Saint-Saëns's "Samson et Dalila." I have seen others whose titles and *dramatis personæ* suggested narratives found in Holy Writ, but in nearly all these cases it would be a profanation of the Book to call them Biblical operas. Those which come to mind are Goldmark's "Königin von Saba," Massenet's "Hérodiade" and Richard Strauss's "Salome." I have heard, in whole or part, but not seen, three of the works which Rubinstein would fain have us believe are operas, but which are not — "Das verlorene Paradies," "Der Thurmbau zu Babel" and "Moses"; and I have a study acquaintance with the books and scores of his "Maccabäer," which is an opera; his "Sulamith," which tries to be one, and his "Christus," which marks the culmination of the vainest effort that a contemporary composer made to parallel Wagner's achievement on a different line. There are other works which are sufficiently known to me through library communion or concert-room contact to enable me to claim enough acquaintanceship to justify converse about them and which must perforce occupy attention in this study. Chiefest and noblest of these are Rossini's "Moses" and Méhul's "Joseph." Finally, there are a few with which I have only a passing or speaking acquaintance; whose faces I can recognize, fragments of whose speech I know, and whose repute is such that I can contrive to guess at their hearts — such as Verdi's "Nabucodonosor" and Gounod's "Reine de Saba."

Rossini's "Moses" was the last of the Italian operas (the last by a significant composer, at least) which used to be composed to ease the Lenten conscience in pleasure-loving Italy. Though written to be played with the adjuncts of scenery and costumes, it has less of action than might easily be infused into a performance of Mendelssohn's "Elijah," and the epical element which finds its exposition in the choruses is far greater than that in any opera of its time with which I am acquainted. In both its aspects, as oratorio and as opera, it harks back to a time when the two forms were essentially the same save in respect of subject matter. It is a convenient working hypothesis to take the classic tragedy of Hellas as the progenitor of the opera. It can also be taken as the prototype of the Festival of the Ass, which was celebrated as long ago as the twelfth century in France; of the miracle plays which were performed in England at the same time; the *Commedia spirituale* of thirteenth-century Italy and the *Geistliche Schauspiele* of fourteenth-century Germany. These mummeries, with their admixture of church song, pointed the way as media of edification to the dramatic representations of Biblical scenes which Saint Philip Neri used to attract audiences to hear his sermons in the Church of St. Mary in Vallicella, in Rome, and the sacred musical dramas came to be called oratorios. While the *camerata* were seeking to revive the classic drama in Florence, Carissimi was experimenting with sacred material in Rome, and his epoch-making allegory, "La Rappresentazione dell' Anima e del Corpo," was brought out, almost simultaneously with Peri's "Euridice," in 1600. Putting off the fetters of plainsong, music became beautiful for its own sake, and as an agent of dramatic expression. His excursions into Biblical story were followed for a century or more by the authors of *sacra azione*, written to take the place of secular operas in Lent. The stories of Jephtha and his daughter, Hezekiah, Belshazzar, Abraham and Isaac, Jonah, Job, the Judgment of Solomon, and the Last Judgment became the staple of opera composers in Italy and Germany for more than a century. Alessandro Scarlatti, whose name looms large in the history of opera, also composed oratorios; and Mr. E. J. Dent, his biographer, has pointed out that "except that the operas are in three acts and the oratorios in two, the only difference is in the absence of professedly comic characters and of the formal statement in which the author protests that the words *fato, dio, dieta,* etc., are only *scherzi poetici* and imply nothing contrary to the Catholic faith." Zeno and Metastasio wrote texts for sacred operas as well as profane, with Tobias, Absalom, Joseph, David, Daniel, and Sisera as subjects.

Presently I shall attempt a discussion of the gigantic attempt made by Rubinstein to enrich the stage with an art-form to which he gave a distinctive name, but which was little else than an inflated type of the old *sacra azione,* employing the larger apparatus which modern invention and enterprise have placed at the command of the playwright, stage manager, and composer. I am compelled to see in his project chiefly a jealous ambition to rival the great and triumphant accomplishment of Richard Wagner, but it is possible that he had a prescient eye on a coming time. The desire to combine pictures with oratorio has survived the practice which prevailed down to the beginning of the nineteenth century. Handel used scenes and costumes when he produced his "Esther," as well as his "Acis and Galatea," in London. Dittersdorf has left for us a description of the stage decorations prepared for his oratorios when they were performed in the palace of the Bishop of Groswardein. Of late years there have been a number of theatrical representations of Mendelssohn's "Elijah." I have witnessed as well as heard a performance of "Acis and Galatea" and been entertained with the spectacle of *Polyphemus* crush-

ing the head of presumptuous *Acis* with a stave
like another *Fafner* while singing "Fly, thou massy
ruin, fly" to the bludgeon which was playing under-
study for the fatal rock.

This diverting incident brings me to a consideration of one of the difficulties which stand in the
way of effective stage pictures combined with
action in the case of some of the most admired
of the subjects for oratorios or sacred opera. It
was not the Lord Chamberlain who stood in the
way of Saint-Saëns's "Samson et Dalila" in the
United States for many years, but the worldly
wisdom of opera managers who shrank from attempting to stage the spectacle of the falling Temple of
Dagon, and found in the work itself a plentiful
lack of that dramatic movement which is to-day
considered more essential to success than beautiful
and inspiriting music. "Samson et Dalila" was
well known in its concert form when the management of the Metropolitan Opera House first attempted to introduce it as an opera. It had a
single performance in the season of 1894–1895 and
then sought seclusion from the stage lamps for
twenty years. It was, perhaps, fortunate for the
work that no attempt was made to repeat it, for,
though well sung and satisfactorily acted, the top-
pling of the pillars of the temple, discreetly sup-
ported by too visible wires, at the conclusion made
a stronger appeal to the popular sense of the ridiculous than even Saint-Saëns's music could with-

stand. It is easy to inveigh against the notion that frivolous fribbles and trumpery trappings should receive more attention than the fine music which ought to be recognized as the soul of the work, the vital spark which irradiates an inconsequential material body; but human nature has not yet freed itself sufficiently from gross clogs to attain so ideal an attitude.

It is to a danger similar to that which threatened the original New York "Samson" that the world owes the most popular melody in Rossini's "Mosè." The story is old and familiar to the students of operatic history, but will bear retelling. The plague of darkness opens the opera, the passage of the Red Sea concludes it. Rossini's stage manager had no difficulty with the former, which demanded nothing more than the lowering of the stage lights. But he could evolve no device which could save the final miracle from laughter. A hilarious ending to so solemn a work disturbed the management and the librettist, Totola, who, just before a projected revival in Naples, a year or two after the first production, came to the composer with a project for saving the third act. Rossini was in bed, as usual, and the poet showed him the text of the prayer, " Dal tuo stellato," which he said he had written in an hour. "I will get up and write the music," said Rossini; "you shall have it in a quarter of an hour." And he kept his word, whether literally or not in respect of time does not matter. When the opera was again performed it contained the chorus with its melody which provided Paganini with material for one of his sensational performances on the G-string.

Carpani tells the story and describes the effect upon the audience which heard it for the first time. Laughter was just beginning in the pit when the public was surprised to note that *Moses* was about to sing. The people stopped laughing and prepared to listen. They were awed by the beauty of the minor strain which was echoed by *Aaron* and then by the chorus of *Israelites*. The host marched across the mimic sea and fell on its knees, and the music burst forth again, but now in the major mode. And now the audience joined in the jubilation. The people in the boxes, says Carpani, stood up ; they leaned over the railings ; applauded ; they shouted: "Bello ! bello ! O che bello !" Carpani adds : "I am almost in tears when I think of this prayer." An impressionable folk, those Italians of less than a century ago. "Among other things that can be said in praise of our hero," remarked a physician to Carpani, amidst the enthusiasm caused by the revamped opera, "do not forget that he is an assassin. I can cite to you more than forty attacks of nervous fever or violent convulsions on the part of young women, fond to excess of music, which have no other origin than the prayer of the Hebrews in the third act with its superb change of key !"

Thus music saved the scene in Naples. When the opera was rewritten for London and made to tell a story about Peter the Hermit, the corresponding scene had to be elided after the first performance. Ebers tells the story : " A body of troops was supposed to pass over a bridge which, breaking, was to precipitate them into the water. The troops being made of basketwork and pulled over the bridge by ropes, unfortunately became refractory on their passage, and very sensibly refused, when the bridge was about to give way, to proceed any further; consequently when the downfall of the arches took place the basket men remained very quietly on that part of the bridge which was left standing, and instead of being consigned to the waves had nearly been set on fire. The audience, not giving the troops due credit for their prudence, found no little fault with their compliance with the law of self-preservation. In the following representations of the opera the bridge and basket men which, *en passant* (or *en restant* rather), had cost fifty pounds, were omitted." [1] When "Moïse" was

[1] *Op. cit.*, p. 160.

prepared in Paris 45,000 francs were sunk in the Red Sea.

I shall recur in a moment to the famous *preghiera* but, having Ebers' book before me, I see an anecdote so delightfully illustrative of the proverbial spirit of the lyric theatre that I cannot resist the temptation to repeat it. In the revised "Moses" made for Paris there occurs a quartet beginning "Mi manca la voce" ("I lack voice") which Chorley describes as "a delicious round." Camporese had to utter the words first and no sooner had she done so than Ronzi di Begnis, in a whisper, loud enough to be heard by her companion, made the comment "E vero !" ("True !") — "a remark," says Mr. Ebers, "which produced a retort courteous somewhat more than verging on the limit of decorum, though not proceeding to the extremity asserted by rumor, which would have been as inconsistent with propriety as with the habitual dignity and self-possession of Camporese's demeanor."

Somebody, I cannot recall who, has said that the success of "Dal tuo stellato" set the fashion of introducing prayers into operas. Whether this be true or not, it is a fact that a prayer occurs in four of the operas which Rossini composed for the Paris Grand Opéra and that the formula is become so common that it may be set down as an operatic convention, — a convention, moreover, which even the iconoclast Wagner left undisturbed. One might think that the propriety of prayer in a religious

drama would have been enforced upon the mind
of a classicist like Goethe by his admiration for the
antique, but it was the fact that Rossini's opera
showed the Israelites upon their knees in supplication to God that set the great German poet against
"Mosè." In a conversation recorded by Ecker-
mann as taking place in 1828, we hear him uttering
his objection to the work: "I do not understand
how you can separate and enjoy separately the
subject and the music. You pretend here that the
subject is worthless, but you are consoled for it
by a feast of excellent music. I wonder that your
nature is thus organized that your ear can listen
to charming sounds while your sight, the most perfect of your senses, is tormented by absurd objects.
You will not deny that your 'Moses' is in effect
very absurd. The curtain is raised and people are
praying. This is all wrong. The Bible says that
when you pray you should go into your chamber
and close the door. Therefore, there should be no
praying in the theatre. As for me, I should have
arranged a wholly different 'Moses.' At first I
should have shown the children of Israel bowed
down by countless odious burdens and suffering
from the tyranny of the Egyptian rulers. Then
you would have appreciated more easily what
Moses deserved from his race, which he had delivered from a shameful oppression." "Then,"
says Mr. Philip Hale, who directed my attention
to this interesting passage, "Goethe went on to

c

reconstruct the whole opera. He introduced, for instance, a dance of the Egyptians after the plague of darkness was dispelled."

May not one criticise Goethe? If he so greatly reverenced prayer, according to its institution under the New Dispensation, why did he not show regard also for the Old and respect the verities of history sufficiently to reserve his ballet till after the passage of the Red Sea, when Moses celebrated the miracle with a song and "Miriam, the prophetess, the sister of Aaron, took a timbrel in her hand; and all the women went out after her with timbrels and with dances"?

CHAPTER II

IT was the fond belief of Dr. Chrysander, born of his deep devotion to Handel, in whose works he lived and moved and had his being, that the heroic histories of the Jews offered no fit material for dramatic representation. In his view the Jews never created dramatic poetry, partly because of the Mosaic prohibition against plastic delineation of their Deity, partly because the tragic element, which was so potent an influence in the development of the Greek drama, was wanting in their heroes. The theory that the Song of Songs, that canticle of canticles of love, was a pastoral play had no lodgment in his mind ; the poem seemed less dramatic to him than the Book of Job. The former sprang from the idyllic life of the northern tribes and reflected that life ; the latter, much more profound in conception, proved by its form that the road to a real stage-play was insurmountably barred to the Hebrew poet. What poetic field was open to him then ? Only the hymning of a Deity, invisible, omnipresent and omnipotent, the swelling call to combat for the glory of God against an inimical world, and the celebration of an ideal consisting in

19

a peaceful, happy existence in the Land of Promise under God's protecting care. This God presented Himself occasionally as a militant, all-powerful warrior, but only in moments when the fortunes of His people were critically at issue. These moments, however, were exceptional and few; as a rule, God manifested Himself in prophecy, through words and music. The laws were promulgated in song; so were the prophetic promises, denunciations, and calls to repentance; and there grew up a magnificent liturgical service in the temple.

Hebrew poetry, epic and lyrical, was thus antagonistic to the drama. So, also, Dr. Chrysander contends, was the Hebrew himself. Not only had he no predilection for plastic creation, his life was not dramatic in the sense illustrated in Greek tragedy. He lived a care-free, sensuous existence, and either fell under righteous condemnation for his transgressions or walked in the way prescribed of the Lord and found rest at last in Abraham's bosom. His life was simple; so were his strivings, his longings, his hopes. Yet when it came to the defence or celebration of his spiritual possessions his soul was filled with such a spirit of heroic daring, such a glow of enthusiasm, as are not to be paralleled among another of the peoples of antiquity. He thus became a fit subject for only one of the arts — music; in this art for only one of its spheres, the sublime, the most appropriate and efficient vehicle of which is the oratorio.

ENRICO CARUSO. (In "Samson et Dalila.")

One part of this argument seems to me irrelevant; the other not firmly founded in fact. It does not follow that because the Greek conscience evolved the conceptions of rebellious pride and punitive Fate while the Hebrew conscience did not, therefore the Greeks were the predestined creators of the art-form out of which grew the opera and the Hebrews of the form which grew into the oratorio. Neither is it true that because a people are not disposed toward dramatic creation themselves they can not, or may not, be the cause of dramatic creativeness in others. Dr. Chrysander's argument, made in a lecture at the Johanneum in Hamburg in 1896, preceded an analysis of Handel's Biblical oratorios in their relation to Hebrew history, and his exposition of that history as he unfolded it chronologically from the Exodus down to the Maccabæan period was in itself sufficient to furnish many more fit operatic plots than have yet been written. Nor are there lacking in these stories some of the elements of Greek legend and mythology which were the mainsprings of the tragedies of Athens. The parallels are striking: Jephtha's daughter and Iphigenia; Samson and his slavery and the servitude of Hercules and Perseus; the fate of Ajax and other heroes made mad by pride, and the lycanthropy of Nebuchadnezzar, of whose vanity Dr. Hanslick once reminded Wagner, warning him against the fate of the Babylonian king who became like unto an ox, "ate grass and was

composed by Verdi"; think reverently of Alcestis
and the Christian doctrine of atonement!

The writers of the first Biblical operas sought
their subjects as far back in history, or legend, as
the written page permitted. Theile composed an
"Adam and Eve" in 1678; but our first parents
never became popular on the serious stage. Perhaps the fearful soul of the theatrical costumer was
frightened and perplexed by the problem which the
subject put up to him. Haydn introduced them
into his oratorio "The Creation," but, as the custom
goes now, the third part of the work, in which they
appear, is frequently, if not generally omitted in
performance. Adam, to judge by the record in
Holy Writ, made an uneventful end: "And all the
days that Adam lived were nine hundred and thirty
years: and he died"; but this did not prevent
Lesueur from writing an opera on his death ten
years after Haydn's oratorio had its first performance. He called it "La Mort d'Adam et son Apo-
théose," and it involved him in a disastrous quarrel
with the directors of the Conservatoire and the
Académie. Pursuing the search chronologically,
the librettists next came upon Cain and Abel,
who offered a more fruitful subject for dramatic
and musical invention. We know very little about
the sacred operas which shared the list with works
based on classical fables and Roman history in the
seventeenth and eighteenth centuries; inasmuch,
however, as they were an outgrowth of the pious

plays of the Middle Ages and designed for edifying
consumption in Lent, it is likely that they adhered
in their plots pretty close to the Biblical accounts.
I doubt if the sentimental element which was in
vogue when Rossini wrote "Mosè in Egitto" played
much of a rôle in such an opera as Johann Philipp
Förtsch's "Kain und Abel ; oder der verzweifelnde
Brudermörder," which was performed in Hamburg
in 1689, or even in "Abel's Tod," which came along
in 1771. The first fratricidal murder seems to
have had an early and an enduring fascination for
dramatic poets and composers. Metastasio's "La
Morte d'Abele," set by both Caldara and Leo
in 1732, remained a stalking-horse for composers
down to Morlacchi in 1820. One of the latest of
Biblical operas is the "Kain" of Heinrich Bulthaupt
and Eugen d'Albert. This opera and a later lyric
drama by the same composer, "Tote Augen" (under
which title a casual reader would never suspect that
a Biblical subject was lurking), call for a little attention because of their indication of a possible drift
which future dramatists may follow in treating
sacred story.

Wicked envy and jealousy were not sufficient
motives in the eyes of Bulthaupt and d'Albert for
the first fratricide ; there must be an infusion of
psychology and modern philosophy. *Abel* is an
optimist, an idealist, a contented dreamer, joying
in the loveliness of life and nature ; *Cain,* a pessimist,
a morose brooder, for whom life contained no beau-

tiful illusions. He gets up from his couch in the
night to question the right of God to create man for
suffering. He is answered by *Lucifer*, who proclaims himself the benefactor of the family in having
rescued them from the slothful existence of Eden
and given them a Redeemer. The devil discourses
on the delightful ministrations of that Redeemer,
whose name is Death. In the morning *Abel* arises
and as he offers his sacrifice he hymns the sacred
mystery of life and turns a deaf ear to the new-
found gospel of his brother. An inspiring thought
comes to *Cain;* by killing *Abel* and destroying himself he will save future generations from the sufferings to which they are doomed. With this be-
nevolent purpose in mind he commits the murder.
The blow has scarcely been struck before a multitude of spirit-voices call his name and God
thunders the question: "Where is Abel, thy
brother?" *Adam* comes from his cave and looks
upon the scene with horror. Now *Cain* realizes
that his work is less than half done: he is himself
still alive and so is his son *Enoch*. He rushes forward to kill his child, but the mother throws herself
between, and *Cain* discovers that he is not strong-
willed enough to carry out his design. God's curse
condemns him to eternal unrest, and while the elements rage around him *Cain* goes forth into the
mountain wilderness.

Herr Bulthaupt did not permit chronology to
stand in the way of his action, but it can at least

be said for him that he did not profane the Book as
Herr Ewers, Mr. d'Albert's latest collaborator, did
when he turned a story of Christ's miraculous healing of a blind woman into a sensational melodrama.
In the precious opera, "Tote Augen" ("Dead
Eyes"), brought out in March, 1916, in Dresden,
Myrocle, the blind woman, is the wife of *Arcesius*,
a Roman ambassador in Jerusalem. Never having
seen him, *Myrocle* believes her husband to be a
paragon of beauty, but he is, in fact, hideous of
features, crook-backed, and lame; deformed in
mind and heart, too, for he has concealed the truth
from her. *Christ* is entering Jerusalem, and *Mary
of Magdala* leads *Myrocle* to him, having heard of
the miracles which he performs, and he opens the
woman's eyes at the moment that the multitude
is shouting its hosannahs. The first man who fills
the vision of *Myrocle* is *Galba*, handsome, noble,
chivalrous, who had renounced the love he bore
her because she was the wife of his friend. In
Galba the woman believes she sees the husband
whom in her fond imagination she had fitted out
with the charms of mind and person which his
friend possesses. She throws herself into his arms,
and he does not repel her mistaken embraces; but
the misshapen villain throws himself upon the pair
and strangles his friend to death. A slave en-
lightens the mystified woman; the murderer, not
the dead hero at his feet, is her husband. Singularly
enough, she does not turn from him with hatred

and loathing, but looks upon him with a great pity. Then she turns her eyes upon the sun, which *Christ* had said should not set until she had cursed him, and gazes into its searing glow until her sight is again dead. Moral : it is sinful to love the loveliness of outward things; from the soul must come salvation. As if she had never learned the truth, she returns to her wifely love for *Arcesius*. The story is as false to nature as it is sacrilegious; its trumpery theatricalism is as great a hindrance to a possible return of Biblical opera as the disgusting celebration of necrophilism in Richard Strauss's "Salome."

In our historical excursion we are still among the patriarchs, and the whole earth is of one language and of one speech. Noah, the ark, and the deluge seem now too prodigious to be essayed by opera makers, but, apparently, they did not awe the Englishman Edward Eccleston (or Eggleston), who is said to have produced an opera, "Noah's Flood, or the Destruction of the World," in London in 1679, nor Seyfried, whose "Libera me" was sung at Beethoven's funeral, and who, besides Biblical operas entitled "Saul," "Abraham," "The Maccabees," and "The Israelites in the Desert," brought out a "Noah" in Vienna in 1818. Halévy left an unfinished opera, "Noé," which Bizet, who was his son-in-law, completed. Of oratorios dealing with the deluge I do not wish to speak further than to express my admiration for the manner in which Saint-Saëns opened the musical floodgates in "Le Déluge."

On the plain in the Land of Shinar the families of the sons of Noah builded them a city and a tower whose top they arrogantly hoped might reach unto heaven. But the tower fell, the tongues of the people were confounded, and the people were scattered abroad on the face of the earth. Rubinstein attempted to give dramatic representation to the tremendous incident, and to his effort and vain dream I shall revert in the next chapter of this book. Now I must on with the history of the patriarchs. The story of Abraham and his attempted offering of Isaac has been much used as oratorio material, and Joseph Elsner, Chopin's teacher, brought out a Polish opera, "Ofiara Abrama," at Warsaw in 1827.

A significant milestone in the history of the Hebrews as well as Biblical operas has now been reached. The sojourn of the Jews in Egypt and their final departure under the guidance of Moses have already occupied considerable attention in this study. They provided material for the two operas which seem to me the noblest of their kind — Méhul's "Joseph" and Rossini's "Mosè in Egitto." Méhul's opera, more than a decade older than Rossini's, still holds a place on the stages of France and Germany, and this despite the fact that it foregoes two factors which are popularly supposed to be essential to operatic success — a love episode and woman's presence and participation in the action. The opera, which is in three acts, was

brought forward at the Théâtre Feydeau in Paris
on February 17, 1807. It owed its origin to a
Biblical tragedy entitled "Omasis," by Baour Lormian. The subject — the sale of Joseph by his
brothers into Egyptian slavery, his rise to power,
his forgiveness of the wrong attempted against
him, and his provision of a home for the people of
Israel in the land of Goshen — had long been popular
with composers of oratorios. The list of these
works begins with Caldara's "Giuseppe" in 1722.
Metastasio's "Giuseppe riconosciuto" was set by
half a dozen composers between 1733 and 1788.
Handel wrote his English oratorio in 1743; G. A.
Macfarren's was performed at the Leeds festival of
1877. Lormian thought it necessary to introduce
a love episode into his tragedy, but Alexander
Duval, who wrote the book for Méhul's opera,
was of the opinion that the diversion only enfeebled
the beautiful if austere picture of patriarchal domestic life delineated in the Bible. He therefore
adhered to tradition and created a series of scenes
full of beauty, dignity, and pathos, simple and
strong in spite of the bombast prevalent in the
literary style of the period. Méhul's music is
marked by grandeur, simplicity, lofty sentiment,
and consistent severity of manner. The composer's
predilection for ecclesiastical music, created, no
doubt, by the blind organist who taught him in his
childhood and nourished by his studies and labors
at the monastery under the gifted Hauser, found

opportunity for expression in the religious sentiments of the drama, and his knowledge of plain
chant is exhibited in the score "the simplicity,
grandeur, and dramatic truth of which will always
command the admiration of impartial musicians,"
remarks Gustave Choquet. The enthusiasm of M.
Tiersot goes further still, for he says that the music
of "Joseph" is more conspicuous for the qualities
of dignity and sonority than that of Handel's
oratorio. The German Hanslick, to whom the absence from the action of the "salt of the earth,
women" seemed disastrous, nevertheless does not
hesitate to institute a comparison between "Joseph"
and one of Mozart's latest operas. "In its mild,
passionless benevolence the entire rôle of Joseph in
Méhul's opera," he says, "reminds one strikingly
of Mozart's 'Titus,' and not to the advantage of
the latter. The opera 'Titus' is the work of an
incomparably greater genius, but it belongs to a
partly untruthful, wholly modish, tendency (that
of the old *opera seria*), while the genre of 'Joseph'
is thoroughly noble, true, and eminently dramatic.
'Joseph' has outlived 'Titus.'" [1] Carl Maria von
Weber admired Méhul's opera greatly, and within
recent years Felix Weingartner has edited a German
edition for which he composed recitatives to take
the place of the spoken dialogue of the original book.

There is no story of passion in "Joseph." The
love portrayed there is domestic and filial; its

[1] "Die Moderne Opera," p. 92.

objects are the hero's father, brothers, and country
— "Champs eternels, Hebron, douce vallée." It
was not until our own day that an author with a
perverted sense which had already found gratification
in the stench of mental, moral, and physical decay
exhaled by "Salome" and "Elektra" nosed the
piquant, pungent odor of the episode of Potiphar's
wife and blew it into the theatre. Joseph's temptress
did not tempt even the prurient taste which gave
us the Parisian operatic versions of the stories of
Phryne, Thaïs and Messalina. Richard Strauss's
"Josephslegende" stands alone in musical literature. There is, indeed, only one reference in the
records of oratorio or opera to the woman whose
grovelling carnality is made the foil of Joseph's
virtue in the story as told in the Book. That reference is found in a singular trilogy, which was
obviously written more to disclose the possibilities
of counterpoint than to set forth the story — even
if it does that, which I cannot say; the suggestion
comes only from a title. In August, 1852, Pietro
Raimondi produced an oratorio in three parts entitled, respectively, "Putifar," "Giuseppe giusto"
and "Giacobbe," at the Teatro Argentina, in Rome.
The music of the three works was so written that
after each had been performed separately, with individual principal singers, choristers, and orchestras,
they were united in a simultaneous performance.
The success of the stupendous experiment in contrapuntal writing was so great that the composer fell

in a faint amidst the applause of the audience and died less than three months afterward.

In the course of this study I have mentioned nearly all of the Biblical characters who have been turned into operatic heroes. Nebuchadnezzar appeared on the stage at Hamburg in an opera of Keiser's in 1704; Ariosti put him through his bovine strides in Vienna in 1706. He was put into a ballet by a Portuguese composer and made the butt of a French opéra bouffe writer, J. J. Debillement, in 1871. He recurs to my mind now in connection with a witty fling at "Nabucco" made by a French rhymester when Verdi's opera was produced at Paris in 1845. The noisy brass in the orchestration offended the ears of a critic, and he wrote:

> Vraiment l'affiche est dans son tort ;
> En faux, ou devrait la poursuivre.
> Pourquoi nous annoncer Nabuchodonos — or
> Quand c'est Nabuchodonos — cuivre?

Judas Maccabæus is one of the few heroes of ancient Israel who have survived in opera, Rubinstein's "Makkabäer" still having a hold, though not a strong one, on the German stage. The libretto is an adaptation by Mosenthal (author also of Goldmark's "Queen of Sheba") of a drama by Otto Ludwig. In the drama as well as some of its predecessors some liberties have been taken with the story as told in Maccabees II, chapter 7. The tale of the Israelitish champion of freedom and his brothers Jonathan and Simon, who lost their lives in the struggle against the tyranny of the kings of Syria, is intensely dramatic. For stage purposes the dramatists have associated the massacre of a mother and her seven sons and the martyrdom of the aged Eleazar, who caused the uprising of the Jews, with the family history of Judas himself. J. W. Franck produced "Die Maccabäische Mutter" in Hamburg in 1679, Ariosti composed "La Madre dei Maccabei" in 1704, Ignaz von Seyfried brought out "Die Makkabäer, oder Salmonäa" in 1818, and Rubinstein his opera in Berlin on April 17, 1875.

The romantic career of Jephtha, a natural son, banished from home, chief of a band of roving marauders, mighty captain and ninth judge of Israel, might have fitted out many an opera text, irrespective of the pathetic story of the sacrifice of his daughter in obedience to a vow, though this episode springs first to mind when his name is mentioned, and has been the special subject of the Jephtha operas. An Italian composer named Pollarolo wrote a "Jefte" for Vienna in 1692; other operas dealing with the history are Rolle's "Mehala, die Tochter Jephthas" (1784), Meyerbeer's "Jephtha's Tochter" (Munich, 1813), Generali, "Il voto di Jefte" (1827), Sanpieri, "La Figlia di Jefte" (1872). Luis Cepeda produced a Spanish opera in Madrid in 1845, and a French opera, in five acts and a prologue, by Monteclaire, was prohibited, after one performance, by Cardinal de Noailles in 1832.

Judith, the widow of Manasseh, who delivered her native city of Bethulia from the Assyrian Holofernes, lulling him to sleep with her charms and then striking off his drunken head with a falchion, though an Apocryphal personage, is the most popular of Israelitish heroines. The record shows the operas "Judith und Holofernes" by Leopold Kotzeluch (1799), "Giuditta" by S. Levi (1844), Achille Peri (1860), Righi (1871), and Sarri (1875). Naumann wrote a "Judith" in 1858, Doppler another in 1870, and Alexander Seroff a Russian opera under the same title in 1863. Martin Röder, who used to live in Boston, composed a "Judith," but it was never performed, while George W. Chadwick's "Judith," half cantata, half opera, which might easily be fitted for the stage, has had to rest content with a concert performance at a Worcester (Mass.) festival.

The memory of Esther, the queen of Ahasuerus, who saved her people from massacre, is preserved and her deed celebrated by the Jews in their gracious festival of Purim. A gorgeous figure for the stage, she has been relegated to the oratorio platform since the end of the eighteenth century. Racine's tragedy "Athalie" has called out music from Abbé Vogler, Gossec, Boïeldieu, Mendelssohn, and others, and a few oratorios, one by Handel, have been based on the story of the woman through whom idolatry was introduced into Judah; but I have no record of any Athalia opera.

D

CHAPTER III

I HAVE a strong belief in the essential excellence of Biblical subjects for the purposes of the lyric drama — at least from an historical point of view. I can see no reason against but many reasons in favor of a return to the stage of the patriarchal and heroic figures of the people who are a more potent power in the world to-day, despite their dispersal and loss of national unity, than they were in the days of their political grandeur and glory. Throughout the greater part of his creative career Anton Rubinstein was the champion of a similar idea. Of the twenty works which he wrote for the theatre, including ballets, six were on Biblical subjects, and to promote a propaganda which began with the composition of "Der Thurmbau zu Babel," in 1870, he not only entered the literary field, but made personal appeal for practical assistance in both the Old World and the New. His, however, was a religious point of view, not the historical or political. It is very likely that a racial predilection had much to do with his attitude on the subject, but in his effort to bring religion into

34

the service of the lyric stage he was no more Jew than Christian : the stories to which he applied his greatest energies were those of Moses and Christ.

Much against my inclination (for Rubinstein came into my intellectual life under circumstances and conditions which made him the strongest personal influence in music that I have ever felt) I have been compelled to believe that there were other reasons besides those which he gave for his championship of Biblical opera. Smaller men than he, since Wagner's death, have written trilogies and dreamed of theatres and festivals devoted to performances of their works. Little wonder if Rubinstein believed that he had created, or could create, a kind of art-work which should take place by the side of "Der Ring des Nibelungen," and have its special home like Bayreuth; and it may have been a belief that his project would excite the sympathetic zeal of the devout Jew and pious Christian alike, as much as his lack of the capacity for self-criticism, which led him like a will-o'-the-wisp along the path which led into the bogs of failure and disappointment.

While I was engaged in writing the programme book for the music festival given in New York in 1881, at which "The Tower of Babel" was performed in a truly magnificent manner, Dr. Leopold Damrosch, the conductor of the festival, told me that Rubinstein had told him that the impulse to use Biblical subjects in lyrical dramas had come to him while witnessing a ballet based on a Bible story many years before in Paris. He said that he had seldom been moved so profoundly by any spectacle as by this ballet, and it suggested to him the propriety of treating sacred subjects in a manner worthy of them, yet different from the conventional oratorio. The explanation has not gotten into the books, but is not inconsistent with the genesis of his Biblical operas, as related by Rubinstein in his essay on the subject printed by Joseph Lewinsky in his book "Vor den Coulissen," published in 1882 after at least three of the operas had been written. The composer's defence of his works and his story of the effort which he made to bring about a realization of his ideals deserve to be rehearsed in justice to his character as man and artist, as well as in the interest of the works themselves and the subjects, which, I believe, will in the near future occupy the minds of composers again.

"The oratorio," said Rubinstein, "is an art-form which I have always been disposed to protest against. The best-known masterpieces of this form have, not during the study of them but when hearing them performed, always left me cold; indeed, often positively pained me. The stiffness of the musical and still more of the poetical form always seemed to me absolutely incongruous with the high dramatic feeling of the subject. To see and hear gentlemen in dress coats, white cravats, yellow gloves, holding music books before them,

or ladies in modern, often extravagant, toilets singing the parts of the grand, imposing figures of the
Old and New Testaments has always disturbed
me to such a degree that I could never attain to
pure enjoyment. Involuntarily I felt and thought
how much grander, more impressive, vivid, and
true would be all that I had experienced in the
concert-room if represented on the stage with costumes, decorations, and full action."

The contention, said Rubinstein in effect, that
Biblical subjects are ill adapted to the stage because of their sacred character is a testimony of
poverty for the theatre, which should be an agency
in the service of the highest purposes of culture.
The people have always wanted to see stage representations of Bible incidents; witness the mystery
plays of the Middle Ages and the Passion Play at
Oberammergau to-day. But yielding to a prevalent feeling that such representations are a profanation of sacred history, he had conceived an
appropriate type of art-work which was to be produced in theatres to be specially built for the purpose
and by companies of artists to be specially trained
to that end. This art-work was to be called Sacred
Opera (*geistliche Oper*), to distinguish it from secular
opera, but its purpose was to be purely artistic and
wholly separate from the interests of the Church.
He developed ways and means for raising the necessary funds, enlisting artists, overcoming the difficulties presented by the *mise en scène* and the

polyphonic character of the choral music, and set forth his aim in respect of the subject-matter of the dramas to be a representation in chronological order of the chief incidents described in the Old and New Testaments. He would be willing to include in his scheme Biblical operas already existing, if they were not all, with the exception of Méhul's "Joseph," made unfit by their treatment of sacred matters, especially by their inclusion of love episodes which brought them into the domain of secular opera.

For years, while on his concert tours in various countries, Rubinstein labored to put his plan into operation. Wherever he found a public accustomed to oratorio performances he inquired into the possibility of establishing his sacred theatre there. He laid the project before the Grand Duke of Weimar, who told him that it was feasible only in large cities. The advice sent him to Berlin, where he opened his mind to the Minister of Education, von Mühler. The official had his doubts; sacred operas might do for Old Testament stories, but not for New; moreover, such a theatre should be a private, not a governmental, undertaking. He sought the opinion of Stanley, Dean of Westminster Abbey, who said that he could only conceive a realization of the idea in the oldtime popular manner, upon a rude stage at a country fair.

For a space it looked as if the leaders of the Jewish congregations in Paris would provide funds for the enterprise so far as it concerned itself with subjects taken from the Old Dispensation; but at the last they backed out, fearing to take the initiative in a matter likely to cause popular clamor. "I even thought of America," says Rubinstein, "of the daring transatlantic impresarios, with their lust of enterprise, who might be inclined to speculate on a gigantic scale with my idea. I had indeed almost succeeded, but the lack of artists brought it to pass that the plans, already in a considerable degree of forwardness, had to be abandoned. I considered the possibility of forming an association of composers and performing artists to work together to carry on the enterprise materially, intellectually, and administratively; but the great difficulty of enlisting any considerable number of artists for the furtherance of a new idea in art frightened me back from this purpose also." In these schemes there are evidences of Rubinstein's willingness to follow examples set by Handel as well as Wagner. The former composed "Judas Maccabæus" and "Alexander Balus" to please the Jews who had come to his help when he made financial shipwreck with his opera; the latter created the Richard Wagner Verein to put the Bayreuth enterprise on its feet.

Of the six sacred operas composed by Rubinstein three may be said to be practicable for stage representation. They are "Die Makkabäer," "Sulamith" (based on Solomon's Song of Songs) and

"Christus." The first has had many performances in Germany; the second had a few performances in Hamburg in 1883; the last, first performed as an oratorio in Berlin in 1885, was staged in Bremen in 1895. It has had, I believe, about fourteen representations in all. As for the other three works, "Der Thurmbau zu Babel" (first performance in Königsberg in 1870), "Das verlorene Paradies" (Düsseldorf, 1875), and "Moses" (still awaiting theatrical representation, I believe), it may be said of them that they are hybrid creations which combine the oratorio and opera styles by utilizing the powers of the oldtime oratorio chorus and the modern orchestra, with the descriptive capacity of both raised to the highest power, to illustrate an action which is beyond the capabilities of the ordinary stage machinery. In the character of the forms employed in the works there is no startling innovation; we meet the same alternation of chorus, recitative, aria, and *ensemble* that we have known since the oratorio style was perfected. A change, however, has come over the spirit of the expression and the forms have all relaxed some of their rigidity. In the oratorios of Handel and Haydn there are instances not a few of musical delineation in the instrumental as well as the vocal parts; but nothing in them can be thought of, so far at least as the ambition of the design extends, as a companion piece to the scene in the opera which pictures the destruction of the tower of Babel. This is as far

beyond the horizon of the fancy of the old masters
as it is beyond the instrumental forces which they
controlled.

"Paradise Lost," the text paraphrased from
portions of Milton's epic, is an oratorio pure and
simple. It deals with the creation of the world
according to the Mosaic (or as Huxley would have
said, Miltonic) theory and the medium of expression is an alternation of recitatives and choruses,
the latter having some dramatic life and a characteristic accompaniment. It is wholly contemplative; there is nothing like action in it. "The
Tower of Babel" has action in the restricted sense
in which it enters into Mendelssohn's oratorios,
and scenic effects which would tax the utmost
powers of the modern stage-machinist who might
attempt to carry them out. A mimic tower of
Babel is more preposterous than a mimic temple
of Dagon; yet, unless Rubinstein's stage directions
are to be taken in a Pickwickian sense, we ought
to listen to this music while looking at a stage-setting
more colossal than any ever contemplated by dramatist before. We should see a wide stretch of the
plain of Shinar; in the foreground a tower so tall
as to give color of plausibility to a speech which
prates of an early piercing of heaven and so large
as to provide room for a sleeping multitude on its
scaffoldings. Brick kilns, derricks, and all the apparatus and machinery of building should be on all
hands, and from the summit of a mound should

grow a giant tree, against whose trunk should
hang a brazen shield to be used as a signal gong.
We should see in the progress of the opera the bustling activity of the workmen, the roaring flames
and rolling smoke of the brick kilns, and witness
the miraculous spectacle of a man thrown into the
fire and walking thence unharmed. We should
see (in dissolving views) the dispersion of the races
and behold the unfolding of a rainbow in the sky.
And, finally, we should get a glimpse of an open
heaven and the Almighty on His throne, and a
yawning hell, with Satan and his angels exercising
their dread dominion. Can such scenes be mim-
icked successfully enough to preserve a serious
frame of mind in the observer? Hardly. Yet the
music seems obviously to have been written in the
expectation that sight shall aid hearing to quicken
the fancy and emotion and excite the faculties to
an appreciation of the work.

"The Tower of Babel" has been performed upon
the stage; how I cannot even guess. Knowing,
probably, that the work would be given in concert
form oftener than in dramatic, Rubinstein tries to
stimulate the fancy of those who must be only
listeners by profuse stage directions which are
printed in the score as well as the book of words.
"Moses" is in the same case. By the time that
Rubinstein had completed it he evidently realized
that its hybrid character as well as its stupendous
scope would stand in the way of performances of

any kind. Before even a portion of its music had been heard in public, he wrote in a letter to a friend: "It is too theatrical for the concert-room and too much like an oratorio for the theatre. It is, in fact, the perfect type of the sacred opera that I have dreamed of for years. What will come of it I do not know; I do not think it can be performed entire. As it contains eight distinct parts, one or two may from time to time be given either in a concert or on the stage."

America was the first country to act on the suggestion of a fragmentary performance. The first scene was brought forward in New York by Walter Damrosch at a public rehearsal and concert of the Symphony Society (the Oratorio Society assisting) on January 18 and 19, 1889. The third scene was performed by the German Liederkranz, under Reinhold L. Herman, on January 27 of the same year. The third and fourth scenes were in the scheme of the Cincinnati Music Festival, Theodore Thomas, conductor, on May 25, 1894.

Each of the eight scenes into which the work is divided deals with an episode in the life of Israel's lawgiver. In the first scene we have the incident of the finding of the child in the bulrushes; in the second occurs the oppression of the *Israelites* by the Egyptian taskmasters, the slaying of one of the overseers by *Moses*, who, till then regarded as the king's son, now proclaims himself one of the oppressed race. The third scene discloses *Moses*

protecting *Zipporah*, daughter of *Jethro*, a Midianit-
ish priest, from a band of marauding Edomites,
his acceptance of *Jethro's* hospitality and the scene
of the burning bush and the proclamation of his
mission.   Scene IV deals with the plagues, those of
blood, hail, locusts, frogs, and vermin being delineated
in the instrumental introduction to the part, the
action beginning while the land is shrouded in the
"thick darkness that might be felt."   The *Egyptians* call upon Osiris to dispel the darkness, but
are forced at last to appeal to *Moses*.   He demands
the liberation of his people as the price to be paid
for the removal of the plague ; receiving a promise
from *Pharaoh*, he utters a prayer ending with "Let
there be light."   The result is celebrated in a brilliant choral acclamation of the returning sun.   The
scene has a parallel in Rossini's opera.   *Pharaoh* now
equivocates ; he will free the sons of Jacob, but not
the women, children, or chattels.   *Moses* threatens
punishment in the death of all of Egypt's first-
born, and immediately solo and chorus voices be-
wail the new affliction.   When the king hears that
his son is dead he gives his consent, and the *Israelites*
depart with an ejaculation of thanks to Jehovah.
The passage of the Red Sea, *Miriam's* celebration
of that miracle, the backsliding of the *Israelites*
and their worship of the golden calf, the reception
of the Tables of the Law, the battle between the
Israelites and *Moabites* on the threshold of the
Promised Land, and the evanishment and apotheosis

of *Moses* are the contents of the remainder of the work.

*

*   *

It is scarcely to be wondered at that the subjects which opera composers have found adaptable to their uses in the New Testament are very few compared with those offered by the Old. The books written by the evangelists around the most stupendous tragical story of all time set forth little or nothing (outside of the birth, childhood, teachings, miracles, death, and resurrection of Jesus of Nazareth) which could by any literary ingenuity be turned into a stage play except the parables with which Christ enforced and illustrated His sermons. The sublime language and imagery of the Apocalypse have furnished forth the textual body of many oratorios, but it still transcends the capacity of mortal dramatist.

In the parable of the Prodigal Son there is no personage whose presentation in dramatic garb could be looked upon as a profanation of the Scriptures. It is this fact, probably, coupled with its profoundly beautiful reflection of human nature, which has made it a popular subject with opera writers. There was an Italian "Figliuolo Prodigo" as early as 1704, composed by one Biffi; a French melodrama, "L'Enfant Prodigue," by Morange about 1810; a German piece of similar character by Joseph Drechsler in Vienna in 1820. Pierre Gaveaux, who composed "Léonore, ou l'Amour

Conjugal," which provided Beethoven with his "Fidelio," brought out a comic opera on the subject of the Prodigal Son in 1811, and Berton, who had also dipped into Old Testament story in an oratorio, entitled "Absalon," illustrated the parable in a ballet. The most recent settings of the theme are also the most significant: Auber's five-act opera "L'Enfant Prodigue," brought out in Paris in 1850, and Ponchielli's "Il Figliuolo Prodigo," in four acts, which had its first representation at La Scala in 1880.

The mediæval mysteries were frequently interspersed with choral songs, for which the liturgy of the Church provided material. If we choose to look upon them as incipient operas or precursors of that art-form we must yet observe that their monkish authors, willing enough to trick out the story of the Nativity with legendary matter drawn from the Apocryphal New Testament, which discloses anything but a reverential attitude toward the sublime tragedy, nevertheless stood in such awe before the spectacle of Calvary that they deemed it wise to leave its dramatic treatment to the church service in the Passion Tide. In that service there was something approaching to characterization in the manner of the reading by the three deacons appointed to deliver, respectively, the narrative, the words of Christ, and the utterances of the Apostles and people; and it may be that this and the liturgical solemnities of Holy Week were reverently thought sufficient by them and the authors of the first sacred operas. Nevertheless, we have Keiser's "Der Blutige und Sterbende Jesus," performed at Hamburg, and Metastasio's "La Passione di Gesù Christi," composed first by Caldara, which probably was an oratorio.

Earlier than these was Theile's "Die Geburt Christi," performed in Hamburg in 1681. The birth of Christ and His childhood (there was an operatic representation of His presentation in the Temple) were subjects which appealed more to the writers of the rude plays which catered to the popular love for dramatic mummery than did His crucifixion. I am speaking now more specifically of lyric dramas, but it is worthy of note that in the Coventry mysteries, as Hone points out in the preface to his book, "Ancient Mysteries Described," [1] there are eight plays, or pageants, which deal with the Nativity as related in the canon and the pseudo-gospels. In them much stress was laid upon the suspicions of the Virgin Mother's chastity, for here was material that was good for rude diversion as well as instruction in righteousness.

*

* *

That Rubinstein dared to compose a Christ drama must be looked upon as proof of the pro-

[1] "Ancient Mysteries Described, especially the English Miracle Plays Founded on Apocryphal New Testament Story," London, 1823.

found sincerity of his belief in the art-form which
he fondly hoped he had created; also, perhaps, as
evidence of his artistic ingenuousness. Only a
brave or naïve mind could have calmly contemplated
a labor from which great dramatists, men as great
as Hebbel, shrank back in alarm. After the completion of "Lohengrin" Wagner applied himself
to the creation of a tragedy which he called "Jesus
of Nazareth." We know his plan in detail, but
he abandoned it after he had offered his sketches
to a French poet as the basis of a lyric drama which
he hoped to write for Paris. He confesses that
he was curious to know what the Frenchman would
do with a work the stage production of which would
"provoke a thousand frights." He himself was
unwilling to stir up such a tempest in Germany;
instead, he put his sketches aside and used some of
their material in his "Parsifal."

Wagner ignored the religious, or, let us say, the
ecclesiastical, point of view entirely in "Jesus of
Nazareth." His hero was to have been, as I have
described him elsewhere,[2] "a human philosopher
who preached the saving grace of Love and sought
to redeem his time and people from the domination of conventional law — the offspring of selfishness. His philosophy was socialism imbued by
love." Rubinstein proceeded along the lines of
history, or orthodox belief, as unreservedly in his
"Christus" as he had done in his "Moses." The
work may be said to have brought his creative activ-

[1] "A Book of Operas," p. 288.

ities to a close, although two compositions (a set
of six pianoforte pieces and an orchestral suite)
appear in his list of numbered works after the sacred
opera. He died on November 20, 1894, without
having seen a stage representation of it. Nor did
he live to see a public theatrical performance of his
"Moses," though he was privileged to witness a
private performance arranged at the German National Theatre in Prague so that he might form an
opinion of its effectiveness. The public has never
been permitted to learn anything about the impression which the work made.

On May 25, 1895, a series of representations of
"Christus" was begun in Bremen, largely through
the instrumentality of Professor Bulthaupt, a potent
and pervasive personage in the old Hanseatic town.
He was not only a poet and the author of the book
of this opera and of some of Bruch's works, but also
a painter, and his mural decorations in the Bremen
Chamber of Commerce are proudly displayed by
the citizens of the town. It was under the super-
vision of the painter-poet that the Bremen representations were given and, unless I am mistaken,
he painted the scenery or much of it. One of the
provisions of the performances was that applause
was prohibited out of reverence for the sacred
character of the scenes, which were as frankly set
forth as at Oberammergau. The contents of the
tragedy in some scenes and an epilogue briefly outlined are these: The first scene shows the temptation

E

of Christ in the wilderness, where the devil "shewed
unto him all the kingdoms of the world in a moment
of time." This disclosure is made by a series of
scenes, each opening for a short time in the background — castles, palaces, gardens, mountains of
gold, and massive heaps of earth's treasures. In the
second scene *John the Baptist* is seen and heard
preaching on the banks of the Jordan, in whose
waters he baptizes *Jesus*. This scene at the Bremen
representations was painted from sketches made
by Herr Handrich in Palestine, as was also that of
the "Sermon on the Mount" and "The Miracle
of the Loaves and Fishes," which form the subject
of the next part. The fourth tableau shows the
expulsion of the money changers from the Temple;
the fifth the Last Supper, with the garden of Geth-
semane as a background; the sixth the trial and
the last the crucifixion. Here, as if harking back
to his "Tower of Babel," Rubinstein brings in
pictures of heaven and hell, with angels and devils
contemplating the catastrophe. The proclamation
of the Gospel to the Gentiles by *St. Paul* is the subject of the epilogue.

CHAPTER IV

"SAMSON ET DALILA"

THERE are but two musical works based on the story of Samson on the current list to-day, Handel's oratorio and Saint-Saëns's opera; but lyric drama was still in its infancy when the subject first took hold of the fancy of composers and it has held it ever since. The earliest works were of the kind called sacred operas in the books and are spoken of as oratorios now, though they were doubtless performed with scenery and costumes and with action of a sort. Such were "Il Sansone" by Giovanni Paola Colonna (Bologna, 1677), "Sansone accecato da Filistri" by Francesco Antonio Uri (Venice, about 1700), "Simson" by Christoph Graupner (Hamburg, 1709), "Simson" by Georg von Pasterwitz (about 1770), "Samson" by J. N. Lefroid Mereaux (Paris, 1774), "Simson" by Johann Heinrich Rolle (about 1790), "Simson" by Franz Tuczek (Vienna, 1804), and "Il Sansone" by Francesco Basili (Naples, 1824). Two French operas are associated with great names and have interesting histories. Voltaire wrote a dramatic text on the subject at the request of La Popelinière, the farmer-general, who, as poet, musician, and artist, exercised a tremendous influence in his day. Rameau was in his service as household clavecinist and set Voltaire's poem. The authors looked forward to a production on the stage of the Grand Opéra, where at least two Biblical operas, an Old Testament "Jephté" and a New Testament "Enfant prodigue" were current; but Rameau had powerful enemies, and the opera was prohibited on the eve of the day on which it was to have been performed. The composer had to stomach his mortification as best he could; he put some of his Hebrew music into the service of his Persian "Zoroastre."

The other French *Samson* to whom I have referred had also to undergo a sea-change like unto Rameau's, Rossini's *Moses*, and Verdi's *Nebuchadnezzar*. Duprez, who was ambitious to shine as a composer as well as a singer (he wrote no less than eight operas and also an oratorio, "The Last Judgment"), tried his hand on a Samson opera and succeeded in enlisting the help of Dumas the elder in writing the libretto. When he was ready to present it at the door of the Grand Opéra the Minister of Fine Arts told him that it was impracticable, as the stage-setting of the last act alone would cost more than 100,000 francs. Duprez then followed the example set with Rossini's "Mosè" in London and changed the book to make it tell a story of the crusades which he called "Zephora." Nevertheless the original form was restored in German and

CAMILLE SAINT-SAENS.

Italian translations of the work, and it had concert performances in 1857. To Joachim Raff was denied even this poor comfort. He wrote a German "Simson" between 1851 and 1857. The conductor at Darmstadt to whom it was first submitted rejected it on the ground that it was too difficult for his singers. Raff then gave it to Liszt, with whom he was sojourning at Weimar, and who had taken pity on his "König Alfred"; but the tenor singer at the Weimar opera said the music was too high for the voice. Long afterward Wagner's friend, Schnorr von Carolsfeld, saw the score in the hands of the composer. The heroic stature of the hero delighted him, and his praise moved Raff to revise the opera; but before this had been done Schnorr died of the cold contracted while creating the rôle of Wagner's *Tristan* at Munich in 1865. Thus mournfully ended the third episode. As late as 1882 Raff spoke of taking the opera in hand again, but though he may have done so his death found the work unperformed and it has not yet seen the light of the stage-lamps.

Saint-Saëns's opera has also passed through many vicissitudes, but has succumbed to none and is probably possessed of more vigorous life now than it ever had. It is the recognized operatic masterpiece of the most resourceful and fecund French musician since Berlioz. Saint-Saëns began the composition of "Samson et Dalila" in 1869. The author of the book, Ferdinand Lemaire, was a cousin

of the composer. Before the breaking out of the
Franco-Prussian War the score was so far on the
way to completion that it was possible to give its
second act a private trial. This was done, an incident of the occasion — which afterward introduced one element of pathos in its history — being
the singing of the part of *Samson* by the painter
Henri Regnault, who soon after lost his life in the
service of his country. A memorial to him and
the friendship which existed between him and the
composer is the "Marche Héroique," which bears
the dead man's name on its title-page. Toward
the end of 1872 the opera was finished. For two
years the score rested in the composer's desk. Then
the second act was again brought forth for trial,
this time at the country home of Mme. Viardot,
at Croissy, the illustrious hostess singing the part of
Dalila. In 1875 the first act was performed in
concert style by M. Edouard Colonne in Paris.
Liszt interested himself in the opera and secured
its acceptance at the Grand Ducal Opera House of
Weimar, where Eduard Lassen brought it out on
December 2, 1877. Brussels heard it in 1878; but
it did not reach one of the theatres of France until
March 3, 1890, when Rouen produced it at its Thé-
âtre des Arts under the direction of M. Henri Verd-
hurt. It took nearly seven months more to reach
Paris, where the first representation was at the
Eden Theatre on October 31 of the same year.
Two years later, after it had been heard in a number

of French and Italian provincial theatres, it was given at the Académie Nationale de Musique under the direction of M. Colonne. The part of *Dalila* was taken by Mme. Deschamps-Jehin, that of *Samson* by M. Vergnet, that of the *High Priest* by M. Lassalle. Eight months before this it had been performed as an oratorio by the Oratorio Society of New York. There were two performances, on March 25 and 26, 1892, the conductor being Mr. Walter Damrosch and the principal singers being Frau Marie Ritter-Goetze, Sebastian Montariol, H. E. Distelhurst, Homer Moore, Emil Fischer, and Purdon Robinson. London had heard the work twice as an oratorio before it had a stage representation there on April 26, 1909, but this performance was fourteen years later than the first at the Metropolitan Opera House on February 8, 1895. The New York performance was scenically inadequate, but the integrity of the record demands that the cast be given here: *Samson*, Signor Tamagno; *Dalila*, Mme. Mantelli; *High Priest*, Signor Campanari; *Abimelech* and *An Old Hebrew*, M. Plançon; *First Philistine*, Signor Rinaldini; *Second Philistine*, Signor de Vachetti; conductor, Signor Mancinelli. The Metropolitan management did not venture upon a repetition until the opening night of the season 1915–1916, when its success was such that it became an active factor in the repertory of the establishment; but by that time it had been made fairly familiar to the New York public by

performances at the Manhattan Opera House under
the management of Mr. Oscar Hammerstein, the
first of which took place on November 13, 1908.
Signor Campanini conducted and the cast embraced
Mme. Gerville-Réache as *Dalila*, Charles Dal-
morès as *Samson*, and M. Dufranne as *High Priest*.
The cast at the Metropolitan Opera House's revival
of the opera on November 15, 1915, was as follows:
Dalila, Mme. Margarete Matzenauer; *Samson*,
Signor Enrico Caruso; *High Priest*, Signor Pas-
quale Amato; *Abimelech*, Herr Carl Schlegel;
An Old Hebrew, M. Léon Rothier; *A Philistine
Messenger*, Herr Max Bloch; *First Philistine*, Pietro
Audisio; *Second Philistine*, Vincenzo Reschiglian;
conductor, Signor Polacco.

*
* *

It would be a curious inquiry to try to determine
the source of the fascination which the story of
Manoah's son has exerted upon mankind for centuries. It bears a likeness to the story of the son of
Zeus and Alcmene, and there are few books on
mythology which do not draw a parallel between
the two heroes. Samson's story is singularly brief.
For twenty years he "judged Israel," but the Biblical history which deals with him consists only of
an account of his birth, a recital of the incidents in
which he displayed his prodigious strength and
valor, the tale of his amours, and, at the end, the

account of his tragical destruction, brought about by the weak element in his character.

Commentators have been perplexed by the tale, irrespective of the adornments which it has received at the hands of the Talmudists. Is Samson a Hebrew form of the conception personified by the Greek Herakles? Is he a mythical creature, born in the human imagination of primitive nature worship — a variant of the Tyrian sun-god Shemesh, whose name his so curiously resembles?[1] Was he something more than a man of extraordinary physical strength and extraordinary moral weakness, whose patriotic virtues and pathetic end have kept his memory alive through the ages? Have a hundred generations of men to whom the story of Herakles has appeared to be only a fanciful romance, the product of that imagination heightened by religion which led the Greeks to exalt their supreme heroes to the extent of deification, persisted in hearing and telling the story of Samson with a sympathetic interest which betrays at least a subconscious belief in its verity? Is the story only a parable enforcing a moral lesson which is as old as humanity? If so, how got it into the canonical Book of Judges, which, with all its mythical and legendary material, seems yet to contain a large substratum of unquestionable history?

There was nothing of the divine essence in Samson as the Hebrews conceived him, except that

[1] In Hebrew he is called *Shimshon*, and the sun *shemesh*.

spirit of God with which he was directly endowed in supreme crises. There is little evidence of his possession of great wisdom, but strong proof of his moral and religious laxity. He sinned against the laws of Israel's God when he took a Philistine woman, an idolater, to wife; he sinned against the moral law when he visited the harlot at Gaza. He was wofully weak in character when he yielded to the blandishments of Delilah and wrought his own undoing, as well as that of his people. The disgraceful slavery into which Herakles fell was not caused by the hero's incontinence or uxoriousness, but a punishment for crime, in that he had in a fit of madness killed his friend Iphitus. And the three years which he spent as the slave of Omphale were punctuated by larger and better deeds than those of Samson in like situation — bursting the new cords with which the men of Judah had bound him and the green withes and new ropes with which Delilah shackled him. The record that Samson "judged Israel in the days of the Philistines twenty years" leads the ordinary reader to think of him as a sage, judicial personage, whereas it means only that he was the political and military leader of his people during that period, lifted to a magisterial position by his strength and prowess in war. His achievements were muscular, not mental.

Rabbinical legends have magnified his stature and power in precisely the same manner as the imagination of the poet of the "Lay of the Nibelung" magnified the stature and strength of Siegfried. His shoulders, says the legend, were sixty ells broad; when the Spirit of God came on him he could step from Zorah to Eshtaol although he was lame in both feet; the hairs of his head arose and clashed against one another so that they could be heard for a like distance; he was so strong that he could uplift two mountains and rub them together like two clods of earth. Herakles tore asunder the mountain which, divided, now forms the Straits of Gibraltar and Gates of Hercules.

The parallel which is frequently drawn between Samson and Herakles cannot be pursued far with advantage to the Hebrew hero. Samson rent a young lion on the road to Timnath, whither he was going to take his Philistine wife; Herakles, while still a youthful herdsman, slew the Thespian lion and afterward strangled the Nemean lion with his hands. Samson carried off the gates of Gaza and bore them to the top of a hill before Hebron; Herakles upheld the heavens while Atlas went to fetch the golden apples of Hesperides. Moreover, the feats of Herakles show a higher intellectual quality than those of Samson, all of which, save one, were predominantly physical. The exception was the trick of tying 300 foxes by their tails, two by two, with firebrands between and turning them loose to burn the corn of the Philistines. An ingenious way to spread a conflagration, probably, but primitive, decidedly primitive. Herakles was a scientific

engineer of the modern school; he yoked the rivers
Alpheüs and Peneüs to his service by turning their
waters through the Augean stables and cleansing
them of the deposits of 3000 oxen for thirty years.
Herakles had excellent intellectual training; Rhada-
manthus taught him wisdom and virtue, Linus
music. We know nothing about the bringing up of
Samson save that "the child grew and the Lord
blessed him. And the Lord began to move him at
times in the camp of Dan between Zorah and Eshtaol." Samson made little use of his musical
gifts, if he had any, but that little he made well;
Herakles made little use of his musical training,
and that little he made ill. He lost his temper and
killed his music master with his lute; Samson, after
using an implement which only the black slaves
of our South have treated as a musical instrument,
to slay a thousand Philistines, jubilated in song:—

> With the jawbone of an ass
>   Heaps upon heaps!
> With the jawbone of an ass
>   Have I slain a thousand men!

The vast fund of human nature laid bare in the
story of Samson is, it appears to me, quite sufficient
to explain its popularity, and account for its origin.
The hero's virtues — strength, courage, patriotism
— are those which have ever won the hearts of men,
and they present themselves as but the more admirable, as they are made to appear more natural,

by pairing with that amiable weakness, susceptibility
to woman's charms.

After all Samson is a true type of the tragic hero,
whatever Dr. Chrysander or another may say.
He is impelled by Fate into a commission of the
follies which bring about the wreck of his body.
His marriage with the Philistine woman in Timnath
was part of a divine plot, though unpatriotic and
seemingly impious. When his father said unto
him: "Is there never a woman among the daughters
of thy brethren or among all my people that thou
goest to take a wife of the uncircumcised Philistines?" he did not know that "it was of the Lord
that he sought an occasion against the Philistines."
Out of that wooing and winning grew the first of
the encounters which culminated in the destruction of the temple of Dagon, when "the dead which
he slew at his death were more than they which he
slew in his life." So his yielding to the pleadings
of his wife when she betrayed the answer to his
riddle and his succumbing to the wheedling arts
of Delilah when he betrayed the secret of his strength
(acts incompatible with the character of an ordinary
strong and wise man) were of the type essential
to the machinery of the Greek drama.

A word about the mythological interpretation
of the characters which have been placed in parallel:
It may be helpful to an understanding of the Hellenic
mind to conceive Herakles as a marvellously strong
man, first glorified into a national hero and finally

deified. So, too, the theory that Herakles sinking
down upon his couch of fire is but a symbol of the
declining sun can be entertained without marring
the grandeur of the hero or belittling Nature's
phenomenon; but it would obscure our understanding of the Hebrew intellect and profane the
Hebrew religion to conceive Samson as anything
but the man that the Bible says he was; while
to make of him, as Ignaz Golziher suggests, a symbol of the setting sun whose curly locks (*crines
Phoebi*) are sheared by Delilah-Night, would bring
contumely upon one of the most beautiful and impressive of Nature's spectacles. Before the days
of comparative mythology scholars were not troubled
by such interpretations. Josephus disposes of the
Delilah episode curtly: "As for Samson being en-
snared by a woman, that is to be ascribed to human
nature, which is too weak to resist sin."

*

* *

It is not often that an operatic figure invites
to such a study as that which I have attempted
in the case of Samson, and it may be that the side-
wise excursion in which I have indulged invites
criticism of the kind illustrated in the metaphor
of using a club to brain a gnat. But I do not think
so. If heroic figures seem small on the operatic
stage, it is the fault of either the author or the actor.
When genius in a creator is paired with genius in an

interpreter, the hero of an opera is quite as deserving of analytical study as the hero of a drama which is spoken. No labor would be lost in studying the character of Wagner's heroes in order to illuminate the impersonations of Niemann, Lehmann, or Scaria; nor is Maurel's *Iago* less worthy of investigation than Edwin Booth's.

The character of Delilah presents even more features of interest than that of the man of whom she was the undoing, and to those features I purpose to devote some attention presently.

There is no symbolism in Saint-Saëns's opera. It is frankly a piece for the lyric theatre, albeit one in which adherence to a plot suggested by the Biblical story compelled a paucity of action which had to be made good by spectacle and music. The best element in a drama being that which finds expression in action and dialogue, and these being restricted by the obvious desire of the composers to avoid such extraneous matter as Rossini and others were wont to use to add interest to their Biblical operas (the secondary love stories, for instance), Saint-Saëns could do nothing else than employ liberally the splendid factor of choral music which the oratorio form brought to his hand.

We are introduced to that factor without delay. Even before the first scene is opened to our eyes we hear the voice of the multitude in prayer. The *Israelites*, oppressed by their conquerors and sore stricken at the reflection that their God has deserted

them, lament, accuse, protest, and pray. Before
they have been heard, the poignancy of their woe
has been published by the orchestra, which at once
takes its place beside the chorus as a peculiarly
eloquent expositor of the emotions and passions
which propel the actors in the drama.   That mission
and that eloquence it maintains from the beginning
to the final catastrophe, the instrumental band
doing its share toward characterizing the opposing
forces, emphasizing the solemn dignity of the Hebrew
religion and contrasting it with the sensuous and
sensual frivolity of the worshippers of Dagon.   The
choral prayer has for its instrumental substructure
an obstinate syncopated figure,

which rises with the agonized cries of the people
and sinks with their utterances of despair.   The
device of introducing voices before the disclosure
of visible action in an opera is not new, and in this
case is both uncalled for and ineffective.   Gounod
made a somewhat similar effort in his "Roméo et

Juliette," where a costumed group of singers presents
a prologue, vaguely visible through a gauze curtain.
Meyerbeer tried the expedient in "Le Pardon de
Ploërmel," and the siciliano in Mascagni's "Cavalleria rusticana" and the prologue in Leoncavallo's
"Pagliacci" are other cases in point. Of these
only the last can be said to achieve its purpose in
arresting the early attention of the audience. When
the curtain opens we see a public place in Gaza
in front of the temple of Dagon. The *Israelites*
are on their knees and in attitudes of mourning,
among them *Samson*. The voice of lamentation
takes a fugal form —

as the oppressed people tell of the sufferings which
they have endured : —

> Nous avons vu nos cités renversées
> Et les gentils profanants ton autel, etc.

The expression rises almost to the intensity of
sacrilegious accusation as the people recall to God
the vow made to them in Egypt, but sinks to accents
of awe when they reflect upon the incidents of their
former serfdom. Now *Samson* stands forth. In a
broad arioso, half recitative, half cantilena, wholly
in the oratorio style when it does not drop into the

F

mannerism of Meyerbeerian opera, he admonishes his brethren of their need to trust in God, their duty to worship Him, of His promises to aid them, of the wonders that He had already wrought in their behalf; he bids them to put off their doubts and put on their armor of faith and valor. As he proceeds in his preachment he develops somewhat of the theatrical pose of *John of Leyden* in "The Prophet." The *Israelites* mutter gloomily of the departure of their days of glory, but gradually take warmth from the spirit which has obsessed *Samson* and pledge themselves to do battle with the foe with him under the guidance of Jehovah.

Now *Abimelech*, Satrap of Gaza, appears surrounded by Philistine soldiers. He rails at the *Israelites* as slaves, sneers at their God as impotent and craven, lifts up the horn of Dagon, who, he says, shall pursue Jehovah as a falcon pursues a dove. The speech fills *Samson* with a divine anger, which bursts forth in a canticle of prayer and prophecy. There is a flash as of swords in the scintillant scale passages which rush upward from the eager, angry, pushing figure which mutters and rages among the instruments. The *Israelites* catch fire from *Samson's* ecstatic ardor and echo the words in which he summons them to break their chains. *Abimelech* rushes forward to kill *Samson*, but the hero wrenches the sword from the Philistine's hand and strikes him dead. The satrap's soldiers would come to his aid, but are held in fear by the hero,

who is now armed. The *Israelites* rush off to make
war on their oppressors. The *High Priest* comes
down from the temple of Dagon and pauses where
the body of *Abimelech* lies. *Two Philistines* tell
of the fear which had paralyzed them when *Samson*
showed his might. The *High Priest* rebukes them
roundly for their cowardice, but has scarcely uttered
his denunciation before a *Messenger* enters to tell
him that *Samson* and his Israelitish soldiers have
overrun and ravaged the country. Curses and vows
of vengeance against Israel, her hero, and her God
from the mouth of Dagon's servant. One of his
imprecations is destined to be fulfilled: —

> Maudit soit le sein de la femme
> Qui lui donna le jour !
> Qu'enfin une compagne infame
> Trahisse son amour !

Revolutions run a rapid course in operatic Palestine. The insurrection is but begun with the slaying of *Abimelech*, yet as the *Philistines*, bearing away
his body, leave the scene, it is only to make room for
the *Israelites*, chanting of their victory. We expect
a sonorous hymn of triumph, but the people of God
have been chastened and awed by their quick deliverance, and their pæan is in the solemn tone of
temple psalmody, the first striking bit of local color
which the composer has introduced into his score —
a reticence on his part of which it may be said that it
is all the more remarkable from the fact that local
color is here completely justified: —

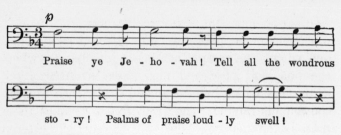

Praise ye Je - ho - vah! Tell all the wondrous sto - ry! Psalms of praise loud - ly swell!

"Hymne de joie, hymne de délivrance
Montez vers l'Eternel!"

It is a fine piece of dramatic characterization, which is followed by one whose serene beauty is heightened by contrast. *Dalila* and a company of singing and dancing Philistine women come in bearing garlands of flowers. Not only *Samson's* senses, our own as well, are ravished by the delightful music:—

Voici le printemps, nous portant des fleurs
Pour orner le front des guerriers vainquers!
Mêlons nos accents aux parfums des roses
A peine écloses!
Avec l'oiseau chantons, mes sœurs!

Now Spring's generous hand, Brings flowers to the land.
Now Spring's generous hand, Brings flowers to the land.

Dalila is here and it is become necessary to say something of her, having said so much about the man whose destruction she accomplished. Let the ingenious and erudite Philip Hale introduce her: "Was Delilah a patriotic woman, to be ranked with Jael and Judith, or was she merely a courtesan, as certain opera singers who impersonate her in the opera seem to think? E. Meier says that the word 'Delilah' means 'the faithless one.' Ewald translates it 'traitress,' and so does Ranke. Knobel characterizes her as *die Zarte*, which means tender, delicate, but also subtle. Lange is sure that she was a weaver woman, if not an out-and-out 'zonah.' There are other Germans who think the word is akin to the verb *einlullen*, to lull asleep. Some liken it to the Arabic *dalilah*, a woman who misguides, a bawd. See in 'The Thousand Nights and a Night' the speech of the damsel to Aziz: 'If thou marry me thou wilt at least be safe from the daughter of Dalilah, the Wily One.' Also 'The Rogueries of Dalilah, the Crafty, and her daughter, Zayrah, the Coney Catcher.'"

We are directly concerned here with the *Dalila* of the opera, but Mr. Hale invites us to an excursion which offers a pleasant occupation for a brief while, and we cheerfully go with him. The Biblical Delilah is a vague figure, except in two respects: She is a woman of such charms that she wins the love of Samson, and such guile and cupidity that she plays upon his passion and betrays him to the

lords of the Philistines for pay. The Bible knows
nothing of her patriotism, nor does the sacred historian give her the title of Samson's wife, though it
has long been the custom of Biblical commentators
to speak of her in this relation. St. Chrysostom
set the fashion and Milton followed it : —

> But who is this?   What thing of sea or land —
> Female of sex it seems —
> That, so bedeck'd, ornate and gay
> Comes this way sailing
> Like a stately ship
> Of Tarsus, bound for the isles
> Of Javan or Gadire,
> With all her bravery on, and tackle trim,
> Sails fill'd and streamers waving,
> Courted by all the winds that hold them play;
> An amber scent of odorous perfume
> Her harbinger, a damsel train behind?
> Some rich Philistian matron she may seem;
> And now, at nearer view, no other certain
> Than Dalila, thy wife.

It cannot be without significance that the author
of the story in the Book of Judges speaks in a different way of each of the three women who play
a part in the tragedy of Samson's life. The woman
who lived among the vineyards of Timnath, whose
murder Samson avenged, was his wife. She was
a Philistine, but Samson married her according to
the conventional manner of the time and, also
according to the manner of the time, she kept her
home with her parents after her marriage. Where-

fore she has gotten her name in the good books of
the sociological philosophers who uphold the mat-
ronymic theory touching early society. The woman
of Gaza whom Samson visited what time he confounded his would-be captors by carrying off the
doors of the gates of the city was curtly "an harlot."
Of the third woman it is said only that it came to
pass that Samson "loved a woman in the Valley
of Sorek, whose name was Delilah." Thereupon
follows the story of her bribery by the lords of the
Philistines and her betrayal of her lover. Evidently a licentious woman who could not aspire
even to the merit of the heroine of Dekker's play.

Milton not only accepted the theory of her wife-
hood, but also attributed patriotic motives to her.
She knew that her name would be defamed "in
Dan, in Judah and the bordering tribes."

> But in my country, where I most desire,
> In Eeron, Gaza, Asdod and in Gath,
> I shall be nam'd among the famousest
> Of women, sung at solemn festivals,
> Living and dead recorded, who to save
> Her country from a fierce destroyer, chose
> Above the faith of wedlock bands; my tomb
> With odours visited and annual flowers;
> Not less renown'd than in Mount Ephraim
> Jael, who, with inhospitable guile,
> Smote Sisera sleeping.

In the scene before us *Dalila* is wholly and simply
a siren, a seductress who plays upon the known love

of *Samson* from motives which are not disclosed. As yet one may imagine her moved by a genuine passion. She turns her lustrous black eyes upon him as she hails him a double victor over his foes and her heart, and invites him to rest from his arms in her embraces in the fair valley of Sorek. Temptation seizes upon the soul of *Samson*. He prays God to make him steadfast; but she winds her toils the tighter: It is for him that she has bound a coronet of purple grapes upon her forehead and entwined the rose of Sharon in her ebon tresses. *An Old Hebrew* warns against the temptress and *Samson* agonizingly invokes a veil over the beauty that has enchained him.

"Extinguish the fires of those eyes which enslave me." — thus he.

"Sweet is the lily of the valley, pleasant the juices of mandragora, but sweeter and more pleasant are my kisses!" — thus she.

The *Old Hebrew* warns again: "If thou give ear to her honeyed phrases, my son, curses will alight on thee which no tears that thou may'st weep will ever efface."

But still the siren song rings in his ears. The maidens who had come upon the scene with *Dalila* (are they priestesses of Dagon?) dance, swinging their floral garlands seductively before the eyes of *Samson* and his followers. The hero tries to avoid the glances which *Dalila*, joining in the dance, throws upon him. It is in vain; his eyes follow

her through all the voluptuous postures and movements of the dance.

And *Dalila* sings "Printemps qui commence" —
a song often heard in concert-rooms, but not so
often as the air with which the love-duet in the
second act reaches its culmination, which is popularly held also to mark the climax of the opera.
That song is wondrously insinuating in its charm;
it pulsates with passion, so much so, indeed, that
it is difficult to conceive that its sentiments are
feigned, but this is lovelier in its fresh, suave, graceful, and healthy beauty : —

As *Dalila* leaves the scene her voice and eyes repeat their lure, while *Samson's* looks and acts betray the trouble of his soul.

It is not until we see and hear *Dalila* in the second act that she is revealed to us in her true character. Not till now does she disclose the motives of her conduct toward her lover. Night is falling in the valley of Sorek, the vale which lies between the hill country which the Israelites entered from the East, and the coast land which the Philistines, supposedly an island people, invaded from the West. *Dalila*, gorgeously apparelled, is sitting on a rock near the portico of her house. The strings of the orchestra murmur and the chromatic figure which we shall hear again in her love-song coos in the wood-winds:

She awaits him whom passion has made her slave in full confidence of her hold upon him.

> Samson, recherchant ma présence,
> Ce soir doit venir en ces lieux.
> Voici l'heure de la vengeance
> Qui doit satisfaire nos dieux !
>
> Amour ! viens aider ma faiblesse !

The vengeance of her gods shall be glutted; it is to that end she invokes the power of love to strengthen her weakness. A passion like his will not down — that she knows. To her comes the *High Priest: Samson's* strength, he says, is supernatural and flows from a vow with which he was consecrated to effect the glory of Israel. Once while he lay in her arms that strength had deserted him, but now, it is said, he flouts her love and doubts his own passion. There is no need to try to awaken

jealousy in the heart of *Dalila;* she hates *Samson* more bitterly than the leader of his enemies. She is not mercenary, like the Biblical woman; she scorns the promise of riches which the *High Priest* offers so she obtain the secret of the Hebrew's strength. Thrice had she essayed to learn that secret and thrice had he set her spell at naught. Now she will assail him with tears — a woman's weapon.

The rumblings of thunder are heard; the scene is lit up by flashes of lightning. Running before

the storm, which is only a precursor and a symbol
of the tempest which is soon to rend his soul, *Samson* comes.   *Dalila* upbraids her lover, rebukes his
fears, protests her grief.   *Samson* cannot withstand her tears.   He confesses his love, but he
must obey the will of a higher power.   "What god
is mightier than Love?"   Let him but doubt
her constancy and she will die.   And she plays her
trump card: "Mon cœur s'ouvre à ta voix," while
the fluttering strings and cooing wood-winds insinu-
ate themselves into the crevices of *Samson's* moral
harness and loosen the rivets that hold it together: —

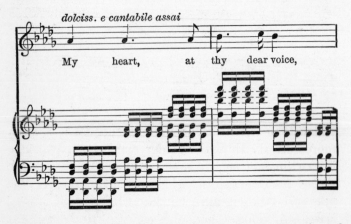

dolciss. e cantabile assai

My   heart,   at   thy   dear voice,

Herein lies the strength and the weakness of
music: it must fain be truthful.   *Dalila's* words
may be hypocritical, but the music speaks the
speech of genuine passion.   Not until we hear
the refrain echoed mockingly in the last scene of

the drama can we believe that the passion hymned in this song is feigned. And we almost deplore that the composer put it to such disgraceful use. *Samson* hears the voice of his God in the growing storm and again hesitates. The storm bursts as *Dalila* shrieks out the hate that fills her and runs toward her dwelling.

Beethoven sought to suggest external as well as internal peace in the "Dona nobis" of his Mass in D by mingling the sounds of war with the prayer for peace; Saint-Saëns pictures the storm in nature and in *Samson's* soul by the music which accompanies the hero as he raises his hands mutely in prayer; then follows the temptress with faltering steps and enters her dwelling. The tempest reaches its climax; *Dalila* appears at the window with a shout to the waiting Philistine soldiery below. The voice of *Samson* cuts through the stormy night: "Trahison!"

Act III. — First scene: A prison in Gaza. *Samson*, shorn of his flowing locks, which as a Nazarite he had vowed should never be touched by shears, labors at the mill. He has been robbed of his eyes and darkness has settled down upon him; darkness, too, upon the people whom his momentary weakness had given back into slavery.

"Total eclipse!" Saint-Saëns has won our admiration for the solemn dignity with which he has invested the penitent confession of the blind hero. But who shall hymn the blindness of Manoah's

son after Milton and Handel? From a crowd of
captive *Hebrews* outside the prison walls come
taunting accusations, mingled with supplications
to God. We recognize again the national mood of
the psalmody of the first act. The entire scene
is finely conceived. It is dramatic in a lofty sense,
for its action plays on the stage of the heart. *Samson*, contrite, humble, broken in spirit, with a prayer
for his people's deliverance, is led away to be made
sport of in the temple of Dagon. There, before
the statue of the god, grouped among the columns and before the altar the *High Priest* and
the lords of the Philistines. *Dalila*, too, with maidens clad for the lascivious dance, and the multitude of Philistia. The women's choral song to
spring which charmed us in the first act is echoed by
mixed voices. The ballet which follows is a prettily exotic one, with an introductory cadence marked
by the Oriental scale, out of which the second dance
melody is constructed — a scale which has the pecul-
iarity of an interval composed of three semitones,
and which we know from the song of the priestesses
in Verdi's " Aïda " : —

The *High Priest* makes mock of the Judge of Israel: Let him empty the wine cup and sing the praise of his vanquisher! *Dalila*, in the pride of her triumph, tauntingly tells him how simulated love had been made to serve her gods, her hate, and her nation. *Samson* answers only in contrite prayer. Together in canonic imitation (the erudite form does not offend, but only gives dignity to the scene) priest and siren offer a libation on the altar of the Fish god.

The flames flash upward from the altar. Now a supreme act of insolent impiety; *Samson*, too, shall sacrifice to Dagon. A boy is told to lead him where all can witness his humiliation. *Samson* feels that the time for retribution upon his enemies

is come. He asks to be led between the marble
pillars that support the roof of the temple. Priests
and people, the traitress and her dancing women,
the lords of the Philistines, the rout of banqueters
and worshippers — all hymn the praise of Dagon.
A brief supplication to Israel's God —

"And Samson took hold.of the two middle pillars
upon which the house stood and on which it was borne
up, of the one with his right hand and of the other with
his left.

"And Samson said, 'Let me die with the Philistines.'
And he bowed himself with all his might : and the house
fell upon the lords and upon all the people that were
therein. So the dead which he slew at his death were
more than they which he slew in his life."

CHAPTER V

"DIE KÖNIGIN VON SABA"

THE most obvious reason why Goldmark's "Königin von Saba" should be seen and heard with pleasure lies in its book and scenic investiture. Thoughtfully considered the book is not one of great worth, but in the handling of things which give pleasure to the superficial observer it is admirable. In the first place it presents a dramatic story which is rational; which strongly enlists the interest if not the sympathies of the observer; which is unhackneyed; which abounds with imposing spectacles with which the imagination of childhood already had made play, that are not only intrinsically brilliant and fascinating but occur as necessary adjuncts of the story. Viewed from its ethical side and considered with reference to the sources whence its elements sprang, it falls under a considerable measure of condemnation, as will more plainly appear after its incidents have been rehearsed.

The title of the opera indicates that the Biblical story of the visit of the Queen of Sheba to Solomon had been drawn on for the plot. This is true, but only in a slight degree. *Sheba's Queen* comes to

G   81

Solomon in the opera, but that is the end of the draft on the Scriptural legend so far as she is concerned. *Sulamith*, who figures in the drama, owes her name to the Canticles, from which it was borrowed by the librettist, but no element of her character nor any of the incidents in which she is involved. The "Song of Songs, which is Solomon's" contributes a few lines of poetry to the book, and a ritualistic service which is celebrated in the temple finds its original text in the opening verses of Psalms lxvii and cxvii, but with this I have enumerated all that the opera owes to the Bible. It is not a Biblical opera, in the degree that Méhul's "Joseph," Rossini's "Moses," or Rubinstein's "Maccabees" is Biblical, to say nothing of Saint-Saëns's "Samson et Dalila." Solomon's magnificent reign and marvellous wisdom, which contribute a few factors to the sum of the production, belong to profane as well as to sacred history and it will be found most agreeable to deeply rooted preconceptions to think of some other than the Scriptural Solomon as the prototype of the *Solomon* of Mosenthal and Goldmark, who, at the best, is a sorry sort of sentimentalist. The local color has been borrowed from the old story; the dramatic motive comes plainly from Wagner's "Tannhäuser."

Assad, a favorite courtier, is sent by *Solomon* to extend greetings and a welcome to the *Queen of Sheba*, who is on the way to visit the king, whose fame for wealth and wisdom has reached her ears in far Arabia. *Assad* is the type (though a milk-and-watery one, it must be confessed) of manhood struggling between the things that are of the earth and the things which are of heaven — between a gross, sensual passion and a pure, exalting love. He is betrothed to *Sulamith*, the daughter of the *High Priest* of the temple, who awaits his return from *Solomon's* palace and leads her companions in songs of gladness. *Assad* meets the *Queen* at Gath, performs his mission, and sets out to return, but, exhausted by the heat of the day, enters the forest on Mount Lebanon and lies down on a bank of moss to rest. There the sound of plashing waters arrests his ear. He seeks the cause of the grateful noise and comes upon a transportingly beautiful woman bathing. The nymph, finding herself observed, does not, like another Diana, cause the death of her admirer, but discloses herself to be a veritable Wagnerian *Venus*. She clips him in her arms and he falls at her feet; but a reed rustles and the charmer flees. These incidents we do not see. They precede the opening of the opera, and we learn of them from *Assad's* narration. *Assad* returns to Jerusalem, where, conscience stricken, he seeks to avoid his chaste bride. To *Solomon*, however, he confesses his adventure, and the king sets the morrow as his wedding day with *Sulamith*.

The *Queen of Sheba* arrives, and when she raises her veil, ostensibly to show unto *Solomon* the first view of her features that mortal man has ever had

vouchsafed him, *Assad* recognizes the heroine of his
adventure in the woods on Lebanon. His mind
is in a maze; bewilderingly he addresses her, and
haughtily he is repulsed. But the woman has felt
the dart no less than *Assad;* she seeks him at night
in the palace garden, whither she had gone to brood
over her love and the loss which threatens her on the
morrow, and the luring song of her slave draws him
again into her arms.

Before the altar in the temple, just as *Assad* is
about to pronounce the words which are to bind him
to *Sulamith,* she confronts him again, on the specious
pretext that she brings gifts for the bride. *Assad*
again addresses her. Again he is denied. Delirium
seizes upon his brain; he loudly proclaims the *Queen*
as the goddess of his devotion. The people are
panic-stricken at the sacrilege and rush from the
temple; the priests cry anathema; *Sulamith* bemoans her fate; *Solomon* essays words of comfort ;
the *High Priest* intercedes with heaven; the soldiery,
led by *Baal-Hanan,* overseer of the palace, enter
to lead the profaner to death. Now *Solomon* claims
the right to fix his punishment. The *Queen,* fearful
that her prey may escape her, begs his life as a boon,
but *Solomon* rejects her appeal; *Assad* must work out
his salvation by overcoming temptation and master-
ing his wicked passion. *Sulamith* approaches amid
the wailings of her companions. She is about to enter
a retreat on the edge of the Syrian desert, but she,
too, prays for the life of *Assad. Solomon,* in a

prophetic ecstasy, foretells *Assad's* deliverance from sin and in a vision sees a meeting between him and his pure love under a palm tree in the desert. *Assad* is banished to the sandy waste; there a simoom sweeps down upon him; he falls at the foot of a lonely palm to die, after calling on *Sulamith* with his fleeting breath. She comes with her wailing maidens, sees the fulfilment of *Solomon's* prophecy, and *Assad* dies in her arms. "Thy beloved is thine, in love's eternal realm," sing the maidens, while a mirage shows the wicked *Queen*, with her caravan of camels and elephants, returning to her home.

The parallel between this story and the immeasurably more poetical and beautiful one of "Tannhäuser" is apparent to half an eye. *Sulamith* is *Elizabeth,* the *Queen* is *Venus, Assad* is *Tannhäuser, Solomon* is *Wolfram von Eschenbach.* The ethical force of the drama — it has some, though very little — was weakened at the performances at the Metropolitan Opera House [1] in New York by the excision

[1] Goldmark's opera was presented for the first time in America at the Metropolitan Opera House on December 2, 1885. Cast: *Sulamith,* Fräulein Lilli Lehmann; *die Königin von Saba,* Frau Krämer-Wiedl; *Astaroth,* Fräulein Marianne Brandt; *Solomon,* Herr Adolph Robinson; *Assad,* Herr Stritt; *Der Hohe Priester,* Herr Emil Fischer; *Baal-Hanan,* Herr-Alexi. Anton Seidl conducted, and the opera had fifteen representations in the season. These performances were in the original German. On April 3, 1888, an English version was presented at the Academy of Music by the National Opera Company, then in its death throes. The opera was revived at the Metropolitan Opera House by Mr. Conried in the season 1905–1906 and had five performances.

from the last act of a scene in which the *Queen*
attempts to persuade *Assad* to go with her to Arabia.
Now *Assad* rises superior to his grosser nature and
drives the temptress away, thus performing the
saving act demanded by *Solomon*.

Herr Mosenthal, who made the libretto of "Die
Königin von Saba," treated this material, not with
great poetic skill, but with a cunning appreciation of
the opportunities which it offers for dramatic effect.
The opera opens with a gorgeous picture of the
interior of *Solomon's* palace, decked in honor of the
coming guest.   There is an air of joyous expectancy
over everything. *Sulamith's* entrance introduces
the element of female charm to brighten the brilliancy of the picture, and her bridal song — in which
the refrain is an excerpt from the Canticles, "Thy
beloved is thine, who feeds among the roses" —
enables the composer to indulge his strong predilection and fecund gift for Oriental melody.   The
action hurries to a thrilling climax. One glittering
pageant treads on the heels of another, each more
gorgeous and resplendent than the last, until the
stage, set to represent a fantastical hall with a bewildering vista of carved columns, golden lions, and
rich draperies, is filled with such a kaleidoscopic mass
of colors and groupings as only an Oriental mind
could conceive.   Finally all the preceding strokes
are eclipsed by the coming of the *Queen*.   But no
time is lost ; the spectacle does not make the action
halt for a moment. *Sheba* makes her gifts and

uncovers her face, and at once we are confronted by the tragical element, and the action rushes on toward its legitimate and mournful end.

In this ingenious blending of play and spectacle one rare opportunity after another is presented to the composer. *Sulamith's* epithalamium, *Assad's* narrative, the choral greeting to the *Queen*, the fateful recognition — all these things are made for music of the inspiring, swelling, passionate kind. In the second act, the *Queen's* monologue, her duet with *Assad*, and, most striking of all, the unaccompanied bit of singing with which *Astaroth* lures *Assad* into the presence of the *Queen*, who is hiding in the shadow of broad-leaved palms behind a running fountain — a melodic phrase saturated with the mystical color of the East — these are gifts of the rarest kind to the composer, which he has enriched to give them in turn to the public. That relief from their stress of passion is necessary is not forgotten, but is provided in the ballet music and the solemn ceremonial in the temple, which takes place amid surroundings that call into active operation one's childhood fancies touching the sacred fane on Mount Moriah and the pompous liturgical functions of which it was the theatre.

Goldmark's music is highly spiced. He was an eclectic, and his first aim seems to have been to give the drama a tonal investiture which should be in keeping with its character, external as well as internal. At times his music rushes along like a lava stream of passion, every measure pulsating with eager, excited, and exciting life. He revels in instrumental color. The language of his orchestra is as glowing as the poetry attributed to the royal poet whom his operatic story celebrates. Many composers before him made use of Oriental cadences, rhythms, and idioms, but to none do they seem to have come so like native language as to Goldmark. It is romantic music, against which the strongest objection that can be urged is that it is so unvaryingly stimulated that it wearies the mind and makes the listener long for a change to a fresher and healthier musical atmosphere.

CHAPTER VI

IN the ballet scene of Gounod's most popular opera *Mephistopheles* conjures up visions of Phryne, Laïs, Aspasia, Cleopatra, and Helen of Troy to beguile the jaded interest of *Faust*. The list reads almost like a catalogue of the operas of Massenet whose fine talent was largely given to the celebration of the famous courtesans of the ancient world. With the addition of a few more names from the roster of antiquity (*Thaïs, Dalila,* and *Aphrodite*), and some less ancient but no less immoral creatures of modern fancy, like *Violetta, Manon Lescaut, Zaza,* and *Louise,* we might make a pretty complete list of representatives of the female type in which modern dramatists and composers seem to think the interest of humanity centres.

When Massenet's "Hérodiade" was announced as the first opera to be given at the Manhattan Opera House in New York for the season of 1909–1910 it looked to some observers as if the dominant note of the year was to be sounded by the Scarlet Woman; but the representation brought a revelation and a surprise. The names of the principal characters

89

were those which for a few years had been filling
the lyric theatres of Germany with a moral stench;
but their bearers in Massenet's opera did little or
nothing that was especially shocking to good taste
or proper morals. *Herod* was a love-sick man of
lust, who gazed with longing eyes upon the physical
charms of *Salomé* and pleaded for her smiles like any
sentimental milksop; but he did not offer her
Capernaum for a dance. *Salomé* may have known
how, but she did not dance for either half a kingdom
or the whole of a man's head. Instead, though
there were intimations that her reputation was not
all that a good maiden's ought to be, she sang pious
hosannahs and waved a palm branch conspicuously
in honor of the prophet at whose head she had
bowled herself in the desert, the public streets, and
king's palaces. At the end she killed herself when
she found that the vengeful passion of *Herodias* and
the jealous hatred of *Herod* had compassed the death
of the saintly man whom she had loved. *Herodias*
was a wicked woman, no doubt, for *John the Baptist*
denounced her publicly as a Jezebel, but her jealousy
of *Salomé* had reached a point beyond her control
before she learned that her rival was her own daughter whom she had deserted for love of the Tetrarch.
As for *John the Baptist* the camel's hair with which
he was clothed must have cost as pretty a penny as
any of the modern kind, and if he wore a girdle of
skins about his loins it was concealed under a really
regal cloak. He was a voice; but not one crying

in the wilderness. He was in fact an operatic tenor *comme il faut,* who needed only to be shut up in a subterranean jail with the young woman who had pursued him up hill and down dale, in and out of season to make love to her in the most approved fashion of the Paris Grand Opéra.

What shall we think of the morals of this French opera, after we have seen and heard that compounded by the Englishman Oscar Wilde and the German Richard Strauss? No wonder that England's Lord Chamberlain asked nothing more than an elimination of the Biblical names when he licensed a performance of "Hérodiade" at Covent Garden. There was no loss of dramatic qualitiy in calling *Herod, Moriame,* and *Herodias, Hesotade,* and changing the scene from Jerusalem to Azoum in Ethiopia; though it must have been a trifle diverting to hear fair-skinned Ethiopians singing *Schma Yisroel, Adonai Elohenu* in a temple which could only be that of Jerusalem. John the Baptist was only *Jean* in the original and needed not to be changed, and *Salomé* is not in the Bible, though Salome, a very different woman is — a fact which the Lord Chamberlain seems to have overlooked when he changed the title of the opera from "Hérodiade" to "Salomé."

Where does Salome come from, anyway? And where did she get her chameleonlike nature? Was she an innocent child, as Flaubert represents her, who could but lisp the name of the prophet when her mother told her to ask for his head? Had she

taken dancing lessons from one of the women of
Cadiz to learn to dance as she must have danced to
excite such lust in Herod? Was she a monster, a
worse than vampire as she is represented by Wilde
and Strauss? Was she an "Israelitish grisette" as
Pougin called the heroine of the opera which it
took one Italian (Zanardini) and three Frenchmen
(Milliet, Grémont, and Massenet) to concoct? No
wonder that the brain of Saint-Saëns reeled when he
went to hear "Hérodiade" at its first performance
in Brussels and found that the woman whom he had
looked upon as a type of lasciviousness and monstrous cruelty had become metamorphosed into a
penitent Magdalen. Read the plot of the opera and
wonder!

Salomé is a maiden in search of her mother whom
John the Baptist finds in his wanderings and be-
friends. She clings to him when he becomes a political as well as a religious power among the Jews,
though he preaches unctuously to her touching the
vanity of earthly love. *Herodias* demands his
death of her husband for that he had publicly insulted her, but *Herod* schemes to use his influence
over the Jews to further his plan to become a real
monarch instead of a Roman Tetrarch. But when
the pro-consul *Vitellius* wins the support of the
people and *Herod* learns that the maiden who has
spurned him is in love with the prophet, he decrees
his decapitation. *Salomé*, baffled in her effort to
save her lover, attempts to kill *Herodias;* but the

wicked woman discloses herself as the maiden's mother and *Salomé* turns the dagger against her own breast.

This is all of the story one needs to know. It is richly garnished with incident, made gorgeous with pageantry, and clothed with much charming music. Melodies which may be echoes of synagogal hymns of great antiquity resound in the walls of the temple at Jerusalem, in which respect the opera recalls Goldmark's "Queen of Sheba." Curved Roman trumpets mix their loud clangors with the instruments of the modern brass band and compel us to think of "Aïda." There are dances of Egyptians, Babylonians, and Phœnicians, and if the movements of the women make us deplore the decay of the choreographic art, the music warms us almost as much as the Spanish measures in "Le Cid." Eyes and ears are deluged with Oriental color until at the last there comes a longing for the graciously insinuating sentimentalities of which the earlier Massenet was a master. Two of the opera's airs had long been familiar to the public from performance in the concert-room — *Salomé's* "Il est doux" and *Herod's* "Vision fugitive" — and they stand out as the brightest jewels in the opera's musical crown; but there is much else which woos the ear delightfully, for Massenet was ever a gracious if not a profound melodist and a master of construction and theatrical orchestration. When he strives for massive effects, however, he sometimes becomes futile, banal where he would be imposing; but he commands a charm which is insinuating in its moments of intimacy.[1]

[1] "Hérodiade" had its first performance in New York (it had previously been given in New Orleans by the French Opera Company) on November 8, 1909. The cast was as follows: *Salomé*, Lina Cavalieri; *Herodias*, Gerville-Reache; *John*, Charles Dalmores; *Herod*, Maurice Renaud; *Vitellius*, Crabbé; *Phanuel*, M. Vallier; *High Priest*, M. Nicolay. Musical director, Henriques de la Fuente.

CHAPTER VII

"LAKMÉ"

Lakmé is the daughter of *Nilakantha*, a fanatical Brahmin priest, who has withdrawn to a ruined temple deep in an Indian forest. In his retreat the old man nurses his wrath against the British invader, prays assiduously to Brahma (thus contributing a fascinating Oriental mood to the opening of the opera), and waits for the time to come when he shall be able to wreak his revenge on the despoilers of his country. *Lakmé* sings Oriental duets with her slave, *Mallika:*—

> Sous le dôme épais où le blanc jasmin
> A la rose s'assemble,
> Sur la rive en fleurs, riant au matin
> Viens, descendons ensemble —

a dreamy, sense-ensnaring, hypnotic barcarole. The opera opens well; by this time the composer has carried us deep into the jungle. The Occident is rude: *Gerald*, an English officer, breaks through a bamboo fence and makes love to *Lakmé*, who, though widely separated from her operatic colleagues from an ethnological point of view like *Elsa* and *Senta*, to expedite the action requites the passion instanter. After the Englishman is gone the father returns and, with an Oriental's cunning which does him credit, deduces from the broken fence that an Englishman has profaned the sacred spot. This is the business of Act I. In Act II the father, disguised as a beggar who holds a dagger ever in readiness, and his daughter, disguised as a street singer, visit a town market in search of the profaner. The business is not to *Lakmé's* taste, but it is not for the like of her to neglect the opportunity offered to win applause with the legend of the pariah's daughter, with its tintinnabulatory charm : —

> Ou va la jeune Hindoue
> Fille des parias;
> Quand la lune se joue
> Dans les grand mimosas?

It is the "Bell song," which has tinkled so often in our concert-rooms. *Gerald* recognizes the singer despite her disguise; and *Nilakantha* recognizes him as the despoiler of the hallowed spot in which he worships and incidentally conceals his daughter. The bloodthirsty fanatic observes sententiously that Brahma has smiled and cuts short *Gerald's* soliloquizing with a dagger thrust. *Lakmé*, with the help of a male slave, removes him to a hut concealed in the forest. While he is convalescing the pair sing duets and exchange vows of undying affection. But the military Briton, who has invaded the country at large, must needs now invade also this cosey abode of love. *Frederick*, a brother officer, discovers *Gerald* and informs him that duty calls (Britain always expects every man to do his duty, no matter what the consequences to him) and he must march with his regiment. *Frederick* has happened in just as *Lakmé* is gone for some sacred water in which she and *Gerald* were to pledge eternal love for each other, to each other. But, spurred on by *Frederick* and the memory that "England expects, etc.," *Gerald* finds the call of the fife and drum more potent than the voice of love. *Lakmé*, psychologist as well as botanist, understands the struggle which now takes place in *Gerald's* soul, and relieves him of his dilemma by crushing a poisonous flower (to be exact, the *Datura stramonium*) between her teeth, dying, it would seem, to the pious delight of her father, who "ecstatically" beholds her dwelling with Brahma.

The story, borrowed by Gondinet and Gille from the little romance "Le Mariage de Loti," is worthless except to furnish motives for tropical scenery, Hindu dresses, and Oriental music. Three English ladies, *Ellen*, *Rose*, and *Mrs. Bentson*, figure in the play, but without dramatic purpose except to take part in some concerted music. They are, indeed, so insignificant in all other respects that when the opera was given by Miss Van Zandt and a French company in London for the first time in 1885 they were omitted, and the excision was commended by the critics, who knew that it had been made. The conversation of the women is all of the veriest stopgap

H

character. The maidens, *Rose* and *Ellen*, are English ladies visiting in the East; *Mrs. Bentson* is their chaperon. All that they have to say is highly unimportant, even when true. "What do you see, *Frederick?*" "A garden." "And you, *Gerald?*" "Big, beautiful trees." "Anybody about?" "Don't know." "Look again." "That's not easy; the fence shuts out the view within." "Can't you make a peephole through the bamboo?" "Girls, girls, be careful." And so on and so on for quantity. But we must fill three acts, and ensemble makes its demands; besides, we want pretty blondes of the English type to put in contrast with the dark-skinned *Lakmé* and her slave. At the first representation in New York by the American Opera Company, at the Academy of Music, on March 1, 1886, the three women were permitted to interfere with what there is of poetical spirit in the play, and their conversation, like that of the other principals, was uttered in the recitatives composed by Delibes to take the place of the spoken dialogue used at the Paris Opéra Comique, where spoken dialogue is traditional. Theodore Thomas conducted the Academy performance, at which the cast was as follows: *Lakmé*, Pauline L'Allemand; *Nilakantha*, Alonzo E. Stoddard; *Gerald*, William Candidus; *Frederick*, William H. Lee; *Ellen*, Charlotte Walker; *Rose*, Helen Dudley Campbell; *Mrs. Bentson*, May Fielding; *Mallika*, Jessie Bartlett Davis; *Hadji*, William H. Fessenden. Few operas have had a more variegated American

history than "Lakmé." It was quite new when it
was first heard in New York, but it had already given
rise to considerable theatrical gossip, not to say
scandal. The first representation took place at the
Opéra Comique in April, 1883, with Miss Marie
Van Zandt, an American girl, the daughter of a
singer who had been actively successful in English
opera in New York and London, as creator of the
part of the heroine. The opera won a pretty triumph and so did the singer. At once there was talk
of a New York performance. Mme. Etelka Gerster
studied the titular rôle with M. Delibes and, as a
member of Colonel Mapleson's company at the
Academy of Music, confidently expected to produce
the work there in the season of 1883–1884, the first
season of the rivalry between the Academy and the
Metropolitan Opera House, which had just opened
its doors; but though she went so far as to offer to
buy the American performing rights from Heugel,
the publisher, nothing came of it. The reason was
easily guessed by those who knew that there has been,
or was pending, a quarrel between Colonel Mapleson
and M. Heugel concerning the unauthorized use by
the impresario of other scores owned by the publisher.
  During the same season, however, Miss Emma
Abbott carried a version (or rather a perversion) of
the opera, for which the orchestral parts had been
arranged from the pianoforte score, into the cities of
the West, and brought down a deal of unmerited
criticism on the innocent head of M. Delibes. In

the season of 1884–1885 Colonel Mapleson came back to the Academy with vouchers of various sorts to back up a promise to give the opera. There was a human voucher in the person of Miss Emma Nevada, who had also enjoyed the instruction of the composer and who had trunkfuls and trunkfuls and trunkfuls of Oriental dresses, though *Lakmé* needs but few. There were gorgeous uniforms for the British soldiers, the real article, each scarlet coat and every top boot having a piece of history attached, and models of the scenery which any doubting Thomas of a newspaper reporter might inspect if he felt so disposed. When the redoubtable colonel came it was to be only a matter of a week or so before the opera would be put on the stage in the finest of styles; it was still a matter of a week or so when the Academy season came to an end. When Delibes's exquisite and exotic music reached a hearing in the American metropolis, it was sung to English words, and the most emphatic success achieved in performance was the acrobatic one of Mme. L'Allemand as she rolled down some uncalled-for pagoda steps in the death scene.

Mme. Adelina Patti was the second *Lakmé* heard in New York. After the fifth season of German opera at the Metropolitan Opera House had come to an end in the spring of 1890, Messrs. Abbey and Grau took the theatre for a short season of Italian opera by a troupe headed by Mme. Patti. In that season "Lakmé" was sung once — on April 2, 1890. Now came an opportunity for the original representative of the heroine. Abbey and Grau resumed the management of the theatre in 1891, and in their company was Miss Van Zandt, for whom the opera was "revived" on February 22. Mr. Abbey had great expectations, but they were disappointed. For the public there was metal more attractive than Miss Van Zandt and the Hindu opera in other members of the company and other operas. It was the year of Emma Eames's coming and also of Jean de Reszke's (they sang together in Gounod's "Roméo et Juliette") and "Cavalleria rusticana" was new. Then Delibes's opera hibernated in New York for fifteen years, after which the presence in the Metropolitan company of Mme. Marcella Sembrich led to another "revival." (Operas which are unperformed for a term of two or three years after having been once included in the repertory are "revived" in New York.) It was sung three times in the season of 1906–1907. It also afforded one of Mr. Hammerstein's many surprises at the Manhattan Opera House. Five days before the close of his last season, on March 21, 1910, it was precipitated on the stage ("pitchforked" is the popular and professional term) to give Mme. Tetrazzini a chance to sing the bell song. Altogether I know of no more singular history than that of "Lakmé" in New York.

*

* *

Lakmé is a child of the theatrical boards, who inherited traits from several predecessors, the strong-

est being those deriving from *Aïda* and *Selika*. Like
the former, she loves a man whom her father believes
to be the arch enemy of his native land, and, like her,
she is the means of betraying him into the hands of
the avenger. Like the heroine of Meyerbeer's post-
humous opera, she has a fatal acquaintance with
tropical botany and uses her knowledge to her own
destruction. Her scientific attainments are on about
the same plane as her amiability, her abnormal
sense of filial duty, and her musical accomplishments.
She loves a man whom her father wishes her to lure
to his death by her singing, and she sings entrancingly
enough to bring about the meeting between her
lover's back and her father's knife. That she does
not warble herself into the position of *particeps
criminis* in a murder she owes only to the bungling
of the old man. Having done this, however, she
turns physician and nurse and brings the wounded
man back to health, thus sacrificing her love to the
duty which her lover thinks he owes to the invaders
of her country and oppressors of her people. After
this she makes the fatal application of her botanical
knowledge. Such things come about when one goes
to India for an operatic heroine.

The feature of the libretto which Delibes has used
to the best purpose is its local color. His music is
saturated with the languorous spirit of the East.
Half a dozen of the melodies are lovely inventions,
of marked originality in both matter and treatment,
and the first half hour of the opera is apt to take one's

fancy completely captive. The drawback lies in the oppressive weariness which succeeds the first trance, and is brought on by the monotonous character of the music. After an hour of "Lakmé" one yearns for a few crashing chords of C major as a person enduring suffocation longs for a gush of fresh air. The music first grows monotonous, then wearies. Delibes's lyrical moments show the most numerous indications of beauty; dramatic life and energy are absent from the score. In the second act he moves his listeners only once — with the attempted repetition of the bell song after *Lakmé* has recognized her lover. The odor of the poppy invites to drowsy enjoyment in the beginning, and the first act is far and away the most gratifying in the opera, musically as well as scenically. It would be so if it contained only *Lakmé's* song "Pourquoi dans les grands bois," the exquisite barcarole — a veritable treasure trove for the composer, who used its melody dramatically throughout the work — and *Gerald's* air, "Fantaisie aux divins mensonges." Real depth will be looked for in vain in this opera; superficial loveliness is apparent on at least half its pages.

CHAPTER VIII

"PAGLIACCI"

FOR a quarter of a century "Cavalleria rusticana" and "Pagliacci" have been the Castor and Pollux of the operatic theatres of Europe and America. Together they have joined the hunt of venturesome impresarios for that Calydonian boar, success; together they have lighted the way through seasons of tempestuous stress and storm. Of recent years at the Metropolitan Opera House in New York efforts have been made to divorce them and to find associates for one or the other, since neither is sufficient in time for an evening's entertainment; but they refuse to be put asunder as steadfastly as did the twin brothers of Helen and Clytemnestra. There has been no operatic Zeus powerful enough to separate and alternate their existences even for a day; and though blasé critics will continue to rail at the "double bill" as they have done for two decades or more, the two fierce little dramas will "sit shining on the sails" of many a managerial ship and bring it safe to haven for many a year to come.

Twins the operas are in spirit; twins in their capacity as supreme representatives of *verismo;*

RUGGIERO LEONCAVALLO.

twins in the fitness of their association; but twins
they are not in respect of parentage or age. "Cavalleria rusticana" is two years older than "Pagliacci"
and as truly its progenitor as Weber's operas were the
progenitors of Wagner's. They are the offspring of
the same artistic movement, and it was the phe-

nomenal success of Mascagni's opera which was the
spur that drove Leoncavallo to write his. When
"Cavalleria rusticana" appeared on the scene, two
generations of opera-goers had passed away without
experiencing anything like the sensation caused
by this opera. They had witnessed the production,
indeed, of great masterpieces, which it would be

almost sacrilegious to mention in the same breath with Mascagni's turbulent and torrential tragedy, but these works were the productions of mature masters, from whom things monumental and lasting were expected as a matter of course; men like Wagner and Verdi. The generations had also seen the coming of "Carmen" and gradually opened their minds to an appreciation of its meaning and beauty, while the youthful genius who had created it sank almost unnoticed into his grave; but they had not seen the advent of a work which almost in a day set the world on fire and raised an unknown musician from penury and obscurity to affluence and fame. In the face of such an experience it was scarcely to be wondered at that judgment was flung to the winds and that the most volatile of musical nations and the staidest alike hailed the young composer as the successor of Verdi, the regenerator of operatic Italy, and the pioneer of a new school which should revitalize opera and make unnecessary the hopeless task of trying to work along the lines laid down by Wagner.

And this opera was the outcome of a competition based on the frankest kind of commercialism — one of those "occasionals" from which we have been taught to believe we ought never to expect anything of ideal and lasting merit. "Pagliacci" was, in a way, a fruit of the same competition. Three years before "Cavalleria rusticana" had started the universal conflagration Ruggiero Leoncavallo, who at sixteen years of age had won his diploma at the Naples Conservatory and received the degree of Doctor of Letters from the University of Bologna at twenty, had read his dramatic poem "I Medici" to the publisher Ricordi and been commissioned to set it to music. For this work he was to receive 2400 francs. He completed the composition within a year, but there was no contract that the opera should be performed, and this hoped-for consummation did not follow. Then came Mascagni's triumph, and Leoncavallo, who had been obliged meanwhile to return to the routine work of an operatic *repétiteur*, lost patience. Satisfied that Ricordi would never do anything more for him, and become desperate, he shut himself in his room to attempt "one more work" — as he said in an autobiographical sketch which appeared in "La Reforme," a journal published in Alexandria. In five months he had written the book and music of "Pagliacci," which was accepted for publication and production by Sonzogno, Ricordi's business rival, after a single reading of the poem. Maurel, whose friendship Leoncavallo had made while coaching opera singers in Paris, used his influence in favor of the opera, offered to create the part of *Tonio*, and did so at the first performance of the opera at the Teatro dal Verme, Milan, on May 17, 1892.

Leoncavallo's opera turns on a tragical ending to a comedy which is incorporated in the play. The comedy is a familiar one among the strolling players who perform at village fairs in Italy, in which Colombina, Pagliaccio, and Arlecchino (respectively the Columbine, Clown, and Harlequin of our pantomime) take part. Pagliaccio is husband to Colombina and Arlecchino is her lover, who hoodwinks Pagliaccio. There is a fourth character, Taddeo, a servant, who makes foolish love to Columbina and, mingling imbecile stupidity with maliciousness, delights in the domestic discord which he helps to foment. The first act of the opera may be looked upon as an induction to the conventional comedy which comes to an unconventional and tragic end through the fact that the Clown (*Canio*) is in real life the husband of Columbine (*Nedda*) and is murderously jealous of her; wherefore, forgetting himself in a mad rage, he kills her and her lover in the midst of the mimic scene. The lover, however, is not the Harlequin of the comedy, but one of the spectators whom *Canio* had vainly sought to identify, but who is unconsciously betrayed by his mistress in her death agony. The Taddeo of the comedy is the clown of the company, who in real life entertains a passion for *Nedda*, which is repulsed, whereupon he also carries his part into actuality and betrays *Nedda's* secret to *Canio*. It is in the ingenious interweaving of these threads — the weft of reality with the warp of simulation — that the chief dramatic value of Leoncavallo's opera lies.

Actual murder by a man while apparently playing a part in a drama is older as a dramatic *motif* than

"Pagliacci," and Leoncavallo's employment of it
gave rise to an interesting controversy and a still more
interesting revelation in the early days of the opera.
Old theatre-goers in England and America remember
the device as it was employed in Dennery's "Pail-
laisse," known on the English stage as "Belphegor,
the Mountebank." In 1874 Paul Ferrier produced
a play entitled "Tabarin," in which Coquelin appeared at the Théâtre Français. Thirteen years
later Catulle Mendès brought out another play
called "La Femme de Tabarin," for which Chabrier
wrote the incidental music. The critics were prompt
in charging Mendès with having plagiarized Ferrier,
and the former defended himself on the ground that
the incident which he had employed, of actual
murder in a dramatic performance, was historical
and had often been used. This, however, did not
prevent him from bringing an accusation of theft
against Leoncavallo when "Pagliacci" was announced for production in French at Brussels and of
beginning legal proceedings against the composer
and his publisher on that score. The controversy
which followed showed very plainly that Mendès
did not have a leg to stand upon either in law or
equity, and he withdrew his suit and made a handsome *amende* in a letter to the editor of "Le Figaro."
Before this was done, however, Signor Leoncavallo
wrote a letter to his publisher, which not only established that the incident in question was based upon
fact but directed attention to a dramatic use of the

motif in a Spanish play written thirty-five years before the occurrence which was in the mind of Leoncavallo. The letter was as follows: —

Lugano, Sept. 3, 1894.

Dear Signor Sonzogno.

I have read Catulle Mendès's two letters. M. Mendès goes pretty far in declaring *a priori* that "Pagliacci" is an imitation of his "Femme de Tabarin." I had not known this book, and only know it now through the accounts given in the daily papers. You will remember that at the time of the first performance of "Pagliacci" at Milan in 1892 several critics accused me of having taken the subject of my opera from the "Drama Nuevo" of the well known Spanish writer, Estebanez. What would M. Mendès say if he were accused of having taken the plot of "La Femme de Tabarin" from the "Drama Nuevo," which dates back to 1830 or 1840? As a fact, a husband, a comedian, kills in the last scene the lover of his wife before her eyes while he only appears to play his part in the piece.

It is absolutely true that I knew at that time no more of the "Drama Nuevo" than I know now of "La Femme de Tabarin." I saw the first mentioned work in Rome represented by Novelli six months after "Pagliacci's" first production in Milan. In my childhood, while my father was judge at Montalto, in Calabria (the scene of the opera's plot), a jealous player killed his wife after the performance. This event made a deep and lasting impression on my childish mind, the more since my father was the judge at the criminal's trial; and later, when I took up dramatic work, I used this episode for a drama. I left the frame of the piece as I saw it, and it can be seen now at the Festival of Madonna della Serra, at Montalto. The clowns arrive a week or ten days before the festival, which takes place on August 15, to put up their tents and booths in the open space which reaches from the church toward the fields. I have not even invented the coming of the peasants from Santo Benedetto, a neighboring village, during the chorale.

What I write now I have mentioned so often in Germany and other parts that several opera houses, notably that of Berlin, had printed on their bills "Scene of the true event." After all this, M. Mendès insisted on his claim, which means that he does not believe my words. Had I used M. Mendès's ideas I would not have hesitated to open correspondence with him before the first representation, as I have done now with a well known writer who has a subject that I wish to use for a future work. "Pagliacci" is my own, entirely my own. If in this opera, a scene reminds one of M. Mendès's book, it only proves that we both had the same idea which Estebanez had before us. On my honor and conscience I assure you that I have read but two of M. Mendès's books in my life — "Zo Hur" and "La Première Maîtresse." When I read at Marienbad a little while ago the newspaper notices on the production of "La Femme de Tabarin" I even wrote to you, dear Signor Sonzogno, thinking this was an imitation of "Pagliacci." This assertion will suffice, coming from an honorable man, to prove my loyalty. If not, then I will place my undoubted rights under the protection of the law, and furnish incontestable proof of what I have stated here.

I have the honor, etc., etc.

At various times and in various manners, by letters and in newspaper interviews, Leoncavallo reiterated the statement that the incident which he had witnessed as a boy in his father's courtroom had suggested his drama. The chief actor in the inci-

dent, he said, was still living. After conviction he
was asked if he felt penitent. The rough voice
which rang through the room years before still
echoed in Leoncavallo's ears: "I repent me of
nothing! On the contrary, if I had it to do over
again I'd do it again!" (*Non mi pento del delitto!
Tutt altro. Se dovessi ricominciare, ricomincerei!*)
He was sentenced to imprisonment and after the
expiration of his term took service in a little Calabrian
town with Baroness Sproniere. If Mendès had pros-
ecuted his action, "poor Alessandro" was ready to
appear as a witness and tell the story which Leoncavallo had dramatized.

I have never seen "La Femme de Tabarin" and
must rely on Mr. Philip Hale, fecund fountain of
informal information, for an outline of the play which
"Pagliacci" called back into public notice: Francisquine, the wife of Tabarin, irons her petticoats in the
players' booth. A musketeer saunters along, stops
and makes love to her. She listens greedily. Tabarin enters just after she has made an appointment
with the man. Tabarin is drunk — drunker than
usual. He adores his wife; he falls at her feet; he
entreats her; he threatens her. Meanwhile the
crowd gathers to see the "parade." Tabarin mounts
the platform and tells openly of his jealousy. He
calls his wife; she does not answer. He opens the
curtain behind him; then he sees her in the arms of
the musketeer. Tabarin snatches up a sword, stabs
his wife in the breast and comes back to the stage

with starting eyes and hoarse voice. The crowd marvels at the passion of his play. Francisquine, bloody, drags herself along the boards. She chokes; she cannot speak. Tabarin, mad with despair, gives her the sword, begs her to kill him. She seizes the sword, raises herself, hiccoughs, gasps out the word "Canaille," and dies before she can strike.

Paul Ferrier and Emanuel Pessard produced a grand opera in two acts entitled "Tabarin" in Paris in 1885; Alboiz and André a comic opera with the same title, music by Georges Bousquet, in 1852. Gilles and Furpilles brought out an operetta called "Tabarin Duelliste," with music by Léon Pillaut, in 1866. The works seem to have had only the name of the hero in common. Their stories bear no likeness to those of "La Femme de Tabarin" or "Pagliacci." The Spanish play, "Drama Nuevo," by Estebanez, was adapted for performance in English by Mr. W. D. Howells under the title "Yorick's Love." The translation was made for Mr. Lawrence Barrett and was never published in book form. If it had the dénouement suggested in Leoncavallo's letter to Sonzogno, the fact has escaped the memory of Mr. Howells, who, in answer to a letter of inquiry which I sent him, wrote: "So far as I can remember there was no likeness between 'Yorick's Love' and 'Pagliacci.' But when I made my version I had not seen or heard 'Pagliacci.'"

The title of Leoncavallo's opera is "Pagliacci," not "I Pagliacci" as it frequently appears in books

I

and newspapers. When the opera was brought out in the vernacular, Mr. Frederick E. Weatherly, who made the English adaptation, called the play and the character assumed by *Canio* in the comedy "Punchinello." This evoked an interesting comment from Mr. Hale: "'Pagliacci' is the plural of Pagliaccio, which does not mean and never did mean Punchinello. What is a Pagliaccio? A type long known to the Italians, and familiar to the French as Paillasse. The Pagliaccio visited Paris first in 1570. He was clothed in white and wore big buttons. Later, he wore a suit of bedtick, with white and blue checks, the coarse mattress cloth of the period. Hence his name. The word that meant straw was afterward used for mattress which was stuffed with straw and then for the buffoon, who wore the mattress cloth suit. In France the Paillasse, as I have said, was the same as Pagliaccio. Sometimes he wore a red checked suit, but the genuine one was known by the colors, white and blue. He wore blue stockings, short breeches puffing out *à la blouse*, a belted blouse and a black, close-fitting cap. This buffoon was seen at shows of strolling mountebanks. He stood outside the booth and by his jests and antics and grimaces strove to attract the attention of the people, and he told them of the wonders performed by acrobats within, of the freaks exhibited. Many of his jests are preserved. They are often in dialogue with the proprietor and are generally of vile indecency. The lowest of the strollers, he was abused

by them. The Italian Pagliaccio is a species of
clown, and Punchinello was never a mere buffoon.
The Punch of the puppet-show is a bastard descendant of the latter, but the original type is still seen
in Naples, where he wears a white costume and a
black mask. The original type was not necessarily
humpbacked. Punchinello is a shrewd fellow, intellectual, yet in touch with the people, cynical; not
hesitating at murder if he can make by it; at the
same time a local satirist, a dealer in gags and quips.
Pagliacci is perhaps best translated by 'clowns';
but the latter word must not be taken in its restricted circus sense. These strolling clowns are
pantomimists, singers, comedians."

At the first performance of "Pagliacci" in Milan
the cast was as follows: *Canio*, Geraud; *Tonio*,
Maurel; *Silvio*, Ancona; *Peppe*, Daddi; *Nedda*,
Mme. Stehle. The first performance in America was
by the Hinrichs Grand Opera Company, at the Grand
Opera House, New York, on June 15, 1893; Selma
Kronold was the *Nedda*, Montegriffo the *Canio*, and
Campanari the *Tonio*. The opera was incorporated
in the Metropolitan repertory in the season of 1893-
1894.

*

* *

Rinuccini's "Dafne," which was written 300
years ago and more, begins with a prologue which
was spoken in the character of the poet Ovid. Leoncavallo's "Pagliacci" also begins with a prologue,

but it is spoken by one of the people of the play; whether in his character as *Tonio* of the tragedy or *Pagliaccio* of the comedy there is no telling. He speaks the sentiments of the one and wears the motley of the other. Text and music, however, are ingeniously contrived to serve as an index to the purposes of the poet and the method and material of the composer. In his speech the prologue tells us that the author of the play is fond of the ancient custom of such an introduction, but not of the old purpose. He does not employ it for the purpose of proclaiming that the tears and passions of the actors are but simulated and false. No! He wishes to let us know that his play is drawn from life as it is — that it is true. It welled up within him when memories of the past sang in his heart and was written down to show us that actors are human beings like unto ourselves.

An unnecessary preachment, and if listened to with a critical disposition rather an impertinence, as calculated to rob us of the pleasure of illusion which it is the province of the drama to give. Closely analyzed, *Tonio's* speech is very much of a piece with the prologue which *Bully Bottom* wanted for the play of "Pyramus" in Shakespeare's comedy. We are asked to see a play. In this play there is another play. In this other play one of the actors plays at cross-purposes with the author — forgets his lines and himself altogether and becomes in reality the man that he seems to be in the first play.

The prologue deliberately aims to deprive us of the thrill of surprise at the unexpected dénouement, simply that he may tell us what we already know as well as he, that an actor is a human being.

Plainly then, from a didactic point of view, this prologue is a gratuitous impertinence. Not so its music. Structurally, it is little more than a loose-jointed pot-pourri; but it serves the purpose of a thematic catalogue to the chief melodic incidents of the play which is to follow. In this it bears a faint resemblance to the introduction to Berlioz's "Romeo and Juliet" symphony. It begins with an energetic figure,

which is immediately followed by an upward scale-passage with a saucy flourish at the end — not unlike the crack of a whiplash: —

It helps admirably to picture the bustling activity of the *festa* into which we are soon to be precipitated.

The bits of melody which are now introduced might all be labelled in the Wolzogen-Wagner manner with reference to the play's peoples and their passions if it were worth while to do so, or if their beauty and eloquence were not sufficient unto themselves. First we have the phrase in which *Canio* will tell us how a clown's heart must seem merry and make laughter though it be breaking : —

Next the phrase from the love music of *Nedda* and *Silvio* : —

The bustling music returns, develops great energy, then pauses, hesitates, and makes way for *Tonio*, who, putting his head through the curtain, politely asks permission of the audience, steps forward and delivers his homily, which is alternately declamatory and broadly melodious. One of his melodies later becomes the theme of the between-acts music, which

separates the supposedly real life of the strolling
players from the comedy which they present to the
mimic audience : —

Ah think then, sweet peo - ple, when ye
E - vo piut - to - sto che le

look on us clad in our mot - ley
no - stre po ve - re gab - ba ne

At last *Tonio* calls upon his fellow mountebanks
to begin their play. The curtain rises. We are in
the midst of a rural celebration of the Feast of the
Assumption on the outskirts of a village in Calabria.
A perambulant theatre has been set up among the
trees and the strolling actors are arriving, accompanied by a crowd of villagers, who shout greetings
to Clown, Columbine, and Harlequin. *Nedda* arrives in a cart drawn by a donkey led by *Beppe*.
Canio in character invites the crowd to come to the
show at 7 o'clock (*ventitre ore*). There they shall
be regaled with a sight of the domestic troubles of
Pagliaccio and see the fat mischief-maker tremble.
Tonio wants to help *Nedda* out of the cart, but *Canio*
interferes and lifts her down himself ; whereupon the
women and boys twit *Tonio*. *Canio* and *Beppe*

wet their whistles at the tavern, but *Tonio* remains behind on the plea that he must curry the donkey. The hospitable villager playfully suggests that it is *Tonio's* purpose to make love to *Nedda*. *Canio*, half in earnest, half in jest, points out the difference between real life and the stage. In the play, if he catches a lover with his wife, he flies into a mock passion, preaches a sermon, and takes a drubbing from the swain to the amusement of the audience. But there would be a different ending to the story were *Nedda* actually to deceive him. Let *Tonio* beware! Does he doubt *Nedda's* fidelity? Not at all. He loves her and seals his assurance with a kiss. Then off to the tavern.

Hark to the bagpipes! Huzza, here come the *zampognari!* Drone pipes droning and chaunters skirling — as well as they can skirl in Italian!

Now we have people and pipers on the stage and there's a bell in the steeple ringing for vespers. Therefore a chorus. Not that we have anything to say that concerns the story in any way. "Din, don!" That would suffice, but if you must have more: "Let's to church. Din, don. All's right with love and the sunset. Din, don! But mamma has her eye on the young folk and their inclination for kissing. Din, don!" Bells and pipes are echoed by the singers.

Her husband is gone to the tavern for refreshment and *Nedda* is left alone. There is a little trouble in her mind caused by the fierceness of *Canio's* voice and looks. Does he suspect? But why yield to such fancies and fears? How beautiful the mid-August sun is! Her hopes and longings find expression in the Ballatella — a waltz tune with twitter of birds and rustle of leaves for accompaniment. Pretty birds, where are you going? What is it you say? Mother knew your song and used once to tell it to her babe. How your wings flash through the ether! Heedless of cloud and tempest, on, on, past the stars, and still on! Her wishes take flight with the feathered songsters, but *Tonio* brings her rudely to earth. He pleads for a return of the love which he says he bears her, but she bids him postpone his protestations till he can make them in the play. He grows desperately urgent and attempts to rape a kiss. She cuts him across the face with a donkey whip, and he goes away blaspheming and swearing vengeance.

Then *Silvio* comes — *Silvio*, the villager, who loves her and who has her heart. She fears he will be discovered, but he bids her be at peace; he had left *Canio* drinking at the tavern. She tells him of the scene with *Tonio* and warns him, but he laughs at her fears. Then he pleads with her. She does not love her husband; she is weary of the wandering

life which she is forced to lead; if her love is true
let her fly with him to happiness. No. 'Tis folly,
madness; her heart is his, but he must not tempt
her to its destruction. *Tonio* slinks in and plays
eavesdropper. He hears the mutual protestations
of the lovers, hears *Nedda* yield to *Silvio's* wild pleadings, sees them locked in each other's arms, and hurries off to fetch *Canio*. *Canio* comes, but not in time
to see the man who had climbed over the wall, yet
in time to hear *Nedda's* word of parting: *A stanotte
— e per sempre tua saro —* "To-night, and forever,
I am yours!" He throws *Nedda* aside and gives
chase after the fugitive, but is baffled. He demands
to be told the name of her lover. *Nedda* refuses to
answer. He rushes upon her with dagger drawn,
but *Beppe* intercepts and disarms him. There is
haste now; the villagers are already gathering for
the play. *Tonio* insinuates his wicked advice: Let
us dissemble; the gallant may be caught at the play.
The others go out to prepare for their labors. *Canio*
staggers toward the theatre. He must act the merry
fool, though his heart be torn! Why not? What
is he? A man? No; a clown! On with the
motley! The public must be amused. What
though Harlequin steals his Columbine? Laugh,
Pagliaccio, though thy heart break!

The between-acts music is retrospective; it comments on the tragic emotions, the pathos foretold
in the prologue. Act II brings the comedy which is
to have a realistic and bloody ending. The villagers

gather and struggle for places in front of the booth.
Among them is *Silvio*, to whom *Nedda* speaks a word
of warning as she passes him while collecting the
admission fees. He reminds her of the assignation;
she will be there. The comedy begins to the music
of a graceful minuet: —

Columbine is waiting for Harlequin. Taddeo is
at the market buying the supper for the mimic lovers.
Harlequin sings his serenade under the window:
"O, Colombina, il tenero fido Arlecchin" — a pretty
measure! Taddeo enters and pours out his admiration for Colombina in an exaggerated cadenza as
he offers her his basket of purchases. The audience
shows enjoyment of the sport. Taddeo makes love
to Colombina and Harlequin, entering by the window, lifts him up by the ears from the floor where he
is kneeling and kicks him out of the room. What
fun! The mimic lovers sit at table and discuss the
supper and their love. Taddeo enters in mock alarm
to tell of the coming of Pagliaccio. Harlequin

decamps, but leaves a philtre in the hands of Columbine to be poured into her husband's wine. At the window Columbine calls after him: *A stanotte — e per sempre io saro tua!* At this moment *Canio* enters in the character of Pagliaccio. He hears again the words which *Nedda* had called after the fleeing *Silvio*, and for a moment is startled out of his character. But he collects himself and begins to play his part. "A man has been here!" "You've been drinking!" The dialogue of the comedy continues, but ever and anon with difficulty on the part of Pagliaccio, who begins to put a sinister inflection into his words. Taddeo is dragged from the cupboard in which he had taken hiding. He, too, puts color of verity into his lines, especially when he prates about the purity of Columbine. *Canio* loses control of himself more and more. "Pagliaccio no more, but a man — a man seeking vengeance. The name of your lover!" The audience is moved by his intensity. *Silvio* betrays anxiety. *Canio* rages on. "The name, the name!" The mimic audience shouts, "Bravo!" *Nedda:* if he doubts her she will go. "No, by God! You'll remain and tell me the name of your lover!" With a great effort *Nedda* forces herself to remain in character. The music, whose tripping dance measures have given way to sinister mutterings in keeping with *Canio's* mad outbursts, as the mimic play ever and anon threatens to leave its grooves and plunge into the tragic vortex of reality, changes to a gavotte: —

Columbine explains: she had no idea her husband could put on so tragical a mask. It is only harmless Harlequin who has been her companion. "The name! *The name!!* THE NAME!!!" *Nedda* sees catastrophe approaching and throws her character to the winds. She shrieks out a defiant "No!" and attempts to escape from the mimic stage. *Silvio* starts up with dagger drawn. The spectators rise in confusion and cry "Stop him!" *Canio* seizes *Nedda* and plunges his knife into her: "Take that! And that! With thy dying gasps thou'lt tell me!" Woful intuition! Dying, *Nedda* calls: "Help, Silvio!" *Silvio* rushes forward and receives *Canio's* knife in his heart. "Gesumaria!" shriek the women. Men throw themselves upon *Canio.* He stands for a moment in a stupor, drops his knife and speaks the words: "The comedy is ended." "Ridi Pagliaccio!" shrieks the orchestra as the curtain falls.

"Plaudite, amici," said Beethoven on his death bed, "la commedia finita est!" And there is a tradition that these, too, were the last words of the arch-jester Rabelais. "When 'Pagliacci' was first sung here (in Boston), by the Tavary company," says Mr. Philip Hale, "*Tonio* pointed to the dead bodies and uttered the sentence in a mocking way. And there is a report that such was Leoncavallo's original intention. As the *Tonio* began the piece in explanation so he should end it. But the tenor (de Lucia) insisted that he should speak the line. I do not believe the story. (1) As Maurel was the original *Tonio* and the tenor was comparatively unknown, it is doubtful whether Maurel, of all men, would have allowed of the loss of a fat line. (2) As *Canio* is chief of the company it is eminently proper that he should make the announcement to the crowd. (3) The ghastly irony is accentuated by the speech when it comes from *Canio's* mouth."

CHAPTER IX

"CAVALLERIA RUSTICANA"

HAVING neither the patience nor the inclination to paraphrase a comment on Mascagni's "Cavalleria rusticana" which I wrote years ago when the opera was comparatively new, and as it appears to me to contain a just estimate and criticism of the work and the school of which it and "Pagliacci" remain the foremost exemplars, I quote from my book, "Chapters of Opera"[1]: "Seventeen years ago 'Cavalleria rusticana' had no perspective. Now, though but a small portion of its progeny has been brought to our notice, we nevertheless look at it through a vista which looks like a valley of moral and physical death through which there flows a sluggish stream thick with filth and red with blood. Strangely enough, in spite of the consequences which have followed it, the fierce little drama retains its old potency. It still speaks with a voice which sounds like the voice of truth. Its music still makes the nerves tingle, and carries our feelings unresistingly on its turbulent current. But the stage-picture is less sanguinary than it looked in the beginning. It

[1] "Chapters of Opera," by H. E. Krehbiel, p. 223.

127

seems to have receded a millennium in time. It
has the terrible fierceness of an Attic tragedy, but
it also has the decorum which the Attic tragedy
never violated. There is no slaughter in the presence
of the audience, despite the humbleness of its personages. It does not keep us perpetually in sight of the
shambles. It is, indeed, an exposition of chivalry ;
rustic, but chivalry nevertheless. It was thus Clytemnestra slew her husband, and Orestes his mother.
Note the contrast which the duel between *Alfio* and
Turiddu presents with the double murder to the
piquant accompaniment of comedy in 'Pagliacci,'
the opera which followed so hard upon its heels.
Since then piquancy has been the cry ; the piquant
contemplation of adultery, seduction, and murder
amid the reek and stench of the Italian barnyard.
Think of Cilèa's 'Tilda,' Giordano's 'Mala Vita,'
Spinelli's 'A Basso Porto,' and Tasca's 'A Santa
Lucia' !

"The stories chosen for operatic treatment by the
champions of *verismo* are all alike. It is their filth
and blood which fructifies the music, which rasps
the nerves even as the plays revolt the moral stomach.
I repeat : Looking back over the time during which
this so-called veritism has held its orgies, 'Cavalleria
rusticana' seems almost classic. Its music is highly
spiced and tastes 'hot i' th' mouth,' but its eloquence
is, after all, in its eager, pulsating, passionate melody
— like the music which Verdi wrote more than half
a century ago for the last act of 'Il Trovatore.' If

neither Mascagni himself nor his imitators have succeeded in equalling it since, it is because they have thought too much of the external devices of abrupt and uncouth change of modes and tonalities, of exotic scales and garish orchestration, and too little of the fundamental element of melody which once was the be-all and end-all of Italian music. Another fountain of gushing melody must be opened before 'Cavalleria rusticana' finds a successor in all things worthy of the succession. Ingenious artifice, reflection, and technical cleverness will not suffice even with the blood and mud of the slums as a fertilizer."

How Mascagni came to write his opera he has himself told us in a bright sketch of the early part of his life-history which was printed in the "Fanfulla della Domenica" of Rome shortly after he became famous. Recounting the story of his struggle for existence after entering upon his career, he wrote : —

In 1888 only a few scenes (of "Ratcliff") remained to be composed ; but I let them lie and have not touched them since. The thought of "Cavalleria rusticana" had been in my head for several years. I wanted to introduce myself with a work of small dimensions. I appealed to several librettists, but none was willing to undertake the work without a guarantee of recompense. Then came notice of the Sonzogno competition and I eagerly seized the opportunity to better my condition. But my salary of 100 lire, to which nothing was added, except the fees from a few pianoforte lessons in Cerignola and two lessons in the Philharmonic Society of Canosa (a little town a

K

few miles from Cerignola), did not permit the luxury of a libretto. At the solicitation of some friends Targioni, in Leghorn, decided to write a "Cavalleria rusticana" for me. My mind was long occupied with the finale. The words: *Hanno ammazzato compare Turiddu!* (They have killed Neighbor Turiddu!) were forever ringing in my ears. I needed a few mighty orchestral chords to give characteristic form to the musical phrase and achieve an impressive close. How it happened I don't know, but one morning, as I was trudging along the road to give my lessons at Canosa, the idea came to me like a stroke of lightning, and I had found my chords. They were those seventh chords, which I conscientiously set down in my manuscript.

Thus I began my opera at the end. When I received the first chorus of my libretto by post (I composed the Siciliano in the prelude later) I said in great good humor to my wife:

"To-day we must make a large expenditure."

"What for?"

"An alarm clock."

"Why?"

"To wake me up before dawn so that I may begin to write on 'Cavalleria rusticana.'"

The expenditure caused a dubious change in the monthly budget, but it was willingly allowed. We went out together, and after a good deal of bargaining spent nine lire. I am sure that I can find the clock, all safe and sound, in Cerignola. I wound it up the evening we bought it, but it was destined to be of no service to me, for in that night a son, the first of a row of them, was born to me. In spite of this I carried out my determination, and in the morning began to write the first chorus of "Cavalleria." I came to Rome in February, 1890, in order to permit the jury to hear my opera; they decided that it was worthy of performance. Returning to Cerignola in a state of the greatest excitement, I noticed that I did not have a penny in my pocket for the return trip to Rome when my opera was to be rehearsed. Signor Sonzogno helped me out of my embarrassment with a few hundred francs.

Those beautiful days of fear and hope, of discouragement and confidence, are as vividly before my eyes as if they were now. I see again the Constanzi Theatre, half filled; I see how, after the last excited measures of the orchestra, they all raise their arms and gesticulate, as if they were threatening me; and in my soul there awakens an echo of that cry of approval which almost prostrated me. The effect made upon me was so powerful that at the second representation I had to request them to turn down the footlights in case I should be called out; for the blinding light seemed a hell to me, like a fiery abyss that threatened to engulf me.

It is a rude little tale which Giovanni Verga wrote and which supplied the librettists, G. Targioni-Tozzetti and G. Menasci, with the plot of Mascagni's opera. Sententious as the opera seems, it is yet puffed out, padded, and bedizened with unessential ornament compared with the story. This has the simplicity and directness of a folk-tale or folksong, and much of its characteristic color and strength were lost in fitting it out for music. The play, which Signora Duse presented to us with a power which no operatic singer can ever hope to match, was more to the purpose, quicker and stronger in movement, fiercer in its onrush of passion, and more pathetic in its silences than the opera with its music, though the note of pathos sounded by Signor Mascagni is the most admirable element of the score. With half a dozen homely touches Verga conjures up the life of a Sicilian village and strikes out his characters in bold outline. Turiddu Macca, son of Nunzia, is a *bersagliere* returned from service. He struts about the village streets in his uniform, smoking a pipe carved with an image of the king on horseback, which he lights with a match fired by a scratch on the seat of his trousers, "lifting his leg as if for a kick." Lola, daughter of Massaro Angelo, was his sweetheart when he was conscripted, but meanwhile she has promised to marry Alfio, a teamster from Licodia, who has four Sortino mules in his stable. Now Turiddu could do nothing better than sing spiteful songs under her window.

Lola married the teamster, and on Sundays she would sit in the yard with her hands posed on her hips to show off the thick gold rings which her husband had given her. Opposite Alfio's house lived Massaro Cola, who was as rich as a hog, as they said, and who had an only daughter named Santa. Turiddu, to spite Lola, paid his addresses to Santa and whispered sweet words into her ear.

"Why don't you go and say these nice things to Lola?" asked Santa one day.

"Lola is a fine lady now; she has married a crown prince. But you are worth a thousand Lolas; she isn't worthy of wearing your old shoes. I could just eat you up with my eyes, Santa"—thus Turiddu.

"You may eat me with your eyes and welcome, for then there will be no leaving of crumbs."

"If I were rich I would like to have a wife just like you."

"I shall never marry a crown prince, but I shall have a dowry as well as Lola when the good Lord sends me a lover."

The tassel on his cap had tickled the girl's fancy. Her father disapproved of the young soldier, and turned him from his door; but Santa opened her window to him until the village gossips got busy with her name and his. Lola listened to the talk of the lovers from behind a vase of flowers. One day she called after Turiddu: "Ah, Turiddu! Old friends are no longer noticed, eh?"

"He is a happy man who has the chance of seeing you, Lola."

"You know where I live," answered Lola. And now Turiddu visited Lola so often that Santa shut her window in his face and the villagers began to smile knowingly when he passed by. Alfio was making a round of the fairs with his mules. "Next Sunday I must go to confession," said Lola one day, "for last night I dreamt that I saw black grapes."

"Never mind the dream," pleaded Turiddu.

"But Easter is coming, and my husband will want to know why I have not confessed."

Santa was before the confessional waiting her turn when Lola was receiving absolution. "I wouldn't send you to Rome for absolution," she said. Alfio came home with his mules, and money and a rich holiday dress for his wife.

"You do well to bring presents to her," said Santa to him, "for when you are away your wife adorns your head for you."

"Holy Devil!" screamed Alfio. "Be sure of what you are saying, or I'll not leave you an eye to cry with!"

"I am not in the habit of crying. I haven't wept even when I have seen Turiddu going into your wife's house at night."

"Enough!" said Alfio. "I thank you very much."

The cat having come back home, Turiddu kept off the streets by day, but in the evenings consoled himself with his friends at the tavern. They were enjoying a dish of sausages there on Easter eve. When Alfio came in Turiddu understood what he wanted by the way he fixed his eyes on him. "You know what I want to speak to you about," said Alfio when Turiddu asked him if he had any commands to give him. He offered Alfio a glass of wine, but it was refused with a wave of the hand.

"Here I am," said Turiddu. Alfio put his arms around his neck. "We'll talk this thing over if you will meet me to-morrow morning."

"You may look for me on the highway at sunrise, and we will go on together."

They exchanged the kiss of challenge, and Turiddu, as an earnest that he would be on hand, bit Alfio's ear. His companions left their sausages uneaten and went home with Turiddu. There his mother was sitting up for him.

"Mamma," Turridu said to her, "do you remember that when I went away to be a soldier you thought I would never come back? Kiss me as you did then, mamma, for to-morrow I am going away again."

Before daybreak he took his knife from the place in the haymow where he had hidden it when he went soldiering, and went out to meet Alfio.

"Holy Mother of Jesus!" grumbled Lola when her husband prepared to go out; "where are you going in such a hurry?"

"I am going far away," answered Alfio, "and it will be better for you if I never come back!"

The two men met on the highway and for a while walked on in silence. Turiddu kept his cap pulled down over his face. "Neighbor Alfio," he said after a space, "as true as I live I know that I have wronged you, and I would let myself be killed if I had not seen my old mother when she got up on the pretext of looking after the hens. And now, as true as I live, I will kill you like a dog so that my dear old mother may not have cause to weep."

"Good!" answered Alfio; "we will both strike hard!" And he took off his coat.

Both were good with the knife. Turiddu received the first blow in his arm, and when he returned it struck for Alfio's heart.

"Ah, Turiddu! You really do intend to kill me?"

"Yes, I told you so.   Since I saw her in the hen-yard I have my old mother always in my eyes."

"Keep those eyes wide open," shouted Alfio, "for I am going to return you good measure !"

Alfio crouched almost to the ground, keeping his left hand on the wound, which pained him.   Suddenly he seized a handful of dust and threw it into Turiddu's eyes.

"Ah !" howled Turiddu, blinded by the dust, "I'm a dead man !"   He attempted to save himself by leaping backward, but Alfio struck him a second blow, this time in the belly, and a third in the throat.

"That makes three — the last for the head you have adorned for me !"

Turiddu staggered back into the bushes and fell. He tried to say, "Ah, my dear mother !" but the blood gurgled up in his throat and he could not.

*
*   *

Music lends itself incalculably better to the cele-bration of a mood accomplished or achieved by action, physical or psychological, than to an expres-sion of the action itself.   It is in the nature of the lyric drama that this should be so, and there need be no wonder that wherever Verga offered an oppor-tunity for set lyricism it was embraced by Mascagni and his librettists.   Verga tells us that Turiddu, having lost Lola, comforted himself by singing spite-

ful songs under her window. This suggested the
Siciliano, which, an afterthought, Mascagni put into
his prelude as a serenade, not in disparagement, but
in praise of Lola. It was at Easter that Alfio returned to discover the infidelity of his wife, and
hence we have an Easter hymn, one of the musical
high lights of the work, though of no dramatic value.
Verga aims to awaken at least a tittle of extenuation and a spark of sympathy for Turiddu by showing us his filial love in conflict with his willingness to
make reparation to Alfio; Mascagni and his librettists do more by showing us the figure of the young
soldier blending a request for a farewell kiss from his
mother with a prayer for protection for the woman
he has wronged. In its delineation of the tender
emotions, indeed, the opera is more generous and
kindly than the story. *Santuzza* does not betray
her lover in cold blood as does Santa, but in the
depth of her humiliation and at the climax of her
jealous fury created by *Turiddu's* rejection of her
when he follows *Lola* into church. Moreover, her
love opens the gates to remorse the moment she
realizes what the consequence of her act is to be.
The opera sacrifices some of the virility of Turiddu's
character as sketched by Verga, but by its classic
treatment of the scene of the killing it saves us from
the contemplation of Alfio's dastardly trick which
turns a duel into a cowardly assassination.

The prelude to the opera set the form which Leoncavallo followed, slavishly followed, in "Pagliacci."

The orchestral proclamation of the moving passions of the play is made by the use of fragments of melody which in the vocal score mark climaxes in the dialogue. The first high point in the prelude is reached in the strain to which *Santuzza* begs for the love of *Turiddu,* even after she has disclosed to him her knowledge of his infidelity : —

the second is the broad melody in which she pleads
with him to return to her arms:—

Between these expositions falls the Siciliano, which interrupts the instrumental flood just as *Lola's* careless song, the Stornello, interrupts the passionate rush of *Santuzza's* protestations, prayers, and lamentations in the scene between her and her faithless lover : —

O Lo - la, bian-ca co - me flor di spi - no . .

effrett. *a tempo*

quan-do t'af-fac - ci te s'affaccio il so - le,

These sharp contrasts, heightened by the device of surprise, form one of the marked characteristics of Mascagni's score and one of the most effective. We meet it also in the instrumentation — the harp accompaniment to the serenade, the pauses which give piquancy to *Lola's* ditty, the unison violins, harp arpeggios, and sustained organ chords of the intermezzo.

When the curtain rises it discloses the open square of a Sicilian village, flanked by a church and the inn of *Lucia, Turiddu's* mother. It is Easter morning and villagers and peasants are gathering for the Paschal mass. Church bells ring and the orchestra breaks into the eager melody which a little later we hear combined with the voices which are hymning the pleasant sights and sounds of nature : —

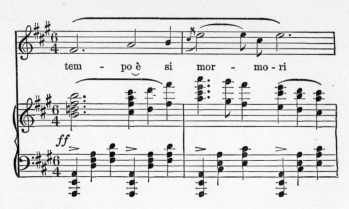

tem - po è si mor - mo - ri

A charming conception is the regular beat and flux and reflux of the women's voices as they sing

Gli a - ran - ci o - lez - za - no sui ver - di mar - gi - ni

can-tan le al-lo do le tra i mir-ti in fior. . . . . .

Delightful and refreshing is the bustling strain of the men. The singers depart with soft exclamations of rapture called out by the contemplation of nature and thoughts of the Virgin Mother and Child in their hearts. Comes *Santuzza*, sore distressed, to *Mamma Lucia*, to inquire as to the whereabouts of her son *Turiddu*. *Lucia* thinks him at Francofonte; but *Santuzza* knows that he spent the night in the village.

In pity for the maiden's distress, *Lucia* asks her to enter her home, but *Santuzza* may not — she is excommunicate. *Alfio* enters with boisterous jollity, singing of his jovial carefree life as a teamster and his love of home and a faithful wife. It is a paltry measure, endurable only for its offering of contrast, and we will not tarry with it, though the villagers echo it merrily. *Alfio*, too, has seen *Turiddu*, and *Lucia* is about to express her surprise when *Santuzza* checks her. The hour of devotion is come, and the choir in the church intones the "Regina cœli," while the people without fall on their knees and sing the Resurrection Hymn. After the first outburst, to which the organ appends a brief postlude, *Santuzza* leads in the canticle, "Innegiamo il Signor non è morte":

> Let us sing of our Lord ris'n victorious !
> Let us sing of our Lord ever glorious : —

The instrumental basses supply a foundation of
Bachian granite, the chorus within the church inter-
polates shouts of "Alleluia!" and the song swells
until the gates of sound fly wide open and we forget
the theatre in a fervor of religious devotion. Only
the critic in his study ought here to think of the
parallel scene which Leoncavallo sought to create in
his opera.

Thus far the little dramatic matter that has been

introduced is wholly expository; yet we are already near the middle of the score. All the stage folk enter the church save *Santuzza* and *Lucia*, and to the mother of her betrayer the maiden tells the story of her wrongs. The romance which she sings is marked by the copious use of one of the distinguishing devices of the veritist composers — the melodic triplet, an efficient help for the pushing, pulsating declamation with which the dramatic dialogue of Mascagni, Leoncavallo, and their fellows is carried on. *Lucia* can do no more for the unfortunate than commend her to the care of the Virgin. She enters the church and *Turiddu* comes. He lies as to where he has been. *Santuzza* is quick with accusation and reproach, but at the first sign of his anger and a hint of the vengeance which *Alfio* will take she abases herself. Let him beat and insult her, she will love and pardon though her heart break. She is in the extremity of agony and anguish when *Lola* is heard trolling a careless song: —

Fior di giag-gio - lo. . . gli an-ge- li bel - li

stan - no a mil -le in cie - lo. . .

She is about to begin a second stanza when she enters and sees the pair. She stops with an excla-

mation. She says she is seeking *Alfio*. Is *Turiddu*
not going to mass? *Santuzza*, significantly: "It is
Easter and the Lord sees all things! None but the
blameless should go to mass." But *Lola* will go,
and so will *Turiddu*. Scorning *Santuzza's* pleadings
and at last hurling her to the ground, he rushes into
the church. She shouts after him a threat of Easter
vengeance and fate sends the agent to her in the
very moment. *Alfio* comes and *Santuzza* tells him
that *Turiddu* has cuckolded him and *Lola* has robbed
her of her lover:—

> Turiddu mi tolse, mi tolse l'onore,
> E vostra moglie lui rapiva a me!

Largo

Tu - rid - du mi tol - se mi, tol - se l'o - no - re!

The oncoming waves of the drama's pathos have
risen to a supreme height, their crests have broken,
and the wind-blown spume drenches the soul of the
listeners; but the composer has not departed from
the first principle of the master of whom, for a time,
it was hoped he might be the legitimate successor.
Melody remains the life-blood of his music as it is
that of Verdi's from his first work to his last;—as
it will be so long as music endures.

Terrible is the outbreak of Alfio's rage:—

> Infami lero, ad esse non perdono,
> Vendetta avro pria che tra monti il di.

ι

Upon this storm succeeds the calm of the intermezzo — in its day the best abused and most hackneyed piece of music that the world knew; yet a
triumph of simple, straightforward tune. It echoes
the Easter hymn, and in the midst of the tumult of
earthly passion proclaims celestial peace. Its instrumentation was doubtless borrowed from Hell-

mesberger's arrangement of the air "Ombra mai fù" from "Serse," known the world over as Handel's "Largo" — violins in unison, harp arpeggios, and organ harmonies. In nothing artistically distinguished it makes an unexampled appeal to the multitude. Some years ago a burlesque on "Cavalleria rusticana" was staged at a theatre in Vienna. It

was part of the witty conceit of the author to have the intermezzo played on a handorgan. Up to this point the audience had been hilarious in its enjoyment of the burlesque, but with the first wheezy tones from the grinder the people settled down to silent attention; and when the end came applause for the music rolled out wave after wave. A burlesque performance could not rob that music of its charm.

Ite missa est. Mass is over. The merry music of the first chorus returns. The worshippers are about to start homeward with pious reflections, when *Turiddu* detains *Lola* and invites his neighbors to a glass of *Mamma Lucia's* wine. We could spare the drinking song as easily as *Alfio,* entering, turns aside the cup which *Turiddu* proffers him. *Turiddu* understands. "I await your pleasure." Some of the women apprehend mischief and lead *Lola* away. The challenge is given and accepted, Sicilian fashion. *Turiddu* confesses his wrong-doing to *Alfio,* but, instead of proclaiming his purpose to kill his enemy, he asks protection for *Santuzza* in case of his death. Then, while the violins tremble and throb, he calls for his mother like an errant child: —

He has been too free with the winecup, he says, and must leave her. But first her blessing, as when he went away to be a soldier. Should he not return, *Santa* must be her care: "Voi dovrete fare; da

madre a Santa !" It is the cry of a child. "A kiss !
Another kiss, mamma ! Farewell !" *Lucia* calls after
him. He is gone, *Santuzza* comes in with her phrase
of music descriptive of her unhappy love. It grows
to a thunderous crash. Then a hush ! A fateful
chord ! A whispered roll of the drums ! A woman
is heard to shriek: "They have killed Neighbor
Turiddu !" A crowd of women rush in excitedly;
Santuzza and *Lucia* fall in a swoon. "Hanno ammazzato compare Turiddu !" The tragedy is ended.

CHAPTER X

THE CAREER OF MASCAGNI

I⊤ would be foolish to question or attempt to deny the merits of the type of Italian opera established by Mascagni's lucky inspiration. The brevity of the realistic little tragedy, the swiftness of its movement, its adherence to the Italian ideal of melody first, its ingenious combination of song with an illuminative orchestral part — these elements in union created a style which the composers of Italy, France, and Germany were quick to adopt. "Pagliacci" was the first fruit of the movement and has been the most enduring; indeed, so far as America and England are concerned, "Cavalleria rusticana" and "Pagliacci" are the only products of the school which have obtained a lasting footing. They were followed by a flood of Italian, French, and German works in which low life was realistically portrayed, but, though the manner of composition was as easily copied as the subjects were found in the slums, none of the imitators of Mascagni and Leoncavallo achieved even a tithe of their success. The men themselves were too shrewd and wise to attempt to repeat the experiment which had once been triumphant.

In one respect the influence of the twin operas was deplorable. I have attempted to characterize that influence in general terms, but in order that the lesson may be more plainly presented it seems to me best to present a few examples in detail. The eagerness with which writers sought success in moral muck, regardless of all artistic elements, is strikingly illustrated in an attempt by a German writer, Edmund von Freihold,[1] to provide "Cavalleria rusticana" with a sequel. Von Freihold wrote the libretto for a "music drama" which he called "Santuzza," the story of which begins long enough after the close of Verga's story for both the women concerned in "Cavalleria rusticana" to have grown children. *Santuzza* has given birth to a son named *Massimo*, and *Lola* to a daughter, *Anita*. The youthful pair grow up side by side in the Sicilian village and fall in love with one another. They might have married and in a way expiated the sins of their parents had not *Alfio* overheard his wife, *Lola*, confess that *Turiddu*, not her husband, is the father of *Anita*. The lovers are thus discovered to be half brother and sister. This reminder of his betrayal by *Lola* infuriates *Alfio* anew. He rushes upon his wife to kill her, but *Santuzza*, who hates him as the slayer of her lover, throws herself between and plunges her dagger in *Alfio's* heart. Having thus taken revenge for *Turiddu's* death, *Santuzza* dies out of hand, *Lola*, as an inferior character, falls

[1] I owe this illustration to Ferdinand Pfohl's book "Die Moderne Oper."

in a faint, and *Massimo* makes an end of the delectable story by going away from there to parts unknown.

In Cilèa's "Tilda" a street singer seeks to avenge her wrongs upon a faithless lover. She bribes a jailor to connive at the escape of a robber whom he is leading to capital punishment. This robber she elects to be the instrument of her vengeance. Right merrily she lives with him and his companions in the greenwood until the band captures the renegade lover on his wedding journey. *Tilda* rushes upon the bride with drawn dagger, but melts with compassion when she sees her victim in the attitude of prayer. She sinks to her knees beside her, only to receive the death-blow from her seducer. There are piquant contrasts in this picture and Ave Marias and tarantellas in the music.

Take the story of Giordano's "Mala Vita." Here the hero is a young dyer whose dissolute habits have brought on tuberculosis of the lungs. The principal object of his amours is the wife of a friend. A violent hemorrhage warns him of approaching death. Stricken with fear he rushes to the nearest statue of the Madonna and registers a vow; he will marry a wanton, effect her redemption, thereby hoping to save his own miserable life. The heroine of the opera appears and she meets his requirements. He marries her and for a while she seems blest. But the siren, the *Lola* in the case, winds her toils about him as the disease stretches him on the floor at her feet. Piquancy again, achieved now without that poor palliative, punishment of the evil-doer.

Tasca's "A Santa Lucia" has an appetizing story about an oysterman's son who deserts a woman by whom he has a child, in order to marry one to whom he had previously been affianced. The women meet. There is a dainty brawl, and the fiancée of *Cicillo* (he's the oysterman's son) strikes her rival's child to the ground. The mother tries to stab the fiancée with the operatic Italian woman's ever-ready dagger, and this act stirs up the embers of *Cicillo's* love. He takes the mother of his child back home — to his father's house, that is. The child must be some four years old by this time, but the oysterman — dear, unsuspecting old man ! — knows nothing about the relation existing between his son and his housekeeper. He is thinking of marriage with his common law daughter-in-law when in comes the old fiancée with a tale for *Cicillo's* ears of his mistress's unfaithfulness. "It is not true !" shrieks the poor woman, but the wretch, her seducer, closes his ears to her protestations; and she throws herself into the sea, where the oysters come from. *Cicillo* rushes after her and bears her to the shore, where she dies in his arms, gasping *in articulo mortis,* "It is not true !"

*

*   *

The romantic interest in Mascagni's life is confined to the period which preceded his sudden rise to fame. His father was a baker in Leghorn, and there he was born on December 7, 1863. Of humble origin and occupation himself, the father, nevertheless, had large ambitions for his son; but not in the line of art. Pietro was to be shaped intellectually for the law. Like Handel, the boy studied the pianoforte by stealth in the attic. Grown in years, he began attending a music-school, when, it is said, his father confined him to his house; thence his uncle freed him and took over his care upon himself. Singularly enough, the man who at the height of his success posed as the most Italian of Italian masters had his inspiration first stirred by German poetry. Early in his career Beethoven resolved to set Schiller's "Hymn to Joy"; the purpose remained in his mind for forty years or so, and finally became a realization in the finale of the Ninth Symphony. Pietro Mascagni resolved as a boy to compose music for the same ode; and did it at once. Then he set to work upon a two-act opera, "Il Filanda." His uncle died, and a Count Florestan (here is another Beethovenian echo!) sent him to the Conservatory at Milan, where, like nearly all of his native contemporaries, he imbibed knowledge (and musical ideas) from Ponchielli.

After two years or so of academic study he yielded to a gypsy desire and set out on his wanderings, but not until he had chosen as a companion Maffei's translation of Heine's "Ratcliff" — a gloomy romance which seems to have caught the fancy of many composers. There followed five years of as checkered a life as ever musician led. Over and over again he was engaged as conductor of an itinerant or stationary operetta and opera company, only to have the enterprise fail and leave him stranded. For six weeks in Naples his daily ration was a plate of macaroni. But he worked at his opera steadily, although, as he once remarked, his dreams of fame were frequently swallowed up in the growls of his stomach, which caused him more trouble than many a millionaire suffers from too little appetite or too much gout. Finally, convinced that he could do better as a teacher of the pianoforte, he ran away from an engagement which paid him two dollars a day, and, sending off the manuscript of "Ratcliff" in a portmanteau, settled down in Cerignola. There he became director of a school for orchestral players, though he had first to learn to play the instruments; he also taught pianoforte and thoroughbass, and eked out a troublous existence until his success in competition for the prize offered by Sonzogno, the Milanese publisher, made him famous in a day and started him on the road to wealth.

It was but natural that, after "Cavalleria rusticana" had virulently affected the whole world with what the enemies of Signor Mascagni called "Mascagnitis," his next opera should be looked forward to with feverish anxiety. There was but a year to wait, for "L'Amico Fritz" was brought

forward in Rome on the last day of October, 1891.
Within ten weeks its title found a place on the programme of one of Mr. Walter Damrosch's Sunday
night concerts in New York; but the music was a
disappointment. Five numbers were sung by Mme.
Tavary and Signor Campanini, and Mr. Damrosch,
not having the orchestral parts, played the accom-
paniments upon a pianoforte. As usual, Mr. Gustav
Hinrichs was to the fore with a performance in
Philadelphia (on June 8, 1892), the principal singers
being Mme. Koert-Kronold, Clara Poole, M. Guille,
and Signor Del Puente. On January 31, 1893, the
Philadelphia singers, aided by the New York Symphony Society, gave a performance of the opera,
under the auspices of the Young Men's Hebrew
Association, for the benefit of its charities, at the
Carnegie Music Hall, New York. Mr. Walter
Damrosch was to have conducted, but was de-
tained in Washington by the funeral of Mr. Blaine,
and Mr. Hinrichs took his place. Another year
elapsed, and then, on January 10, 1894, the opera
reached the Metropolitan Opera House. In spite
of the fact that Madame Calvé sang the part
of *Suzel*, only two performances were given to the
work.

The failure of this opera did not dampen the
industry of Mascagni nor the zeal of his enterprising
publishers. For his next opera the composer went
again to the French authors, Erckmann-Chatrian,
who had supplied him with the story of "L'Amico

Fritz." This time he chose "Les deux Frères," which they had themselves turned into a drama with the title of "Rantzau." Mascagni's librettist retained the title. The opera came out in Florence in 1892. The tremendous personal popularity of the composer, who was now as much a favorite in Vienna and Berlin as he was in the town of his birth which had struck a medal in his honor, or the town of his residence which had created him an honorary citizen, could not save the work.

Now he turned to the opera which he had laid aside to take up his "Cavalleria," and in 1895 "Guglielmo Ratcliff," based upon the gloomy Scotch story told by Heine, was brought forward at La Scala, in Milan. It was in a sense the child of his penury and suffering, but he had taken it up inspired by tremendous enthusiasm for the subject, and inasmuch as most of its music had been written before success had turned his head, or desire for notoriety had begun to itch him, there was reason to hope to find in it some of the hot blood which surges through the score of "Cavalleria." As a matter of fact, critics who have seen the score or heard the work have pointed out that portions of "I Rantzau" and "Cavalleria" are as alike as two peas. It would not be a violent assumption that the composer in his eagerness to get his score before the Sonzogno jury had plucked his early work of its best feathers and found it difficult to restore plumage of equal brilliancy when he attempted to make restitution. In the same year, 1895, his next opera, "Silvano," made a fiasco in Milan. A year later there appeared "Zanetto," which seems like an effort to contract the frame of the lyric drama still further than is done in "Cavalleria." It is a *bozzetto*, a sketch, based on Coppée's duologue "Le Passant," a scene between a strumpet who is weary of the world and a young minstrel. Its orchestration is unique — there are but strings and a harp. It was brought out at Pesaro, where, in 1895, Mascagni had been appointed director of the Liceo Musicale Rossini.

As director of the music-school in Rossini's native town Mascagni's days were full of trouble from the outset. He was opposed, said his friends, in reformatory efforts by some of the professors and pupils, whose enmity grew so virulent that in 1897 they spread the story that he had killed himself. He was deposed from his position by the administration, but reinstated by the Minister of Fine Arts. The criticism followed him for years that he had neglected his duties to travel about Europe, giving concerts and conducting his operas for the greater glory of himself and the profit of his publisher. At the time of the suicide story it was also said that he was in financial straits; to which his friends replied that he received a salary of 60 lire ($12) a day as director, 1000 lire ($200) a month from Sonzogno, and lived in a princely dwelling.

After "Zanetto" came "Iris," to which, as the
one opera besides "Cavalleria rusticana" which
has remained in the American repertory, I shall
devote the next chapter in this book. "Iris" was
followed by "Le Maschere," which was brought out
on January 17, 1901, simultaneously in six cities
— Rome, Milan, Venice, Genoa, Turin, and Naples.
It made an immediate failure in all of these places
except Rome, where it endured but a short time.
Mascagni's next operatic work was a lyric drama,
entitled "Vistilia," the libretto of which, based
upon an historical novel by Racco de Zerbi, was
written by Menasci and Targioni-Tozzetti, who
collaborated on the book of "Cavalleria rusticana."
The action goes back to the time of Tiberius and
deals with the loves of Vistilia and Helius. Then
came another failure in the shape of "Amica,"
which lived out its life in Monte Carlo, where it
was produced in March, 1905.

In the winter of 1902–1903 Signor Mascagni was
in the United States for the purpose of conducting
performances of some of his operas and giving concerts. The company of singers and instrumental-
ists which his American agents had assembled for
his purpose was, with a few exceptions, composed
of the usual operatic flotsam and jetsam which can
be picked up at any time in New York. The enterprise began in failure and ended in scandal. There
had been no adequate preparation for the operas
announced, and one of them was not attempted.

This was "Ratcliff." "Cavalleria rusticana," "Zanetto," and "Iris" were poorly performed at the
Metropolitan Opera House in October, and an
attempt at Sunday night concerts was made.
Signor Mascagni's countrymen labored hard to
create enthusiasm for his cause, but the general
public remained indifferent. Having failed miser-
ably in New York, Mascagni, heavily burdened with
debt, went to Boston. There he was arrested for
breach of contract. He retaliated with a suit for
damages against his American managers. The
usual amount of crimination and recrimination followed, but eventually the difficulties were compounded and Mascagni went back to his home a
sadly disillusionized man.[1]

"Zanetto" was produced along with "Cavalleria
rusticana" at the Metropolitan Opera House on
October 8, 1902, and "Iris" on October 16. Signor
Mascagni conducted and the parts were distributed
as follows among the singers of the company:
Iris, Marie Farneti; *Osaka*, Pietro Schiavazzi;
Kyoto, Virgilio Bollati; *Il Cieco*, Francesco
Navarrini; *Una Guecha*, Dora de Filippe; *Un
Mercianola*, Pasquale Blasio; *Un Cencianola*, Ber-
nardino Landino. The opera was not heard of
again until the season of 1907–1908, when, just be-

---

[1] The story of this visit is told in greater detail in my "Chapters of Opera," as is also the story of the rivalry among American managers to be first in the field with "Cavalleria rusticana."

fore the end of the administration of Heinrich Conried, it was incorporated into the repertory of the
Metropolitan Opera House apparently for the purpose of giving Mme. Emma Eames an opportunity
to vie with Miss Geraldine Farrar in Japanese opera.

CHAPTER XI

"IRIS"

"LIGHT is the language of the eternal ones — hear it!" proclaims the librettist of "Iris" in that portion of his book which is neither said nor sung nor played. And it is the sun that sings with divers voices after the curtain has risen on a nocturnal scene, and the orchestra has sought to depict the departure of the night, the break of day, the revivification of the flowers and the sunrise. As Byron sang of him, so Phœbus Apollo celebrates himself as "the god of life and poetry and light," but does not stop there. He is also Infinite Beauty, Cause, Reason, Poetry, and Love. The music begins with an all but inaudible descending passage in the basses, answered by sweet concordant harmonies. A calm song tells of the first streaks of light; woodwind and harp add their voices; a mellifluous hymn chants the stirring flowers, and leads into a rhythmically, more incisive, but still sustained, orchestral song, which bears upon its surface the choral proclamation of the sun: "I am! I am life! I am Beauty infinite!" The flux and reflux of the instrumental surge grows in intensity, the music begins to glow

162

with color and pulsate with eager life, and reaches
a mighty sonority, gorged with the crash of a
multitude of tamtams, cymbals, drums, and bells,
at the climacteric reiteration of *"Calore! Luce!
Amor!"* The piece is thrillingly effective, but as
little operatic as the tintinnabulatory chant of the
cherubim in the prologue of Boito's "Mefistofele."

And now allegory makes room for the drama.
To the door of her cottage, embowered on the banks
of a quiet stream, comes *Iris*. The peak of Fujiyama glows in the sunlight. *Iris* is fair and youthful and innocent. A dream has disturbed her.
"Gorgons and Hydras and Chimæras dire" had
filled her garden and threatened her doll, which she
had put to sleep under a rose-bush. But the sun's
rays burst forth and the monsters flee. She lifts
her doll and moves its arms in mimic salutation to
the sun. *Osaka*, a wealthy rake, and *Kyoto*, a
pander, play spy on her actions, gloat on her loveliness and plot to steal her and carry her to the
Yoshiwara. To this end they go to bring on a
puppet show, that its diversion may enable them to
steal her away without discovery. Women come
down to the banks of the river and sing pretty meta-
phors as they wash their basketloads of muslins.
Gradually the music of samisens, gongs, and drums
approaches. *Osaka* and *Kyoto* have disguised
themselves as travelling players, gathered together
some geishas and musicians, and now set up a
marionette theatre. *Iris* comforts her blind father,

the only object of her love, besides her doll, and promises to remain at his side. The puppet play tells the story of a maiden who suffers abuse from a cruel father, who threatens to sell her to a merchant. *Iris* is much affected by the sorrows of the puppet. The voice of Jor, the son of the sun, is heard — it is *Osaka*, singing without. The melody is the melody of *Turridu's* Siciliano, but the words are a promise of a blissful, kissful death and thereafter life everlasting. The puppet dies and with Jor dances off into Nirvana. Now three geishas, representing Beauty, Death, and the Vampire, begin a dance. *Kyoto* distracts the attention of the spectators while the dancers flaunt their skirts higher and wider until their folds conceal *Iris,* and *Osaka's* hirelings seize her and bear her off toward the city. *Kyoto* places a letter and money at the cottage door for the blind father. Through a pedler and the woman he learns that his daughter is gone to be an inmate of the Yoshiwara. He implores the people who had been jeering him to lead him thither, that he may spit in her face and curse her.

Iris is asleep upon a bed in the "Green House" of the district, which needs no description. A song, accompanied by the twanging of a samisen and the clanging of tamtams, is sung by three geishas. *Kyoto* brings in *Osaka* to admire her beauty, and sets a high price upon it. *Osaka* sends for jewels. *Iris* awakes and speculates in philosophical vein touching the question of her existence. She cannot be dead, for death brings knowledge and paradise joy; but she weeps. *Osaka* appears. He praises her rapturously — her form, her hair, her eyes, her mouth, her smile. *Iris* thinks him veritably Jor, but he says his name is "Pleasure." The maiden recoils in terror. A priest had taught her in an allegory that Pleasure and Death were one! *Osaka* loads her with jewels, fondles her, draws her to his breast, kisses her passionately. *Iris* weeps. She knows nothing of passion, and longs only for her father, her cottage, and her garden. *Osaka* wearies of his guest, but *Kyoto* plans to play still further upon his lust. He clothes her in richer robes, but more transparent, places her upon a balcony, and, withdrawing a curtain, exhibits her beauty to the multitude in the street. Amazed cries greet the revelation. *Osaka* returns and pleads for her love.

"*Iris!*" It is the cry of the blind man hunting the child whom he thinks has sold herself into disgraceful slavery. The crowd falls back before him, while *Iris* rushes forward to the edge of the veranda and cries out to him, that he may know her presence. He gathers a handful of mud from the street and hurls it in the direction of her voice. "There! In your face! In your forehead! In your mouth! In your eyes! *Fango!*" Under the imprecations of her father the mind of *Iris* gives way. She rushes along a corridor and hurls herself out of a window.

The third act is reached, and drama merges again into allegory. In the wan light of the moon ragpickers, men and women, are dragging their hooks through the slimy muck that flows through the open sewer beneath the fatal window. They sing mockingly to the moon. A flash of light from Fujiyama awakens a glimmer in the filth. Again. They rush forward and pull forth the body of *Iris* and begin to strip it of its adornments. She moves and they fly in superstitious fear. She recovers consciousness, and voices from invisible singers tell her of the selfish inspirations of *Osaka*, *Kyoto*, and her blind father; *Osaka's* desire baffled by fate — such is life! *Kyoto's* slavery to pleasure and a hangman's reward; — such is life! The blind man's dependence on his child for creature comforts; — such is life! *Iris* bemoans her fate as death comes gently to her. The sky grows rosy and the light brings momentary life. She stretches out her arms to the sun and acclaims the growing orb. As once upon Ida —

> Glad earth perceives and from her bosom pours
> Unbidden herbs and voluntary flow'rs!

A field of blossoms spreads around her, into which she sinks, while the sun, again many-voiced and articulate, chants his glory as in the beginning.

The story is perhaps prettier in the telling than in the performance. What there is in its symbolism and its poetical suggestion that is ingratiating is more effective in the fancy than in the experience. There are fewer clogs, fewer stagnant pools, fewer eddies which whirl to no purpose. In the modern school, with its distemper music put on in splotches, there must be more merit and action. Psychological delineation in music which stimulates action, or makes one forget the want of outward movement, demands a different order of genius than that which Signor Mascagni possesses. Mere talent for artful device will not suffice. There are many effective bits of expressive writing in the score of "Iris," but most of them are fugitive and aim at coloring a word, a phrase, or at best a temporary situation. There is little flow of natural, fervent melody. What the composer accomplished with tune, characteristic but fluent, eloquent yet sustained, in "Cavalleria rusticana," he tries to achieve in "Iris" with violent, disjointed shifting of keys and splashes of instrumental color. In this he is seldom successful, for he is not a master of orchestral writing — that technical facility which nearly all the young musicians have in the same degree that all pianists have finger technic. His orchestral stream is muddy; his effects generally crass and empty of euphony. He throws the din of outlandish instruments of percussion, a battery of gongs, big and little, drums, and cymbals into his score without achieving local color. Once only does he utilize it so as to catch the ears and stir the fancy of his listeners — in the beginning of the second act, where there is a murmur of real Japanese melody. As a rule, however, Signor Mascagni seems to have been careless in the matter of local color, properly so, perhaps, for, strictly speaking, local color in the lyric drama is for comedy with its petty limitations, not for tragedy with its appeal to large and universal passions. Yet it is in the lighter scenes, the scenes of comedy, like the marionette show, the scenes of mild pathos, like the monologues of *Iris*, and the scenes of mere accessory decoration, like that of the laundresses, the *mousmés* in the first act, with its purling figure borrowed from "Les Huguenots" and its unnecessarily uncanny col legno effect conveyed from "L'Africaine" that it is most effective.

CHAPTER XII

THIS is the book of the generation of "Madama Butterfly": An adventure in Japan begat Pierre Loti's "Madame Chrysanthème"; "Madame Chrysanthème" begat John Luther Long's "Madame Butterfly," a story; "Madame Butterfly," the story, begat "Madame Butterfly," a play by David Belasco; "Madame Butterfly," the play, begat "Madama Butterfly," the opera by Giacomo Puccini. The heroine of the roving French romanticist is therefore seen in her third incarnation in the heroine of the opera book which L. Illica and G. Giacosa made for Puccini. But in operatic essence she is still older, for, as Dr. Korngold, a Viennese critic, pointed out, *Selica* is her grandmother and *Lakmé* her cousin.

Even this does not exhaust her family history; there is something like a bar sinister in her escutcheon. Mr. Belasco's play was not so much begotten, conceived, or born of admiration for Mr. Long's book as it was of despair wrought by the failure of another play written by Mr. Belasco. This play was a farce entitled "Naughty Anthony," created by Mr. Belasco in a moment of æsthetic aberration

for production at the Herald Square Theatre, in
New York, in the spring of 1900. Mr. Belasco
doesn't think so now, but at the time he had a
notion that the public would find something humorous and attractive in the spectacle of a popular
actress's leg swathed in several layers of stocking.
So he made a show of Blanche Bates. The public
refused to be amused at the farcical study in comparative anatomy, and when Mr. Belasco's friends
began to fault him for having pandered to a low
taste, and he felt the smart of failure in addition,
he grew heartily ashamed of himself. His affairs,
moreover, began to take on a desperate aspect;
the season threatened to be a ruinous failure, and
he had no play ready to substitute for "Naughty
Anthony." Some time before a friend had sent
him Mr. Long's book, but he had carelessly tossed
it aside. In his straits it came under his eyes
again, and this time he saw a play in it — a play
and a promise of financial salvation. It was late at
night when he read the story, but he had come to
a resolve by morning and in his mind's eye had already seen his actors in Japanese dress. The drama
lay in the book snugly enough; it was only necessary to dig it out and materialize it to the vision.
That occupation is one in which Mr. Belasco is at
home. The dialogue went to his actors a few pages
at a time, and the pictures rose rapidly in his mind.
Something different from a stockinged leg now !

Glimpses of Nippon — its mountains, waters,

DAVID BELASCO.

bridges, flowers, gardens, geishas; as a foil to their grace and color the prosaic figures of a naval officer and an American Consul. All things tinged with the bright light of day, the glories of sunset or the super-glories of sunrise. We must saturate the fancy of the audience with the atmosphere of Japan, mused Mr. Belasco. Therefore, Japanese scenes, my painter! Electrician, your plot shall be worked out as carefully as the dialogue and action of the play's people. "First drop discovered; house-lights down; white foots with blue full work change of color at back of drop; white lens on top of mountain; open light with white, straw, amber, and red on lower part of drop; when full on lower footlights to blue," and so on. Mr. Belasco's emotions, we know, find eloquent expression in stage lights. But the ear must be carried off to the land of enchantment as well as the eye. "Come, William Furst, recall your experiences on the Western coast. For my first curtain I want a quaint, soft Japanese melody, *pp* — you know how!"

And so "Madame Butterfly," the play, was made. In two weeks all was ready, and a day after the first performance at the Herald Square Theatre, on March 5, 1900, the city began to hum with eager comment on the dramatic intensity of the scene of a Japanese woman's vigil, of the enthralling eloquence of a motionless, voiceless figure, looking steadily through a hole torn through a paper partition, with a sleeping child and a nodding maid at her feet, while a mimic night wore on, the lanterns on the floor flickered out one by one and the soft violins crooned a melody to the arpeggios of a harp.

The season at the Herald Square Theatre was saved. Some time later, when Mr. Belasco accompanied Mr. Charles Frohman to London to put on "Zaza" at the Garrick Theatre, he took "Madame Butterfly" with him and staged it at the Duke of York's Theatre, hard by. On the first night of "Madame Butterfly" Mr. Frohman was at the latter playhouse, Mr. Belasco at the former. The fall of the curtain on the little Japanese play was followed by a scene of enthusiasm which endured so long that Mr. Frohman had time to summon his colleague to take a curtain call. At a stroke the pathetic play had made its fortune in London, and, as it turned out, paved the way for a new and larger triumph for Mr. Long's story. The musical critics of the London newspapers came to the house and saw operatic possibilities in the drama. So did Mr. Francis Nielson, at the time Covent Garden's stage manager, who sent word of the discovery to Signor Puccini. The composer came from Milan, and realized on the spot that the successor of "Tosca" had been found. Signori Illica and Giacosa, librettists in ordinary to Ricordi & Co., took the work of making the opera book in hand. Signor Illica's fancy had roamed in the Land of Flowers before; he had written the libretto for Mascagni's "Iris." The ephemeral life of

Cho-Cho-San was over in a few months, but by that time "Madama Butterfly," glorified by music, had lifted her wings for a new flight in Milan.

It is an old story that many operas which are recognized as masterpieces later, fail to find appreciation or approval when they are first produced. "Madama Butterfly" made a fiasco when brought forward at La Scala on February 17, 1904.[1]

So complete was the fiasco that in his anxiety to withdraw the work Signor Puccini is said to have offered to reimburse the management of the theatre for the expenditures entailed by the production.

[1] At this *première* Campanini was the conductor and the cast was as follows: *Butterfly*, Storchio; *Suzuki*, Giaconia; *Pinkerton*, Zenatello; *Sharpless*, De Luca; *Goro*, Pini-Corsi; *Bonzo*, Venturini; *Yakuside*, Wulmann. At the first performance in London, on July 10, 1905, at Covent Garden, the cast was: *Butterfly*, Destinn; *Suzuki*, Lejeune; *Pinkerton*, Caruso; *Sharpless*, Scotti; *Goro*, Dufriche; *Bonzo*, Cotreuil; *Yakuside*, Rossi. Conductor, Campanini. After the revision it was produced at Brescia on May 28, 1904, with Zenatello, of the original cast, Krusceniski as *Butterfly*, and Bellati as *Sharpless*. The first American performances were in the English version, made by Mrs. R. H. Elkin, by the Savage Opera Company, which came to the Garden Theatre, New York, after a trial season in Washington, on November 12, 1906. It had a run of nearly three months before it reached the Metropolitan Opera House, on February 11, 1907. Mr. Walter Rothwell conducted the English performance, in which there were several changes of casts, the original *Butterfly* being Elza Szamozy (a Hungarian singer); *Suzuki*, Harriet Behne; *Pinkerton*, Joseph F. Sheehan, and *Sharpless*, Winifred Goff. Arturo Vigna conducted the first Italian performance at the Metropolitan, with Geraldine Farrar as *Butterfly*, Louise Homer as *Suzuki*, Caruso as *Pinkerton*, Scotti as *Sharpless*, and Albert Reiss as *Goro*.

Failures of this kind are frequently inexplicable, but it is possible that the unconventional character of the story and the insensibility of the Italians to national musical color other than their own, had a great deal to do with it in this case. Whatever the cause, the popular attitude toward the opera was displayed in the manner peculiar to Italy, the discontented majority whistling, shrilling on house keys, grunting, roaring, bellowing, and laughing in the good old-fashioned manner which might be set down as possessed of some virtuous merit if reserved for obviously stupid creations.

"The Pall Mall Gazette" reported that at the time the composer told a friend that on this fateful first night he was shut up in a small room behind the scenes, where he could hear nothing of what was going on on the stage or in the audience-room. On a similar occasion, nearly a century before, when "The Barber of Seville" scored an equally monumental failure, Rossini, in the conductor's chair, faced the mob, shrugged his shoulders, and clapped his hands to show his contempt for his judges, then went home and composedly to bed. Puccini, though he could not see the discomfiture of his opera, was not permitted to remain in ignorance of it. His son and his friends brought him the news. His collaborator, Giacosa, rushed into the room with dishevelled hair and staring eyes, crying: "I have suffered the passion of death!" while Signorina Storchio burst into such a flood of

tears and sobs that it was feared she would be ill.
Puccini was cut to the heart, but he did not lose
faith in the work. He had composed it in love
and knew its potentialities. His faith found jus-
tification when he produced it in Brescia three
months later and saw it start out at once on a
triumphal tour of the European theatres. His
work of revision was not a large or comprehensive
one. He divided the second act into two acts,
made some condensations to relieve the long strain,
wrote a few measures of introduction for the final
scene, but refused otherwise to change the music.
His fine sense of the dramatic had told him correctly
when he planned the work that there ought not to
be a physical interruption of the pathetic vigil out
of which Blanche Bates in New York and Evelyn
Millard in London had made so powerful a scene,
but he yielded to the compulsion of practical considerations, trying to save respect for his better
judgment by refusing to call the final scene an act,
though he permitted the fall of the curtain; but
nothing can make good the loss entailed by the
interruption. The mood of the play is admirably
preserved in the music of the intermezzo, but the
mood of the listeners is hopelessly dissipated with
the fall of the curtain. When the scene of the
vigil is again disclosed, the charm and the pathos
have vanished, never to return. It is true that a
rigid application of the law of unities would seem
to forbid that a vigil of an entire night from eve

till morning be compressed into a few minutes; but poetic license also has rights, and they could have been pleaded with convincing eloquence by music, with its marvellous capacity for publishing the conflicting emotions of the waiting wife.

*
* *

His ship having been ordered to the Asiatic station, *Benjamin Franklin Pinkerton*, Lieutenant in the United States Navy, follows a custom (not at all unusual among naval officers, if Pierre Loti is to be believed) and for the summer sojourn in Japan leases a Japanese wife. (The word "wife" is a euphemism for housekeeper, companion, play-fellow, mistress, what not.) This is done in a manner involving little ceremony, as is known to travellers and others familiar with the social customs of Nippon, through a *nakodo*, a marriage broker or matrimonial agent. M. Loti called his man Kangourou; Mr. Long gave his the name of Goro. That, however, and the character of the simple proceeding before a registrar is immaterial. M. Loti, who assures us that his book is merely some pages from a veritable diary, entertains us with some details preliminary to his launch into a singular kind of domestic existence, which are interesting as bearing on the morals of the opera and as indicative of the fact that he is a closer observer of Oriental life than his American confrère. He lets us see how merchantable "wives" are chosen, permits M. Kangourou to exhibit his wares and expatiate on their merits. There is the daughter of a wealthy China merchant, a young woman of great accomplishments who can write "commercially" and has won a prize in a poetic contest with a sonnet. She is, consequently, very dear — 100 *yen*, say $100 — but that is of no consequence; what matters is that she has a disfiguring scar on her cheek. She will not do. Then there is Mlle. Jasmin, a pretty girl of fifteen years, who can be had for $18 or $20 a month (contract cancellable at the end of any month for non-payment), a few dresses of fashionable cut and a pleasant house to live in. Mlle. Jasmin comes to be inspected with one old lady, two old ladies, three old ladies (mamma and aunts), and a dozen friends and neighbors, big and little. Loti's moral stomach revolts at the thought of buying for his uses a child who looks like a doll, and is shocked at the public parade which has been made of her as a commodity. He has not yet been initiated into some of the extraordinary customs of Japan, nor yet into some of the distinctions attendant upon those customs. He learns of one of the latter when he suggests to the broker that he might marry a charming geisha who had taken his fancy at a tea house. The manner in which the suggestion was received convinced him that he might as well have purposed to marry the devil himself as a professional dancer and singer. Among

N

the train of Mlle. Jasmin's friends is one less young than Mlle. Jasmin, say about eighteen, and already more of a woman; and when Loti says, "Why not her?" M. Kangourou trots her out for inspection and, discreetly sending Loti away, concludes the arrangement between night-fall and 10 o'clock, when he comes with the announcement: "All is arranged, sir; her parents will give her up for $20 a month — the same price as Mlle. Jasmin."

So Mlle. Chrysanthème became the wife of Pierre Loti during his stay at Nagasaki, and then dutifully went home to her mother without breaking her heart at all. But she was not a geisha, only a *mousmé* — "one of the prettiest words in the Nipponese language," comments M. Loti, "it seems almost as if there must be a little *moue* in the very sound, as if a pretty, taking little pout, such as they put on, and also a little pert physiognomy, were described by it."

Lieutenant Pinkerton, equally ignorant with Lieutenant Loti but uninstructed evidently, marries a geisha whose father had made the happy dispatch at the request of the Son of Heaven after making a blunder in his military command. She is *Cio-Cio-San*, also *Madama Butterfly*, and she comes to her wedding with a bevy of geishas or *mousmés* (I do not know which) and a retinue of relations. All enjoy the hospitality of the American officer while picking him to pieces, but turn from their kinswoman when they learn from an uncle, who is a

Buddhist priest and comes late to the wedding like the wicked fairy in the stories, that she has attended the Mission school and changed her religion. Wherefore the *bonze* curses her: "Hou, hou! *Cio-Cio-San*, hou, hou!"

Sharpless, United States Consul at Nagasaki, had not approved of *Pinkerton's* adventure, fearing that it might bring unhappiness to the little woman; but *Pinkerton* had laughed at his scruples and emptied his glass to the marriage with an American wife which he hoped to make some day. Neither Loti nor Long troubles us with the details of so prosaic a thing as the marriage ceremony; but Puccini and his librettists make much of it, for it provides the only opportunity for a chorus and the musician had found delightfully mellifluous Japanese gongs to add a pretty touch of local color to the music. *Cio-Cio-San* has been "outcasted" and *Pinkerton* comforts her and they make love in the starlight (after *Butterfly* has changed her habiliments) like any pair of lovers in Italy. "Dolce notté! Quante stelle! Vieni, vieni!" for quantity.

This is the first act of the opera, and it is all expository to Belasco's "Tragedy of Japan," which plays in one act, with the pathetic vigil separating the two days which form its period of action. When that, like the second act of the opera, opens, *Pinkerton* has been gone from Nagasaki and his "wife" three years, and a baby boy of whom he has never heard, but who has his eyes and hair has come to bear *Butterfly* company in the little house on the hill. The money left by the male butterfly when he flitted is all but exhausted. *Madama Butterfly* appears to be lamentably ignorant of the customs of her country, for she believes herself to be a wife in the American sense and is fearfully wroth with *Suzuki*, her maid, when she hints that she never knew a foreign husband to come back to a Japanese wife. But *Pinkerton* when he sailed away had said that he would be back "when the robins nest again," and that suffices *Cio-Cio-San*. But when *Sharpless* comes with a letter to break the news that his friend is coming back with an American wife, he loses courage to perform his mission at the contemplation of the little woman's faith in the truant. Does he know when the robins nest in America? In Japan they had nested three times since *Pinkerton* went away. The consul quails at that and damns his friend as a scoundrel. Now *Goro*, who knows *Butterfly's* pecuniary plight, brings *Yamadori* to her. *Yamadori* is a wealthy Japanese citizen of New York in the book and play and a prince in the opera, but in all he is smitten with *Butterfly's* beauty and wants to add her name to the list of wives he has conveniently married and as conveniently divorced on his visits to his native land. *Butterfly* insists that she is an American and cannot be divorced Japanese fashion, and is amazed when *Sharpless* hints that *Pinkerton* might have forgotten her and she would better accept *Yamadori's* hand.

First she orders him out of the house, but, repenting her of her rudeness, brings in the child to show him something that no one is likely to forget. She asks the consul to write to his friend and tell him that he has a son, so fine a son, indeed, that she indulges in a day dream of the Mikado stopping at the head of his troops to admire him and make him a prince of the realm. *Sharpless* goes away with his mission unfulfilled and *Suzuki* comes in dragging *Goro* with her, for that he had been spreading scandalous tales about the treatment which children born like this child receive in America. *Butterfly* is tempted to kill the wretch, but at the last is content to spurn him with her foot.

At this moment a cannon shot is heard. A man-of-war is entering the harbor. Quick, the glasses! "Steady my hand, *Suzuki*, that I may read the name." It is the Abraham Lincoln, *Pinkerton's* ship! Now the cherry tree must give up its every blossom, every bush or vine its violets and jessamines to garnish the room for his welcome! The garden is stripped bare, vases are filled, the floor is strewn with petals. Perfumes exhale from the voices of the women and the song of the orchestra. Here local color loses its right; the music is all Occidental. *Butterfly* is dressed again in her wedding gown of white and her pale cheeks are touched up with carmine. The paper partitions are drawn against the night. *Butterfly* punctures the *shoji* with three holes — one high up for herself

to look through, standing; one lower for the maid
to look through, sitting; one near the floor for the
baby. And so *Butterfly* stands in an all-night vigil.
The lanterns flicker and go out. Maid and babe
sink down in sleep. The gray dawn creeps over
the waters of the harbor. Human voices, transformed into instruments, hum a barcarolle. (We
heard it when *Sharpless* tried to read the letter.)
A Japanese tune rises like a sailors' chanty from
the band. Mariners chant their "Yo ho!" Day
is come. *Suzuki* awakes and begs her mistress to
seek rest. *Butterfly* puts the baby to bed, singing
a lullaby. *Sharpless* and *Pinkerton* come and
learn of the vigil from *Suzuki*, who sees the form
of a lady in the garden and hears that it is the
American wife of *Pinkerton*. *Pinkerton* pours out
his remorse melodiously. He will be haunted forever by the picture of his once happy home and
Cio-Cio-San's reproachful eyes. He leaves money
for *Butterfly* in the consul's hands and runs away
like a coward. *Kate*, the American wife, and
Suzuki meet in the garden. The maid is asked
to tell her mistress the meaning of the visit, but
before she can do so *Butterfly* sees them. Her questions bring out half the truth; her intuition tells
her the rest. *Kate* (an awful blot she is on the
dramatic picture) begs forgiveness and asks for the
baby boy that her husband may rear him. *Butterfly*
says he shall have him in half an hour if he will
come to fetch him. She goes to the shrine of

Buddha and takes from it a veil and a dagger, reading the words engraved on its blade: "To die with honor when one can no longer live with honor." It is the weapon which the Mikado had sent to her father. She points the weapon at her throat, but at the moment *Suzuki* pushes the baby into the room. *Butterfly* addresses it passionately; then, telling it to play, seats it upon a stool, puts an American flag into its hands, a bandage around its eyes. Again she takes dagger and veil and goes behind a screen. The dagger is heard to fall. *Butterfly* totters out from behind the screen with a veil wound round her neck. She staggers to the child and falls, dying, at its feet. *Pinkerton* rushes in with a cry of horror and falls on his knees, while *Sharpless* gently takes up the child.

*

* *

I have no desire to comment disparagingly upon the *dénouement* of the book of Mr. Long or the play of Mr. Belasco which Puccini and his librettists followed; but in view of the origin of the play a bit of comparative criticism seems to be imperative. Loti's "Madame Chrysanthème" was turned into an opera by André Messager. What the opera was like I do not know. It came, it went, and left no sign; yet it would seem to be easy to guess at the reason for its quick evanishment. If it followed the French story, as no doubt it did, it was too faithful to the actualities of Japanese life to awaken a throb of emotion in the Occidental heart. Without such a throb a drama is naught — a sounding brass and tinkling cymbal. The charm of Loti's book lies in its marvellously beautiful portrayal of a country, a people, and a characteristic incident in the social life of that people. Its interest as a story, outside of the charm of its telling, is like that excited by inspection of an exotic curio. In his dedication of the book the author begged Mme. la Duchesse de Richelieu not to look for any meaning in it, but to receive it in the same spirit in which she would receive "some quaint bit of pottery, some grotesque carved ivory idol, or some preposterous trifle brought back from the fatherland of all preposterousness." It is a record of a bit of the wandering life of a poet who makes himself a part of every scene into which fortune throws him. He has spent a summer with a Japanese *mousmé*, whom he had married Japanese fashion, and when he has divorced her, also in Japanese fashion, with regard for all the conventions, and sailed away from her forever, he is more troubled by thoughts of possible contamination to his own nature than because of any consequences to the woman. Before the final farewell he had felt a touch of pity for the "poor little gypsy," but when he mounted the stairs to her room for the last time he heard her singing, and mingled with her voice was a strange metallic sound, *dzinn,*

dzinn! as of coins ringing on the floor. Is she amusing herself with quoits, or the *jeu du crapaud*, or pitch and toss? He creeps in, and there, dressed for the departure to her mother's, sitting on the floor is Chrysanthème; and spread out around her all the fine silver dollars he had given her according to agreement the night before. "With the competent dexterity of an old money changer she fingers them, turns them over, throws them on the floor, and armed with a little mallet *ad hoc*, rings them vigorously against her ear, singing the while I know not what little pensive, birdlike song, which I dare say she improvises as she goes along. Well, after all, it is even more completely Japanese than I could possibly have imagined it — this last scene of my married life! I feel inclined to laugh." And he commends the little gypsy's worldly wisdom, offers to make good any counterfeit piece which she may find, and refuses to permit her to see him go aboard of his ship. She does, nevertheless, along with the Japanese wives of four of his fellow officers, who peep at their flitting husbands through the curtains of their sampans. But when he is far out on the great Yellow Sea he throws the faded lotus flowers which she had given him through the porthole of his cabin, making his best excuses for "giving to them, natives of Japan, a grave so solemn and so vast"; and he utters a prayer: "O Ama-Térace-Omi-Kami, wash me clean from this little marriage of mine in the waters of the river of Kamo!"

The story has no soul, and to give his story, which borrowed its motive from Loti's, a soul, Mr. Long had to do violence to the verities of Japanese life. Yet might not even a geisha feel a genuine passion?

*

* *

The use of folk-tunes in opera is older than "Madama Butterfly," but Puccini's score stands alone in the extent of the use and the consistency with which Japanese melody has been made the foundation of the music. When Signor Illica, one of the librettists, followed Sâr Péladan and d'Annunzio into Nippon seeking flowers for "Iris," he took Mascagni with him — metaphorically, of course. But Mascagni was a timid gleaner. Puccini plucked with a bolder hand, as indeed he might, for he is an incomparably greater adept in the art of making musical nosegays. In fact, I know of only one score that is comparable with that of "Madama Butterfly" in respect of its use of national musical color, and that is "Boris Godounoff." Moussorgsky, however, had more, richer, and a greater variety of material to work with than Puccini. Japanese music is arid and angular, and yet so great is Puccini's skill in combining creative imagination and reflection that he knew how to make it blossom like a rose. Pity that he could not wholly overcome its rhythmical monotony. Japanese melody runs almost uninterruptedly through his instrumental score, giving way at intervals to the Italian style of lyricism when the characters and passions become universal rather than local types. Structurally, his score rests on the Wagnerian method, in that the vocal part floats on an uninterrupted instrumental current. In the orchestral part the tunes which he borrowed from the popular music of Japan are continuously recurrent, and fragments of them are used as the connecting links of the whole fabric. He uses also a few typical themes (*Leitmotive*) of his own invention, and to them it might be possible, by ingenious study of their relation to text and situation, to attach significances in the manner of the Wagnerian handbooks; but I do not think that such processes occupied the composer's mind to any considerable extent, and the themes are not appreciably characteristic. His most persistent use of a connecting link, arbitrarily chosen, is found in the case of the first motive of the theme, which he treats fugally in the introduction, and which appears thereafter to the end of the chapter (*a*, in the list of themes printed herewith). What might be called personal themes are the opening notes of "The Star-Spangled Banner" for *Pinkerton* and the melody (*d*) which comes in with *Yamadori*, in which the Japanese tune used by Sir Arthur Sullivan in "The Mikado" is echoed. The former fares badly throughout the score (for which no blame need attach to Signor Puccini), but the latter is used with capital effect, though not always in connection with the character.

If Signor Puccini had needed the suggestion that Japanese music was necessary for a Japanese play (which of course he did not), he might have received it when he saw Mr. Belasco's play in London. For the incidental music in that play Mr. William Furst provided Japanese tunes, or tunes made over the very convenient Japanese last. Through Mr. Belasco's courtesy I am able to present here a relic of this original "Butterfly" music. The first melody (*a*) was the theme of the curtain-music; (*b*) that accompanying *Cho-Cho-San*, when discovered at the beginning spraying flowers, presenting an offering at the shrine and burning incense in the house at the foot of Higashi hill; (*c*) the *Yamadori* music; (*d*) the music accompanying the first production of the sword; (*e*) the music of the vigil. There were also two Occidental pieces — the melody of a little song which *Pinkerton* had taught *Cho-Cho-San*, "I Call Her the Belle of Japan," and "Rock-a-bye, Baby."

Themes from Puccini's "Butterfly" music

By permission of Ricordi & Co.

Melodies from Mr. Furst's "Butterfly" music

By permission of Mr. David Belasco

CHAPTER XIII

"DER ROSENKAVALIER"

In the beginning there was "Guntram," of which we in America heard only fragmentary echoes in our concert-rooms. Then came "Feuersnot," which reached us in the same way, but between which and the subject which is to occupy me in this chapter there is a kinship through a single instrumental number, the meaning of which no commentator has dared more than hint at. It is the music which accompanies the episode, politely termed a "love scene," which occurs at the climax of the earlier opera, but is supposed to take place before the opening of the curtain in the later. Perhaps I shall recur to them again — if I have the courage.

These were the operas of Richard Strauss which no manager deemed it necessary or advisable to produce in New York. Now came "Salome." Popular neurasthenia was growing. Oscar Wilde thought France might accept a glorification of necrophilism and wrote his delectable book in French. France would have none of it, but when it was done into German, and Richard Strauss accentuated its sexual perversity by his hysterical music, lo ! Berlin ac-

RICHARD STRAUSS.

cepted it with avidity. The theatres of the Prussian capital were keeping pace with the pathological spirit of the day, and were far ahead of those of Paris, where, it had long been the habit to think, moral obliquity made its residence. If Berlin, then why not New York? So thought Mr. Conried, saturated with German theatricalism, and seeing no likely difference in the appeal of a "Parsifal," which he had successfully produced, and a "Salome," he prepared to put the works of Wagner and Strauss on the same footing at the Metropolitan Opera House. An influence which has not yet been clearly defined, but which did not spring from the director of the opera nor the gentlemen who were his financial backers, silenced the maunderings of the lust-crazed *Herod* and paralyzed the contortions of the lascivious dancer to whom he was willing to give one-half his kingdom.[1]

Now Mr. Hammerstein came to continue the artistic education which the owners of the Metropolitan Opera House had so strangely and unaccountably checked. *Salome* lived out her mad life in a short time, dying, not by the command of *Herod*, but crushed under the shield of popular opinion. The operation, though effective, was not as swift as it might have been had operatic conditions been different than they are in New York, and before it was accomplished a newer phase of Strauss's pathological

[1] For the story of "Salome" in New York, see my "Chapters of Opera" (Henry Holt & Co., New York), p. 343 *et seq.*

art had offered itself as a nervous excitation. It was "Elektra," and under the guise of an ancient religious ideal, awful but pathetic, the people were asked to find artistic delight in the contemplation of a woman's maniacal thirst for a mother's blood. It is not necessary to recall the history of the opera at the Manhattan Opera House to show that the artistic sanity of New York was proof against the new poison.

Hugo von Hoffmannsthal had aided Strauss in this brew and collaborated with him in the next, which, it was hoped, probably because of the difference in its concoction and ingredients, would make his rein even more taut than it had ever been on theatrical managers and their public. From the Greek classics he turned to the comedy of the Beaumarchais period. Putting their heads together, the two wrote "Der Rosenkavalier." It was perhaps shrewd on their part that they avoided all allusion to the *opera buffa* of the period and called their work a "comedy for music." It enabled them, in the presence of the ignorant, to assume a virtue which they did not possess; but it is questionable if that circumstance will help them any. It is only the curious critic nowadays who takes the trouble to look at the definition, or epithet, on a title page. It is the work which puts the hallmark on itself; not the whim of the composer. It would have been wise, very wise indeed, had Hoffmannsthal avoided everything which might call up a comparison between himself and Beaumarchais. It was simply fatal to Strauss that he tried to avoid all comparison between his treatment of an eighteenth century comedy and Mozart's. One of his devices was to make use of the system of musical symbols which are irrevocably associated with Wagner's method of composition. Mozart knew nothing of this system, but he had a better one in his Beaumarchaisian comedy, which "Der Rosenkavalier" recalls; it was that of thematic expression for each new turn in the dramatic situation — a system which is carried out so brilliantly in "Le Nozze di Figaro" that there is nothing, even in "Die Meistersinger," which can hold a candle to it. Another was to build up the vocal part of his comedy on orchestral waltzes. Evidently it was his notion that at the time of Maria Theresa (in whose early reign the opera is supposed to take place) the Viennese world was given over to the dance. It was so given over a generation later, so completely, indeed, that at the meetings in the ridotto, for which Mozart, Haydn, Gyrowetz, Beethoven, and others wrote music, retiring rooms had to be provided for ladies who were as unprepared for possible accidents as was one of those described by Pepys as figuring in a court ball in his time; but to put scarcely anything but waltz tunes under the dialogue of "Der Rosenkavalier" is an anachronism which is just as disturbing to the judicious as the fact that Herr Strauss, though he starts his half-dozen or more of waltzes most insinuatingly, never lets them run the natural course which Lanner and the Viennese

o

Strauss, who suggested their tunes, would have made them do.   Always, the path which sets out so prettily becomes a byway beset with dissonant thorns and thistles and clogged with rocks.

All of this is by way of saying that "Der Rosen-kavalier" reached New York on December 9, 1913, after having endured two years or so in Europe, under the management of Mr. Gatti-Casazza, and was treated with the distinction which Mr. Conried gave "Parsifal" and had planned for "Salome."   It was set apart for a performance outside the subscription, special prices were demanded, and the novelty dressed as sumptuously and prepared with as lavish an expenditure of money and care as if it were a work of the very highest importance.   Is it that? The question is not answered by the fact that its music was composed by Richard Strauss, even though one be willing to admit that Strauss is the greatest living master of technique in musical composition, the one concerning whose doings the greatest curiosity is felt and certainly the one whose doings are the best advertised.   "Der Rosenkavalier," in spite of all these things, must stand on its merits — as a comedy with music.   The author of its book has invited a comparison which has already been suggested by making it a comedy of intrigue merely and placing its time of action in Vienna and the middle of the eighteenth century.   He has gone further; he has invoked the spirit of Beaumarchais to animate his people and his incidents.   The one thing which he could not do, or did not do, was to supply the satirical scourge which justified the Figaro comedies of his great French prototype and which, while it made their acceptance tardy, because of royal and courtly opposition, made their popular triumph the more emphatic. "Le Nozze di Figaro" gave us more than one figure and more than one scene in the representation, and "Le Nozze di Figaro" is to those who understand its text one of the most questionable operas on the current list. But there is a moral purpose underlying the comedy which to some extent justifies its frank salaciousness. It is to prevent the *Count* from exercising an ancient seigniorial right over the heroine which he had voluntarily resigned, that all the characters in the play unite in the intrigue which makes up the comedy. Moreover, there are glimpses over and over again of honest and virtuous love between the characters and beautiful expressions of it in the music which makes the play delightful, despite its salaciousness. Even *Cherubino*, who seems to have come to life again in *Octavian*, is a lovable youth if for no other reason than that he represents youth in its amorousness toward all womankind, with thought of special mischief toward none.

"Der Rosenkavalier" is a comedy of lubricity merely, with what little satirical scourge it has applied only to an old roué who is no more deserving of it than most of the other people in the play. So much of its story as will bear telling can be told very

briefly. It begins, assuming its instrumental introduction (played with the scene discreetly hidden)
to be a part of it, with a young nobleman locked in
the embraces of the middle-aged wife of a field
marshal, who is conveniently absent on a hunting
expedition. The music is of a passionate order, and
the composer, seeking a little the odor of virtue, but
with an oracular wink in his eye, says in a descriptive note that it is to be played in the spirit of parody
(*parodistisch*). Unfortunately the audience cannot
see the printed direction, and there is no parody in
music except extravagance and ineptitude in the
utterance of simple things (like the faulty notes of
the horns in Mozart's joke on the village musicians,
the cadenza for violin solo in the same musical joke,
or the twangling of *Beckmesser's* lute) ; so the introduction is an honest musical description of things
which the composer is not willing to confess, and
least of all the stage manager, for when the curtain
opens there is not presented even the picture called
for by the German libretto. Nevertheless, morn is
dawning, birds are twittering, and the young lover,
kneeling before his mistress on a divan, is bemoaning
the fact that day is come and that he cannot publish his happiness to the world. The tête-à-tête is
interrupted by a rude boor of a nobleman, who comes
to consult his cousin (the princess) about a messenger to send with the conventional offering of a silver
rose to the daughter of a vulgar plebeian just ele-
vated to the nobility because of his wealth. The

conversation between the two touches on little more than old amours, and after the lady has held her levee designed to introduce a variety of comedy effects in music as well as action, the princess recommends her lover for the office of rosebearer. Meanwhile the lover has donned the garments of a waiting maid and been overwhelmed with the wicked attentions of the roué, *Lerchenau*. When the lovers are again alone there is a confession of renunciation on the part of the princess, based on the philosophical reflection that, after all, her *Octavian* being so young would bring about the inevitable parting sooner or later.

In the second act what the princess in her prescient abnegation had foreseen takes place. Her lover carries the rose to the young woman whom the roué had picked out for his bride and promptly falls in love with her. She with equal promptness, following the example of Wagner's heroines, bowls herself at his head. The noble vulgarian complicates matters by insisting that he receive a dowry instead of paying one. The young hot-blood adds to the difficulties by pinking him in the arm with his sword, but restores order at the last by sending him a letter of assignation in his first act guise of a maid servant of the princess.

This assignation is the background of the third act, which is farce of the wildest and most vulgar order. Much of it is too silly for description. Always, however, there is allusion to the purpose of the meeting on the part of *Lerchenau*, whose plans are spoiled by apparitions in all parts of the room, the entrance of the police, his presumptive bride and her father, a woman who claims him as her husband, four children who raise bedlam (and memories of the contentious Jews in "Salome"), by shouting "Papa! papa!" until his mind is in a whirl and he rushes out in despair. The princess leaves the new-found lovers alone.

They hymn their happiness in Mozartian strains (the melody copied from the second part of the music with which *Papageno* sets the blackamoors to dancing in "Die Zauberflöte"), the orchestra talks of the matronly renunciation of the princess, enthusiastic Straussians of a musical parallel with the quintet from Wagner's "Meistersinger," and the opera comes to an end after three and one-half hours of more or less unintelligible dialogue poised on waltz melodies.

I have said unintelligible dialogue. For this unintelligibility there are two reasons — the chief one musical, the other literary. Though Strauss treats his voices with more consideration in "Der Rosenkavalier" than in his tragedies, he still so overburdens them that the words are distinguishable only at intervals. Only too frequently he crushes them with orchestral voices, which in themselves are not overwhelming — the voices of his horns, for instance, for which he shows a particular partiality. His style of declamation is melodic, though it is only at the end of the opera that he rises to real vocal melody; but it seems to be put over an orchestral part, and not the orchestral part put under it. There is no moment in which he can say, as Wagner truthfully and admiringly said of the wonderful orchestral music of the third act of "Tristan und Isolde," that all this swelling instrumental song existed only for the sake of what the dying *Tristan* was saying upon his couch. All of Strauss's waltzes seem to exist for their own sake, which makes the disappointment greater that they are not carried through in the spirit in which they are begun; that is, the spirit of the naïve Viennese dance tune.

A second reason for the too frequent unintelligibility of the text is its archaic character. Its idioms are eighteenth century as well as Viennese, and its persistent use of the third person even among individuals of quality, though it gives a tang to the libretto when read in the study, is not welcome when heard with difficulty. Besides this, there is use of dialect — vulgar when assumed by *Octavian*, mixed when called for by such characters as *Valzacchi* and his partner in scandal mongery, *Annina*. To be compelled to forego a knowledge of half of what such a master of diction as Mr. Reiss was saying was a new sensation to his admirers who understand German. Yet the fault was as little his as it was Mr. Goritz's that so much of what he said went for nothing; it was all his misfortune, including the fact that much of the music is not adapted to his voice.

The music offers a pleasanter topic than the

action and dialogue.   It is a relief to those listeners
who go to the opera oppressed with memories of
"Salome" and "Elektra."   It is not only that their
ears are not so often assaulted by rude sounds, they
are frequently moved by phrases of great and genuine
beauty.   Unfortunately the Straussian system of
composition demands that beauty be looked for in
fragments.   Continuity of melodic flow is impossible
to Strauss — a confession of his inability either to
continue Wagner's method, to improve on it, or invent anything new in its place.   The best that has
been done in the Wagnerian line belongs to
Humperdinck.[1]

[1] "Der Rosenkavalier" had its first American production at
the Metropolitan Opera House, New York, on December 9,
1913, the cast being as follows:—

Feldmarschallin Fürstin Werdenberg	Frieda Hempel
Baron Ochs auf Lerchenau	Otto Goritz
Octavian, genannt Quinquin	Margarete Ober
Herr von Faninal	Hermann Weil
Sophie, seine Tochter	Anna Case
Jungfer Marianne Leitmetzerin	Rita Fornia
Valzacchi, ein Intrigant	Albert Reiss
Annina, seine Begleiterin	Marie Mattfeld
Ein Polizeikommissär	Carl Schlegel
Haushofmeister der Feldmarschallin	Pietro Audisio
Haushofmeister bei Faninal	Lambert Murphy
Ein Notar	Basil Ruysdael
Ein Wirt	Julius Bayer
Ein Sänger	Carl Jorn
Drei adelige Waisen	{ Louise Cox / Rosina Van Dyck / Sophie Braslau }
Eine Modistin	Jeanne Maubourg
Ein Lakai	Ludwig Burgstaller
Ein kleiner Neger	Ruth Weinstein

Conductor — Alfred Hertz

CHAPTER XIV

"KÖNIGSKINDER"

ONCE upon a time a witch cast a spell upon a king's daughter and held her in servitude as a goose-herd. A prince found her in the forest and loved her. She loved him in return, and would gladly have gone away from her sordid surroundings with him, though she had spurned the crown which he had offered her in exchange for her wreath of flowers; but when she escaped from her jailer she found that she could not break the charm which held her imprisoned in the forest. Then the prince left the crown lying at her feet and continued his wanderings. Scarcely had he gone when there came to the hut of the witch a broommaker and a woodchopper, guided by a wandering minstrel. They were ambassadors from the city of Hellabrunn, which had been so long without a king that its boorish burghers themselves felt the need of a ruler in spite of their boorishness. To the wise woman the ambassadors put the questions: Who shall be this ruler and by what sign shall they recognize him? The witch tells them that their sovereign shall be the first person who enters their gates after the bells have rung the noon hour on the morrow, which is the day of the Hella festival. Then the minstrel catches sight of the lovely goose-girl, and through the prophetic gift possessed by poets he recognizes in her a rightly born princess for his people. By the power of his art he is enabled to put aside the threatening spells of the witch and compel the hag to deliver the maiden into his care. He persuades her to break the enchantment which had held her bound hitherto and defy the wicked power.

Meanwhile, however, grievous misfortunes have befallen the prince, her lover. He has gone to Hella-brunn, and desiring to learn to serve in order that he might better know how to rule, he had taken ser-vice as a swineherd. The daughter of the innkeeper becomes enamoured of the shapely body of the prince, whose proud spirit she cannot understand, and who has repulsed her advances. His thoughts go back to the goosegirl whose wreath, with its fresh fra-grance, reminds him of his duty. He attempts to teach the burghers their own worth, but the wench whose love he had repulsed accuses him of theft, and he is about to be led off to prison when the bells peal forth the festal hour.

Joyfully the watchmen throw open the strong town gates and the multitude and gathered coun-cillors fall back to receive their king. But through the doors enters the gooseherd, proudly wearing her crown and followed by her flock and the minstrel. The lovers fall into each other's arms, but only the poet and a little child recognize them as of royal blood. The boorish citizens, who had fancied that their king would appear in regal splendor, drive the youth and maiden out with contumely, burn the witch and cripple the minstrel by breaking one of his legs on the wheel. Seeking his home, the prince and his love lose their way in the forest during a snowstorm and die of a poisoned loaf made by the witch, for which the prince had bartered his broken crown, under the same tree which had sheltered them on their first meeting; but the children of Hellabrunn, who had come out in search of them, guided by a bird, find their bodies buried under the snow and give them royal acclaim and burial. And the prescient minstrel hymns their virtues.

This is the story of Engelbert Humperdinck's opera "Königskinder," which had its first performance on any stage at the Metropolitan Opera House, New York, on December 28, 1910, with the following cast:

Der Königssohn...................Herman Jadlowker
Die Gänsemagd.....................Geraldine Farrar
Der Spielmann.........................Otto Goritz
Die Hexe..............................Louise Homer
Der Holzhacker.......................Adamo Didur
Der Besenbinder........................Albert Reiss
Zwei Kinder............Edna Walter and Lotte Engel
Der Ratsälteste......................Marcel Reiner
Der Wirt.........................Antonio Pini-Corsi
Die Wirtstochter..................Florence Wickham
Der Schneider.........................Julius Bayer
Die Stallmagd.......................Marie Mattfeld
Zwei Torwächter......Ernst Maran and William Hinshaw
Conductor: Alfred Hertz

To some in the audience the drama was new only in the new operatic dress with which Humperdinck had clothed it largely at the instance of the Metropolitan management. It had been known as a spoken play for twelve years and three of its musical numbers — the overture and two pieces of between-acts music — had been in local concert-lists for the same length of time. The play had been presented with incidental music for many of the scenes as well as the overture and *entr'actes* in 1898 in an extremely interesting production at the Irving Place Theatre, then under the direction of Heinrich Conried, in which Agnes Sorma and Rudolf Christians had carried the principal parts. It came back four years later in an English version at the Herald Square Theatre, but neither in the German nor the English performance was it vouchsafed us to realize what had been the purpose of the author of the play and the composer of the music.

The author, who calls herself Ernst Rosmer, is a woman, daughter of Heinrich Porges, for many years a factotum at the Bayreuth festivals. It was her father's devotion to Wagner which gave her the name of Elsa. She married a lawyer and littérateur in Munich named Bernstein, and has written a number of plays besides "Königskinder," which she published in 1895, and afterward asked Herr Humperdinck (not yet a royal Prussian professor, but a simple musician, who had made essays in criticisms and tried to make a composer out of Siegfried Wagner)

GERALDINE FARRAR.   (IN " KÖNIGSKINDER.")

to provide with incidental music. Mr. Humperdinck took his task seriously. The play, with some
incidental music, was two years old before Mr.
Humperdinck had his overture ready. He had tried
a new experiment, which proved a failure. The
second and third acts had their preludes, and the
songs of the minstrel had their melodies and accom-
paniments, and all the principal scenes had been
provided with illustrative music in the Wagnerian
manner, with this difference, that the dialogue had
been "pointed," as a church musician would say —
that is, the rhythm was indicated with exactness,
and even the variations of pitch, though it was understood that the purpose was not to achieve song, but
an intensified utterance, halfway between speech
and song. This was melodrama, as Herr Humperdinck conceived it and as it had no doubt existed
for ages — ever since the primitive Greek drama, in
fact. It is easy to understand how Herr Humperdinck came to believe in the possibility of an art-
form which, though accepted, for temporary effect,
by Beethoven and Cherubini, and used for ballads
with greater or less success by Schumann, had been
harshly rejected by his great model and master,
Wagner. Humperdinck lives in Germany, where
in nearly every theatre there is more or less of an
amalgamation of the spoken drama and the opera —
where choristers play small parts and actors, though
not professional singers, sing when not too much is
required of them. And yet Herr Humperdinck

found out that he had asked too much of his actors
with his "pointed" and at times intoned declamation, and "Königskinder" did not have to come to
America to learn that the compromise was a failure.
No doubt Herr Humperdinck thought of turning so
beautiful a play into an opera then, but it seems to
have required the stimulus which finally came from
New York to persuade him to carry out the operatic
idea, which is more than suggested in the score as
it lies before me in its original shape, into a thorough
lyric drama.   The set pieces which had lived in the
interim in the concert-room were transferred into
the opera-score with trifling alterations and condensations and so were the set songs.   As for the
rest it needed only that note-heads be supplied to
some of the portions of the dialogue which Humperdinck had designed for melodic declamation to have
those portions ready for the opera.   Here an example : —

Willst du mein Mai-en-buh-le sein,   du Blu-men-wei-che?

A German opera can generally stand severer criticism than one in another language, because there is
a more strict application of principles in Germany
when it comes to writing a lyric drama than in any
other country.   So in the present instance there is no
need to conceal the fact that there are outbreaks of
eroticism and offences against the German language

which are none the less flagrant and censurable because they are, to some extent, concealed under the thin veneer of the allegory and symbolism which every reader must have recognized as running through the play. This is, in a manner, Wagnerian, as so much of the music is Wagnerian — especially that of the second act, which because it calls up scenes from the "Meistersinger" must also necessarily call up music from the same comedy. But there is little cause here for quarrel with Professor Humperdinck. He has applied the poetical principle of Wagner to the fairy tale which is so closely related to the myth, and he has with equal consistency applied Wagner's constructive methods musically and dramatically. It is to his great honor that, of all of Wagner's successors, he has been the only one to do so successfully.

The story of "Königskinder," though it belongs to the class of fairy tales of which "Hänsel und Gretel" is so striking and beautiful an example, is not to be found as the author presents it in the literature of German *Märchen*. Mme. Bernstein has drawn its elements from many sources and blended them with the utmost freedom. To avoid a misunderstanding Germans will insist that the title be used without the article, for "Die Königskinder" or "Zwei Königskinder" both suggest the simple German form of the old tale of Hero and Leander, with which story, of course, it has nothing whatever to do. But if literary criticism forbids association between Humperdinck's two operas, musical criticism compels it. Many of the characters in the operas are close relations, dramatically as well as musically — the royal children themselves, the witches, of course, and the broom-makers. The rest of the characters have been taken from Wagner's "Meistersinger" picture book; the citizens of Hellabrunn are Nuremberg's burghers, the city's councillors, the old master singers. The musical idiom is Humperdinck's, though its method of employment is Wagner's. But here lies its charm: Though the composer hews to a theoretical line, he does it freely, naturally, easily, and always with the principle of musical beauty as well as that of dramatic truthfulness and propriety in view. His people's voices float on a symphonic stream, but the voices of the instruments, while they sing on in endless melody, use the idiom which nature gave them. There is admirable characterization in the orchestral music, but it is music for all that; it never descends to mere noise, designed to keep up an irritation of the nerves.

CHAPTER XV

FROM whatever point of view it may be considered Mossourgsky's opera "Boris Godounoff" is an extraordinary work. It was brought to the notice of the people of the United States by a first performance at the Metropolitan Opera House, in New York, on March 19, 1913, but intelligence concerning its character had come to observers of musical doings abroad by reports touching performances in Paris and London. It is possible, even likely, that at all the performances of the work outside of Russia those who listened to it with the least amount of intellectual sophistication derived the greatest pleasure from it, though to them its artistic deficiencies must also have been most obvious. Against these deficiencies, however, it presented itself, first of all, as a historical play shot through and through with a large theme, which, since it belongs to tragedy, is universal and unhampered by time or place or people. To them it had something of the sweep, dignity, and solemnity and also something of the dramatic incongruity and lack of cohesion of a Shakespearian drama as contradistinguished from the coherence of purpose and manner of a modern drama.

To them also it had much strangeness of style, a style which was not easily reconciled to anything with which the modern stage had made them familiar. They saw and heard the chorus enter into the action, not for the purpose of spectacular pageantry, nor as hymners of the achievements of the principal actors in the story, but as participants. They heard unwonted accents from these actors and saw them behave in conduct which from moment to moment appeared strangely contradictory. There were mutterings of popular discontent, which, under threats, gave way to jubilant acclamation in the first great scenes in the beginning of the opera. There were alternate mockeries and adulations in the next scene in which the people figured; and running through other scenes from invisible singers came ecclesiastical chants, against which were projected, not operatic song in the old conception, but long passages of heightened speech, half declamatory, half musical. A multitude cringed before upraised knouts and fell on its knees before the approach of a man whose agents swung the knotted cords; anon they acclaimed the man who sought to usurp a throne and overwhelmed with ridicule a village imbecile, who was yet supposed because of his mental weakness to be possessed of miraculous prescience, and therefore to have a prevision of what was to follow the usurpation. They saw the incidents of the drama moving past their eyes within a framework of barbaric splendor typical of a wonderful political past. an amazing political present, and possibly prophetic of a still more amazing political future.

These happily ingenuous spectators saw an historical personage racked by conscience, nerve-torn by spectres, obsessed by superstitions, strong in position achieved, yet pathetically sweet and moving in his exhibition of paternal love, and going to destruction through remorse for crime committed. They were troubled by no curious questionings as to the accuracy of the historical representation. The *Boris Godounoff* before them was a remorse-stricken regicide, whose good works, if he did any, had to be summed up for their imagination in the fact that he loved his son. In all this, and also in some of its music, the new opera was of the opera operatic. But to the unhappily disingenuous (or perhaps it would be better to say, to the instructed) there was much more in the new opera; and it was this more which so often gave judgment pause, even while it stimulated interest and irritated curiosity. It was a pity that a recent extraordinary outburst of enthusiasm about a composer and an opera should have had the effect of distorting their vision and disturbing their judgment.

There was a reason to be suspicious touching this enthusiasm, because of its origin. It came from France and not from the home land of the author of the play or the composer of the music. Moreover, it was largely based upon an element which has as little genuineness in France as a basis of judgment (and which must therefore be set down largely as an affectation) as in America. Loud hallelujahs have been raised in praise of Moussorgsky because, discarding conventional law, he vitalized the music of the lyric poem and also the dramatic line, by making it the emotional flowering of the spoken word. When it became necessary for the precious inner brotherhood of Frenchmen who hold burning incense sticks under each others' noses to acclaim "Pelléas et Mélisande" as a new and beautiful thing in dramatic music, it was announced that Moussorgsky was like Debussy in that he had demonstrated in his songs and his operas that vocal melody should and could be written in accordance with the rhythm and accents of the words. We had supposed that we had learned that lesson not only from Gluck and Wagner, but from every true musical dramatist that ever lived! And when the Frenchmen (and their feeble echoers in England and America) began to cry out that the world make obeisance to Moussorgsky on that score, there was no wonder that those whose eagerness to enjoy led them to absorb too much information should ask how this marvellous psychical assonance between word and tone was to be conveyed to their unfortunate sense and feeling after the original Russian word had been transmogrified into French or English. In New York the opera, which we know to be saturated in some respects with Muscovitism, or Slavicism, and which we have every reason to believe is also so saturated in its musico-verbal essence, was sung in Italian. With the change some of the character that ought to make it dear to the Russian heart must have evaporated. It is even likely that vigorous English would have been a better vehicle than the "soft, bastard Latin" for the forceful utterances of the operatic people.

It is a pity that a suspicion of disingenuousness and affectation should force itself upon one's thoughts in connection with the French enthusiasm over Moussorgsky; but it cannot be avoided. So far as Moussorgsky reflects anything in his art, it is realism or naturalism, and the latter element is not dominant in French music now, and is not likely to be so long as the present tendency toward sublimated subjectivism prevails. Debussy acclaimed Moussorgsky enthusiastically a dozen years ago, but for all that Moussorgsky and Debussy are antipodes in art — they represent extremes.

It is much more likely that outside of its purely literary aspect (a large aspect in every respect in France) the Moussorgsky cult of the last few years was a mere outgrowth of the political affiliation between France and Russia; as such it may be looked upon in the same light as the sudden appreciation of Berlioz which was a product of the Chauvinism which followed the Franco-Prussian War. It is easy even for young people of the day in which I write to remember when a Wagner opera at the Académie Nationale raised a riot, and when the dances at the Moulin Rouge and such places could not begin until the band had played the Russian national hymn.

Were it not for considerations of this sort it would be surprising to contemplate the fact that Moussorgsky has been more written and talked about in France than he was in his native Russia, and that even his friend Rimsky-Korsakoff, to whose revision of the score "Boris Godounoff" owes its continued existence, has been subjected to much rude criticism because of his work, though we can only think of it as taken up in a spirit of affection and admiration. He and the Russians, with scarcely an exception, say that his labors were in the line of purification and rectification; but the modern extremists will have it that by remedying its crudities of harmonization and instrumentation he weakened it — that what he thought its artistic blemishes were its virtues. Of that we are in no position to speak, nor ought any one be rash enough to make the proclamation until the original score is published, and then only a Russian or a musician familiar with the Russian tongue and its genius. The production of the opera outside of Russia and in a foreign language ought to furnish an occasion to demand a stay of the artistic cant which is all too common just now in every country.

We are told that "Boris Godounoff" is the first real Russian opera that America has ever heard. In a sense that may be true. The present generation has heard little operatic music by Russian composers. Rubinstein's "Nero" was not Russian music in any respect. "Pique Dame," by Tschaïkowsky, also performed at the Metropolitan Opera House, had little in it that could be recognized as characteristically Russian. "Eugene Onegin" we know only from concert performances, and its Muscovitism was a negligible quantity. The excerpts from other Russian operas have been few and they demonstrated nothing, though in an intermezzo from Tschaïkowsky's "Mazeppa," descriptive of the battle of Poltava, which has been heard here, we met with the strong choral tune which gives great animation to the most stirring scene in "Boris" — the acclamation of the Czar by the populace in the first act. Of this something more presently. There were American representations, however, of a Russian opera which in its day was more popular than "Boris" has ever been; but that was so long ago that all memories of it have died, and even the records are difficult to reach. Some fifty years ago a Russian company came to these shores and performed Verstoffsky's "Askold's Tomb," an opera which was republished as late as 1897 and which within the first twenty-five years of its existence had 400 performances in Moscow and 200 in St. Petersburg. Some venturesome critics have hailed Verstoffsky as even more distinctively a predecessor of Moussorgsky than Glinka; but the clamor of those who are preaching loudly that art must not exist for art's sake, and that the ugly is justified by the beauty of ugliness, has silenced the voices of these critical historians.

This may thus far have seemed a long and discursive disquisition on the significance of the new opera; but the questions to which the production of "Boris Godounoff" give rise are many and grave, especially in the present state of our operatic activities. They have a strong bearing on the problem of nationalism in opera, of which those in charge of our operatic affairs appear to take a careless view. Aside from all æsthetic questions, "Boris Godounoff" bears heavily on that problem. It is a work crude and fragmentary in structure, but it is tremendously puissant in its preachment of nationalism; and it is strong there not so much because of its story and the splendid barbarism of its external integument as because of its nationalism, which is proclaimed in the use of Russian folk-song. All previous experiments in this line become insignificant in comparison with it, and it is questionable if any other body of folk-song offers such an opportunity to the operatic composer as does the Russian. The hero of the opera is in dramatic stature (or at least in emotional content) a *Macbeth* or a *Richard III*; his utterances are frequently poignant and heart searching in the extreme; his dramatic portrayal by M. Chaliapine in Europe and Mr. Didur in America is so gripping as to call up memories of some of the great English tragedians of the past. But we cannot speak of the psychology of the musical setting of his words because we have been warned that it roots deeply in the accents and inflections of a language with which we are unfamiliar and which was not used in the performance. But the music of the choral masses, the songs sung in the intimacy of the *Czar Boris's* household, the chants of the monks, needed not to be strange to any student of folk-song, nor could their puissance be lost upon the musically unlettered. In the old Kolyáda Song "Sláva" [1] with which *Boris* is greeted by the populace, as well as in the wild shoutings of the Polish vagrom men and women in the scene before the last, it is impossible not to hear an outpouring of that spirit of which Tolstoi wrote: "In it is yearning without end, without hope; also power invincible, the fateful stamp of destiny, iron preordination, one of the fundamental principles of our nationality with which it is possible to explain much that in Russian life seems incomprehensible."

No other people have such a treasure of folk-song to draw on as that thus characterized, and it is not likely that any other people will develop a national school of opera on the lines which lie open to the Russian composer, and which the Russian composer has been encouraged to exploit by his government for the last twenty years or more.

It is possible that some critics, actuated by political rather than artistic considerations, will find reasons

[1] Lovers of chamber music know this melody from its use in the allegretto in Beethoven's E minor Quartet dedicated to Count Rasoumowski, where it appears thus:—

for the present condition of Moussorgsky's score in the attitude of the Russian government. It is said that court intrigues had much to do with the many changes which the score had to undergo before it became entirely acceptable to the powers that be in the Czar's empire. Possibly. But every change which has come under the notice of this reviewer has been to its betterment and made for its practical presentation. It is said that the popular scenes were curtailed because they represented the voice of the democracy. But there is still so much choral work in the opera that the judgment of the operatic audiences of to-day is likely to pronounce against it measurably on that account. For, splendid as the choral element in the work is, a chorus is not looked upon with admiration as a dramatic element by the ordinary opera lover. There was a lack of the feminine element in the opera, and to remedy this Moussorgsky had to introduce the Polish bride of the *False Dmitri* and give the pair a love scene, and incidentally a polonaise; but the love scene is uninteresting until its concluding measures, and these are too Meyerbeerian to call for comment beyond the fact that Meyerbeer, the much contemned, would have done better. As for the polonaise, Tschaikowsky has written a more brilliant one for his "Eugene Onegin."

The various scores of the opera which have been printed show that Moussorgsky, with all his genius, was at sea even when it came to applying the prin-

ADAMO DIDUR AS CZAR BORIS.

ciples of the Young Russian School, of which he is set down as a strong prop, to dramatic composition. With all his additions, emendations, and rearrangements, his opera still falls much short of being a dramatic unit. It is a more loosely connected series of scenes, from the drama of Boris Godounoff and the false Dmitri, than Boito's "Mefistofele" is of Goethe's "Faust." Had he had his own way the opera would have ended with the scene in which *Dmitri* proceeds to Moscow amid the huzzas of a horde of Polish vagabonds, and we should have had neither a *Boris* nor a *Dmitri* opera, despite the splendid opportunities offered by both characters. It was made a *Boris* opera by bringing it to an end with the death of *Boris* and leaving everything except the scenes in which the *Czar* declines the imperial crown, then accepts it, and finally dies of a tortured conscience, to serve simply as intermezzi, in which for the moment the tide of tragedy is turned aside. This and the glimpse into the paternal heart of the *Czar* is the only and beautiful purpose of the domestic scene, in which the lighter and more cheerful element of Russian folk-song is introduced.

At the first American performance of "Boris Godounoff" the cast was as follows: —

Boris	Adamo Didur
Theodore	Anna Case
Xenia	Lenora Sparkes
The Nurse	Maria Duchêne
Marina	Louise Homer

Schouisky.................................Angelo Bada
Tchelkaloff......................Vincenzo Reschiglian
Pimenn...............................Léon Rothier
Dmitri.....................Paul Althouse (his debut)
Varlaam.....................Andrea de Segurola
Missail...............................Pietro Audisio
The Innkeeper.....................Jeanne Maubourg
The Simpleton..........................Albert Reiss
A Police Officer.........................Giulio Rossi
A Court Officer.................... Leopoldo Mariani
Lovitzky...... } Two Jesuits.......... { V. Reschiglian
Tcerniakowsky   Louis Kreidler

Conductor: Arturo Toscanini

CHAPTER XVI

"MADAME SANS-GÊNE" AND OTHER OPERAS BY GIORDANO

THE opera-goers of New York enjoyed a novel experience when Giordano's "Madame Sans-Gêne" had its first performance on any stage in their presence at the Metropolitan Opera House on January 25, 1915. It was the first time that a royal and imperial personage who may be said to live freshly and vividly in the minds of the people of this generation as well as in their imaginations appeared before them to sing his thoughts and feelings in operatic fashion. At first blush it seemed as if a singing Bonaparte was better calculated to stir their risibilities than their interest or sympathies; and this may, indeed, have been the case; but at any rate they had an opportunity to make the acquaintance of Napoleon before he rose to imperial estate. But, in all seriousness, it is easier to imagine the figure which William II of Germany would cut on the operatic stage than the "grand, gloomy, and peculiar" Corsican. The royal people with whom the operatic public is familiar as a rule are sufficiently surrounded by the mists of antiquity and obscurity that the

221

contemplation of them arouse little thought of the incongruity which their appearance as operatic heroes ought to create. *Henry the Fowler* in "Lohengrin," *Mark* in "Tristan und Isolde," the unnumbered *Pharaoh* in "Aïda," *Herod* in "Salomé" and "Hérodiade," and the few other kings, if there are any more with whom the present generation of opera-goers have a personal acquaintance, so to speak, are more or less merely poetical creations whom we seldom if ever think of in connection with veritable history. Even *Boris Godounoff* is to us more a picture out of a book, like the *Macbeth* whom he so strongly resembles from a theatrical point of view, than the monarch who had a large part in the making of the Russian people. The Roman censorship prevented us long ago from making the acquaintance of the Gustavus of Sweden whom Ankerström stabbed to death at a masked ball, by transmogrifying him into the absurdly impossible figure of a *Governor of Boston;* and the *Claudius* of Ambroise Thomas's opera is as much a ghost as *Hamlet's* father, while Debussy's blind *King* is as much an abstraction as is *Mélisande* herself.

Operatic dukes we know in plenty, though most of them have come out of the pages of romance and are more or less acceptable according to the vocal ability of their representatives. When Caruso sings "La donna è mobile" we care little for the profligacy of Verdi's *Duke of Mantua* and do not inquire whether or not such an individual ever lived. Moussorgsky's

Czar Boris ought to interest us more, however. The great bell-tower in the Kremlin which he built, and the great bell — a shattered monument of one of his futile ambitions — have been seen by thousands of travellers who never took the trouble to learn that the tyrant who had the bell cast laid a serfdom upon the Russian people which endured down to our day. Boris, by the way, picturesque and dramatic figure that he is as presented to us in history, never got upon the operatic stage until Moussorgsky took him in hand. Two hundred years ago a great German musician, Mattheson, as much scholar as composer if not more, set him to music, but the opera was never performed. Peter the Great, who came a century after Boris, lived a life more calculated to invite the attention of opera writers, but even he escaped the clutches of dramatic composers except Lortzing, who took advantage of the romantic episode of Peter's service as ship carpenter in Holland to make him the hero of one of the most sparkling of German comic operas. Lortzing had a successor in the Irishman T. S. Cooke, but his opera found its way into the limbo of forgotten things more than a generation ago, while Lortzing's still lives on the stage of Germany. Peter deserved to be celebrated in music, for it was in his reign that polyphonic music, albeit of the Italian order, was introduced into the Russian church and modern instrumental music effected an entrance into his empire. But I doubt if Peter was sincerely musical; in his youth he heard only music of the rudest kind. He was partial to the bagpipes and, like Nero, played upon that instrument.

To come back to Bonaparte and music. "Madame Sans-Gêne" is an operatic version of the drama which Sardou developed out of a little one-act play dealing with a partly fictitious, partly historical story in which Napoleon, his marshal Lefèbvre, and a laundress were the principal figures. Whether or not the great Corsican could be justified as a character in a lyric drama was a mooted question when Giordano conceived the idea of making an opera out of the play. It is said that Verdi remarked something to the effect that the question depended upon what he would be called upon to sing, and how he would be expected to sing it. The problem was really not a very large or difficult one, for all great people are turned into marionettes when transformed into operatic heroes.

In the palmy days of *bel canto* no one would have raised the question at all, for then the greatest characters in history moved about the stage in stately robes and sang conventional arias in the conventional manner. The change from old-fashioned opera to regenerated lyric drama might have simplified the problem for Giordano, even if his librettist had not already done so by reducing Napoleon to his lowest terms from a dramatic as well as historical point of view. The heroes of eighteenth-century opera were generally feeble-minded lovers and nothing more;

Giordano's Napoleon is only a jealous husband who helps out in the dénouement of a play which is concerned chiefly with other people.

In turning Sardou's dramatic personages into operatic puppets a great deal of bloodletting was necessary and a great deal of the characteristic charm of the comedy was lost, especially in the cases of *Madame Sans-Gêne* herself and *Napoleon's* sister; but enough was left to make a practicable opera. There were the pictures of all the plebeians who became great folk later concerned in the historical incidents which lifted them up. There were also the contrasted pictures which resulted from the great transformation, and it was also the ingratiating incident of the devotion of *Lefèbvre* to the stout-hearted, honest little woman of the people who had to try to be a duchess. All this was fair operatic material, though music has a strange capacity for refining stage characters as well as for making them colorless. Giordano could not do himself justice as a composer without refining the expression of *Caterina Huebscher*, and so his *Duchess of Dantzic* talks a musical language at least which Sardou's washer-woman could not talk and remain within the dramatic verities. Therefore we have "Madame Sans-Gêne" with a difference, but not one that gave any more offence than operatic treatment of other fine plays have accustomed us to.

To dispose of the artistic merits of the opera as briefly as possible, it may be said that in more ways

9

than one Giordano has in this work harked back to "Andrea Chenier," the first of his operas which had a hearing in America. The parallel extends to some of the political elements of the book as well as its musical investiture with its echoes of the popular airs of the period of the French Revolution. The style of writing is also there, though applied, possibly, with more mature and refined skill. I cannot say with as much ingenuousness and freshness of invention, however. Its spirit in the first act, and largely in the second, is that of the *opéra bouffe*, but there are many pages of "Madame Sans-Gêne" which I would gladly exchange for any one of the melodies of Lecocq, let us say in "La Fille de Mme. Angot." Like all good French music which uses and imitates them, it is full of crisp rhythms largely developed from the old dances which, originally innocent, were degraded to base uses by the *sans-culottes;* and so there is an abundance of life and energy in the score though little of the distinction, elegance, and grace that have always been characteristic of French music, whether high-born or low. The best melody in the modern Italian vein flows in the second act when the genuine affection and fidelity of *Caterina* find expression and where a light touch is combined with considerable warmth of feeling and a delightful daintiness of orchestral color. Much of this is out of harmony with the fundamental character of Sardou's woman, but music cannot deny its nature. Only a Moussorgsky could make a drunken monk talk truthfully in music.

If Giordano's opera failed to make a profound impression on the New York public, it was not because that public had not had opportunity to learn the quality of his music. His "Andrea Chenier" had been produced at the Academy of Music as long before as November 13, 1896. With it the redoubtable Colonel Mapleson went down to his destruction in America. It was one of the many strange incidents in the career of Mr. Oscar Hammerstein as I have related them in my book entitled "Chapters of Opera" [1] that it should have been brought back by him twelve years later for a single performance at the Manhattan Opera House. In the season of 1916–1917 it was incorporated in the repertory of the Boston-National Opera Company and carried to the principal cities of the country. On December 16, 1906, Mr. Heinrich Conried thought that the peculiar charms of Madame Cavalieri, combined with the popularity of Signor Caruso, might give habitation to Giordano's setting of an opera book made out of Sardou's "Fédora"; but it endured for only four performances in the season of 1906–1907 and three in the next, in which Conried's career came to an end. In reviving "Andrea Chenier" Mr. Hammerstein may have had visions of future triumphs for its composer, for a few weeks before (on February 5, 1908) he had brought forward the same composer's "Siberia," which gave some promise of life, though it died with the season that saw its birth.

[1] New York, Henry Holt & Co.

The critical mind seems disposed to look with kindness upon new works in proportion as they fall back in the corridors of memory; and so I am inclined to think that of the four operas by Giordano which I have heard "Andrea Chenier" gives greatest promise of a long life. The attempt to put music to "Fédora" seemed to me utterly futile. Only those moments were musical in the accepted sense of the word when the action of the drama ceased, as in the case of the intermezzo, or when the old principles of operatic construction waked into life again as in the confession of the hero-lover. Here, moreover, there comes into the score an element of novelty, for the confession is extorted from *Lorris* while a virtuoso is entertaining a drawing-roomful of people with a set pianoforte solo. As for the rest of the opera, it seems sadly deficient in melody beautiful either in itself or as an expression of passion. "Andrea Chenier" has more to commend it. To start with, there is a good play back of it, though the verities of history were not permitted to hamper the imagination of Signor Illica, the author of the book. The hero of the opera is the patriotic poet who fell under the guillotine in 1794 at the age of thirty-two. The place which Saint-Beuve gave him in French letters is that of the greatest writer of classic verse after Racine and Boileau. The operatic story is all fiction, more so, indeed, than that of "Madame Sans-Gêne." As a matter of fact, the veritable Chenier was thrown into prison on the accusation of having sheltered a political criminal, and was beheaded together with twenty-three others on a charge of having engaged in a conspiracy while in prison. In the opera he does not die for political reasons, though they are alleged as a pretext, but because he has crossed the love-path of a leader of the revolution.

When Giordano composed "Siberia," he followed the example of Mascagni and Puccini (if he did not set the example for them) by seeking local color and melodic material in the folk-songs of the country in which his scene was laid. Puccini went to Japan for musical ideas and devices to trick out his "Madama Butterfly" as Mascagni had done in "Iris." Giordano, illustrating a story of political oppression in "Siberia," called in the aid of Russian melodies. His exiles sing the heavy-hearted measures of the bargemen of the Volga, "Ay ouchnem," the forceful charm of which few Russian composers have been able to resist. He introduced also strains of Easter music from the Greek church, the popular song known among the Germans as "Schöne Minka" and the "Glory" song (*Slava*) which Moussorgsky had forged into a choral thunderbolt in his "Boris Godounoff." It is a stranger coincidence that the "Slava" melody should have cropped up in the operas of Giordano and Moussorgsky than that the same revolutionary airs should pepper the pages of "Madame Sans-Gêne" and "Andrea Chenier." These operas are allied in subject and period and the same style of composition is followed in both.

Chenier goes to his death in the opera to the tune of the "Marseillaise" and the men march past the windows of *Caterina Huebscher's* laundry singing the refrain of Roget de Lisle's hymn. But Giordano does not make extensive use of the tune in "Madame Sans-Gêne." It appears literally at the place mentioned and surges up with fine effect in a speech in which the *Duchess of Dantzic* overwhelms the proud sisters of Napoleon; but that is practically all. The case is different with two other revolutionary airs. The first crash of the orchestra launches us into "La Carmagnole," whose melody provides the thematic orchestral substratum for nearly the entire first scene. It is an innocent enough tune, differing little from hundreds of French vaudeville melodies of its period, but Giordano injects vitriol into its veins by his harmonies and orchestration. With all its innocence this was the tune which came from the raucous throats of politically crazed men and women while noble heads tumbled into the bloody sawdust, while the spoils of the churches were carried into the National Convention in 1793, and to which "several members, quitting their curule chairs, took the hands of girls flaunting in priests' vestures" and danced a wild rout, as did other mad wretches when a dancer was worshipped as the Goddess of Reason in the Cathedral of Notre Dame.

Caterina's account of the rude familiarity with which she is treated by the soldiery (I must assume a knowledge of Sardou's play which the opera follows) is set to a melody of a Russian folk-song cast in the treatment of which Russian influences may also be felt; but with the first shouts of the mob attacking the Tuileries in the distance the characteristic rhythmical *motif* of the "Ça ira" is heard muttering in the basses. Again a harmless tune which in its time was perverted to a horrible use; a lively little contradance which graced many a cotillion in its early days, but which was roared and howled by the mob as it carried the beauteous head of the Lamballe through the streets of Paris on a pike and thrust it almost into the face of Marie Antoinette.

Of such material and a pretty little dance ("La Fricassée") is the music of the first act, punctuated by cannon shots, made. It is all rhythmically stirring, it flows spiritedly, energetically along with the current of the play, never retarding it for a moment, but, unhappily, never sweetening it with a grain of pretty sentiment or adorning it with a really graceful contour. There is some graciousness in the court scene, some archness and humor in the scene in which the *Duchess of Dantzic* submits to the adornment of her person, some dramatically strong declamation in the speeches of *Napoleon*, some simulation of passion in the love passages of *Lefèbvre* and of *Neipperg;* but as a rule the melodic flood never reaches high tide.

CHAPTER XVII

TWO OPERAS BY WOLF-FERRARI

WHEN the operas of Ermanno Wolf-Ferrari came to America (his beautiful setting of the "Vita Nuova" was already quite widely known at the time), it was thought singular and somewhat significant that though the operas had all been composed to Italian texts they should have their first Italian performances in this country. This was the case with "Le Donne Curiose," heard at the Metropolitan Opera House, New York, on January 3, 1912; of "Il Segreto di Susanna," which the Chicago-Philadelphia Opera Company brought to New York after giving it a hearing in its home cities, in February, 1912; of "I Giojelli della Madonna" first produced in Berlin in December, 1911, and in Chicago a few weeks later. A fourth opera, "L'Amore Medico," had its first representation at the Metropolitan Opera House, New York, on March 25, 1914.

The circumstance to which I have alluded as worthy of comment was due, I fancy, more to the business methods of modern publishers than to a want of appreciation of the operas in Italy, though

A PAGE OF THE SCORE OF THE GERMAN "DONNE CURIOSE"

Signor Wolf-Ferrari sought to meet the taste of his countrymen (assuming that the son of a German father and a Venetian mother is to be set down as an Italian) when he betrayed the true bent of his genius and sought to join the ranks of the Italian veritists in his "Giojelli della Madonna." However, that is not the question I am desirous to discuss just now when the first impressions of "Le Donne Curiose" come flocking back to my memory. The book is a paraphrase of Goldoni's comedy of the same name, made (and very deftly made) for the composer by Count Luigi Sugana. It turns on the curiosity of a group of women concerning the doings of their husbands and sweethearts at a club from which they are excluded. The action is merely a series of incidents in which the women (the wives by rifling the pockets of their husbands, the maidens by wheedling, cajoling, and playing upon the feelings of their sweethearts) obtain the keys of the club-room, and effect an entrance only to find that instead of gambling, harboring mistresses, seeking the philosopher's stone, or digging for treasure, as is variously suspected, the men are enjoying an innocent supper. In their eagerness to see all that is going on, the women betray their presence. Then there follow scoldings, contrition, forgiveness, a graceful minuet, and the merriment runs out in a wild furlana.

Book and score of the opera hark back a century or more in their methods of expression. The in-

cidents of the old comedy are as loosely strung
together as those of "Le Nozze di Figaro," and the
parallel is carried further by the similarity between
the instrumental apparatus of Mozart and Wolf-
Ferrari and the dependence of both on melody,
rather than orchestral or harmonic device, as the
life-blood of the music upon which the comedy
floats. It is Mozart's orchestra that the modern
composer uses ("the only proper orchestra for
comedy," as Berlioz said), eschewing even those
"epical instruments," the trombones. It would not
do to push the parallel too far, though a keen listener
might feel tempted also to see a point of semblance
in the Teutonism which tinctures the Italian music
of both men; a Teutonism which adds an ingredient
more to the taste of other peoples than that of the
people whose language is employed. But while the
Italianism of Mozart was wholly the product of
the art-spirit of his time, the Teutonism of Wolf-
Ferrari is a heritage from his German father and
its Italianism partakes somewhat of the nature of a
reversion to old ideals from which even his mother's
countrymen have departed. There is an almost
amusing illustration of this in the paraphrase of
Goldoni's comedy which the composer took as a
libretto. The *Leporello* of Da Ponte and Mozart
has his prototype in the *Arlecchino* of the classic
Italian comedy, but he has had to submit to so
great a metamorphosis as to make him scarcely
recognizable. But in the modern "Donne Curiose"

we have not only the old figure down to his conventional dress and antics, but also his companions *Pantaloon* and *Columbine*. All this, however, may be better enjoyed by those who observe them in the representation than those who will only read about them, no matter how deftly the analysis may be made.

It is Mozart's media and Mozart's style which Wolf-Ferrari adopts, but there are traces also of the idioms of others who have been universal musicians rather than specifically Italian. Like Nicolai's "O süsse Anna !" (Shakespeare's "Oh, Sweet Anne Page"), Wolf-Ferrari's *Florindo* breathes out his languishing "Ah, Rosaura !" And in the lively chatter of the women there is frequently more than a suggestion of the lively gossip of Verdi's merry wives in his incomparable "Falstaff." Wolf-Ferrari is neither a Mozart nor a Verdi, not even a Nicolai, as a melodist, but he is worthy of being bracketed with them, because as frankly as they he has spoken the musical language which to him seemed a proper investiture of his comedy, and like them has made that language characteristic of the comedy's personages and illustrative of its incidents. He has been brave enough not to fear being called a reactionary, knowing that there is always progress in the successful pursuit of beauty.

The advocates of opera sung in the language native to the hearers may find an eloquent argument in "Le Donne Curiose," much of whose humor lies in the text and is lost to those who cannot under-

stand it despite the obviousness of its farcical action.
On the other hand, a feeling of gratitude must have
been felt by many others that they were not compelled to hear the awkward commonplaces of the
English translation of the libretto. The German
version, in which the opera had its first hearing in
Munich six years before, is in a vastly different
case — neither uncouth nor halting, even though it
lacks the characteristic fluency essential to Italian
opera buffa; yet no more than did the speech of
most of the singers at the Metropolitan performance.
The ripple and rattle of the Italian *parlando* seem
to be possible only to Italian tongues.

The Mozartian type of music is illustrated not
only in the character of many of its melodies, but
also in the use of *motivi* in what may be called the
dramatic portions — the fleet flood upon which the
dialogue dances with a light buoyancy that is delightfully refreshing. These *motivi* are not used in
the Wagnerian manner, but as every change of
situation or emotion is characterized in Mozart's
marvellous ensembles by the introduction of a
new musical idea, so they are in his modern disciple's.
All of them are finely characteristic, none more so
than the comical cackle so often heard from the
oboe in the scenes wherein the women gossip about
the imaginary doings of the men — an intentional
echo, it would almost seem, of the theme out of
which Rameau made his dainty harpsichord piece
known as "La Poule." The motto of the club,

"Bandie xe le done," is frequently proclaimed with more or less pomposity; *Florindo's* "Ah, Rosaura," with its dramatic descent, lends sentimental feeling to the love music, and the sprightly rhythm which accompanies the pranks of *Colombina* keeps much of the music bubbling with merriment. In the beginning of the third act, not only the instrumental introduction, but much of the delightful music which follows, is permeated with atmosphere and local color derived from a familiar Venetian barcarolle ("La biondina in gondoleta"), but the musical loveliness reaches its climax in the sentimental scenes — a quartet, a solo by *Rosaura*, and a duet, in which there breathes the sympathetic spirit of Smetana as well as Mozart.[1]

[1] The cast at the first performance at the Metropolitan Opera House was as follows:—

Ottavio	Adamo Dfdur
Beatrice	Jeanne Maubourg
Rosaura	Geraldine Farrar
Florindo	Hermann Jadlowker
Pantalone	Antonio Pini-Corso
Lelio	Antonio Scotti
Leandro	Angelo Bada
Colombina	Bella Alten
Eleonora	Rita Fornia
Arlecchino	Andrea de Segurola
Asdrubale	Pietro Audisio
Almoro	Lambert Murphy
Alvise	Charles Hargreaves
Lunardo	Vincenzo Reschiglian
Momolo	Paolo Ananian
Menego	Giulio Rossi
Un Servitore	Stefen Buckreus

Conductor — Arturo Toscanini.

In "Le Donne Curiose," the gondoliers sing their barcarolle and compel even the cynic of the drama to break out into an enthusiastic exclamation: "Oh, beautiful Venice!" The world has heard more of the natural beauties of Naples than of the artificial ones of Venice, but when Naples is made the scene of a drama of any kind it seems that its attractions for librettist and composer lie in the vulgarity and vice, libertinism and lust, the wickedness and wantonness, of a portion of its people rather than in the loveliness of character which such a place might or ought to inspire.

Perhaps it was not altogether surprising that when Wolf-Ferrari turned from Venice and "Le Donne Curiose" to "I Giojelli della Madonna" with Naples as a theatre for his drama he should not only change the style of his music, but also revert to the kind of tale which his predecessors in the field seem to have thought appropriate to the place which we have been told all of us should see once and die out of sheer ecstasy over its beauty. But why are only the slums of Naples deemed appropriate for dramatic treatment?

How many stories of Neapolitan life have been told in operas since Auber wrote his "La Muette di Portici" I do not know; doubtless many whose existence ended with the *stagione* for which they were composed. But it is a singular fact bearing on the present discussion that when the young "veritists" of Italy broke loose after the success of

Mascagni's "Cavalleria rusticana" there came almost a universal desire to rush to the Neapolitan shambles for subjects. New York has been spared all of these operas which I have described in an earlier chapter of this book, except the delectable "A Basso Porto" which Mr. Savage's company gave to us in English sixteen years ago; but never since.

Whether or not Wolf-Ferrari got the subject of "I Giojelli della Madonna" from the sources drawn on by his predecessors, I do not know. I believe that, like Leoncavallo, he has said that the story of his opera has a basis of fact. Be this as it may, it is certain that the composer called on two versifiers to help him out in making the book of the opera and that the story in its essence is not far removed from that of the French opera "Aphrodite," by Baron Erlanger. In that opera there is a rape of the adornments of a statue of Venus; in Wolf-Ferrari's work of the jewels enriching an effigy of the Virgin Mary. The story is not as filthy as the other plots rehearsed elsewhere, but in it there is the same striving after sharp ("piquant," some will say) contrasts, the blending of things sacred and profane, the mixture of ecclesiastical music and dances, and — what is most significant — the generous use of the style of melody which came in with Ponchielli and his pupils. In "I Giojelli della Madonna" a young woman discards the love of an honest-hearted man to throw herself,

out of sheer wantonness, into the arms of a blackguard dandy. To win her heart through her love
of personal adornment the man of faithful mind
(the suggestion having come from his rival) does
the desperate deed of stealing for her the jewels of
the Madonna. It is to be assumed that she rewards him for the sacrilegious act, but without
turning away from the blackguard, to whom she
grants a stolen interview during the time when
her true love is committing the crime. But even
the vulgar and wicked companions of the dandy,
who is a leader among the Camorristi, turn from
her with horror when they discover the stolen
jewels around her neck, and she gives herself to
death in the sea. Then the poor lover, placing the
jewels on the altar, invokes forgiveness, and, seeing
it in a ray of light which illumines them, thrusts a
dagger into his heart and dies at the feet of the
effigy of the goddess whom he had profaned.

The story would not take long in the telling
were it not tricked out with a multitude of incidents
designed to illustrate the popular life of Naples
during a festival. Such things are old, familiar, and
unnecessary elements, in many cases not even
understood by the audience. But with them Signor
Wolf-Ferrari manages to introduce most successfully
the atmosphere which he preserves even throughout
his tragical moments — the atmosphere of Neapolitan life and feeling. The score is saturated with
Neapolitan folk-song. I say Neapolitan rather than

B

Italian, because the mixed population of Naples
has introduced the elements which it would be rash
to define as always Italian, or even Latin. While
doing this the composer surrendered himself unreservedly and frankly to other influences. That
is one of the things which make him admirable in
the estimation of latter-day critics. In "Le Donne
Curiose" he is most lovingly frank in his companionship with Mozart. In "Il Segreto" there is a
combination of all the styles that prevailed from
Mozart to Donizetti. In "I Giojelli" no attempt
seems to have been made by him to avoid comparison with the composer who has made the most
successful attempt at giving musical expression to
a drama which fifty years ago the most farsighted
of critics would have set down as too rapid of movement to admit of adequate musical expression —
Mascagni and his "Cavalleria rusticana," of course.
But I am tempted to say that the most marvellous
faculty of Wolf-Ferrari is to do all these things
without sacrifice of his individuality. He has gone
further. In "La Vita Nuova" there is again an
entirely different man. Nothing in his operas
seems half so daring as everything in this cantata.
How he could produce a feeling of mediævalism in
the setting of Dante's sonnets and yet make use
of the most modern means of harmonization and
orchestration is still a mystery to this reviewer.
Yet, having done it long ago, he takes up the modern
style of Italian melody and blends it with the old

church song, so that while you are made to think one moment of Mascagni, you are set back a couple of centuries by the cadences and harmonies of the hymns which find their way into the merrymakings of the *festa*.   But everything appeals to the ear — nothing offends it, and for that, whatever our philosophical notions, we ought to be grateful to the melodiousness, the euphony, and the rich orchestration of the new opera.[1]

[1] The performances of "I Giojelli della Madonna" by the Chicago-Philadelphia Opera Company, as it was called in Chicago, the Philadelphia-Chicago Opera Company, as it was called in Philadelphia, were conducted by Cleofonte Campanini and the principal parts were in the hands of Carolina White, Louise Bèrat, Amadeo Bassi, and Mario Sammarco.